CASWELL COUNTY, NORTH CAROLINA

Marriage Bonds,
1778-1868

Compiled by
Katharine Kerr Kendall

CLEARFIELD

Copyright © 1981, 1990 by
Katharine Kerr Kendall
All rights reserved.

Originally published 1981
Reprinted in a new format 1990 for
Clearfield Company, Inc. by
Genealogical Publishing Co., Inc.
Baltimore, Maryland

Reprinted for
Clearfield Company, Inc. by
Genealogical Publishing Co., Inc.
Baltimore, Maryland
1999, 2003

International Standard Book Number: 0-8063-1276-9

Made in the United States of America

INTRODUCTION

In 1741 there was enacted in North Carolina a law requiring a prospective groom and his bondsman to post a bond with the clerk of pleas and quarter sessions to certify there was no legal impediment to the marriage. This remained the law of the land until 1868 when a new state constitution changed the marriage laws.

The marriage bonds of Caswell County are in the custody of the North Carolina State Archives, Raleigh, North Carolina. Although Caswell County began its history in 1777, the first extant bonds are dated 1778. The bonds are filed in boxes. In the 1930s they were alphabetized by the staff of the Archives who soon found it necessary to prepare a card file of the bonds in order to preserve the originals. The Genealogical Society of Utah typed the first index and prepared a cross index to brides. One copy of this is at the State Archives and a second at the Caswell County Courthouse, Yanceyville. I am grateful to the State Archives for allowing me to update its copy.

Not all of the marriage bonds remain. The 5,700 bonds of Caswell County in this compilation include fifty-nine bonds which had been filed erroneously with bonds of Stokes County, North Carolina. In addition to brides, the index includes bondsmen, witnesses, and names other than bride and groom found on the bonds. All names on the bonds are included in this edition, but in some cases the names of county officials or issuing officers are omitted to avoid repetition.

Katharine Kerr Kendall
2814 Exeter Circle
Raleigh, N. C. 27608

ABBREVIATIONS

CC	Clerk of Court
CCC	County Clerk of Court
DC	Deputy Clerk
JP	Justice of the Peace
MG	Minister of the Gospel

Col	a person of color
dau	daughter
dpt	deputy
md	married

* An asterisk after the name of a groom indicates bond was filed erroneously in Stokes County.

CLERKS OF COURT OF CASWELL COUNTY

William Moore	1777-1780	Paul A. Haralson	1822-1842
Archibald Murphey	1781-1817	Abisha Slade	1842-1853
Azariah Graves	1817-1819	Thomas Williams Graves	1854-1866
Alexander Murphey	1819-1822	Henry F. Brandon	1866-1873

DEPUTY CLERKS AND OTHER ISSUING OFFICERS

James T. Graves
John H. Graves
John Henry Franklin Graves
Napoleon E. Graves
Herndon Haralson
Leanna H. Haralson, wife of Paul A. Haralson
W. Allen Harrelson
Henderson House, apprentice to Paul A. Haralson
Thomas D. Johnston

J. L. McKee
John G. Murphey
Joseph C. Pinnix
D. W. Simpson
A. Tatom, deputy sheriff
W. A. Vernon
William Wilkerson
John G. Womack
George W. Van Hook

MINISTERS OF THE GOSPEL SIGNING BONDS

A. G. Anderson
C. A. Apple
Solomon Apple
R. G. Barrett
A. B. Brown
William Burns
F. H. Burrings
Thomas S. Campbell
P. J. Carraway
Jacob Doll
James L. Fisher
W. C. Gannon
John S. Grasty
George W. Griffin
A. N. Hall, Elder

E. H. Harding
H. G. Hill
Aaron Jones, Jr.
F. H. Jones
Robert B. Jones
F. M. Jordan, Elder
John H. Lacy
John W. Lewis
John Long
A. McDowell
George W. McNeely
Samuel G. Mason
R. A. Moore
Alfred Norman
F. L. Oakley

Daniel A. Penick
W. S. Penick
John H. Pickard
T. Page Ricaud
Lemmon Shell
James P. Simpson
John Stadler
S. A. Stanfield
Fr. Stanley
M. C. Thomas
Thomas W. Tobey
G. G. Walker, Elder
Q. A. Ward
N. W. Wilson
J. W. Wonycott

Names of ministers did not appear on bonds prior to 1840.

```
_____._____._____._____

         Caswell     Richmond    St. Lawrence    Nash

_____._____X._____._____

        St. David's   Gloucester   St. Luke's    St. James

_____._____._____._____
```

Caswell County 1777-1792 with eight districts

X indicates Caswell Court House, the name being changed to Leasburg in 1788. Person County was formed in 1792 from the eastern part of Caswell. The districts falling into Person were St. Lawrence, St. Luke's, Nash, and St. James. The districts in Caswell after 1792 were Richmond, Caswell, St. David's and Gloucester.

CASWELL COUNTY, NORTH CAROLINA, MARRIAGE BONDS 1778-1868

GROOM	BRIDE	DATE	BONDSMAN OR WITNESS
Abbott Richard M.	Marth A. Baines	9 Apr 1867	H. F. Brandon
Adams Edmon	Patsy Vaden	18 Jun 1818	Lewis Graves
Adams Hannible A.	Mary E. Bird	9 Apr 1862	George W. Riggs
Adams Joel T.	Sarah Fielder	16 Oct 1828	James D. Chandler
Adams John W.	Sally H. McLaughan	21 Nov 1867	H. F. Brandon
Adams Philip	Fanny Powell	24 Jun 1800	Thomas Powell
Adams Richard	Amelia Ann Rucker	30 Mar 1833	John G. Campbell
Adams Sylvester P.	Adaline A. Gunn	3 Oct 1846	James Burton
Adams William	Julia Hodges	15 Nov 1845	Cary W. West
Adams William A.	Pelina Patterson	2 Sep 1858	Wm. B. Patterson
Adams William C.	Emily Williamson	13 Nov 1855	B. Harrelson
Adams William W.	Mary P. Womack (wid)	30 Jul 1842	Edward J. Morriss
Atkin William D.	Talitha J. Rigney	8 Sep 1865	William Coleman
Adkins Akillis	Jemis A. Gipson	21 Jul 1864	James M. Hodges
Adkins Byrd	Anna Yancey	21 Apr 1866	Jas. Graves
Adkins Green	Hannah Kimbro	20 Oct 1866	Jno. K. Adkins
Adkins Henry (Col)	Charity Kimbrough (Col)	9 Mar 1867	James W. Graves
Adkins Henry F.	Frances Oliver	9 Dec 1847	A. Slade
Adkins James	Polly Brookes	2 Apr 1814	Thomas Smith
Adkins William	Nancey Foster	10 Oct 1815	Thomas Smith
Adkins William	Polley Fuller	26 Oct 1815	James Page
Adkins William	Mary Chandler	3 Jun 1828	James Adkins
Akin James	Mary Murphey	9 Jul 1779	Benjamin McIntosh
Akin John	Patience Waddell	3 Aug 1816	Nathl. Pass
Albart William B.	Nancy A. Stadler	21 Nov 1840	John T. Stadler
Alderson James A. (son of Poindexter & Rebecca)	Julia J. Walters (dau of William & Elizabeth)	23 Nov 1867	H. F. Brandon
Aldress William	Elizabeth Smithey	14 Oct 1799	Samuel Smithey
Aldridge Allen*	Jane Hall	3 Dec 1831	Joseph S. Totten
Aldridge Andrew	Patsey Melton	17 Apr 1834	David Melton
Aldridge Joseph	Patsey Graves	25 Dec 1816	Robert Stadler
Aldridge P. H.	E. H. Dameron	6 Mar 1860	James H. Aldridge
Aldridge Richard	Lucy Pleasant	21 Jan 1822	Micajah Pleasant Jr.
Aldrige James	Isabella G. Moore	27 Oct 1824	Thomas W. Graves
Aldrige William J.	Elizabeth Donoho	6 Feb 1856	Franklin Graves
Alexander Benjamin	-------------	24 Jul 1819	Jno. J. Oliver
Alexander Wallace H.	Mary R. Robertson	21 Oct 1850	A. A. Ramsour
Allen Bob	America Denny	6 Jan 1866	Bill Hinton
Allen George W.	Mary A. Turner	26 Dec 1866	Charles W. Wynn
Allen James M.	Mary R. Moore	10 Nov 1854	Benjamin Hines
Allen John	Elizabeth Feagins	29 Jan 1851	John H. Sanders
Allen John	Rebecca Ann Hamlett	10 Jul 1864	Thomas Davis
Allen John W.	Ann E. Woods	3 Oct 1865	John C. Stephens
Allen Moses	Priscilla Ingram	2 May 1795	John Starkey
Allen Randolph J.	Mary J. House	21 Dec 1859	John G. Oliver
Allen Robert	Lucrecia Swann	5 Jan 1867	Hugh Scott
Allen Thomas H.	Frances J. Somers	13 Mar 1862	William Summers
Allen Thomas T.	Martha Pugh	25 Oct 1837	Jno. Kerr Jr.
Allen William	Mary Horton	3 Mar 1866	Yancey Chance
Allison John	Polly Johnston	2 Dec 1799	Thomas Johnston
Allison John J.	Mary E. Hinton	13 Apr 1846	William W. Taylor
Allred William B.	Hannah Aldridge	17 Nov 1845	William P. Anderson
Alverson Azariah J.	Celia White	11 Dec 1841	John Travis
Alverson Azariah J.	Mary Ann Ford	26 Jan 1849	William Alverson
Alverson Clarborn W.	Matilda J. Swann	30 Nov 1850	John M. Richmond

1

GROOM	BRIDE	DATE	BONDSMAN OR WITNESS
Alverson Jesse	Henny Wright	20 Jul 1816	Elisha Ingram
Alverson Jesse	Salley Kiersey	2 Sep 1818	Henson Alverson
Alverson William L.	Mary McKinney	20 Jan 1853	Rufus Y. Graves
Amos William T.	Mary P. Evans	26 Sep 1859	B. Harralson
Anderson Albert JB	Fanny H. Kirby	6 Aug 1860	Benjamin W. Kirby
Anderson Dennis (Col)	Margaret Williamson (Col)	25 Dec 1865	Ellick Williamson
Anderson James	Margret Cadal	9 Jul 1782	Andrew Caddel
Anderson James	Martha M. Flood	2 Feb 1839	B. C. West Sr.
Anderson John*	Jane T. Lampkin	21 Nov 1831	William Vaughan
Anderson Jno. Q.	Minerva J. Rice	26 Nov 1863	Ezekiel Sawyer
Anderson Moses G.	Rachel Scoggins	25 Dec 1867	H. F. Brandon clk
Anderson Nelson (Col)	China Brown (Col)	22 Dec 1865	Paul Windsor
Anderson Nelson S.	Frances A. Jones	18 Jan 1853	William A. Anderson
Anderson Quinten A.	Mary A. Taite	6 Mar 1862	Alfred A. Mitchell
Anderson Quinten T.	Virginia A. Walker	5 Feb 1866	John E. Covington
Anderson William	Sarah L. Hightower	25 Sep 1834	William Hightower
Anderson William	Paulina Ann Keesee	14 Mar 1836	Dr. Allen Gunn
Anderson William A.	Elizabeth A. Jones	18 Jan 1853	A. Slade clk
Anderson Wm. B.	Sophia Williams	14 Dec 1858	George W. Eubank
Anderson William R. (Col)	Polly Jones (Col)	19 Nov 1860	William Mangram
Anglin Caleb	Hannah Powell	9 Nov 1809	James Powell
Anglin William	Kerin H. Rice (dau of Wright)	15 Nov 1789	John Anglin
Anthoney James	Elizabeth Corder	7 Feb 1781	Hudson Berry
Anthony Johnson	Rebecca Berry	7 Nov 1781	Hudson Berry
Anthony Joseph	Hannah Cantrel	17 Feb 1802	Thomas Gooch
Anthony William	Sally Simmons	30 Jul 1794	Thomas Yancey
Apple Samuel	Mary Ann Somers	22 Oct 1851	William Somers
Apple William	Sarah Carlen	14 Feb 1840	L. A. Gwyn
Archer Richard F.	Elizabeth Brown	19 May 1819	John Massey
Armfield Jacob	Louisa Benton	28 Jan 1837	Jones W. Collins
Arnett Stephen	Teletha Trigg	17 Apr 1837	William Trigg
Arnn George W.	Julina F. Witcher	26 Mar 1851	Jesse Fuller
Arnold James W.	Sarah M. Rice	6 Jan 1840	William B. Stadler
Arnold Luke	Susannah Stadler	21 Feb 1810	Lewis Corbett
Arnold Richard	Patsy Cock (Cook?)	30 Sep 1814	Thomas Burns
Arnold Richard	Mary Melton	24 Mar 1818	Thomas Graves
Arnold Thomas	Polley Sewell	16 Dec 1812	Daniel Sewell
Arnold Wiett	Fannie Austin	6 Jan 1836	John McDaniel
Artwell Richard	Sarah Tennesson	8 Dec 1803	Ignatius Tenneson
Ashburn Lewis	Elizabeth Hamlett	5 Dec 1797	Richard Hamlett
Ashford Willis	Nancey Massey	9 May 1812	William Massey
Ashwell William A.	Misura E. Sheon	18 Feb 1857	James B. Lynch
Aspin Thomas	Sarah Stafford	14 Mar 1782	Henry McNiell
Astin Wilson J.	Kesiah A. Hodges	24 Jan 1846	William Adams
Atkinson James H.	Martha A. Prather	14 Nov 1836	Henderson House
Atkinson Jesse T.	Mary Burton (dau of Jas. & Mary)	13 Feb 1827	Matthew Dodson
Atkinson John	Sarah Lea	15 Sep 1782	Benjn. Hatcher
Atkinson John	Fanny Waren	6 Mar 1816	Edward Wilson
Atkinson Johnson E.	Elizabeth Ingram	5 May 1832	Robert Knight
Atkinson Leroy	Annis Sneed	2 Mar 1835	Thomas C. Green
Atkinson Thomas	Betsy Pain Samuel	14 Aug 1822	Ambrose L. Bennett
Atwell John	----------------	20 Dec 1807	Ignatius Tennison
Atwell John	Beney Smith	8 Dec 1810	Richard Smith

GROOM	BRIDE	DATE	BONDSMAN OR WITNESS
Atwell Lock	Polley Smith	5 Dec 1807	David Powell
Austin John H.	Elizabeth Riggs	16 Dec 1863	A. L. Pleasants
Austin Ransom B.	Lucey Scott	18 Apr 1854	Noel W. Lyon
Ayres William	Julia Ann Henderson	11 Oct 1834	Owen McAleer

- B -

GROOM	BRIDE	DATE	BONDSMAN OR WITNESS
Badgett Henry	Martha S. Glass	2 Jan 1830	John D. Glass
Badgett Jno.	Ann Howard	16 Jan 1817	Robert Madding
Badgett Peter	Nancy Pindexter	16 Sep 1820	William Canon
Badgett Ranson	Nancy Carloss	15 Jan 1803	Ibzan Rice
Badgett William	Polly Sergant	14 Nov 1801	Bird Hamlett
Bagley George	-------------	11 May 1808	Archy Dill
Bailey Noah	Betsy Ransom	5 Sep 1809	Charles Earley
Baines Willis	Sabine Rudd	12 Jan 1867	Bethel Rudd
Bains James	Ebby Willis	29 Dec 1810	Cartre Ball
Baker General	Lucy Jones	11 Nov 1819	Thomas Oakly
Baldwin Henry S.	Mary Ray	22 Oct 1824	Richard Estes
Baldwin John C.	Sarah B. Pennick	27 Nov 1866	Wm. Thomas
Ball Alfred L.	Elizabeth M. Smith	5 Feb 1852	Samuel B. Holder
Ball David	Frances L. Clark	20 Jul 1819	Sterling F. Vaughan
Ball G. S.	Margarett Taylor	27 Sep 1864	David Longwell
Ball Rufus (Col)	Celestia Lea (Col)	16 Feb 1866	Caleb A. Johnston
Ballad Larkin	Polly Ferrell	1 Jan 1846	Robert Joseph King
Ballard Andrew	Haley Reed	23 Dec 1809	John Reed
Ballard Larkin	Jincey Loafman	2 Jan 1812	Anthony Foster
Ballard Lewis	Salley Wray	23 Dec 1812	Lewis Barton
Ballard Mourning	Dilley Bush	8 Feb 1802	Pleasant Childress
Barber James	Jane Johnston	9 Jan 1802	James Johnston
Barber N. S.	Annie Dalton	29 Apr 1848	William Picknel
Barksdale Squire (Col)	Lucy Washington (Col)	29 Sep 1867	H. F. Brandon
Barker Burnley	---------------	25 Apr 1809	Henry Williams
Barker David	Sarah Cochran	20 Apr 1790	William Cochran
Barker Eaton B.	Mary C. Farley	6 Oct 1865	W. T. Farley
Barker George	Frankey Kerr	18 Oct 1783	William Henslee
Barker James	Susana Johnston	26 Jan 1779	Charles Taylor
Barker James	Nancey Taylor	14 Dec 1807	Hiram Taylor
Barker James M.	Dorithy Hensley	2 Nov 1846	Samuel Bethel
Barker John	Kezia Barton	19 Nov 1806	Aquila Barton
Barker Josiah	Mary F. Dodson	14 Nov 1865	Robert T. Vernon
Barker Mjnyard	Marthy E. Wilkerson	14 Nov 1865	RobertT. Vernon
Barker Stephen Y.	Martha J. Slayton	8 Dec 1864	R. W. Wilkinson
Barker Tolbert	Margret J. Jackson	10 Jul 1864	Samuel W. Taylor
Barker William	Nancey Brinckle (Brintle?)	11 Jan 1820	Azariah Graves
Barksdale Armistead	Ailcey Lydnar	26 May 1824	Thomas Jeffreys
Barlow Caloway	Mary Adams	27 Jan 1846	John W. Dameron
Barnard William	Susan Holoway	15 Feb 1842	John Holoway
Barnard William L.	Jamima Jane Withers	30 Jun 1857	E. B. Withers
Barner John (Col)	Amanda Garland (Col)	27 Dec 1865	Woodly Henderson
Barnet Hugh	Margurete McFarland	26 Jan 1784	Thomas Barnett
Barnett Andrew	Agness Haralson	21 Jun 1851	George F. Connally
Barnett John (Col)	Julia Jones (Col)	23 Jun 1866	Anthony Barnett
Barnett Thomas	Fanny Hargass	6 Jun 1830	William Forrest
Barnett William	Jane Breeze	18 Feb 1795	John Pogue
Barnett William	Betsy Sanders	27 Oct 1798	William Currie
Barnwell Carter	Caroline Prendergast	2 Aug 1837	Bird H. Bateman
Barnwell David	Judith Roberts	19 Dec 1804	William Barnwell
Barnwell Edward	Lucy Bevill	21 Feb 1804	Robert Barnwell
Barnwell John	Sarah Muze	31 Dec 1792	Joseph McReynolds
Barnwell Robert	Rebeccah Love	28 May 1796	Richard Arwin
Barnwell Robert S.	Mary F. Smith	26 Feb 1850	Lemuel R. Tate

3

GROOM	BRIDE	DATE	BONDSMAN OR WITNESS
Barnwell William	Elizabeth Enochs	16 Dec 1812	George Lloyd
Barnwell William H.	Mary C. V. Nelson	21 Sep 1844	Bird H. Bateman
Barricks David G.	Mary J. Barricks	14 Feb 1843	Jesse Owen
Barrow Henry	Letitia Ward	9 Nov 1835	Thomas Heydon
Barry Edward H.	Mary Ann Goodwin	20 Jan 1837	John S. Oglesby
Bartlett Edward	Elizabeth Muzzall	24 Feb 1814	David Mitchell
Bartlett Thompson M.	Susan Moore	19 Jun 1826	Jonathan Terrell
Barton Abraham	Mary Burch	20 Jun 1826	Elie Massey
Barton Aquila	Sally Hensle	20 Jan 1842	Chesley L. Barton
Barton Aquilla	Elizabeth Kennebrew	10 Feb 1813	William Kennebrew
Barton Chesley L.	Mary Page	15 May 1855	William A. Turner
Barton Elisha	Polley Cochran	9 Jan 1799	Reuben Cochran
Barton Lewis	Margret Willson	24 Jul 1804	Nowell Massey
Barton Lewis	Sarah Harrelson	8 Mar 1827	Lewis Denney
Barton Rice	Elizabeth Burch	31 Oct 1826	Thomas Barton
Barton Thomas	Frances Burch	20 Jan 1813	Burnley Barker
Barts Allen	Almedia Smith (dau of Catherine)	26 May 1866	Richd. S. Smith
Barts James H.	Margaret Mangum	13 Jan 1861	John H. Hall
Barutt Jno. B.	Rebeca H. Dodson	7 Jul 1846	M. P. Huntington
Bass Alex.	Sally A. Flintoff	8 Jul 1866	Kinchen Duncible
Bass John B.	Mary J. Gallion	8 Apr 1859	Thos. A. Hudson
Bass William	Martha Tolbert	31 May 1841	Jeremiah Tolbert
Bastin Henry	Kitty Hobbs	10 Jul 1823	Brockman Nichols
Bastin Thomas	Judath Hodge	15 Dec 1823	Henry Bastin
Bateman John	Susannah Evans	23 Nov 1807	James Darby
Bates Lemuel	Jane Chamberlin	30 Dec 1840	Wm. F. Chambers
Batman Bird H.	Mary Barnhill	14 Nov 1833	James Cooper
Baugh John J. (of Va.)	Lucey Ann Atkinson (dau of Mary)	20 Jun 1857	James M. Williams
Baugh John J.	R. C. Rodenhizer (of Danville, Va.)	17 Jan 1867	Simon T. Wilkinson
Baugh Peter	Jane P. Gordon	15 Jan 1821	John Gordon
Bauldwin Henry	Martha Murphey	26 Nov 1825	Lewis V. Whittemore
Bauldwin John	Betsey Murphey	26 Sep 1808	Daniel Darby
Bauldwin John	Frances Murphey	11 Apr 1825	Josiah Womack
Baxter James	Nancey Stone	3 Jul 1804	Hnry Stone
Baxter John Jr.	Martha Ware	15 Aug 1825	Henry A. Burton
Baxter Thomas	Jenny Dennis	5 Mar 1793	William Baxter
Bayes Robert J.	Isabella G. Nance (wid)	5 Jun 1866	Turner Patterson
Bayes Thompson (Col)	----------------	9 Oct 1850	Geo. Yates
Baynes Archibald	Barbary Morton	22 Feb 1840	David M. Murray
Baynes John	Sarah Lea	10 Sep 1845	Lindsey Roberts
Baynes Sidney Y.	Mary L. Fuller	11 May 1855	F. A. Wiley
Baynes Thornton Y.	Elizabeth B. Patillo	8 May 1854	Joseph C. Pinnix
Bayns Eaton	Elizabeth Shacford (dau of Nance Shacford)	26 Jul 1810	Philip Baynes
Beadles John W. (of Pittsylvania Co. Va.)	Frances K. Slayden	26 Mar 1828	Lewis Simpson
Beaver Humphrey	Jemima Sanders	24 Nov 1835	Ransome Sanders
Beaver James P.	Nancy E. Rice	23 Aug 1859	Leroy Sanders
Beaver Jesse	Mary Richardson	13 Feb 1786	John Beaver
Beaver Jesse	Jerusha Wynn	25 Jun 1810	Nathan Browning
Beaver Johnston	Polly Nunnary	3 Jul 1792	Alexr. Nunnary
Beaver Joshua	Polly Carroll	5 Oct 1793	Sterling Carroll
Beaver Solomon	Nancey Browning	24 Feb 1809	Nathan Browning
Beevers William T.	Sarah Jane Smithy	6 Nov 1854	Jess Sanders
Belew Daniel	Sally Hall	1 Nov 1794	Joseph McCain

GROOM	BRIDE	DATE	BONDSMAN OR WITNESS
Bell David	Agness Jones	22 Dec 1812	Thompson McKissack
Bellsire Thomas	Mary Thompson	25 Aug 1807	Archibald Rice
Benett Warren E.	Ann A. Shackelford	27 Dec 1855	R. A. Newbell
Bennatt Ambrose L.	Susannah Donoho	18 Feb 1804	William S. Webb
Bennatt Richard	Elizabeth Buckingham	15 Jan 1830	John Lennox
Bennatt Richard	Rebecca Pirant	18 Feb 1836	Charles Pirant
Bennatt William T.	Kitty C. Thorn	16 Jul 1814	Silas C. Cornwell
Bennett Ambrose L.	Frances Watlington	8 Nov 1822	Josiah Samuel
Bennett Ambrose L.	Vienna Rudd	30 Nov 1836	Owen McAleer
Bennett Ambrose L. Jr.	Leathy Taylor	23 Feb 1830	Joel Bolton
Bennett Henry	Nancey Hamner	17 Jan 1828	Starling H. Gunn
Bennett James	Delilah Peterson	14 Nov 1833	Owen McAleer
Bennett James W.	Betty W. Phelps	20 Feb 1866	William A. Oliver
Bennett Jesse	Patsey Paul	25 Nov 1788	John Bennett
Bennett John	Eliza M. Shelton	24 Dec 1839	Barzilla Graves
Bennett John A.	Elizabeth A. Smith	16 Jan 1854	William P. Browning
Bennett John N.	Julia Bennett	9 Nov 1857	Jesse C. Young
Bennett Mumford	Nancy Lumpkin (of Pittsylvania Co. Va.)	17 Feb 1821	Ludwell Worsham
Bennett Richard	Rachel R. Roper	21 Jan 1845	William L. Foster
Bennett Thomas	Anne Shacklford	6 Feb 1813	Holloway Pass
Bennett Thomas	Mildred Givings	26 Oct 1826	Alexander Gillaspe
Bennett William D.	Mary H. Shackleford	27 Dec 1853	John T. Shackleford
Benson Alexander	Patty Pleasant	10 Feb 1802	Lewis Corbett
Benson John	Nancey Pleasant	25 Feb 1828	Ruffin Pleasant
Benson John	Francis Lyon	24 Dec 1841	James Gunn
Benton Daniel (son of Abram & Charity Vincen)	Fannie Price (dau of Allen Kelly & Isbel Price)	6 Sep 1867	H. F. Brandon clk
Benton Joseph	Sarah Foster	2 Mar 1798	Lewis Foster
Benton Richard	Winifred Hopper	28 Dec 1787	John Murphy
Benton Richard	Salley Kitchen	20 Apr 1819	Barzillai Graves
Benton Robert	Nancey Cate	25 Oct 1790	Epaphroditus Benton
Benton Thomas	Isabella Groom	23 Sep 1828	Carter Groom
Benton Thomas*	Isabella Rice	26 Feb 1831	John M. Walker
Benton Titus	Mary Cates	9 Jan 1789	William McIntosh
Benton William	Bestey Groom	1 Jan 1820	Thomas Groom
Benton Zachariah	Mary Nunn	11 Jan 1843	Henry Cotton
Berry Elisha	Frances Bozwell	3 Jan 1826	Clement Nance
Bethell William*	Elizabeth A. Brown	19 Sep 1831	Alfred B. Johnston
Bethell William (Col)	Julia Williamson (Col)	12 Jan 1867	Lindsay Williamson
Bethell William P.	Mary S. Price	15 Jun 1865	George O. Williamson
Beusey John	Nancey Baldwin	3 Jul 1822	Charles Beusey
Bevil Peter	Margaret Brown	23 Sep 1866	Albert Brown
Bevill John	Salley Childs	29 Oct 1815	Thomas Childs
Bevill Robert	Nancey Smith	28 Nov 1810	Francis Smith
Bevins Grief	Sally Coats	3 Aug 1816	Thomas Burch
Bewsey Charles	Polly Hodge	9 Jun 1817	Severn Bewsey
Bigelow Calvin (Col)	Candice Williamson (Col)	28 May 1867	H. F. Brandon clk
Bigelow Willis (Col)	Harriet Bigelow (Col)	28 Dec 1866	Geo. Bigelow
Binion John	Ann Burton	17 Jan 1785	James Burton
Binion William	Jane Burton	19 Nov 1784	Saml. Paul
Bird Joel	Mary Hubbard (wid)	17 Aug 1866	Zachariah Hooper
Bird John	Jane Walker	3 Dec 1867	H. F. Brandon
Bird Thomas	Elizabeth Boldin	13 Apr 1824	William Walker
Bird Willie	Jane Jeffreys	8 Dec 1866	Bob Pattillo
Bird William A.	Susan F. Enock	25 Aug 1858	Levi A. Vincent
Birk Anderson	Nancy Rice	20 Nov 1804	Wylie Yancy
Birk Archibald R.	Isabella L. Graves	18 Oct 1836	Lewis S. Morton
Birk Benjamin	Nancy Vaughan	28 Sep 1800	James Birk

GROOM	BRIDE	DATE	BONDSMAN OR WITNESS
Birk James	Cisley Gooch	31 Jul 1802	Henry Williams
Birk James Jr.	Polley Porter	8 Apr 1809	Maddison Birk
Birk Matterson	Dolly Ellis	17 Oct 1804	James Wilson
Birk Tompson	Nancy Massey	9 Aug 1805	James Wilson
Birk Wiley	Elizabeth Compton	12 Dec 1826	Nathan Massie
Birks James A.	Susanna Shepard	22 Jan 1852	md by John Stadler
Birks Johnson	Betsey Woods	24 Aug 1802	Reuben Cochran
Black Hardy	Frances Basdall	6 Feb 1821	David Basdall
Black Robert	Lucy Gill	8 Feb 1792	Samuel Glaze
Black Samuel	Frances Delone	24 Dec 1802	Flemman Carnal
Blackard Aaron C.	Mary Harrison	19 Dec 1836	Dr. Allen Gunn
Blackard Charles	Nancy Vermillion	18 Jul 1780	William Blackard
Blackard Jobe	Jean Hargiss	31 Jan 1792	Henry Walters
Blacklock John	Polly Peterson	15 Dec 1818	Ambrose L. Bennett
Blackwell Carter	Isabella Brackin	28 Apr 1797	Thomas Jouett
Blackwell Elias (Col)	Eliza Withers (Col)	26 Mar 1867	H. F. Brandon
Blackwell Garland	Polly Scott	2 Dec 1811	Lewis Malone
Blackwell Garland	Sarah Brooks	22 Feb 1839	Cary A. Howard
Blackwell George (Col)	Julia Bouldin (Col)	13 Dec 1866	Joseph Bouldin
Blackwell Henry	Fannie Weatherford	8 Jun 1866	Robert Weatherford
Blackwell James (son of Chas. & Cindy)	Winnie Hooper	2 Nov 1867	H. F. Brandon
Blackwell James M.	Aniva E. Whittemore	16 Sep 1856	R. L. Wright
Blackwell John N.	Nancy B. Withers	6 Oct 1862	A. Sidney Badgett
Blackwell Levi	Patsey Smith	16 Feb 1799	William Whelton
Blackwell Marshal	Betsey Strador	25 Aug 1818	Christian Strador
Blackwell Milton	Nancey Mitchell	27 Dec 1820	John Blackwell
Blackwell Milton	Nancy Mitchell	26 Apr 1823	Richard Mitchell
Blackwell N. L.	Martha E. Siddle	18 Jun 1859	Thos. J. Mills
Blackwell Nathaniel L.	Ann E. Cobb	16 Oct 1847	J. B. Siddle
Blackwell Robert	Matilda Simpson	11 Jan 1813	Thomas Williamson
Blackwell Robert	Elmira J. Nunnally	19 May 1838	Lewis W. Withers
Blackwell Robert A.	Alice Stubblefield	12 Oct 1865	J. Bedford Siddle
Blackwell Samuel (Col-son of Nickolas & Agnes)	Frances King (Col- dau of Rogers & Matilda)	7 Mar 1868	H. F. Brandon
Blackwell Thomas I.*	Nancy Womack	6 Jan 1831	Richard Mitchell
Blackwell Whitson G.	Sally Rice	7 Apr 1853	James M. Neal
Blair Thomas	Letty Fanning	28 Nov 1791	Midleton Fanning
Blair William	Eliza A. Right	16 Aug 1834	John S. Price
Blair William Thomas	Manerva A. Hooper	29 Nov 1858	Robt. M. Price
Blake Ellis G.	Elizabeth Leachmond	19 Feb 1830	John J. Fielder
Blalock Alfred	Harriet Harrison	3 Feb 1843	Logan Brooks
Bland Richard	Elisabeth Dickins	22 Sep 1790	Jesse Dickins
Blankenship Archa. F.	Catherine C. Corbin	13 Nov 1866	Lafayette Womack
Blanks Joseph	Martha M. Clark	6 Feb 1857	Nathaniel Vaser
Blare (Blair) Josiah*	Frances Penick	14 Nov 1831	Wm. G. Penick
Boaz David R.	Susanna Stubblefield	3 Dec 1816	Geo. W. Stubblefield
Bohanan Ludwell	Elizabeth Spratten (dau of George)	25 Nov 1816	Thomas Wilds
Bohannan Ambrose	Elizabeth Marriable (dau of Nancy)	9 Jul 1810	Thos. Bouldin
Bohannan J. M.	Elizabeth Bains	8 Oct 1856	Mainyard Bohannan
Bohannan Nathaniel	Betsy Akin	7 May 1802	John Tharp

GROOM	BRIDE	DATE	BONDSMAN OR WITNESS
Bohannan Thomas (Col)	Martha Hightower (Col)	10 Jun 1867	H. F. Brandon
Bohannon Maynard	Nancy Baynes	23 Sep 1841	James F. Sikes
Bohannon Yancey	Martha Cox (dau of Mary & Philip)	17 Nov 1823	Alexander Gillaspy
Boles James M.	Nisey L. Fuller	8 Sep 1830	George Smith
Boley Parham A.	Esther D. Fair	23 Aug 1854	Thos W. Graves clk
Boling George or Bonds George	Syrena Collins	11 Jun 1832	James Currie
Bolton Joel	Elizabeth Watlington	7 Feb 1820	Thomas Donoho Jr.
Bolton Lewis	Elizabeth H. Lansdown	18 Sep 1826	Charles Willson
Boman James W.	Nancy D. Nicholson	7 Jan 1860	William J. Mustain
Boman John	Salley Cooper	29 Apr 1806	Ephraim Noel
Boman John	Nancy Somers	28 Dec 1807	Samuel Boman
Boman Joseph	Elizabeth Dixon	1 Mar 1790	Robert Boman
Boman Samuel	Betsey Carloss	30 Jun 1798	Simon Roberts
Boman Siar	Elizabeth Morton	3 May 1793	Zachariah Wright
Boman Thomas P. or Boman Will. P.	Thursday Ann Kennon	22 Dec 1856	James W. Cannaday
Bond Balaam	Prisciller Cook	23 Jan 1891	Thomas Donoho
Bonds George (see Boling George)			
Booz Henry	Matilda Hite	2 Aug 1820	Hugh Campbell
Boswell Abner	Mary Stainback	22 Nov 1838	Stephen Neal
Boswell Amza	Martha Herndon	14 Oct 1846	Mitchell Walker
Boswell Andrew J.	Melissa Watlington	7 Sep 1866	John R. Boswell
Boswell Antiochus	Mary Siddle	8 Nov 1836	John Harrison
Boswell Bedford A.	Nancy Boswell	17 Nov 1842	John R. Boswell
Boswell Brown	Manilla Graves	15 Oct 1829	John Boswell
Boswell Calvin G.	Lucinda Bird	15 Jan 1844	James M. Brookes
Boswell Craven	Rebecca Windsor	15 Feb 1812	Joseph Windsor
Boswell Howel	Susannah Gooch	22 Dec 1813	John Gooch
Boswell Howell Jr.	Ann E. Thompson	12 Aug 1856	Thomas M. Thompson
Boswell James	Mary Merony	21 Oct 1819	Robert Swift
Boswell James	Nanny Simpson	11 Dec 1823	Thomas W. Graves
Boswell James	Mary G. Brookes	3 Dec 1832	Thomas Bigelow
Boswell James M.	Julia Brannock	3 Apr 1849	William M. Russell
Boswell John	Citty Simpson	5 Oct 1805	Craven Boswell
Boswell John	Sarah Turner	11 Dec 1826	Col. Tho. Graves
Boswell John A.	Elizabeth J. Miles	23 Jan 1867	John A. Smith
Boswell Moses	Mary Martin	1 Dec 1866	Henry Corbett
Boswell Romulus S.	Louisa J. West	25 Aug 1856	James M. Neal
Boswell Thomas	Mary Sims	27 Nov 1802	Edward Sims
Boswell Thomas	Eliza Ann Bird	28 Sep 1861	Alfred A. Malone
Boswell William	Lucinda Page	19 Dec 1837	James P. Page
Bouldin Edward	Hariet Parks	3 Jul 1838	James M. McMenamy
Bouldin George T.	Susan Leath	12 May 1840	Henry C. Tapscott
Bouldin James	Sally Conally	24 Nov 1802	David Brandon
Bouldin James O.	Hannah Ann Simpson	7 Feb 1860	Thompson H. Boswell
Bouldin John	Frances Connally	20 Sep 1817	John Clendennin
Bouldin John	Catherine Garner	28 Feb 1843	Henry C. Tapscott
Bouldin Lewis P.	Sarah J. Vincent	8 Oct 1846	Geo. T. Bouldin
Bouldin W. L.	J. T. Simpson	12 Feb 1866	Wm. S. Walker
Bouldin William J.	Sarah L. Montgomery	12 May 1837	James M. McMenamy
Boulton Charles	Elizabeth Farley	7 Oct 1791	Samuel Johnston
Boulton George (Col)	Mary Richmond (Col)	26 Jan 1867	Abb Morton
Boulton William	Polly Dixon	18 Nov 1799	Tho. Jeffreys
Bowden John	Kitty Harriway	26 Nov 1817	William Mitchell
Bowe George	Mary Phillips	26 Dec 1866	Edmund Long
Bowe George	Huldah Jackson	9 Mar 1867	Saml. Bowe
Bowe Geo. (son of Jesse Hooper & Cely Bowe)	Malissa Rose Willis (dau of Peter & Hannah)	14 Nov 1867	H. F. Brandon

GROOM	BRIDE	DATE	BONDSMAN OR WITNESS
Bowe William B.*	Mary A. Miles	15 Dec 1831	Dr. Allen Gunn
Bowe William B.	Amy James	8 Jun 1858	Tho. W. Graves
Bowers John	Mariann Evans	15 Jun 1803	Elijah Evans
Bowers Lemual	Phebe Lea	11 Jan 1810	Samuel Woods
Bowers William	Nancy Christenbury	26 Jul 1817	Richard Burch
Bowler Ellis G.	Mary Slayton	14 Oct 1850	James M. Fernor
Bowles Henry	Nancey Dickey	13 Nov 1813	William Dickie
Bowles Stephen	Mary Eubank	16 Oct 1818	Miles Wells Jr.
Bowles Thomas	Susan Y. Gwyn	28 Nov 1853	John W. Gwyn
Bowls John	Maryann Boswell	21 Oct 1850	H. J. Boswell
Boyd Alexander Jr.	Nancey L. Harrison	9 Dec 1819	John P. Harrison
Boyd David	Jane Gwynn	1 Dec 1801	Robert Holderness
Boyd Lindsey J.	Elizabeth J. Gravett	11 Jan 1813	Daniel S. Farley
Boyd William	Polley Williamson	13 Feb 1795	James Williamson
Boykin Drury D.	Cornelia D. Currie	20 May 1849	William P. Graves
Boyles Abel	Mary L. Roper (wid)	6 Nov 1848	Geo. W. Simpson
Bozes Jno. Thos.	Sallie Ann Webster	26 Jul 1854	Thomas Solomon
Bozwell Kindall	Betsy Stokes	9 Jan 1817	Richard Bozwell
Bozwell Thomas	Elizabeth Yancey	22 Dec 1819	Nathaniel Gooch
Brackin John H.	Martha Womack	1 Dec 1835	Thomas J. Blackwell
Brackin Joseph	Sinna Womack	28 Jan 1795	Samuel Brackin
Brankin Joseph	Jenny Dixon	10 Jun 1802	William King
Brackin Joseph	Nancy Hooper	5 Jan 1841	Paul A. Haralson
Brackin Julius A. (son of John H. & Martha S.)	Martha J. Hubbard (dau of A. D. & Malinda)	9 Dec 1867	H. F. Brandon
Brackin Samuel	Rebeccah Reed	29 Oct 1799	Alex. Murphey
Bradford David	Elinor Faucet	3 Jun 1806	Jehu Bird
Bradley James	Dorrithy Burton	13 Sep 1788	Thomas Bradley
Bradley Samuel	Sarah Ray	26 Dec 1837	Francis Ray
Bradshaw James M.	Mary F. Hodges	17 Jan 1863	Will S. Eaton
Bradsher Henderson (Col-son of James Henderson & Jinny Bradsher)	Martha Poteat (Col-dau of Jack Wmson. & Leaned Poteat)	7 Dec 1867	H. F. Brandon clk
Bradsher Henry (Col-son of David & Nelly)	Leander Ragsdale (Col-dau of Elex & Mary)	27 Sep 1867	H. F. Brandon clk
Bradsher John Jr.	Cynthia Stafford	13 Mar 1830	John N. Fuller
Bradsher Moses	Elizabeth Wallis	11 Jan 1825	Vincent Bradsher
Bradsher Richard	Phebe Nellson	31 Oct 1817	Isaac Vanhook
Bradsher W. G.	Mattie E. Bradshear	8 Jul 1865	Weldon H. Lunsford
Bradsher Wilson A.	Martha Martin	11 Feb 1858	William S. Yarbrough
Brady Thomas	Marguret Morton	21 Dec 1791	James Robinson
Bragg Cicero	Mary Patterson	7 Feb 1855	John M. Swann
Bragg John	Seluda Strader	19 Nov 1866	Wm. F. Durham
Brandon David	Rebecca Conley	15 Dec 1800	Thomas Connally
Brandon David G.	Mary J. McAdin	14 Apr 1821	Jeremiah Dixon
Brandon Francis	Sarah Scott	13 Feb 1786	Septimus Taylor
Brandon Henry F.	Fannie P. Norflett	20 Oct 1856	Tho. W. Graves
Brandon Irvin	Judah Fanning	28 Jan 1788	John Jeffers
Brandon Isaac (Col)	Elizabeth Hughes (Col)	20 Nov 1866	Peter Brandon
Brandon Jacob (Col)	Harriett Cuningham (Col)	22 Dec 1866	Benja. Brandon
Brandon John	Peggy Foster	20 Dec 1809	Thomas Word
Brandon Joseph (son of Frank & Rhoda)	Sally Farmer (dau of Coleman & Ricey)	20 Dec 1867	H. F. Brandon
Brandon Louis	Nancy Woody	17 Feb 1867	Jefferson Brandon (Col)
Brandon Reubin (Col-son of Rufus & Delphy)	July Stamps (Col-dau Hugh White & Clary)	18 Nov 1867	H. F. Brandon clk

GROOM	BRIDE	DATE	BONDSMAN OR WITNESS
Brandon Thomas Jr.	Jane Allin Pullham	8 Jan 1785	Thomas Brandon Sr.
Brandon Thomas S. Jr.	Frances C. Roper	16 Dec 1846	William L. Brandon
Brandon William	Rebecca Scott	15 Aug 1785	Francis Brandon Jr.
Brandon William	Mary Langley	12 Jan 1796	John Langley
Brandon William	Esther Wiley	14 Dec 1811	Moses Langley
Brandon William L.	Mary A. Connally	11 Apr 1842	Spencer Connally
Brann John	Patsey Foster	6 Jan 1800	Thomas Brann
Brann Peter D.	Martha T. Standfield	17 Jan 1859	George Carter
Brann Vincent	Rebeca Johnston	9 Aug 1856	Peter D. Brann
Brannock Samuel T.	Francis Boswell	21 Dec 1850	James M. Brooks
Braughton Jeremiah	Parrizetta Foley	17 Oct 1809	Henry Burch
Brechen William Jr.	Elsey Wheeler	12 Jan 1807	William Brechen
Breeze James	Rebeccah McMullin	1 Nov 1797	James Neely
Brewer James	Elizabeth Buttery	28 Apr 1816	Hardy Brewer
Briggs Silas	Lucinda Grogan	1 Jun 184-	Dr. Willie Jones
Brightwell Wm. C.	Mary J. Adams	2 Sep 1859	John A. Mohr
Brigman James	Patsey Anderson	8 Mar 1816	John Brandon
Brincefield A. J.	Martha E. Matkins	1 Nov 1865	Jno. Chatham
Brincefield Bartlet Y.	Jane Gwyn	20 Dec 1858	Anderson Brincefield
Brincefield Colmon W.	Francis Morton	11 Aug 1858	John Hall
Brinsfield Anderson	Francis Dye	13 Dec 1815	George Dilworth
Brinsfield Calvin	Mary Shelton	2 Jul 1847	Noel Burton
Brinsfield Dennard	----------	13 Oct 1806	James Leath
Brintle John*	Nancy Childress	24 Sep 1831	Roland Roberts
Brintle Oliver	Salley Brown	24 Feb 1816	Spencer Jackson
Brintle Solomon	Sarah Bell	29 May 1810	Jesse Brintle
Brintle William	Lucy Heston	15 Nov 1798	John Jackson
Brintle William	Aggy Massy	13 May 1802	John Jackson
Brintle William	Elizabeth Cantrell	30 Jun 1854	George W. Pinnix
Brintle Zachariah	Eliza A. Smith	1 Jan 1866	John C. Chatham
Broche George	Jenny Burch or Broach	19 Mar 1803	James Broache
Brodie Thomas	Christian Mathison	13 May 1779	William Campbell
Broocks Dr. Wm. M.	Virginia Word	1 Dec 1841	Jas. R. Callum
Brookes Christopher W.	Isbel Kerr	28 Nov 1812	Jaes Graves
Brookes Iverson I. W.	Rebecca H. Paschal	5 Feb 1861	W. L. Brookes
Brookes Jeremiah	Elisabeth Thomas	18 Mar 1795	Thomas Thomas
Brookes John	Mary B. Watlington	17 Nov 1824	James Watlington
Brookes Robert H.	Sinthy Boswell	6 Dec 1842	James N. Parks
Brookes Samuel	Betsey Wood	10 Nov 1792	Thomas Cheatham
Brookes Thomas	Susanna Adkins	24 Dec 1816	James Atkins
Brookes Thomas	Huldath Mitchell	28 May 1823	Jonathan B. Watlington
Brookes Thomas Jr.	Jane Flipping	26 Feb 1791	Armistead Watlington
Brookes William L.	Mary J. Pinnix	28 Jan 1864	A. R. Paschal
Brooks Andrew P.	Jereney Wedding	15 Jun 1850	William Matlock
Brooks Christopher	Salley Holderness	9 Feb 1810	James Scott
Brooks Christopher	Melesia Moore	9 May 1848	Augustus Gwyn
Brooks Christopher	Eliza Lewis	16 Sep 1858	James H. Evans
Brooks David	Betsy Terrell	6 Oct 1816	Thomas Brooks
Brooks James	Elisabeth Traylor	26 Dec 1782	John H. Simpson
Brooks John K.	Celenis B. Simpson	3 Nov 1845	John H. Simpson
Brooks John K.	Eliza Malone	28 Jun 1847	George Robertson
Brooks William	Catharine Gipson	17 Nov 1816	Philip Jones
Broughton Jerremiah	Caty Bird	21 Sep 1805	Baylor Byrd
Browder David A.	Sarah Eubaley	6 Mar 1846	Thomas Eudeleyse
Brower Lewis S.	Lucy P. Stinson	25 Mar 1846	Jarvis Friou
Brown Bedford	Mary Glenn	6 Jul 1816	Griffin Gunn

GROOM	BRIDE	DATE	BONDSMAN OR WITNESS
Brown Cicero	Frances Bowes	12 Sep 1866	L. L. Wilson
Brown Clark H.	Wyeney B. Fourd	20 Feb 1834	John McDaniel
Brown Edward	Susannah Flinn	31 Mar 1798	Thomas Cambell
Brown Franklin (Col)	Susan Windsor (Col)	25 Jan 1866	Paul Windsor
Brown Green Lea	Nancey Simpson	1 Jan 1802	John Worsham
Brown Green W.	Mary Ann Richmond	14 Mar 1857	Saml. P. Hill
Brown Henry	Elizabeth Stacy	27 Nov 1815	Thomas Stacy
Brown Hudson	Henrietta Simms	16 Apr 1796	George Sims Jr.
Brown Isham (Col)	Jinny Gunn (Col)	3 Jul 1866	A. Gunn
Brown James*	Biddy Massey	17 Feb 1831	Archibald R. Birke
Brown James	Susanna Brown	4 Feb 1808	Jesse Hollis
Brown James	Sally Shackleford	12 Jan 1815	Joseph Roe
Brown James (Col)	Juliann Kersey (Col)	11 Aug 1866	James Hodges (Col)
Brown James W.	Mary A. C. Carter	30 Jul 1818	Thomas Harrelson
Brown Jethro	Lucey Williamson	28 May 1788	John Buchanan
Brown John	Salley Jones	29 Dec 1786	Joseph Farrar
Brown John	Lidia Tait	2 Nov 1801	Zachariah Tate
Brown John	Mary Barker	9 Apr 1814	John Stadler
Brown John E.	Elizabeth B. Carter	20 Apr 1827	George Williamson
Brown John T.	Julia Ann Purkins	7 Jan 1861	John T. Hodges
Brown Jonathan	Eliza Butler	1 Jan 1844	Joseph S. Blackwell
Brown Madison	Ella Boswell	2 Dec 1866	Anderson Brown
Brown Michael	Mary H. Lea	11 Feb 1840	Joseph F. Cornwell
Brown Nathan	Mary Walker	30 Nov 1842	William Herndon
Brown Ned	Edy Graves	15 Feb 1867	Marshall Willis
Brown Obediah	F. Elington	22 Jan 1861	S. T. Sparks
Brown Richard	Patsey Ballard	11 Sep 1810	Benjamin Cantrill
Brown Richard H.	Mary P. Johnson	25 Sep 1841	Alfred M. Nash
Brown Robert	Lydia Harris	19 Dec 1795	William Shelton
Brown Robert	Parthney Brintle	23 Feb 1818	William W. Lyon
Brown Robert A.	Lucy Ann Faulks	3 May 1830	Jno. Blackwell
Brown Samuel	Perthena Farley	16 Sep 1813	William Woods
Brown Stephen E.	Eliza G. Lea	2 Nov 1846	Harrison Lea
Brown Tarlton W.	Lucy Hilliard	13 Jul 1830	James W. Jeffreys
Brown Thomas M.	Mary F. Stanley	18 Dec 1847	William R. Stanley
Brown William	Elizabeth Stadler	19 mar 1803	James Taylor
Brown William	Mary Jeffreys	23 Feb 1867	Geo. Pass
Brown William J.	Sarah Hailey	11 Dec 1857	O. F. Terry
Brown William V.	Frances Lyon	20 Nov 1812	William Lyon
Browning Edmon	Sarah Allen	13 Feb 1790	Solomon Parks
Browning Edmund	Maryan Murphey	9 Sep 1800	William Culberson
Browning Edmund E.	Susan Pitts	13 Oct 1841	Levi Sawyers
Browning Elijah C.	Mary C. Stadler	11 Feb 1859	Thomas B. Smith
Browning Francis	Mary Morton	22 Dec 1838	Allen Scott
Browning James S.	Drady Parks	12 Nov 1826	Josiah Page
Browning John K.	Mary Smith	6 Apr 1825	Zephaniah T. Kerr
Browning John R.	S. W. Dameron	17 Dec 1860	James R. Aldridge
Browning Martin	Polley Gomer	20 Feb 1870	Charles Earley
Browning Martin	Nancy Hubbard	22 Dec 1852	Julius C. Watlington
Browning Nathan	Rilla Mullens	26 Dec 1810	William Scott
Browning Nimrod	Rachel Parks	21 Aug 1789	Solomon Parks
Browning Reubin	Polley Robinson	9 Feb 1802	Ziza Rice
Browning Richard	Polley Street	16 Oct 1798	William Kerr
Browning Richard	Sophiah Cantrel	12 Mar 1816	Solomon Browning
Browning Robert	Hannah Browning	28 Jan 1786	Joseph McReynolds
Browning Sanders	Leatha Warren	15 Oct 1823	Zephaniah T. Kerr
Browning Sanders	Sarah Oakely	6 Oct 1857	James Terrell
Browning Simeon	Mary Brown	23 Dec 1819	John Massee
Browning Thomas	Elizabeth Allin	19 Sep 1795	Edmond Browning
Browning Thomas	Polly Lay	9 Nov 1801	Humphrey Roberts
Browning William	Cathrine Anglin	24 Aug 1797	Humphrey Roberts
Browning William	Permelia Nelson	12 Nov 1823	Zephaniah T. Kerr
Browning William	Jane Estes	13 Feb 1837	Richard Jackson

GROOM	BRIDE	DATE	BONDSMAN OR WITNESS
Bruce David	Prudence Zachary	23 Aug 1795	Richard Jones
Bruce James	Peggy Cobb	7 Oct 1808	John Cooper
Bruce John	Nelly Browning	28 Dec 1796	Jacob Ayard
Bruce Levi L.	Henritta Brooks	29 Jan 1841	John Evans
Bruce Robert	Tabitha Cochran	2 Feb 1789	James Hayes
Bruce Robert	Letty Turner	29 Dec 1801	Jacob A. Hart
Bruce Scott (Col- son of Barney Scott & Betsy Walker)	Millie Reid (Col-dau of Nick & Amy)	2 Nov 1867	H. F. Brandon
Bruce Thomas	Jenny Perry	7 Jul 1792	Starling Carrol
Bruce William	Betsey A. Hart (Ahart?)	4 Sep 1797	James Carrel
Bruce William	Mary Sawyer	18 Oct 1806	James Bruce
Brumit Pleasant	Barbara Jones	11 Jan 1837	Hiram Lockard
Brummit William	Mary Hightower	30 Nov 1832	Marmaduke Norfleet
Brummitt Anderson	Eliza O. Evans	7 Nov 1838	Henderson House
Bryan James	Sally Carrell	22 Jan 1783	Joseph Smith
Bryan John	Rebeccah Farley	11 Aug 1797	William Frasure
Bryant Fleming B.	Elizabeth Snody	21 Dec 1837	Philip Hawker
Bryant Harrison	Betsey Cook	17 Mar 1810	William Stimpson
Bryant John	Heathy Shearman	31 Oct 1783	James Bryant
Bryant W. W. R.	V. E. Poteat	11 Feb 1867	Thos. P. Neal
Bucey Isaac F.	Margarett Astin	25 Oct 1830	Allen Halcomb
Buchanan John	Catherine Ledford	27 Feb 1799	Joseph Payne
Buchanan Washington	Mary M. Murphey	30 Dec 1856 8 Jan 1857	Albert A. Malone md
Buckingham Bird	Frances Elam	24 Mar 1834	Peter E. Hooper
Buckingham Bird	Mary Allen	10 Aug 1866	Henry H. Gordon
Buckingham George	Joicy Tallaw	26 Nov 1833	William J. Connally
Buckingham James	Mary Basdell	16 Nov 1819	Mathis Moore Stokes
Buckley John	Margret Swainey	26 Nov 1780	John Sweaney
Buckley Nathan	Sarah Poyner (dau of John)	4 Jan 1792	William Chambers
Buckley Peyton	Zebba Mallory	23 Aug 1811	Moses Simpson
Buckley Randolph	Ann Roper (dau of Jno.)	15 Nov 1803	James Samuel Jr.
Buckner James	Frances Phelps	3 Feb 1849	Lawson Earp
Buckner John	Sarah Kursey	15 Apr 1830	Henry Thomas
Buckner Thomas S.	Cathern A. Brandon	31 Aug 1854 17 Sep 1854	James A. Childress md by T. L. Lea JP
Bull Jacob	Judith Chambers	6 May 1781	John Chambers
Bull Jacob	Elisabeth Walker	12 Jul 1784	James Chambers
Bulles John	Philadelphia Pearce	30 Apr 1794	Reuben Cochran
Bullock John	Catherine Baxter	23 Mar 1791	Thomas Gaddiss
Bullock John C.	Eliza Poindexter	20 Dec 1815	Richard C. Overton
Burch A. J.	Mary Moore	5 Mar 1853	Rufus A. Lockard
Burch Baylor	Lucy Crisp	11 Oct 1790	George Burch
Burch Ephraim	Frances Hendshaw	15 Mar 1825	Allin Cooper
Burch George	Betsy Crisp	16 Nov 1789	John Crisp
Burch Henry	Aggy Stuart	21 Dec 1807	Brittain Moore
Burch James	Mary Burch	26 Jan 1829	Robert Malone
Burch James S.	Nancey Colemon	17 Feb 1819	John Crisp Jr.
Burch Jesse	Nancy Moore	8 Jan 1834	William Moore
Burch John	Elisabeth Shermon	12 Apr 1791	Jon Winningham
Burch John W.	Nannie J. Gosney	29 May 1862	Richard A. Newbell
Burch Larkin	Salley Puttery (Buttery?)	22 Jan 1812	George Burch
Burch Peter L.	Martha Ann Adams	29 Apr 1842	Jesse Owen
Burch Richard	Maryan Crisp	23 Feb 1790	John Crisp
Burch Richard	Polley McKee	2 Jan 1815	Phillip Burch
Burch Samuel	Peggy Stokes	24 Aug 1802	Bluford Warren
Burch Squire	Sarah Moore	28 Jan 1826	Henry D. Fuqua
Burch Thomas	Polly Brown	26 Sep 1798	John Dobbin

GROOM	BRIDE	DATE	BONDSMAN OR WITNESS
Burch William	Nancy Dobbin	10 Oct 1792	Derritt Richards
Burch William	Betsey Eubank	21 Jun 1805	William Hester
Burch William	Mary A. Warren	10 Oct 1850	William S. Tate
Burge John	Cathrine Smith	8 Oct 1787	William Brown
Burgess William	Elizabeth Price	20 Aug 1816	Joseph Langley
Burgiss John	Polly Cox	28 Mar 1795	James Willson
Burk Granderson	Agness Warren	26 Mar 1840	John Davis
Burk William A.	Martha Dameron	4 Oct 1842	William W. Richardson
Burke James A.	Susan W. Sheppard	20 Jan 1852	William Miles
Burke John	Elizabeth Russell	5 Mar 1842	Thomas Campbell
Burke Johnson	Mary Bird	17 Dec 1837	Archibald Birk
Burke William A.	Jane Aldridge	4 Jan 1845	Iverson Foulks
Burke William A.	Martha Ann West	23 Sep 1854	William J. Aldrige
Burke William T.	Nancey Boswell	3 May 1858	William B. Smith
		4 May 1858	md by John Stadler
Burke Wyly M.	Mary Frances Stanback	31 Mar 1862	William Gooch
Burks Joseph F.	Marthy Jane Hall	21 Sep 1866	Benjamin H. Burks
Burks Richard	Susan S. Yuille	27 Nov 1852	Lindsey M. Shumaker
H. Jr.		28 Nov 1852	md by S. S. Harrison JP
Burne Thomas	Sally Cox	6 Feb 1813	Jacob Ahart
Burris Rawzel	Pamilia Kirk	16 Jan 1810	Amos Satterfield
Burroughs Bennett	Salley Raimey	16 Feb 1820	James Harris
Burton Absalom	Priscilla Jackson	2 Oct 1815	Moses Langley
Burton Allin	Nancey Cleton	19 Jan 1791	Francis Scoggins
Burton Benjamin	Rebecca Gunn	9 Dec 1801	Nathl. Pass
Burton David	Susanna Simpson (dau of Richd.)	7 Feb 1780	Tyree Harris William Campbell
Burton David S.	Nancy J. Burton	14 Dec 1842	Thomas W. Burton Jr.
Burton Drury	Jenney Hughston	4 Oct 1808	Thomas Burton
Burton Drury	Peggy Richmond	3 Dec 1816	Jonathan Huston
Burton Drury	Sally Baynes	5 Apr 1864	James L. McKee
		7 Apr	md by John D. Long JP
Burton Francis A.	Jane Baynes	2 Feb 1856	Thomas W. Burton
		2 Feb	md by Thos. Covington JP
Burton Francis H.	Zilphah Love	17 Dec 1810	Thomas Burton
Burton Franklin X.	Harriet Ware	22 Oct 1847	Allen Gunn
Burton George M.	F. E. Smith	24 Sep 1866	George & Jerry Smith
		29 Sep	md by Jerry Smith JP
Burton Henry	Keziah Farley	20 Nov 1786	John Burton
Burton Henry A.	Nancy G. Slade	21 Dec 1823	S. H. Gunn
Burton Hutchens	Eliza B. Malone	2 Nov 1813	Drury Burton
Burton Hutchens	Louisa Burton	22 Dec 1828	Azariah Graves
Burton Isaac	Laney Burch	8 Aug 1838	John M. Brown B. C. West Sr.
Burton James	Sarah Gunn	19 Jan 1800	Elijah Graves
Burton James	Phillisse B. Doson	30 Jan 1838	Isaac Burton B. C. West Sr.
Burton James	Mary Walker	17 Oct 1861	John Scott
Burton James M.	Agness S. Richmond	20 Oct 1848	George W. Simpson
Burton John	Judy Russell	20 Jan 1867	John Yarbrough
Burton John (Col)	Frances Dameron (Col)	12 Nov 1867	H. F. Brandon clk
		14 Nov	md by Jerry mith JP
Burton John A.	Allice W. Roper	18 Oct 1865	William H. Kersey
		22 Oct	md by R. G. Barrett MG
Burton John J.	Mary Kernal	13 Nov 1839	John Johnston
Burton Noel	Nancey Dobbins	5 Jun 1817	Newman Durham
Burton Noel	Priscilla Payne	8 Apr 1822	H. Hooper
Burton Noel	Nannie Thompson	24 Nov 1857	William Lockhart J. H. F. Graves, D.C.
		26 Nov	md by J. M. Allen JP
Burton Richd.	------------	1787	Daniel Burton
Burton Samuel	Amey Oldham	19 May 1784	Jeremiah Poston

GROOM	BRIDE	DATE	BONDSMAN OR WITNESS
Burton Thomas	Jenney Brandon	29 Dec 1802	Drury Burton
Burton Thomas	Susan Enochs	21 Oct 1843	Francis A. Burton
Burton Thomas F.*	Nancey Burton	10 Feb 1831	Hutchins Burton
Burton Thomas W.	Nancy E. Bradsher	25 Jun 1845	Jno. W. Roan
Burton William	Jane Love	17 Nov 1818	John Love
			Iverson Graves
Burton William	Judeth Pinix	11 Dec 1827	Bartlett Y. Slade
Busby James	Elizabeth Mann	1 Jun 1863	William H. Hodges
			md by J. A. Hodges JP
Busey Samuel	Betsey Trigg	26 Dec 1823	William Busey
Busey William	Patsey Holloway	6 Feb 1808	William Holloway
Bush Bennet	Betsy Brintle	14 Aug 1809	Buckner Duke
Bush Ezanus	Liddey Rice	14 Jun 1797	Thomas Harrelson
Bush Jeremiah	Rebecah Dickins	6 Dec 1794	William Darnell
Bush Zenas	Patsey Brooks	27 Nov 1805	Jeremiah Graves
			Wm. Wilkinson
Butcher George	Lucy Deboe	30 Jan 1828	James Woodall
Butler Hudson	Jincy Farmer	26 Mar 1795	William Ragland
Butler J. H.	Candis J. Walton	23 Sep 1857	H. A. Maynard
			J. H. G. Graves D.C.
		23 Sep	md by J. Doll, MG
Butler Moses M.	Elizabeth Summers	16 Feb 1855	Saml. Apple
		18 Feb	md by Lancelot Johnston
Butler Thomars	Susan Paschael	27 Mar 1839	Zera Sommers
Butt Ambrose	Sophia Curles	1 Jul 1803	John T. Curl
Buttery John	Narcissia Foley	9 Nov 1812	George Burch
Buzwell John	Delphia Rice	19 Mar 1799	James Hamlett
Byrd Albert G.	Mary Bouldin	23 Jan 1838	James Vincent
Byrd James T.	Caroline Connally	11 Feb 1847	William A. Lea
Byrd John	Mary Brookes	21 Jul 1795	Thos. Cheatham
Byrd Temple	Salley McMenemy	28 May 1809	Jeremiah Braughton
Byrd Temple	Nancey Fuller	14 Jul 1809	John Price Jr.
Byrd Thomas	Anne Browning	11 Oct 1784	Isaac Boran
Byrd Thomas	Rebecca Johnston	25 Oct 1816	William Fitch
Bysor John	Polly Dixon	28 Jan 1799	Peter Bysor
Bysor Peter	Betsey Bennett	22 Feb 1800	Joseph Payne

- C -

Cabell P. B.	Jane B. Lanier	3 Sep 1857	A. S. Cabell
Caldwell Alexander	Betsey Nickleson	13 Feb 1811	Abraham B. Morton
Caldwell Jno. M. M.	Caroline E. Levy	7 Jun 1844	Saml. Moore
Camel Edley	Jincey Jones	27 Nov 1812	John Covington
Campbell Allen C.	Manerva E. Browning	11 Jun 1855	James P. Boswell
Campbell Archibald	Joannah Sheppard	22 Sep 1846	James M. Boswell
Campbell Banister	Rhody Pinson	9 Dec 1815	Smith Murphey
Campbell Edley	Jincey Jones	27 Nov 1812	John Covington
Campbell Hugh	Nelly Robinson	27 Jun 1812	John Covington
Campbell James Bedford	Susanna Hancock	22 Jul 1855	Thomas N. Davis md by C. H. Richmond JP
Campbell John	Lucey Moore	26 Jan 1785	Archld. Murphey
Campbell William	Patsey Hunter	14 Apr 1816	John Chandler
Canaday A. L.	Margarett Gibson	19 Dec 1865	James Combs
			B. Harrelson
Canaday James	Sina Whalebone	27 Mar 1804	Smith Sutton
Cannaday John	Elizabeth Boswell	16 Dec 1828	Ezekiel Paschal
Cannon William	Usrly Pirkins	29 Oct 1783	John Cannon
Cantrell Joseph	Lettice Florence	11 Nov 1814	Tolifer Florence
			Math. G. Muzzall
Cantrell Alexander	Nancy Foster	17 Dec 1834	Ezekiel Sawyer
			L(eannah) Haralson

GROOM	BRIDE	DATE	BONDSMAN OR WITNESS
Cape Thomas R.	Harriet J. Lashly	18 Mar 1865	C. W. Prendergast
Capes George	Mary Dobbs	3 Aug 1863	James M. Smith
		4 Aug	md by M. F. Adams MP
Cardwell Richard M.	Salley Crowder	19 Apr 1817	David Northington
Cardwell William (Col-son of Randol Dodson & Thomas & Nancy Cardwell)	Emily Hunt (Col-dau of Essex) Jennie Burton)	23 Jul 1868	H. F. Brandon md by N. M. Lewis JP
Cardwell William W. (son of Thomas & Nancy Cardwell)	Martha J. Russell (dau of P. H. & Sarah Womack)	7 Jan 1868	H. F. Brandon clk
Carlen Richard	Mary Midleton	18 Nov 1780	Hugh Dobbin
Carman Archibald	Polley Rose	11 Feb 1795	John Cameron
Carman Elijah	Rachel Standsbury	19 Sep 1796	Saml. Stafford
Carman Elijah	Betsey Ponds	11 Jul 1797	Thomas Climer
Carman William	Sarah Quine	27 Mar 1792	Travis Graham
Carmichel William	Elizabeth Williams	1 Jun 1818	Alfred M. Nash
Carmikel William	Salley Smith	25 Oct 1799	Thomas Smith
Carnal Flemman	Frankey Warrin	22 Oct 1804	Clem Deshazo
Carnal Hubbard	Elisabeth Dixon	21 Jan 1797	Henry Mitchell
Carnal Patrick	Anness Warrin	17 Dec 1790	Henry Mitchell
Carnal Wm. Jr.	Ellin Dunn	26 Jan 1818	Richd. Burch Tho. Slade
Carney Joshua	Lucy Miles	26 Dec 1786	Lewis Shappard
Carr John	Polly Zachary	15 Mar 1797	Zachariah Groom
Carral William	Sarah Bryant	5 Jan 1782	William Reed
Carrel Daniel	Suckey Jones	5 Jan 1801	William Jones
Carrell Ellis	Caty Whitlow	14 May 1817	William Lyon
Carrol Edward	Polly Ferrell	19 Jun 1826	John C. Harvey
Carrol Edward	Delilah Baxter	9 Jan 1827	Thomas Ware Jr.
Carrol Jackson	Martha Shelton	12 Apr 1838	Benjamin Evans
Carrol James	Sarah Bruce	29 Nov 1790	James Hays
Carroll James R.	Polly Hubbird	10 Aug 1827	Thomas Johnson
Carroll Lemuel H.	Salley Hooper	11 Sep 1819	Wm. W. Lyon Jr.
Carter Benjamin (son of Albert & Julia Wharton)	Sinai Carter (dau of George Mills & Agness Carter)	10 Aug 1867	H. F. Brandon
Carter Benjamin H.	Almedia A. Cobb	10 May 1859 18 May	N. L. Blackwell md by Jno W. Lewis MG
Carter Braxston	Polley Fuller	24 May 1832	William Carver
Carter Iverson B.	Susan Gatewood	27 Nov 1847	Franklin Knight
Carter James	Matilda Walters	9 Dec 1832	Charles Lucas Henderson House
Carter Jesse	Sally Brown	17 Dec 1809	Alexander Murphey
Carter John	Betty Lea	15 Sep 1784	Owen Lea
Carter John	Sarah Williams	12 Sep 1818	John Lea
Carter John	Adeline Bennett	24 Feb 1849	Lafayett Bennette
Carter John B.	Malinda Cox (dau of Gabriel Cox)	18 Jan 1847	Mastin J. Powell
Carter Joseph	Ann Mallory	18 Dec 1790	Stephen Mallory
Carter Joseph G.	Ann Johnson	25 Jun 1832	B. H. Carter
Carter Martin	Nancy Saterfield	12 Aug 1863	Thomas H. Hudgins
Carter Paton	Elizabeth Eudaly	9 Dec 1819	Thomas Eudaley
Carter Richard T.	Arree Swan	18 Mar 1854 22 Mar	Washington T. Hodges md by Wm. Anderson
Carter Robert H.	Martha J. Thomas	26 Apr 1843	S. B. Holder
Carter Theoderick	Dianah Mallary	16 Apr 1793	Thomas Mallary
Carter Thomas	Anna Powell	27 Feb 1816	Benj. W. Harrelson
Carter Thomas	Martha Walker	18 Apr 1846	William Carter
Carter Thornton	Cathrina Wyne	18 May 1814	Hezh. P. Smithson
Carver Benjamin F.	Ann W. Bastin	15 May 1830	Thomas Bastin
Carver Lemuel	Maria Moor	2 Jan 1838	John Holloway Leannah Haralson

GROOM	BRIDE	DATE	BONDSMAN OR WITNESS
Carver William	Fanny Doowns	7 Jul 1835	John Holloway
Case John J.	Willey Nelson	22 Jun 1841	Richard McAdams
Case Luther A.	Lucy A. Perkins	11 Feb 1856	A. L. Ball
		13 Feb	md R. A. Newell
Casey John (or Kiersey)	Agniss Hightower	2 Dec 1794	Epaphroditus Hightower
Cash Moses	---------	16 Jun	Millinton Blalock
Casort John H.	Harriet Glasco	23 Feb 1843	William P. Graves
Casort Wylie	Margaret Campbell	19 Apr 1847	John H. Casort
Cates John	Elizabeth Foster	25 Sep 1804	Richard Cates
Cates Richard	Lucy Grant	26 Mar 1801	William Cannon
Caynor John H.	Artelia Hensley	27 Apr 1847	Henry Cotton
Cazort Squire	Maseniah Fowler	19 Feb 1833	Richard Gates
Cearnal Robert V.	Margaret A. Woods	4 Dec 1837	Archibald S. Woods
Challes John	Milley Rice	25 Nov 1786	Hezekiah Rice Jr.
Chalmers Joseph W.	Frances M. Henderson	8 Sep 1829	Henry E. Coleman
Chalmers John G.	Mary W. Henderson	2 Oct 1827	Jno. E. Lewis
Chamberlin Ebenezer	Sarah Wells	31 Aug 1819	Thos. Mitchel
Chamberlin John	Polley Burch	16 Sep 1819	Simeon C. Barton
Chambers Abner	Jemima Walker	8 Jan 1789	John Rogers Jr.
Chambers Anthony (Col)	Lucy Swann (Col)	13 Apr 1867	H. F. Brandon md by Thomas J. Brown JP
Chambers James	Nancey Chambers	8 Apr 1787	John Chambers
Chambers Joshua	Nancy M. Powell	17 Feb 1832	James Greenwood
Chambers Josias	Nanny Stanfield	20 Jun 1780	Jno. Chambers
Chambers William P.	Mary J. Price	19 Jul 1843	Albert G. Wiley
Chance David	Frances Lyon	24 Jun 1853	Samuel Davis
Chance James	Frances Jackson	30 Sep 1848	Henry N. Holden
Chance Yancy	Martha Horton	8 Jan 1864	Tho. W. Graves clk md by John J. Jones JP
Chandler Charles G.	Rachael Clempson	14 Oct 1837	John Jeffreys
Chandler Daniel	Polley Groom	19 Dec 1821	Bennet Malone
Chandler George W.	Elizabeth Boswell	31 Oct 1857 5 Nov	Thomas Slade Jr. md by J. Doll MG
Chandler Hosea A.	Judy Boswell	8 Dec 1847	James M. Boswell R. Y. Graves
Chandler James C.	Susan C. Price	10 Jul 1852 11 Jul	John D. Keesee md by William Anderson
Chandler James D. (or Stephen J.)	Frances Smith	26 Oct 1827	James D. Chandler
Chandler John	Mary J. Kimbro	16 Dec 1822	Anderson Willis
Chandler John J.	Sarah J. Goodson	1 Dec 1840	William C. Page Levi C. Page
Chandler Josiah	Nancey Wiley	23 Mar 1801	Alexander Wiley
Chandler Pleasant	Martha Jeffreys	26 Aug 1816	Wilkins Chandler
Chandler Pleasant	Jemima Cobb	28 Oct 1852	md by John H. Pickard MG
Chandler Rufus W.	Nancy Aldridge	8 Nov 1843	John T. Stadler
Chandler Stephen	Betsy Ingram	21 Dec 1805	John Pinson Wm. Wilkinson
Chandler Stephen J. (or James D.)	Frances Smith	26 Oct 1827	James D. Chandler
Chandler Stephen J.	Nancey Prendergast	28 Dec 1829	William Howard
Chandler Thomas B.	Sarah Hightower	28 Nov 1838	Lewis Morton
Chandler Thomas J.	Louisiana Walters	31 Aug 1852	A. Slade clk md by Theo. L. Lea JP
Chandler Thomas W.	Julia Wiley	12 Oct 1830	Azariah G. Kimbro
Chandler Thomas W.	Sarah Richmond	24 Oct 1843	Robert H. Wiley
Chandler Wilkins	Joicy Willis	29 Nov 1818	Bennet Malone

GROOM	BRIDE	DATE	BONDSMAN OR WITNESS
Chandler William	Salley Bozwell	14 May 1806	John Pinson
			Wm. Wilkinson
Chandler William	Martha B. Walters	23 Nov 1857	A. W. Jeffreys
			R. A. Newbell
Chandler William G.	Virginia Covington (dau of Thomas)	26 Jan 1856 31 Jan	Tho. W. Graves clk md by James K. Lea JP
Chapman John	Betsey Johnston	26 Jul 1796	Henry McAden
Chapman Nelson	Jane Murphey	31 Jan 1849	William Chapman
Chapman Richard	Sally Going	21 Jun 1806	James Vaughan
Chatham John	Lucinda Davis	7 Feb 1829	Thomas Christopher
			Isaac Chatham
Chatham John C.	Annie Saunders	15 Jun 1866	William L. Page
Chatham Joseph	Artelia Underwood	30 Jan 1847	Thomas Moore
Chatman James	Matilda A. Murphey	12 Apr 1866 13 Apr	E. S. Cook md by W. B. Swann JP
Chatman William	Matilda Sourtherd	1 Jan 1840	William Sourtherd
Chavers Evans	Susan Jeffreys	21 Dec 1857 22 Dec	Iverson Jeffreys md by Benj. Wells JP
Cheaney William H.	Elizabeth A. Halcomb	27 May 1846	Abisha Slade
Cheek John W.	Susan A. Rudd	13 Nov 1866 14 Nov	Thomas H. Rudd md by F. L. Oakley MG
Cheek Robert	Tabitha Terrell	6 Dec 1838	John A. Leath
Cheek Robert H.	Mary Sanders	21 Jul 1864 24 Jul	A. S. Williamson md by Stephen Neal JP
Cheek Robert H.	Martha E. Cates	24 Jan 1867 27 Jan	James H. Willis md by Thomas J. Brown JP
Childress James A.	Susan J. Fullinton	22 Feb 1856	James Dismuke md by Wm. J. Moore JP
Childress Jerremiah	Mary Wells	7 Jul 1821	John Sawyer
Childress Salmon	Susannah Bush	-- Sep 1807	Bennet Bush
Childress William*	Parthenia Boman	29 Dec 1831	William Shaw Leannah H. Haralson
Chiles William H.	Julia Fannie Foster	26 Apr 1864 1 May	B. Y. McAden md by P. J. Carraway MG
Chilton Alfred	Eliza Groom	10 Dec 1842	Miller Nunn
Chilton James	Joannah Kennaday	9 Jan 1800	Greenbury Voss
Chilton John	Salley Hamilton	31 Jan 1807	William Swann
Chilton Joshua (L?)	Martha Ann Freman	23 Nov 1836	John McDaniel
Chilton Samuel*	Sina Chambers	1 Jan 1831	William Garrott
Chilton William	Sally Holloway	4 Oct 1800	Walker Dowell
Chissonbury John	Elizabeth Burch	24 Nov 1791	John Winningham
Chisum Joseph	Martha Dillard	17 Aug 1853	Thomas Davis md by J. M. Allen JP
Chresfield James A.	Mary A. Day	28 Feb 1867	Thomas Day J. J. Jones md by S. A. Stanfield
Chrismas Thomas	Margarett Underwood	13 Apr 1811	William Heritage S. D. Watkins
Chrismus John	Mary Bryant	12 Sep 1783	James Bryant
Chumbly Larkin	Elizabeth Montgomery	23 Dec 1835	Archibald W. Worsham
Chuning Richard	Betsey Rice	26 Mar 1802	William Browning
Cinkler James	Elizabeth Haddock	1 Feb 1798	Duncan Kermichael
Claiborne William (Col)	Jane Stamps (Col)	20 Dec 1866	Alexander Irvine md by J. J. Jones JP
Clapsaddle John H.	Louisa F. Baugh	24 Sep 1863	David G. Womack md by S. S. Harrison JP
Clardy William H.	Martha A. Davis	6 Dec 1866	David N. Atkinson md by J. J. Jones JP

GROOM	BRIDE	DATE	BONDSMAN OR WITNESS
Clark Benjamin (Col-son of Ben & Amy Clark)	Francis Dodson (Col-dau of George & Marthy Dodson)	21 Dec 1867	H. F. Brandon clk
Clark John	Anny Hall	17 Apr 1855 18 Apr	E. B. Holden md by J. M. Allen JP
Clark Joseph (Col-son of Hiram & Sarah Bennett)	Amanda Brandon (Col-dau of Edward & Martha)	26 Dec 1867	H. F. Brandon
Clark Martin	Susana Smith	4 Oct 1805	Peter Smith
Clark Peter F.	Mary A. Moore	10 Oct 1856 15 Oct	L. T. Hunt md by J. M. Allen JP
Clark Richard H.	Amy J. Mansfield	6 Jan 1835	Henry N. Holden
Clarke Robert	Hannah Roberts	26 May 1799	George Powel
Clay Henry (Col-son of James Buster & Nancy Lewis)	Ellen Lewis (Col-dau of Antny & Eliza Lewis)	27 Dec 1867	H. F. Brandon
Clay James	Pheobe Johnston	22 Oct 1819	James Holder
Clayton Daniel	Rebeccah Clayton	15 Jan 1789	Allin Burton
Clemson William	Polley Delgs	12 Feb 1800	John Starkey
Clendenin James J.	Susan A. Hodge	15 Dec 1857	W. S. Ector Jno. F. Graves DC
Climer Thomas	Leminah Kermichael	5 Nov 1799	Benjamin Pond
Clowders Samuel	Martha Jourdon (formerly of Halifax Co. Va.)	26 Dec 1829	John O. Brackin
Clyborne George	Lucy Ann Wilkes	2 Feb 1836	William H. Hendrick
Clyce James T.	Nancy Jane McCampbell	13 Jan 1850	William W. Price
Clyft John	Nancy Long	27 Oct 1780	Robert Moore
Cobb Amsa	Nancy Denny	18 Dec 1822	Azariah Denny
Cobb Andrew J.	Jemima Powell	22 Jan 1846	John Evans
Cobb Archey	Martha F. Walker	17 Nov 1863	James Dill
Cobb Archy	Rebecca F. Cannady	28 Jul 1865	Joseph H. Cannaday
Cobb Ebenezer	Hannah Emons	5 Mar 1806	Henry Cobb
Cobb Ebenezar	Nancy Humphreys	4 Dec 1839	Hugh E. Cobb G. W. G. VanHook
Cobb Henry	Martha Nunnaly	7 Dec 1818	William H. Nunnally Azariah Graves CC
Cobb Henry Sr.	Mary Lovelace	14 Jun 1826	Barnett Lovelace John H. Pickard
Cobb Hugh	Elizabeth Murphey	20 Dep 1811	Joseph Bours
Cobb Hugh E.	Sarah Rice	22 Dec 1832	John M. Walker
Cobb James	Louisa Barker	4 Dec 1846	Isaac Barker
Cobb James	Frances Cox	8 Aug 1854	H. F. Adkins
Cobb James N.	Cloe Siddle	25 May 1830	William M. Cobb
Cobb Jesse	Mary Boswell	5 Dec 1817	William Cobb
Cobb Jesse E.	Elizabeth Cobb	26 Dec 1838	Samuel Bethel
Cobb John Jr.	Jane Brackin	18 Dec 1786	Thomas Thaxton H. Haralson DC
Cobb John Jr.	Elizabeth Slade	9 Dec 1826	Jno. G. Womack
Cobb John W.	Elizabeth E. King	11 Dec 1852 14 Dec	Thos. J. Brown md by John H. Pickard MG
Cobb Joseph	Nancy Gennings	9 Nov 1812	William Morgan
Cobb Joseph K.	Kitty Harris	30 Aug 1825	John Cobb Jr.
Cobb Joseph P.	Charlott T. Lipscomb	2 Nov 1860	Archibald W. Jeffreys md by S. A. Stanfield
Cobb Levi	Rebecah Elmore	7 Nov 1808	James Cobb
Cobb Mastin H.	Malvina F. Butler	4 Feb 1850	Ezekiel J. Orr
Cobb Mathew	Polly North	3 Feb 1809	Henry Cobb W. Smith
Cobb Maximin	Pamelia D. Grant	25 Feb 1837	Robert Madding
Cobb Milton	Elizabeth Suthard	25 Oct 1825	Ebenezar Cobb

GROOM	BRIDE	DATE	BONDSMAN OR WITNESS
Cobb Neptha	Martha A. Cobb	13 Sep 1841	Jesse E. Cobb
Cobb Noah	Nancey Walker	23 Oct 1812	William Cobb
Cobb Noah	Phoebe Lovelace	29 Jan 1820	James Lovelace
Cobb Noah Sr.	Jane Dill	23 Nov 1833	Samuel M. Cobb
			John Kerr Jr.
Cobb Samuel B.	Elizabeth C. Burton	10 Nov 1851	Bartlett Y. Cobb
		11 Nov	md by John H. Pickard MG
Cobb Samuel C.	Sarah Harris	7 Dec 1827	Joseph K. Cobb
Cobb Samuel M.	Matilda Powell	3 Jan 1854	Jessey E. Cobb
			James T. Graves DC
		5 Jan	md by John H. Pickard MG
Cobb William	Mary A. Elmore	5 Dec 1821	Levi Cobb
Cobb William M.	Dolpha Groom	25 Jan 1830	Jno. Harrison
Cobbs James S. (son of John Jr. & Mildred A. Cobbs)	Annie E. Wilson (dau of John Wilson)	15 Oct 1867	md by S. A. Stanfield
Cochran Robert	Silvy Scott	25 Aug 1800	Robert Bruce
Cochron Will	Elizabeth Cate	24 Oct 1789	J. Womack
Cock George	Bidsey Miles	9 Dec 1822	Elisha Rudd
Coe Joshua	Rackael Paul	26 Oct 1784	Samuel Paul
Coe William	Susannah Adkerson	5 Feb 1828	Samuel Shelton
			Barzl. Graves
Coil Azariah	Nancey Dunnavan	2 Mar 1826	James A. Kersey
			John H. Graves
Coil Nicholas	Sally Eskridge	9 Feb 1796	Richard Eskridge
Coile Theopolas	Martha Lamb	29 May 1828	Enoch Coyle
Cole Green W.	Susan Smith	18 Nov 1851	Alexander McAlpin md by Howell Boswell JP
Cole Harvie J.	Ann R. Williams	16 Jan 1844	B. L. Cole
Cole Theophilus M.	Willie L. Jerrill	27 Nov 1843	Baley Martin
Cole Thomas	Unity McCoy	21 Sep 1780	George Lea
Cole Tilman	Sarah Frances Smith	22 Oct 1851	Maj. H. Graves
Cole William T.	Nancy T. Crane	25 Nov 1866	Thomas Orander
Coleman Alexander	Mary Hilton	6 Feb 1837	John Hinton
Coleman Alexander	Martha B. Bateman	29 Oct 1855	Robert Smith
Coleman Archibald	Dicey Perkins	13 Feb 1795	William Kannon
Coleman Daniel	Lucy Bumpass	22 Dec 1789	John Satterfield
Coleman George A.	Sarah F. Hagewood	9 Jan 1858	Wm. E. Harrelson
		14 Jan	md by J. S. Totten JP
Coleman George J.	Sarah W. Swan	11 Jan 1847	Danl. W. Swan
Coleman James	Elizabeth Florence	22 Dec 1832	John Coleman
Coleman James E.	Rebecca J. King	12 Oct 1866	James W. Massey
		14 Oct	md by F. L. Oakley MG
Coleman James M.	Agness W. Harrison	5 Jan 1850	Thomas D. Harrison
Coleman Joshua (or Page Whitehead)	Betsey Wright	15 Dec 1809	Whitehead Page
Coleman William*	Elizabeth B. Robertson	3 Jan 1831	Thomas Hagood
Coles Willis (Col)	Letitia Davis (Col)	19 May 1867	H. F. Brandon
Colley Bannister	Sarah Birch	19 Nov 1848	LaFayette Morgan
Collier Henry	Darky Ellis	3 Dec 1815	Robert Stadler
			Sm. Murphey
Collier James	Salley Kimbrough	5 Sep 1810	Garland Cock
Collier James M.	Mary J. Midkiff	26 Dec 1866	Wm. D. Cole
Collier Joseph	Isbel Kimbro	17 Sep 1805	William S. Webb
Collier Joseph	Polley White	6 Jul 1815	Robert Stadler
			Jas. Yancey
Collier Thomas	Dilly Robertson	20 Dec 1804	James Wilson
Collier Thomas	Susanah Pinson	21 Dec 1822	Nathaniel Gooch
Collier William	Patsey Kimbrough	13 Apr 1814	James Collier
Collins Brice	Huldah Tait	17 Dec 1808	Henry Tait

GROOM	BRIDE	DATE	BONDSMAN OR WITNESS
Collins Theophilus J.	Mary Ann Deens	7 Sep 1840	A. H. Clarke
Colquhoun James	Patsey Gatewood (dau of Dudley Gatewood)	19 Dec 1796	James Dix
Combes James	Susan Sanders	1 May 1849	Absalom Canaday
Combes Orrison G.	Missouri S. Braughton	16 Jan 1837	Lewis Malone
Combs James	Mary Rowland	23 Aug 1859	Leroy Sanders
Combs Jesse	Betsy Stephens	2 Nov 1799	James Robinson
Comer John	Mary Brown	26 Oct 1824	Thomas Comer A. D. Montgomery
Comer John	Matilda Moore	4 Jan 1827	Nathaniel M. Roan
Comer William G.	Ann W. Bomar	4 Apr 1836	Booker Bomar
Compton Allen	Lavinia Cooper	17 Feb 1835	Sieria G. Compton Abr. Landers
Compton Aquilla	Salenia Cooper	4 Feb 1832	Robeson McMennamy
Compton John L.	Nancey Burt	24 Oct 1840	Robeson McMenamy
Compton Samuel W.	Rebecka Burt	2 Dec 1833	James N. Landers
Compton Thomas	Nancey Greer	22 May 1811	Aquilla Compton
Conally William J.	Nancy McCain (wid)	21 Jul 1857 23 Jul	James M. Allen md by J. B. Jackson
Connally Charles	Keziah Smith	13 May 1794	Charles Connally
Connally Charls	Nancy Smith	2 Mar 1793	William Williams
Connally George A.	Mary Jane Womack	26 May 1830	James E. Williamson
Connally George O.	Polly Ball	17 Jan 1811	William Evans
Connally George R.	Caroline Owen	5 Oct 1854	John S. Connally md by Thos. L. Lea JP
Connally John S.	Margarett Walker	27 May 1826	George A. Connally
Connally John Spencer	Sarah Roper	28 Nov 1844	Stephen Dodson N. J. Palmer
Connally Solomon (Col)	Emily Connally (Col)	26 Jan 1867	Edward Palmer
Connally William T.	Mary W. Hooper	18 Dec 1854 19 Dec	Robert W. Graves md by J. H. Lacy
Connally William T.	Mary E. Brandon	23 Oct 1858 1 Nov	David T. Elliott md by Jas. P. Simpson MG
Connaly William J.	Cary Ball	23 Mar 1816	William Gattis
Conner William B.	Nancey Garrett	12 Mar 1855 15 Mar	A. Simpson md by L. L. Hendren
Conoley John	Scecily Moore	23 May 1788	George Conoley William Moore
Cook Augustin	Clary Payne	20 Jan 1789	Greenwood Payne
Cook Edmund	Mary Ann O'Brian	15 Feb 1830	David Tyree
Cook George	Lucy Hardy	19 Jul 1844	William W. Price William Cook
Cook Henry	Elizabeth Chapman	22 Dec 1851 23 Dec	Nelson Chapman md by E. K. Withers JP
Cook Johnston	Delilah Stafford	25 Jul 1796	Thomas Stafford
Cook Lemuel	Margarett Downs	10 Mar 1826	Corban Jackson
Cook Owen	Jane Dunervent	27 Jan 1855 29 Jan	Abraham Dunervent md by Thomas Covington
Cook Philip	Elisabeth Richardson	9 Jul 1792	Thoms. Richardson
Cooke William	Unity Richardson	8 Jul 1793	Thomas Richardson
Cooper Allin	Fanney Warren	4 Aug 1800	William Warren
Cooper Harvey W.*	Permelia Baynes	2 Apr 1831	Westley Warren
Cooper Hiram	Nancey Sawyer	15 Jan 1805	James Mitchell
Cooper James	Dililah Simpson	31 Aug 1811	Joseph Neeley
Cooper John	Mary Gibson	13 Jul 1782	Thos. Douglas
Cooper Martin	Elizabeth Parker	20 Jan 1790	Kindal Vanhook J. Womack
Cooper Plumer (Col)	Jane Piles (Col)	24 Mar 1867	Elijah Lewis
Cooper Warren	Elizabeth A. Corbit	1 Jul 1851 17 Jul	J. J. Allen md by Benj. Wells JP

GROOM	BRIDE	DATE	BONDSMAN OR WITNESS
Cooper William	Mary A. Warren	6 Feb 1847	Azariah Dameron
Coram William	Abagail Carmon	10 Apr 1782	Henry Quine
Corbet John	Emily T. Russell	4 Aug 1840	Solomon Corbet
Corbet Pleasant	Sina Brackin	24 May 1839	Solomon Corbett B. Corbett
Corbett Archer (Col-son of David & Jane Hooper)	Littie Williamson (Col- dau of John & Frances Williamson)	26 Dec 1867 27 Dec	H. F. Brandon clk md by Jacob Doll MG
Corbett B. H.	Fannie Cooper	3 Aug 1860 8 Aug	Jno. F. Graves DC md by J. S. Compton JP
Corbett Burel	Susan Miles	16 Dec 1839	Solomon Corbet
Corbett Solomon	Judiah Russel	28 Apr 1842	Lindsay Roberts
Corbett Solomon	Susan Hooper	10 Dec 1844	A. Slade T. H. Miles
Corbin Thomas J. (of Danville, Va.)	Martha E. Rodenhizer (of Danville, Va.)	21 Mar 1866	Thomas J. Lee md by Jacob Doll MG
Corbitt William	Nancey Warren	25 Feb 1830	Christopher W. Brookes
Corder Joel	Jane Anthony	15 Nov 1784	David Enochs
Corham Richard F.	Rachel T. Ellington (wid)	11 Jul 1865	John P. Ellington J. L. McKee clk
Corley Charles S.	Sarah J. Barker	20 Dec 1865	James Harrison md by S. S. Harrison JP
Cornwell Joseph	Margarett Prather	31 Dec 1833	John R. Griffith
Cornwell Samuel	Eliza Boswell	26 Dec 1839	Joseph F. Cornwell
Corum William J.	Frances Cole	14 Apr 1857 30 Apr	James A. Burke md by John Stadler
Cochran Elijah	Letecia Campbell	19 Feb 1822	Joshua Hightower
Cochran James H.	Mary Lovelace	11 Jan 1841	Wm. C. Mitchell
Cotton Henry	Mary Ballard	281 Aug 1838	William Benton Geo. W. VanHook
Courts Jennings H.	Eliza G. Williams	12 Jul 1819	William M. Puryear
Courts William James	Sarah Frances Carter	4 Jan 1858 4 Jan	M. C. Holderby md by John H. Pickard MG
Cousins Alexander (Col)	Celia Jones (Col)	29 Mar 1851	Alexander Hart
Cousins James	Nancy Parks	12 Aug 1820	Herrod Smith
Cousins Thomas	Harriett Good	13 Dec 1859	John F. Turner
Covey James G.	Elizabeth C. Fowler	27 Apr 1847	William C. Paxton
Covington Bird	Phoebe Key	25 May 1826	Dennis Wilsn
Covington Elisha J.	Nancy E. Steel	31 Oct 1866 4 Nov	J. L. McKee md by E. W. Beale
Covington Henry	Margaret Malone	2 Mar 1867	Robin Covington md by James K. Lea JP
Covington John	Martha Holderness	9 Jan 1866	Thomas R. Kimbro
Covington John E.	Nancy A. Enocks	5 Feb 1866	Q. T. Anderson
Covington John J.	Sarah J. Ferguson	29 Dec 1856 30 Dec	David A. Gillispie md by N. M. Lewis JP
Cowan Joseph	Susannah Hart	1 Jun 1808	David Hart Sol Debow
Cowardin Francis C.	Parthana F. Wilkerson	8 Dec 1836	James Duffy Temple Lewis Leroy Rice John W. Carden C. West
Cowman William	Sarah Cox	13 Dec 1838	B. C. West Sr. J. M. Lee
Cox Armstead	Ann Hudson	15 Mar 1834	Willson Cox
Cox Gabriel	Anna Shacklford	10 Dec 1810	William Shacklford
Cox Gabriel	Elizabeth Smith	21 Nov 1846	Richard P. Sanders
Cox Henry	Nancy Shackleford	21 Aug 1827	William Harvill
Cox Henry	Betsy Brinsfield	6 Sep 1845	Martin Browning

GROOM	BRIDE	DATE	BONDSMAN OR WITNESS
Cox Nathaniel	Nancey Green	16 Oct 1838	Williamson Peterson
Cox Reuben	Mary Holcomb	11 Jan 1792	Berryman Watkins
Cox Thomas	Mildred Birk	9 Jan 1823	Jno. Halcom
Cox Whitaker	Pensey Swann	4 Nov 1799	Greenbury Voss
Cox William	Mildred Shackleford	13 Jan 1821	William Halcomb
Cox William	Elizabeth Lumpkins	17 Dec 1853	John B. Carter
Cox William	Frances Kennon	19 Mar 1858	Franklin Graves
		23 Mar	md by Wm.B. Bowe JP
Cozens Tazwell (Col)	Nancy Philips (Col)	21 Apr 1851	Lewis Hill
Cozzens Lewis	Frances Elliott	6 Jan 1855	Zalman J. Jones
Craft Andrew J.	Mary J. Lockard	28 Sep 1859	Andrew J. Lockard
Crawford John (Col-son of Wesley Turner & Caroline Crawford)	Frances Pettiford (Col-dau of Isham Bird)	20 Feb 1868	H. F. Brabdon clk
Crawford William	Rachiel Walker	25 Mar 1833	Jacob G. Walker
Crenshaw John	Rebecca Denney	1 Apr 1818	William Denney Iverson Graves
Crenshaw Thomas E.	Fannie E. Stacy	3 May 1864	A. J. Rahen
Creswell John	Nancey Landers	30 Mar 1810	Abraham Landers
Crews Abediah	Rebecca Cobb	10 Nov 1835	Jesse E. Cobb
Crews Thomas	Elizabeth Ford	23 Apr 1835	John Jeffreys
Crews Thomas	Joicey Willis	21 Jan 1837	Rufus Stamps
Crisp Chesley	Sarah Warren	2 Jan 1827	Yerbey Warren
Crisp Dr. David H.	Betty A. Mitchell	26 Aug 1856	Henderson Terrell
		31 Aug 1856	md by Jno. S. Grasty MG
Crisp John	Janney Burch	12 Apr 1791	George Burch
Crisp John H.	Mary K. Smith	31 Aug 1836	Thomas D. Johnston
Crisp Thomas	Frances Burch	14 Oct 1799	George Burch
Crisp William H.	Sarah M. Batten	9 Jun 1848	John Terell
Critinton Deveraux	Elenor Pyron	3 Jul 1832	Thomas Gossett
Crittenden Richard	Elizabeth Morton	29 Jun 1850	Calvin D. Vernon
Crittenton George	Lucy Cox	11 Oct 1800	Phillip Cox Jr.
Crockett John H.	Frances N. Sneed	7 Dec 1834	Josiah Rainey
Crosset James	Charlotte Johnston	15 Feb 1816	Lemuel Rainey
Crowder Godfrey	Susannah Shelton	23 Feb 1802	pencer Speed Joseph McCain
Crowder Richardson	Anne Samuel	13 Mar 1821	Thomas Jeffreys Jr.
Crowder Robert A. (of Mecklenburg Co. Va.)	Eleanor Robertson (dau of Chrs. Robertson)	23 Jun 1826	Adam Finch
Crowder Thomas J. (son of James & Emaline)	Emily Davis (dau of James & Anna)	29 Jul 1867	md by J. J. Jones JP
Croxton William R.	Elizabeth F. Daniel	2 Jun 1863	William Lockhart
		2 Jun 1863	md by Geo. W. Griffin MG
Crummell Charles	Mary McKnight	19 Mar 1785	Andrew Ferguson
Crumpton Robert T.	Mary C. Slade	23 Mar 1858	Joseph Miller md by Wm. B. Bowe JP
Crutchfield George H.	Eliza A. Garrott	4 Jul 1838	Stapleton Crutchfield
Crutchfield William B.	Barbara Matlock	8 May 1837	Ashley G. Lea
Culberson David	Clary Browning	22 Feb 1782	Isac Boran
Culberson Joseph	Agnes Chittelton	24 Dec 1787	Jas. Smith J. Womack
Culberson William	Mary Browning	28 May 1800	Joseph McReynolds
Culbertson Hiram	Nancey Hightower	15 Dec 1806	Jepthah Parks
Culbertson James	Mary Gillyon	13 Dec 1785	John Currie Jr.
Cummell William	Anne Coleston	8 Mar 1784	William Addington

GROOM	BRIDE	DATE	BONDSMAN OR WITNESS
Cuningham Charles	Mary Hunt	29 Jul 1866	Armstead Hunt
			md by E. Hunt JP
Cuningham Glouster	Sarah Cuningham	27 Jul 1866	Edmond Williamson
			md by E. Hunt JP
Cunningham Moses (Col-son of Moses & Pattie Cunningham)	Nancy Scott (dau of William & Annie Scott)	5 Oct 1867	H. F. Brandon clk md by J. J. Jones JP
Cunningham Nathaniel	Elizabeth Sneed	24 Sep 1790	Benjn. Snead
Cunningham Thomas	Maryan Browning	22 Jun 1808	William Donoho
Curl John T.	Susanah Hightower	29 Aug 1803	George Willson
Currie George	Judith Chandler	9 Sep 1829	John Comer
Currie Isaac R.	Eliza Johnston	8 Mar 1824	John C. Harvey
Currie James	Elizabeth A. Mitchell	15 Oct 1822	Paul A. Haralson
Currie James	Julia Ann Mitchell	24 Feb 1837	John H. Wiley
Currie Jesse	Margarett Chandler	29 Sep 1830	John Currie Shelby Currie
Currie Joseph	Jincey Wiley	1 Sep 1802	Alexander Wiley
Currie Joseph M.	Mary J. Lea	13 Jan 1858 19 Jan	Brice Harrelson md by G. G. Walker, Elder
Currie Mitchell	Catharine Currie	11 Feb 1832	Isaac R. Currie Azariah Graves
Currie William	Frances H. Patellor	28 Dec 1842	Alex. McAlpin
Currie William (son of Charles & Anness Johnson)	Frances Currie (dau of Nepthalin & Betsey Currie)	28 Dec 1867 18 Jan 1868	H. F. Brandon clk md by D. Burch JP
Currie Young (Col)	Amanda Bolton (Col)	20 Nov 1867 23 Dec	H. F. Brandon clk md by David Burch JP
Cutler Joshua	Sally Olridg	18 Jul 1816	Jacob Ahart

- D -

Dabbs Lemuel J.	Nanny J. Chandler	4 Nov 1856 5 Nov	William A. Foster md by James K. Lea JP
Dabbs William J.	Mary Dunaway	24 Sep 1847	Williamson Parkes Rufus Y. Graves
Dabney Samuel	Jane Harrison	8 Apr 1817	James Rainey Warren Williams
Dalton Claiborn	Elizabeth Weatherford	30 Jun 1810	Thomas Weatherford
Dalton John	Mary Ann Weatherford	4 Dec 1838	Jesse E. Cobb Geo. W. VanHook
Damaron James K.	Olive Ann Moore	30 Nov 1840	Zachariah E. Dameron
Dameron Alexander M.	Martha P. Dameron	21 Jul 1821	Drury Mathews
Dameron Azariah	Lucretia Burch	4 Apr 1848	H. A. Richmond
Dameron Bartholomew	Rebecca Malone	27 Aug 1798	Vines Mathis
Dameron Benjamin	Matilda Mathews	20 Nov 1820	William Upton
Dameron Christopher	Salley Ware	6 Jun 1815	Samuel Dameron
Dameron Christopher	Martha A. Camron	1 Apr 1851 2 Apr	Saml. S. Harrison md by H. P. Harrison JP
Dameron Harrison	Martha P. Dameron	17 Dec 1822	Joseph Langley
Dameron Henry W.	Sarah E. Russell	11 Jan 1856 13 Jan	Samuel Pittard md by B. Cooper JP
Dameron James B.	Elizabeth Connally	12 Dec 1829	George A. Connally
Dameron James H.	Sally Thomas (wid)	15 Aug 1846	William Hightower
Dameron James K.	Barsheba Bateman	28 Nov 1829	John Dameron
Dameron John	Nancey Love	22 Jan 1828	Samuel Love Jr.
Dameron John	Jane Richmond	14 Aug 1834	Dr. Nathl. M. Roan

GROOM	BRIDE	DATE	BONDSMAN OR WITNESS
Dameron John W.	Catharine Evans	27 Nov 1841	Williamson M. Stephens
Dameron Joseph	Mary Burton	2 Apr 1790	Thos. Jeffreys
Dameron Joseph C.	Salinda Dameron	20 Sep 1820	Alexander W. Dameron
Dameron Joseph C.	Sarah Roan	14 Apr 1841	Robert M. Wiley
			H. Sawyer
Dameron Samuel	Salley Holcomb	10 Jan 1799	Geroge Dameron
Dameron Samuel	Fanney Samuell	11 Jul 1801	Joseph Dameron
Dameron Samuel	Susan Bateman	3 Mar 1828	Williamson Dameron
Dameron William	Cathrine Dameron	5 Dec 1814	Samuel Kendrick
Dameron William	Mary Malone	26 Aug 1820	John Mathis
Dameron William J.	Alcey S. Travis	28 Sep 1841	Elzey W. Travis
Dameron William M.	Sarah F. Browning	29 Nov 1852	Samuel Pittard
		2 Dec	md by B. Cooper JP
Dameron Williamson	Polley Evans	21 Dec 1813	George B. Dameron
Dameron Willias A.	Martha M. Murry	19 Dec 1853	William McNutt
		22 Dec	md by Benj.Wells JP
Dameron Zachariah E.	Martha Day	18 Jan 1847	Barzillai A. Evans
Daniel Alexander A.	Isabella Brandon	6 Nov 1866	Fleming Daniel
Daniel Elias J.	Susan R. Tirpin (dau of Thomas V. Tirpin)	5 Apr 1843	John R. English
Daniel James	Jane Stewart	13 Aug 1830	Isaac V. Vanhook
Daniel Jno.	Lucy Murphey	25 Jul 1805	Hearndon Haralson
Daniel John	Rebecca Huston	21 Oct 1822	Williamson Moore
Daniel John	Lucy Walters	29 Mar 1844	John Carter
Daniel John	Martha Mangum	5 Feb 1860	David Walker
			md by Wm. B. Swann JP
Daniel John M.	Carnelia A. Carter	6 Jul 1836	John Lenox
Daniel John P.	Jane C. Higgason	30 Apr 1857	D. S. Cates
			Thos. D. Johnston Dpt
		30 Apr	md by Thomas W. Tobey MG
Daniel Martin	Charlotte Mims	11 Aug 1834	Thomas B. Mims
Daniel Martin T.	Susan Conally	18 Dec 1854	Wm. Walter Murry
		19 Dec	by J. M. Allen JP
Daniel Robert	Julia A. Norflet	27 Aug 1842	Henry A. Richmond
Daniel Thomas	Nancy Hardige	16 Dec 1814	Martin Daniel
Daniel William M.	Adaline H. Williamson	14 Aug 1839	A. C. Finley
			R. H. Moss
Darby Archibald L.	Malinda Moore	10 Feb 1830	Richard E. Hornbuckle
Darby Daniel	Elizabeth Gibson	9 Feb 1791	John Darby
Darby George	Betsey Vanhook	12 Nov 1800	Henry Royster
Darby James	Anne Rone	12 Oct 1802	George Darby
Darby John	Elisabeth McDaniel	15 Sep 1794	William Rainey
Davenport Richard S.*	Mary Hubbard	14 Dec 1831	George Farley
Davidson John A.	Mary A. Chilton	20 Dec 1828	Lewis G. Bagley
Davidson Leroy	Adeline S. J. Moore	14 Mar 1828	Richard O. Davidson
			John P. Harrison
Davis Alfred	Elizabeth Warf	26 Feb 1840	Coleman L. Mitchell
			John H. Wiley JP
Davis Ashley	Anney Kennon	8 Sep 1814	Ralph Glaze
Davis David	Jame Montgomery	23 Mar 1808	James Matlock
Davis Elijah	Nancy Warrick	16 Jun 1823	Robert Lyon
			Thomas W. Graves DC
Davis Granville (Col-son of Samuel & Mourning Davis	Louisa Hoge (Col-dau of Wm. & Matilda Hoge)	10 Nov 1867	H. F. Brandon clk
Davis Henry J.	Letetia J. Reid	11 Dec 1852	William A. Stanfield
		15 Dec	md by Tho. L. Lea JP
Davis James	Nelly Quine	23 Oct 1816	Thomas Hooper
Davis James	Susanna Parkes	2 Apr 1822	Hiram Culberson

GROOM	BRIDE	DATE	BONDSMAN OR WITNESS
Davis James M.	Ann Cox	15 Dec 1835	Humphrey Dix
Davis James M.	Elizabeth J. Kimbrough	1 Sep 1847	Jno. K. Graves
Davis James T.	Virginia C. Hill	15 Feb 1866	Thomas D. Hill md by E. Hunt JP
Davis John	Martha Matthews	11 Oct 1817	Luke Matthews
Davis John	Mecay Logan	18 Jan 1859	Henry Logan
Davis Jonarthan	Mary Austen	17 Apr 1781	Basel Davis Solomon Parks
Davis Jonathan	Rachel Wilkerson	-- Oct 1817	Alexander Murphey
Davis Lewis	Kezziah Warf	18 Dec 1832	William Davis
Davis Thomas	Nancy Mallory	23 Aug 1805	Joel Leath
Davis Thomas W.	Frances Stanfield	2 Sep 1848	Jefferson Moore
Davis William*	Elisa Warf	17 Dec 1831	Thomas Bennett
Davis William	Polly Baynes (dau of Nancy Bohannon)	8 Jun 1812	Luke Wild
Davis William F.	Mary C. Evans	24 Jun 1854	William A. Futrell md by J. C. Pinnix JP
Davise James	Crecy Hendrick	25 Dec 1835	Benja Knight
Day Henry	Margery Cate	28 Mar 1788	John Cate J. Womack
Day Isaac	Jeen Oakley	26 Feb 1791	Philip Day J. Womack
Day Philip	Jane Smith	7 Feb 1815	John Smith Herndon Haralson Jr.
Deacon Henry	Betsey Aslum	9 Apr 1857	Joseph I. Watson md by J. Doll MG
Debo Benjamin	Frances Tunks	27 Jul 1790	Alexander Morison
Debow Solomon	Nancey Murphey	22 Mar 1804	Herndon Haralson Ald. Murphey CC
Debruler Charles	Betsey Hargrave	3 Feb 1816	Thomas Hargrave
Debruler Wesley	Lucy Hargreave	4 Nov 1816	Thomas Hargrave
DeJarratte James P.	Martha A. Price	13 Dec 1856	Alfred A. Mitchell W. A. Vernon DC md by Jas. P. Simpson MG
Delaney Davis*	Altena J. Gordon	21 Nov 1831	Joel Gossett
Delps Michael	Elisabeth Starkey	29 Jan 1782	Jonathan Starkey
Denney Azariah	Elizabeth McKinney	26 Sep 1823	Thomas Pinson
Denney Simon	Polly Barton	26 Apr 1796	Lewis Barton
Dennis Franklin J.	Edith A. Vernon	6 Apr 1857 7 Apr	Bartlett Y. McAden md by Thomas W. Tobey MG
Dennis John	Rachel Grant (dau of James Grant Sr.)	3 Feb 1796	Thomas Jeffreys
Denny Lewis	Levina Simmons	19 Apr 1830	Azariah Denney
Denny William	Salley Crenshaw	-- Apr 1818	John Crenshaw
De Nordendorf Charles Chaky	Elizabeth L. V. Hooper	24 Apr 1865	William B. Bowe
Denson Richard	Elizabeth Paul	28 Aug 1828	Cornelius West Joseph Pruitt Lancelott T. Johnston
Denton John	Lucinda Payne	8 Jul 1842	James Lunsford
Deviney Madison	Ary W. Powell	2 Apr 1838	Jerome B. Russell
Deweese Samuel	Rachel White	8 Apr 1782	Elisha Dewees Joshua Guttery
Dewese Isaiah	Rebecca Barnett	6 Dec 1788	Thos. Barnett
Dick John W.	Martha W. Graves	31 May 1822	Paul A. Haralson
Dickens Joseph W.	Mary Sadler	27 Sep 1850	Jarrett Dunn
Dickerson Benjamin G.	Bettie S. Wootson	24 Mar 1864	Smith Brandon
Dickey Jacob	Mary A. Pinnix	17 Dec 1839	James Mebane
Dickey John	Nancy Smithy	10 Oct 1796	Samuel Smythe
Dickie Samuel	Elizabeth Shanks	11 Dec 1787	William Cantrell

GROOM	BRIDE	DATE	BONDSMAN OR WITNESS
Dickin Beverly	Susan Shelton	5 Dec 1840	Eaton P. Dickins
Dickins Henry	Lydia Hews	21 Apr 1791	Will Darnald
Dickins Israel	Francis Ware	4 Mar 1842	Nathl. S. Graves
Dickins Israel	Nancy J. Durham	30 Oct 1844	Jackson Yates
Dickins James	Alley Estridge	28 Mar 1781	James Person
Dickins Jeremiah	Rebeccah Dickins	12 Oct 1802	Gower Whittemore
Dickins Jesse	Frances Moore	7 Nov 1791	Herndon Haralson
Dickins William	Priscilla Poston	6 May 1794	Jesse Brintle
Dickins William	Polly Dickins	30 Mar 1801	Jeremiah Hackson
Dickins William	Nancy Brintle	1802-1805	John Jackson
Dill James	Jane Kennon	20 May 1843	William P. Womack
Dill John H.	Susan Saunders	10 Jun 1841	William P. Womack James Dill
Dill Joseph	Elizabeth Sanders	9 Jan 1858	Archey Cobb
Dill Reubin H. (son of James & Jane)	Martha F. Scott (dau of Asa & Deby)	9 Mar 1868 10 Mar	H. F. Brandon md by Stephen Neal JP
Dillard Richard	Sarah Holt	7 Dec 1796	Nathan Holloway Douglas Oliver
Dillard William	Sarah Ann Claiborne (dau of Johnson Hunt)	10 Nov 1866	Lewis Hunt md by E. Hunt JP
Dinwiddie John	Rachel Newton	1 Nov 1791	Reubin Newton
Dishough George F.	Mary Sawyer	10 Jan 1835	Ezekiel Sawyer Evelina B. Campbell
Dishough Lewis	Elizabeth Pleasant	1 Apr 1845	William C. Page
Dishough Reddick	Elizabeth S. Rainey	12 Dec 1817	Leml. Rainey Isaac Rainey
Dismukes James M.	Nancy G. McAden	11 Apr 1838	William Dismukes Benj. F. Stanfield
Dismukes John	Susan Hubbard	13 Jul 1835	Marcus A. VanHook
Dison Thomas	Lotty Hood	17 Sep 1840	Henry Rose Edward M. Spain
Dix George Washington	Elizabeth Cook	6 Nov 1834	Matthew Earp
Dix Humphrey	Caroline Davis (dau of Fanny Davis)	12 Apr 1832	Thomas Bennett
Dix James (of Va.)	Lucinda Dix (grand- daughter of George Critington)	22 Apr 1846	Jordan Ray
Dix John M.	Patsey A. Tanner	13 Dec 1816	John P. Dix
Dix John M.	Nancey Crittenton (dau of George & Lucy Crittenton of Pittsylvania Co. Va.)	15 Aug 1822	Samuel Adams Jno G. Womack DC
Dix Tandy	Martha L. Saddler	17 Feb 1836	John R. Lester
Dix William	Jane Patterson	28 Jan 1836	William Jeffreys
Dix William	Mary E. Ragsdale	26 Jan 1862	Richard Warf md by E. Hunt JP
Dixon Henry	Polly Burnett	28 May 1802	Joseph Payne
Dixon Henry	Nancy Boulton	8 Mar 1809	William Dixon
Dixon Levi	Sarah W. Boulton	14 Sep 1823	Waller Bolton
Dixon Robert	Jenney Brooks	22 Nov 1796	Lewis Shapard
Dixon Robert	Sinah Brackin	17 Dec 1823	John Cobb Jr.
Dixon Roger	Polley Jouette	16 Dec 1794	Nathaniel Dickerson
Dixson Robert	Mary Barnet	9 Sep 1779	Andrew McNight
Dobbin John	Betsey Hinton	3 Feb 1796	Nathaniel Comer
Dobbins Azariah	Frances Trim	31 May 1828	David Hodge
Dobbins Hugh C.	Sarah Dameron	2 Nov 1824	Thomas Comer
Dodson Carter	Alcy Dodson	23 Feb 1818	James Eudaily
Dodson Hugh H.	Susannah Morris	26 Dec 1816	William H. Lovins Joseph Dodson
Dodson John F.	Isabella Baynes	4 Jul 1817	Daniel S. Farley D. G. Brandon
Dodson Matthew	Prudence Penix	20 Dec 1819	James Boswell

GROOM	BRIDE	DATE	BONDSMAN OR WITNESS
Dodson Thomas	Piety Ferrell	26 Feb 1817	William Dodson
Dodson Thomas C.	Isabella L. Graves	23 Oct 1849	A. A. Pattillo
			R. Y. Graves
Dodson William	Louisa Williamson	25 Dec 1866	John W. Stephens
			md by R. G. Barrett
Dodson William T.	Sally Young	28 Sep 1812	John B. Dodson
Dodson Woodson (Col-son of James Watkins & Lucinda Dodson, Col.)	Jane Richmond (Col-dau of Vilet Richmond, Col.)	26 Dec 1867	H. F. Brandon
Doll Archer	Sarah Mebane	28 Sep 1866	Calvin Jones
			md by Thos. J. Brown JP
Dollarhide John	Nancy Chittington	3 Nov 1784	James Roberts
Dollarhide William	Mary Dollarhide	28 Sep 1789	William Rainey
Dolton Isam	Parmela Bingam	3 Jun 1833	William Dolton
			Benj. C. West Sr.
Donaldson James (Col)	Lydia Jeffreys (Col)	3 Nov 1866	James Pamplet md by J. J. James JP
Donaldson Robert	Elizabeth Richmond	16 Jan 1799	Joshua Richmond
Donaldson William	Margret Motheral	5 Sep 1793	James Richmond
Donelson Andrew	Mary Motheral	18 Jul 1791	James Richmond
Donoho Alexander	Susan H. Raimey	6 Aug 1832	James H. Sidebottom
Donoho Charles D.	Caroline Boswell	7 May 1861	Richd. Miles
		8 May	md by A. G. Anderson MG
Donoho James	Susannah Turner	22 Apr 1802	Jeremiah Harrelson
Donoho T. A.	Isabella Garland	18 Apr 1854	Jno. W. Lewis
Donoho William	Dorcass Haralson	6 Apr 1784	Thomas Harrelson
Donoho William	Nicey Lea	8 Nov 1797	William Lea
Donoho William A.	Huldah G. Wilson	29 Jun 1859	J. L. McKee
		30 Jun	md by J. Doll MG
Donoho William C.	Nancy R. Miles	19 Mar 1833	Thomas D. Connally
Dooley John	Sally Colley	15 May 1806	Joel Mann
			Enoch Dunaway
Doris John	Elizabeth Russel	12 Apr 1804	Samuel Morton Sr.
Doson William H.	Ellin Jones	13 Dec 1837	B. C. West Sr.
			Littleberry W. Melton
Doss Clark H.	Joanna Holloway	2 Jan 1832	John Holloway
Doss Thomas	Betsy Edes	6 Mar 1827	Richard R. Kennon
Douglass David	Mary Benton	5 Nov 1817	Absalom Nutt
Dove William J.	Susan Strader	25 Mar 1853	Thomas Dove
Dowell James	Sarah Fuller	14 Mar 1782	Peter Fuller
			Pulliam Williamson
Dowell Walker	Nancey Thompson	29 Dec 1806	William Swann
Downey John A.	Lucinda S. Martin	8 Aug 1846	Abisha Slade
Downs Rolling L.	Mary E. Lane (dau of Ann P. Lane)	9 Sep 1842	James H. Montgomery
Downs William	Priscilla Marr	9 May 1853	William Patterson
Doyle Edward	Ruth Sargent	17 Apr 1782	John Campbell
Doyle Simon	Elizabeth Sargent	26 Aug 1791	Edwd. Doyle
Drake James M.	Jane Childres	22 Dec 1828	William J. Daniel
Drake Thomas	Rachel Page	27 Jun 1829	Benjamin Bowden
Draper Joshua	Holly Nowles	1 Apr 1796	George Reed
Draper Solomon	Joyce Taylor	4 Jul 1790	William Draper
Druskill Samuel	Ibby Dudley	20 Apr 1820	Abnr Dudley
			Alijah Walker
Dudley Elisha	Joanna Dill	14 Dec 1832	Thomas Taylor
Duest Hezekiah	Anness Tricky	9 Aug 1784	Giles Tricky
Duke Buckner	Nancy Dunivant	30 Aug 1825	Hodge Dunivant
Duvavant Andy D.	Elizabeth Hix	28 Sep 1854	Owen Cook
		1 Oct	md by Tho. Covington JP

GROOM	BRIDE	DATE	BONDSMAN OR WITNESS
Dunaven John	Betsey Duke	13 Jul 1825	Nathan Rice
Dunavent Edward	Susanah Overby	19 Oct 1818	Alexander Kiersey
Dunaway Allen	Mary Ann Paschall	5 Dec 1841	Thomas W. Harrelson Geo. W. Graves
Dunaway James	Cathrine Ferrell	29 Dec 1795	Enoch Dunaway
Dunaway Samuel	Kesiah Barsdale	29 Feb 1792	Richard Green
Duncan Jessee	Hannah Paschall (dau of William Paschal)	14 Jul 1780	Danl. Duncan
Duncan Nathan	Elizabeth Humphreys	5 Sep 1818	Hiram Henderson Azariah Graves CC
Duncan Nathan	Martha Tyre	2 Mar 1827	John Duncan
Duncan Nathaniel	Jane Rainey	6 Nov 1782	William Rainey
Dunervant Abraham	Artemesia Hix	2 Aug 1855 3 Aug	Payton L. Lunsford md by Thos. Covington JP
Dunevant James	Virginia Denevant	31 Dec 1866 31 Dec	A. Dunevant md by M. Oliver JP
Dunevant John H.	Virginia Overby	2 Oct 1866 2 Oct	Thomas Martin md by Jerry Smith JP
Dunn Jarrett	Isabella R. Lockett	22 May 1852	William L. Fowler
Dunnavant Jesse	Frances Overby	25 Oct 1827	Samuel Love Jr.
Dunnavant Thomas	Elizabeth Fuqua	7 Apr 1866	Addison Morgan md by A. A. Patillo JP
Dunnavent Thomas	Mary Toler	26 Aug 1840	William A. Richmond
Dunnaway Allen J.	Martha Hooper	12 Apr 1837	Oliver Foulks
Dunnaway James	Frances Hicks	10 May 1822	Samuel Dunnaway
Duprey John W.	Elizabeth A. Withers	12 Jun 1843	Geo. W. Price
Durham Archibald	Susanna P. Shirly	29 Sep 1830	William Barr
Durham Charles	Sarah Hughs	27 Nov 1862	George Richardson md by N. M. Lewis JP
Durham George	Ann S. Robertson	15 Mar 1841	George W. Price
Durham George	Emily Dicken	11 Sep 1843	Albert Dickens
Durham James	James Strador	14 Dec 1842	Daniel S. Price
Durham John	Catherine Fair	30 Oct 1848	George W. Thompson
Durham John	Mary Ann Strader	5 Dec 1861	William J. Chandler md by W. B. Swann JP
Durham Josephus S.	Caroline Pool	10 Nov 1846	John C. Love
Durham Martin	Lucy Stone	8 Jan 1847	Richard Durham
Durham Nathaniel	Eliza Busey	5 Nov 1822	William Busey
Durham Newman	Cathrine Farly	7 Apr 1804	John Burton
Durham Richard	Hannah Hodge	6 Dec 1824	Thomas Basdil
Durham Richard	Martha Strador	2 Nov 1838	John Jeffreys
Durham Richard	Sarah Stone	11 Oct 1844	Israel Dickins
Durham Samuel	Elizabeth Freeman	9 May 1836	Mathew Terry
Durham William F.	Eliza A. Walker	24 Dec 1866	J. J. Swann md by John D. Keesee
Durrem Daniel	Eleanor Wiley	22 Feb 1808	John Wiley Sol. Debow
Durrett Francis	Betsy Moore	31 Nov 1807	Durrett Richards
Durrum Isaac	Nancy Match	25 Aug 1789	Joseph Lewis
Duty Joseph	Polly Fitch	23 Jul 1826	William Askey Q. Anderson
Duty Richard	Lois McNeill	21 Jul 1791	Thomas McNeill
Duty William	Rachel Warren	13 Feb 1783	Robert Moore
Dyar Samuel	Betsy Matlock	18 Aug 1796	John Dobbins
Dye Abraham	Lattis Coleston	3 Feb 1787	James Randolph
Dye Benjamin B.	Elizabeth W. Dodson	10 May 1823	Charles Willson
Dye Shadrack	Elionar Westly	16 Nov 1802	William Dye
Dye William	Sally Gordon	5 Jun 1799	James Randolph

- E -

| Earp Joel* | Elizabeth Cook | 23 Feb 1831 | Philip Cook |
| Earp Lawson | Sarah Foster | 4 Aug 1832 | James Greenwood |

GROOM	BRIDE	DATE	BONDSMAN OR WITNESS
Earp Smith L.	Rebecca Chancy	13 Mar 1845	Lawson Earp
Easely Charles	Mary Jane Hunt	27 Dec 1866	Beverly Easely E. Hunt JP
Easley John	Harriott E. Henderson	27 Sep 1830	James S. Henderson
Echols Philip J.	Mary E. Jackson	20 Jan 1813	Edward D. Jones
Ector Hugh	Elizabeth Mitchell	19 Oct 1821	James Anderson
Ector James	Jenny Anderson	10 Mar 1808	James Anderson Sol. Debow
Ector Joseph	Caty Anderson	15 Oct 1804	James Anderson
Ector William S.	Ellen T. Hodges	17 Dec 1855 19	George Leath md by John H. Pickard
Eddings Joseph	Elizabeth Holcom	17 Jul 1805	William Holcom Jr.
Eddings William	Polly Johnston	18 Mar 1807	Geo. M. Willson
Edwards Christopher B.	Mary G. Powell	13 Nov 1865 16	Samuel D. McCain md by J. J. Jones JP
Edwards Edward	Eliza Gooch	18 Oct 1859	Wm. F. Smith
Edwards George R.	Jane Fielder	27 Sep 1834	Jesse Meadors
Edwards Gustavus A.	Sarah P. Allen	22 Feb 1830	Edward Carrel
Edwards James	Elvira B. Boley	3 Jan 1829 15 Jan	Parham A. Boley md by Danl. A. Penick MG
Edwards Joseph M.	Martha L. Slade	30 Dec 1853 1 Jan 1854	John J. Lipscomb md by J. M. Allen JP
Edwards N. R.	Martha Jane Zigler	2 Mar 1863	N. N. Curris Jr. md by J. A. Hodges JP
Edwel Harrison	Celia A. Thomas (Col)	29 Jan 1842	John H. Fawcett
Edwel Jim	Sally Griffis (Col)	10 Apr 1845	Tilmon Snow
Edwell Harrison	Leaner Cole	9 Nov 1847	Horace Howard C. D. Vernon
Egmon Lott	Polly Burk	24 Oct 1812	John Slade
Elam Robert	Betsy Carrol	14 Mar 1804	Benjamin Ingram Sol. Debow
Eldridge Daniel B.	Amanda A. Evans	6 Feb 1856 19 Feb	Yancey Jones md by James P. Simpson
Eliott George C.	S. T. Parrish	17 Mar 1860	Robert H. Evans md by J. Doll MG
Elliot George	Julia Hamlet	18 Dec 1824	Thomas M. Hamlet
Elliott Allen W.	Mary F. Turner	10 Dec 1855	John T. Hodges W. A. Vernon DC
Elliott David T.	Sarah L. Conally	5 Nov 1855	Thomas J. Jones
Elliott Granderson (Col)	Ann Pullium (Col)	15 Apr 1867	H. F. Brandon clk md by Solomon Apple MG
Elliott James	Judith T. Slayton (wid)	9 Oct 1862	J. L. McKee DC md by T. Page Ricaud MG
Elliott James A.	Ellen J. Stone	7 Aug 1858	Richard Durham J. H. F. Graves
Elliott John	Zilpah Sims	20 Aug 1785	James Johnson
Elliott John	Polly Donoho	25 Feb 1808	Ambrose L. Bennett
Elliott Martin S.	Nancey Turner	12 Oct 1814	Wm. Donoho
Ellis Andrew	Lucy Terrell	22 Sep 1819	Samuel Hulett Thos. Slade
Ellis John H.	Lucrasey F. Rolen	16 Dec 1856	Lewis Cousins
Ellison David	Lucretia Eubank	24 Dec 1818	Robert McKee
Ellmore Thomas	Betsey Smith	11 May 1801	John Ellmore
Elmore Benjamin	Mary Cobb	23 Jan 1811	Henry Cobb
Elmore John	Marianne Lea	27 Nov 1798	James Farley
Elmore John	Polly Taylor	6 Jan 1829	John McCain
Elmore John	Lucy Ann Elmore	6 Mar 1830	John A. Elmore
Elmore John A.	Ann Eliza Roper	27 Feb 1833	Thomas C. Pass
Elmore William	Delilah Pearce	2 Aug 1819	Harden Winfre Ch. Willson
English George C.	Mary H. Hunly	25 Nov 1856 25	Tho. W. Graves clk md by J. Jennings JP

GROOM	BRIDE	DATE	BONDSMAN OR WITNESS
Enoch Benjamin	Sally Shy	8 Oct 1796	Robert Shy
			John Enoch
Enoch David	Rachel Everet	3 Oct 1803	James Milton
Enoch John	Nancy Shy	30 Jun 1798	Rees Enoch
Enoch John	Nancy Walker	3 Dec 1832	James Walker
Enoch Rees H.	Susan C. Thompson	6 Jan 1859	Andres J. Thompson
			md by James K. Lea JP
Enoch Samuel	Betsy Smith	13 Aug 1804	James Corder
Enochs Andrew	Elizabeth King	11 Mar 1787	Daniel Milton
Enock Walker L.	Mildred A. Everett	4 May 1864	Zachariah Page
		5 May	md by H. F. Adkins JP
Epperson Branch	Martha Hughs	2 Nov 1842	Henderson Standfield
			M. P. Huntington
Epps Lewis (Col)	Nancy Brown (Col)	14 May 1867	H. F. Brandon
		20 May	md by Jas. J. Clendenin
Erwin James	Nancy Nash	10 Oct 1786	Alexr. Murphey
Eskridge Bird	Nancy R. Johnston	27 Nov 1821	Jno. Smith
(Burdett)			Ch. Wilson
Eskridge George	Elizabeth Dobbin	25 Nov 1790	John Dobbin
Eskridge John	Frances Smith	22 Nov 1811	Gabl. R. Lea
			Wm. Lea
Eskridge Robert W.	Mary B. Graves	25 Aug 1849	Byrd W. Buckingham
			T. S. Poore
Eskridge Samuel	Sarah Dobbins	30 Oct 1829	Aaron V. Lea
Eskridge Thomas	Phoebe Stafford	26 Nov 1827	Walker Eskridge
Eskridge Walker	Matilda Lea	4 Aug 1827	Aron V. Lea
Eskridge William	Polly Johnston	4 Jan 1820	John Adams
Esters Daniel	Polly Moton (Morton)	3 Mar 1825	Azariah Morton
Estes Bartlet	Elizabeth Rease	6 Dec 1819	Jno. J. Oliver
Estes Bartlett	Pheby Musick	28 Dec 1790	John Gibbs
Estes Jonathan	Sarah Smith	26 Mar 1834	Isaac Simmons
Estes Marcus E.	Sarah A. Stone	23 Jun 1846	Sylvester P. Adams
			John K. Graves
Estes Micajah	Margery Pyron	8 Jul 1801	Robert Thompson
Estes Nathaniel	Isabella Smith	16 Nov 1830	Richard J. Smith Jr.
Estes Richard	Delpha Sanders	18 May 1822	Jas. Sanders
Estes Samuel	Elemore Holles	25 Dec 1815	Bartlett Estes
			Archabel Day
Estis Richard B.	Susan M. Page	3 Jan 1855	Jaes A. Ferrell
		4 Jan	md by Stephen Neal JP
Eubank George	Dicey Malone	3 Sep 1799	William Burch
Eubank James	Elisabeth Eubanks	1 Dec 1791	Clayton Jones
			J. Womack
Eubank Thomas	Nancey Graves	16 Dec 1828	Abel Faulks
Eudaley David	Salley Baldwin	29 Dec 1817	Henry Baldwin
			Elijah Withers
Evans Allen W.	Adeline A. Owen	30 Sep 1850	William Terrell
Evans Barzillai A.	Phoebe W. Dameron	6 Dec 1845	William G. Chandler
Evans Berry	Nancey Page	1 Dec 1830	Azariah G. Kimbro
Evans Bird	Betsey Smith	11 Dec 1815	Robert Hamlet
Evans Bird	Mary Matlock	23 Dec 1840	James Poteat
Evans Daniel	Pherebe Evans	6 Mar 1782	Thomas Sargent
Evans David H.	Mary Moore	8 Oct 1851	Samuel Pittard
Evans David H.	Lilla Murphey	23 Nov 1860	Joshua Hightower
Evans Edward	Artilia Fitch	19 Apr 1848	William H. Daniel
Evans Elisha	Elizabeth Lea	3 Mar 1789	Benjn. Douglass
			Jane Murphey
Evans Ellis	Polly Martin	25 Apr 1797	Joseph Dameron
Evans Ellis	Martha R. Scott	7 Aug 1838	Joseph F. Cornwell
Evans Francis	Sally Walters	24 Nov 1842	Isaac Patterson
Evans George	Elizabeth Steward	16 May 1859	Archabald B. Glidewell
			md by N. M. Lewis JP
Evans Goodwin	Nancey G. Kimbrough	5 Jan 1814	Elijah Martin
			D. W. Simpson

GROOM	BRIDE	DATE	BONDSMAN OR WITNESS
Evans Henry	Nancy Ferrel	28 Feb 1822	James Page
Evans James	Nicey Fuller	9 Nov 1825	James Lea Jr.
Evans James	Nancy Wright	2 Aug 1837	Bird H. Bateman
Evans James	Frances G. Currie	24 Dec 1851	John Oliver
		26 Dec	md by John H. Pickard
Evans Joel	Mary Hubbard	23 Dec 1846	Jonathan Estes
Evans Madison (Col)	Frances Matlock	7 Oct 1865	Moris Mason J. L. McKee clk
Evans Samuel J.	Barbara Hooper	8 Oct 1836	Ludolphus Henderson
Evans Samuel J. W.	Martha A. Owen	5 Dec 1866	David Perkins md by J. J. Jones JP
Evans Samuel W.	Harriet A. Bowe	10 Oct 1862	S. P. Corbett
		12 Oct	md by T. Page Ricaud MG
Evans Thomas	Abbarellah Willson	26 Nov 1821	James Ingram
Evans Walter	Cathrine Davis	4 Feb 1804	Allen Burton
Evans William	Polley Thomas	17 Dec 1817	Nathaniel Lea
Evans William	Mary Henshaw	30 Mar 1836	William Hawks
Evans Willis R.	Druzey Earp	28 May 1862	Lewis F. Gildewell md by N. M. Lewis JP
Evans Zecheriah	Anne Gibson	3 Jan 1784	Joseph Carney
Evens Samuel	Priscilla Henderson	1 Dec 1835	William Graves
Evens William A. (or G.)	Elizabeth Hall	13 Nov 1855	Charles Hawl B. Harralson
Everet Samuel	Marthy Shy	1 May 1786	Luke Prendergast
Everett Danl.	Ann -------	4 Jul 1843	Charles Hendrick
Everett John	Phebe R. Atkinson	18 Feb 1813	Thomas Prendergast
Evins John	Nancy Swift	15 Mar 1836	Augustus Gwyn

- F -

Fackler Abraham	Harriett F. Seates	23 Oct 1858	Thomas A. Powell md by Lancelot Johnston
Faddis John	Anne Lemorns	31 Jan 1822	Hugh McCaddams
Falkner Franklin (son of Linsey Falkner)	Mary J. Malone (dau of Judy Malone)	9 Nov 1867	H. F. Brandon clk
Fanning Hezekiah	Cloe Jackson	28 Nov 1796	Henry Quine Betsy Murphey
Fanning Midleton	Delpha Moore	13 Dec 1787	Jehu Fanin Wm. Moore
Farely Abner B.	Ann Owen	15 Sep 1835	James Jones
Fergusson John	Polley Wright	1 Feb 1797	Jacob Wright
Faris Thomas D.	Julia A. McHaney	10 Mar 1860	John W. Tucker md by N. M. Lewis JP
Farish Adam T.	Mary W. Prather	16 Mar 1836	Lewis A. Patillo
Farish G. James	Elizabeth T. Turner	22 Nov 1841	James H. Atkinson
Farish Joseph	Gracie Harris	26 Dec 1866	Jim Nunnally
		27 Dec	md by John D. Keesee JP
Farley Abner B.	Elizabeth Gordon	11 Nov 1848	James Jones
Farley Daniel S.	Cathrine Logan	13 Oct 1785	John J. Farley
Farley Danl. S.	Cathrine McAden	16 Jun 1800	John McAden
Farley Isakiah	Martha Burton	28 Nov 1786	Henry Burton
Farley James	Betsey Lea	5 Sep 1793	Will Lea
Farley John	Nancy Fleming	21 Feb 1803	Bluford Warrin
Farley John	Peggy Dobbin	-- --- 1806	William Willson
Farley John B.	Eliza Vaughn	26 Dec 1816	John H. McAden Jr.
Farley John E.	Mary E. Lyon	8 Feb 1867	Robert D. Ferguson
		10 Feb	md by N. M. Lewis JP
Farley Kerr	Susan Cousins	17 Mar 1862	Thomas W. Graves clk md by Wm. B. Bowe JP
Farley William A.	Julia C. Smither	28 Mar 1849	Samuel B. Holder
Farley William T.	Betty Poore	29 Aug 1866	Bevin D. Oliver
Farmer Daniel	Sarah Moore Tapley	7 Aug 1781	John Womack

GROOM	BRIDE	DATE	BONDSMAN OR WITNESS
Farmer Evans	Lucy T. Marr	1 May 1859	A. M. Jones
Farmer Henry R.	Elisabeth H. Farmer	24 Dec 1857	G. G. Walker elder
Farmer James M.	Martha S. Ragland	25 Nov 1849	David A. Nichols
Farmer Joseph (Col)	Mildred C. Steward (Col)	30 Sep 1865 1 Oct	George Farmer md by C. A. Apple MG
Farmer Samuel	Lydia Ann Stewart	25 Dec 1866 26 Dec	Moses Farmer md by Solomon Apple MG
Farmer Stephen	Judy Harper	17 Mar 1791	Hosea Tapley
Farmer William	Hanner Pogue	30 Dec 1790	Demcey Moore
Farquhar Abraham M.	Mary Lipscomb	25 Mar 1823	John Whitlow
Farrar Richard J.	Sarah E. Wright	14 Sep 1856	Joseph Jennings JP
Farrow John	Phebe McNab	20 Dec 1813	John McNab D. W. Simpson
Faucett David L.	Sarah A. Terry	7 Apr 1849	Will D. Faucett
Faukner Osmund B.	Eliza Roberts	24 Dec 1832	James McClarney
Faulkner Joseph T.	Matilda M. Pool	16 Oct 1859	John T. Pool
Faulks Abel	Betsey Rudd	13 Apr 1815	William Rudd
Faulks Edwd. J. R.	Martha A. Windsor	24 Apr 1843	William F. Brown
Fausett James	Elizabeth Douglass	3 Nov 1827	Ashford Walker Henry Tait
Featherston George A.	Elizabeth J. Bowe	11 Dec 1858 15 Dec	Robert Newman md by John W. Lewis MG
Featherston Thomas W.	Virginia C. Richmond (Jinny)	11 Nov 1867 14 Nov	H. F. Brandon md by Lemmon Shell MG
Fegans James W.	Eliza Jane Duke	18 Jan 1847	William Brintle
Feguson Thomas	Polley Beaucey	15 Dec 1810	Charles Beaucey Stephen D. Watkins
Fenn Gabriel	Rebeccah Marshall	5 Jan 1796	Samuel Brooks
Ferguson Albert G.	Sarah Farley	23 Nov 1858	Joseph J. Terrell
Ferguson Bethel (Col-son of Peter Turner & Annie Ferguson)	Ann Fitzgerald (Col)	28 Dec 1867	H. F. Brandon md by Jacob Doll
Ferguson John	Polly Akin	10 Apr 1816	James Covington
Ferguson Joseph	Silvey Lawson	17 Nov 1866	Amos Graves md by Jacob Doll MG
Ferguson Richard	Mary Hooper	20 May 1833	Allen Gunn
Ferguson Samuel D.	Martha A. Rawlins	2 Jan 1858 6 Jan	Jas. M. Rawlins md by Jas. L. Fisher MG
Fergusson John J.	Gerly G. Brown	29 Oct 1853 30 Oct	H. Smith md by Archibald Currie
Ferrall John	Elizabeth Christenbury	9 Nov 1781	William Smith
Ferrell Henry W.	Sally Ann Page	1 Apr 1858	Daniel J. Page md by John H. Pickens MG
Ferrell Hutchings	Ann E. Gatewood (dau of Lewis Gatewood)	11 Oct 1830	John Cahall
Ferrell J. H.	M. J. Fretwell	18 Oct 1866	Ezekiel Slade
Ferrell James A.	Adaline M. Johnston	31 Oct 1859 1 Nov	Washington D. Page md by John W. Lewis MG
Ferrell John O.	Rachael J. Page	2 Feb 1859 3 Feb	Franklin Gooch md by John Stadler
Ferrell Moses (Col-son of Henry & Jennie Ferrell)	Isabella Panton (Col-dau of Alexander & Rhoda Panton)	27 Dec 1867	H. F. Branon clk
Ferrell William	Nancy Williams	18 Nov 1789	Joseph Robertson
Ferrell William	Martha Page	16 Apr 1825	Thomas W. Graves
Ferrill George W.	Cynthia Lynch	10 Nov 1835	James Mebane
Fielder Alfred T.	Isabell Tait	28 Nov 1832	Anthony W. Swift
Fielder John	Willy Rice	28 Sep 1842	William Tulloh

GROOM	BRIDE	DATE	BONDSMAN OR WITNESS
Fielder Leonard L.	Eliza Boswell	12 Sep 1829	Thomas Boswell
Fielder Samuel C.	Elizabeth Henderson	12 Jan 1833	Jacob Henderson
Fielder Benjamin T.	Susanna W. Swift	2 Oct 1810	Thomas Leachman
Fillips Joseph	Elizabeth Walters (dau of Archer Walters)	21 Dec 1812	Barton Terry
Finch George A.	Catherine McOrmick	19 May 1862	M. L. Finch
Finch Samuel	Sarah Dodson	30 Apr 1859	Thomas S. Hawker
Finley Augustus C.	Ann E. Williamson	9 Jun 1836	Thomas D. Connally D. Knott Nathl. Lea
Finley George	Nancey Samuell	7 Feb 1816	Rowzee Samuell
Fisher Anthony	Nancey Turner	6 Sep 1825	Thomas Turner David Montgomery
Fisher Tressy	Catherine Bauldin	12 Jan 1801	John Keen John G. Murphey DC
Fisher William	Polly H. Farley	30 Aug 1814	Haskue Price
Fitch Anderson N.	Susan Page	20 Oct 1860	James R. Aldridge
Fitch Empson	Delilah Hightower	24 Nov 1834	William V. Wilder
Fitch James	Mary Clendening	13 Mar 1830	George Boulding
Fitch Thomas*	Lydia Walker	13 Sep 1831	Thomas Sawyer
Fitch William W.	Cornelia Nash	19 Nov 1866 20 Nov	D. A. Walker md by A. G. Anderson MG
Fitts Marcellus G.	Susan A. Hudgins	1 Mar 1865	James W. Carter md by J. J. Jones JP
Fitz William	Lidia Stadler	16 Feb 1805	Thomas Shanks
Fitzgerald Baniter R.	Maria H. Betts	5 Jan 1829	William Weatherford, JR
Fitzgerald James W.	Elizabeth F. Swann	23 Apr 1847	John W. Foster
Fitzgerald Jno. B.	Sophia A. Land	12 Nov 1867 15 Nov	H. F. Brandon md by W. C. Gannon MG
Fitzgerald Joseph M.	Harriet Terry	7 Dec 1843	Silas Simpson
Fitzgerald Pleasant	Susan Garrett	4 Oct 1853 6 Oct	Tho. W. Graves clk md by F. H.Burrings MG
Fitzgerald Richard	Martha Hooper	31 Jan 1822	Robert Roe
Fitzgerald William	Sarah A. E. Woods	14 Mar 1846	Samuel P. Moore
Fitzgerald William	Elizabeth Nance (dau of Mildred & Jared W. Nance)	27 Jun 1848	Jared W. Nance
Flack Elijah	Fanny Tait	8 May 1801	John Yancey
Fleming Jasper	Rebecca A. Stegall	22 Jan 1861	Saml. H. Hines
Fleming William	Elizabeth Winters	14 Dec 1801	Roterick McDaniel
Flemming Pleasant	Betsey Rush (Bush)	25 Jul 1798	Thomas Harrelson
Fletcher James	Mary Reason	28 Nov 1781	Woolsey Pride
Fletcher Reubin	Betsey Thompson	22 Dec 1802	William Rice
Flintoff John F.	Mary M. Pleasant	11 May 1850	Algernon D. Stephens
Flippin Joseph W.	Susan W. Atkinson	4 Jun 1856	William D. Neal md by John Stadler
Flippo Joseph	Sally Elmore	28 Sep 1801	Thomas Elmore
Flora Melceger R.	Lucy Dunkly	18 Nov 1842	Lewis Smith M. P. Huntington
Florance Empson	Eliza Boswell	7 Dec 1846	Hames M. Brookes
Florence Bennett	Elizabeth Ann Bird	18 Oct 1837	John P. Florence
Florence George W.	Susannah F. Womble	18 Sep 1854 21 Sep	Jefferson H. Walker md by Benj. Wells JP
Florence James	Sarah S. Bouldin	29 Jun 1841	John Q. Anderson
Florence James	Frances H. Dameron	22 Nov 1858	William Nutt
Florence Josiah T.*	Avis Simmons	7 Dec 1831	James Coleman
Florence William	Patcey Pleasant	6 Nov 1808	Moses S. Simpson
Floyd Samuel B.	Permela F. Sailes	21 Jun 1833	Benjamin C. West

GROOM	BRIDE	DATE	BONDSMAN OR WITNESS
Foard Francis	Nancy Stephen	29 Mar 1798	William Rice
Forbes William A. (son of John H. & M. H.)	Virginia V. Powell (dau of John B. & Nancy)	9 May 1867	H. F. Brandon md by John J. Jones JP
Ford Alexander	Pheby Fuller	19 Aug 1806	Mumford Ford
Ford Amos	Frances Rudd	24 Sep 1811	Laban Ford
Ford Eli	Zeporiah Strador	22 Dec 1827	Christian Strador
Ford George	Elizabeth Tennesson	13 Dec 1800	Lemuel Ford
Ford George D.	Mary F. Scott	27 May 1852	Joseph Shields md by Philip Hodnett
Ford John N.	Esther Strador	22 Dec 1827	Christian Strador
Ford John R.	Susan E. Thornton	4 Sep 1851	Robert B. Thornton md by A. McDowell MG
Ford Laban	Patsey Griffin	8 Apr 1813	Zenas Martin Goodwin Evans
Ford Levi	Mary Payne	4 Jan 1814	John Payne
Ford Lewis H.	Elizabeth Gill	21 Sep 1841	John Shields G. W. VanHook
Ford Munford	Rachel McNeely	7 Oct 1806	William Wilkinson
Ford Pleasant L.	Nancy M. Southard	19 Oct 1833	Richard Fitzgerald
Ford Thomas	Elmina Dotson	1 May 1828	Jonathan Pearman
Ford William	Salley Wray	5 Dec 1787	Hearndon Haralson
Forgerson Garrett	Lucy Bays	5 Aug 1841	John Bucey
Forgusson James	Nancey Durham	4 Oct 1816	John Morton
Forod Elijah T.	Martha Crews	22 Dec 1834	Obadiah Cruise
Forrell Enuch	Lucy Stone	3 Nov 1784	William Stone Jr.
Forshee Joseph	Nelley Stafford	15 Apr 1784	John Stafford
Forrest Thomas	Betsey Burton	2 Dec 1809	John Woods
Forster F. K.	S. E. Turner	14 Oct 1848	Philemon Neal
Fossett Robert	Mary Hughes	7 Feb 1800	James Hughes
Foster Anthony	Salley Perkins	1 Oct 1811	William Bruce
Foster Azariah	Nancy King	30 Jun 1828	Richard B. Gunn
Foster Colby	Betsey King	16 Jun 1808	John Sawyer
Foster Franklin	Ibba Manley	7 Oct 1841	Ezekiel Sawyer
Foster Franklin	Lucy Manley	26 Jan 1864 28 Jan ----	Zeneth Page md by Stephen Neal JP
Foster James	Nancey Harden	4 Sep 1812	Jeremiah Jones
Foster Jesse	Polley Adkins	3 Nov 1817	Richard Gunn
Foster John	Nancy Pirkins	22 Dec 1783	Edward Upton
Foster John	Agniss Pulhim	31 Dec 1786	William Taylor
Foster John	Elizabeth Perkins	29 Jul 1816	Thomas Foster
Foster John	Elizabeth Brandon	29 Jan 1820	Shadrack Lewis
Foster Lewis	Cisily Mitchel	2 Sep 1797	Robert Lackey
Foster Madison P.	Nancy Blackwell	17 Jan 1842	Williamson P. Foster
Foster Richard	Lucy Hobbs	28 Feb 1821	Robert Perkins
Foster Robert	Elizabeth Grant	5 Sep 1805	Richard Cates
Foster Samuel P.	Mary Garrott	14 Dec 1829	Barzillai Graves Pleasant Pearman
Foster Thomas	Polley Harrelson	22 Jan 1814	Jacob Henderson
Foster Thomas T.	Mary A. Mitchell	12 Nov 1850	James E. Foster
Foster William A.	Ann P. Jones (wid)	19 Dec 1860	Jos. L. McKee
Foster William L.	Lucinda Taylor	28 Jul 1846	N. J. Palmer Henry Rose
Foster Williamson P.	Sally Montgomery	27 Jan 1845	James M. Neal T. H. Miles
Foulkes Edward M.	Martha Brown	16 Dec 1811	George Williamson
Foulkes Thomas C.	Pennelope Moore	6 Apr 1811	Geo. Washington Jeffreys
Foulkes Oliver	Patience Rudd	11 Oct 1825	Elisha Rudd
Foulks Woodson*	Elizabeth Miles	19 Oct 1831	Oliver Foulks
Fowler Elias	Eliza Glasgow	8 Nov 1834	Barthus J. Crawley
Fowler Harrison (Col)	Sallie Blair (Col)	20 Jan 1866 21 Jan	Jerry Graves Jr. md by Jacob Doll MG

GROOM	BRIDE	DATE	BONDSMAN OR WITNESS
Fowler John	Nancy Fowler	9 Jul 1853 11 Jul	A. Slade clk md by J. S. Totten JP
Fowler William L.	America F. Clay	12 Feb 1853	And. J. McAlpin md by Jno. S. Grasty
Fox Nathan	Mary J. Rend	6 Nov 1848	Nathaniel Broach
Fox Wm.	Nancy Jacob	28 Dec 1820	Richd. Crisp
Frailey John	Patience Dalton	1 Apr 1811	George Frailey Benj. Williamson
Franklin Ambrose	Elizabeth Jones	18 Mar 1826	Jno. P. Womack
Franklin William G. (son of Pleasant Franklin)	Mary E. Burton (dau of Benjamin G. Burton of Halifax Co. Va.)	10 Nov 1859	Henry E. Rodden
Franklin Zeary	Sarah A. Boswell	7 May 1850	Antichus Boswell
Frazier Madison M.	Nancy W. Hightower (dau of Joshua Hightower decd.)	18 Aug 1832	Charles Stephens
Frederick Jesse	Sophia Hicks	11 Jun 1833	Thomas S. Swift
Freeland Charles J.	Margaret E. Barton	30 Aug 1853	Wm. J. Freeland
Freeman John (Col)	Rhody Hendrick (Col)	10 Jan 1856	Henry Mayho R. A. Newbell
Freeman John P.	Deborah Harden	1 Feb 1815	James P. Foster
Freeman Moses (Col)	Betsey Good (Col- dau of Thomas & Elizabeth Good)	30 Oct 1811	Ambrose Bohannon
Freeman Wesley (Col)	Vilet Good (Col)	29 Jan 1862	Byrd Maho md by N. M. Lewis JP
Freeman Willis W.	Jane Piles	6 May 1848	William Bowers
French Benjamin	Salley Turner	10 Nov 1784	James Turner
French James	Mahala Strador	14 May 1818	David Strador Elijah Withers
French John	Agripina Brackin	30 Mar 1833	Charles G. Mitchell
Fretwell William A.	Caroline Locket	23 May 1842	Thomas D. Harrison John B. Powell
Fryer William	Elizabeth Windsor	14 Apr 1815	John Kinnebrugh
Fugerson Andrew J.	Judah F. Willis	26 Nov 1856	R. A. Newbell Felix F. Thornton
Fulcher Henry	Mary Gregory	21 Dec 1786	John Warren
Fulcher William	Alsey Archdeacon	4 Sep 1787	John H. Pryor
Fulington John R.	Patience Mathis	17 Nov 1827	Solomon Whitlow
Fullar Peter	Jane Rosebrough	23 Apr 1781	Wilson Vermillion
Fuller Abraham	Mary Sargent	6 Feb 1786	Stephen Sargent Jr.
Fuller Albert G.	Ann Catharin Powell	11 Oct 1847	John G. Jeffreys
Fuller Henry	Jane Pass	20 Jul 1867 21 Jul	H. F. Brandon md by Solomon Apple MG
Fuller Jesse	Sophronia Moore	24 Nov 1846	Wm. Wisdom
Fuller John	Susannah Clayton	9 Dec 1778	Robert Long Abner Tatom
Fuller John H.	Nancey Cooper	26 Aug 1836	Johnson Scoggins
Fuller Levi	Susannah McDaniel	3 Feb 1810	Saml. Johnston Jr.
Fuller Stephen	Elizabeth Hightower	15 Mar 1825	William Fuller
Fuller William	Elizabeth Wallis	9 Mar 1796	John Wallis
Fullington James	Anna Johnston	25 Oct 1825	Solomon Whitlow
Fullington James G.	Meranda Campbell	22 Nov 1856	L. B. Evans
Fullington William	Milley Page	3 Jan 1825	Adams S. Richmond
Fulton Jno. K.	Louisa M. Harrison (dau of Susan B. Harrison)	10 Jan 1852 15 Jan ----	Thomas P. Harrison md by Wm. Anderson
Fulton Mathias	Jane L. Hunter	9 Jan 1822	Archabald Rice
Fulton William J.	Minerva Coleman	28 Jan 1842	James M. Coleman
Fuqua Henry D.	Mary R. Ferrell	3 Aug 1826	James McClarney

GROOM	BRIDE	DATE	BONDSMAN OR WITNESS
Fuqua John	Rebecca V. Lea	29 Nov 1851	James T. Mitchell
			md by Wm. P. Graves JP
Fuqua William	Elizabeth Ferrell	10 Jul 1833	James McClarney
Furgerson Alexander	Mary Hailey	6 Oct 1856	Washington T. Hodges md by Jas. P. Simpson MG
Furgerson Samuel	Mary L. Arnett (dau of Mary A. Arnett Pittsylvania Co. Va.)	12 Aug 1822	John Furgerson Jno. G. Womack DC
Furgerson William G.	Elizabeth Jane Jeffreys	30 Oct 1848	William C. Page
Furguson James T.	Eliza J. Russell	14 Feb 1866 15 Feb	James C. Williamson md by Geo. W. Thompson
Furguson Robert F.	Harriet M. Richardson	14 Sep 1854	Tho. W. Graves clk

- G -

Gaddis William	Angelico Connelly	16 Nov 1795	George Connally
Gaffard William	Nancey Climpson	30 Oct 1821	Edwin Reamy
Gallangher William	Sarah Dollarhide	26 Nov 1781	George Huston
Galloway Robert	Fanny M. Hill	9 Mar 1852	William C. Brown
Gann William	Rebeccah Pass	3 Mar 1798	William Williams
Gannaway G. T. F. (Col-son of Wm. & Matilda Gannaway)	Sally Paschal (Col- dau of Ned Windsor & China Paschal)	12 Feb 1868	H. F. Brandon
Gant Jesse	Minerva M. Anderson	20 Jun 1840	Allen T. Collilns
Garber A. M. Jr.	A. C. Baldwin	16 Mar 1864	H. T. Tucker md by Jacob Doll MG
Gardner Joseph C. (son of N. W. & Martha H. Gardner)	Martha E. Howard (dau of Alanson & Mary Howard)	4 Sep 1867 5 Sep	H. F. Brandon md by S. G. Mason
Gardner Nathaniel W.	Martha H. Cobb	10 Sep 1832	Samuel B. Cobb
Gardner Starke	Harriot Holladay	13 May 1835	Solomon Corbet
Garland Anderson (son of Isaac & Viney Garland)	Rhoda Guy (dau of Washington & Vilet Guy)	27 Dec 1867	H. F. Brandon md by J. J. Jones JP
Garland Eustace (Col)	Minerva Clark (Col)	4 Oct 1867	H. F. Brandon md by Eustace Hunt JP
Garland Jacob (Col)	Allice Thomas (Col)	20 Apr 1867	H. F. Brandon clk
Garland Jno. T.	Christine J. Glenn	15 May 1821	Jno. E. Lewis P. H. Inge
Garland Nelson (Col)	Neldenna Garland (Col)	16 Jun 1867	md by John J. Jones JP
Garland Oscar (Col)	Pheby Ann Garland (Col)	18 May 1867 19 May	md by R. A. Moore
Garland Peter (Col)	Anna Clay (Col)	5 Dec 1866 6 Dec	Jacob Garland md
Garland William (Col)	Candis Wilson (Col)	8 Oct 1865	Nathaniel Wooding
Garland Wilson	Mary E. Jenings	16 Jul 1860	N. L. Walker
Garlington John L.	Mary E. Oliver	29 May 1857 30 May	John J. Crawley md by Jas. P. Simpson MG
Garner Archibald W.	Ann E. Yancey	26 Dec 1861 9 Jan 1862	Tho. W. Graves clk md by S. G. Mason
Garner James V.	Mary Ann Green	3 Dec 1838	Joseph F. Cornwell
Garrett John W.	Martha Blackwell	2 Feb 1835	Stephen Neal
Garrett R. J.	Mary A. Walker	27 Feb 1855	Jno. P. Rainey Jr. md by L. L. Hendren Jas. T. Graves DC

GROOM	BRIDE	DATE	BONDSMAN OR WITNESS
Garrison Daniel (son of John G. & Sarah Garrison)	Matilda P. Sartin (dau of Elisha Sartin)	21 Aug 1867 22 Aug	md by M. A. Turner JP
Garrison Hall	Catherine Cantrel	20 May 1809	Joseph Anthony
Garrison George	Frances Herndon	29 Nov 1847	George Herndon
Garrod John C.	Mary E. Reaves	11 Apr 1867	H. F. Brandon
Garrott Mansell	Ann Frazer	4 Jul 1790	Jno. Hall
Garrott Stephen	Martha B. Bradsher	18 Jan 1823	Vincent Bradsher
Gates James M.	Nancy B. Smith	10 Feb 1824	David G. Leigh
Gates John*	Lucy M. Merritt	11 Jan 1831	Richard Yarbrough
Gates John	Lucy Richardson	10 Mar 1821	Thomas Richardson
Gates Richard	Aggy Williams	6 Aug 1798	Robert Willson
Gates Richard	Rebecca Fowler	12 Nov 1837	Thomas Richardson
Gatewood Lewis	Sally Stokes (dau of Silvs. Stokes)	1 Feb 1811	Contract between Gatewood & Stokes
Gatewood Robert A.	Eliza Hodges	18 Nov 1842	Cary W. West
Gatewood Thomas	Pamilia Farley	23 Sep 1806	John McAden
Gatewood Thomas L.	Martha T. Bennett	31 May 1853	James B. Peabody md by J. M. Allen JP
Gatewood William D.	Mary W. Badgett	6 Feb 1856 13 Feb 1856	Robert W. Graves md by John S. Grasty MG
Gatewood William H.	Mary Hodges	23 Nov 1847	Alexander Pinix
Gatley John	Mime Messer	30 Jan 1787	John Pyron J. Womack
Gattis Rev. Alexander	Sarah E. F. Womble	12 Nov 1857 24 Nov 1857	James W. Lea md by N. M. D. Wilson
Gattis W. A.	Alice V. Hawkins	17 Dec 1866	Thos. Dickson md by S. G. Mason
Gattis William	Rebecca Montgomery	18 Mar 1820	John Hughes
Gatty Joseph	Elizabeth Ragsdale	22 Dec 1789	James Messer
Geary Bengemin	Appy Caldwell	11 Aug 1817	Charles D. Taylor William Moore
George Isaac	Frankey Henslee	4 Nov 1805	Enoch Henslee Wm. Wilkinson
Gibbs John	Hannah Muchmore	18 Jan 1783	Shadrack Hudson
Gibes Shadrack	Ester Robinson	11 May 1785	Charles McIntosh
Gibson Benjn.	Susannah Tate	20 Oct 1795	Richard Simpson
Gibson Iveson	Frances Cobb	3 Feb 1841	Franklin J. Wilson
Gibson John	Juda Hogg	8 Jun 1779	John Brockman Wm. Campbell
Gibson Samuel	Jane Davis	11 Nov 1834	William A. Sneed
Gibson Thomas	Margaret Boswell	28 Dec 1819	Richard Smith
Gill Richard D.	Sarah Lampkin	18 Nov 1822	Thomas Graves
Gill Robert	Elisabeth Davey	5 Jan 1784	Francis Lawson
Gillam Joseph	Sarah Walker	21 Jan 1839	Abner Walker Jr.
Gillam Robert	Martha Walker	24 Apr 1837	Abner Walker Jr.
Gillaspie Edward R.	Mary F. Austin	13 Jul 1855	William O. Gillaspie md by Wm. J. Moore JP
Gillaspy Gidel	Martha Pass	24 Nov 1817	Nathaniel W. Pass
Gillaspy James	Rhody Hubbard	18 Feb 1799	Alexander Gillaspy
Gillaspy William	Patty Jeffrys	26 Oct 1782	Joseph Kelley
Gillespie William	Susannah Mannen	13 Jun 1805	Thomas Slade Jr.
Gilliam R. C.	Virginia M. Rucks	30 Nov 1863	James R. Warren md by Jacob Doll MG
Gilliam Wm. M.	J. B. Watson	1 Nov 1860	W. M. Caldwell W. Allen Harralson dpt md by J. Doll MG
Gillispie David A.	Rebecca F. Powell	30 Sep 1848	James T. Mitchell
Gillispie David A.	Mary F. Colly	30 Mar 1852	John W. Ames md by Tho. L. Lea JP
Gillispie Joseph M.	Sophia J. Hendrick	30 Aug 1865	M. J. Powell md by J. J. Jones JP

GROOM	BRIDE	DATE	BONDSMAN OR WITNESS
Gillispie William O.	Mary F. Walters	29 Nov 1851	James T. Mitchell
		2 Dec 1851	md by Wm. J. Moore JP
Glasgow William T.	Nancey Howel	20 Mar 1815	Benjamin Howell
Glass Iverson M.	Sallie M. Fuller	8 Oct 1853	John C. Harvey
Glass John D.	Margaret E. Powell	3 Feb 1854	Saml. P. Hill
		14 Feb 1854	md by Aaron Jones Jr. MG
Glass Joshua S.	Elizabeth Richardson	24 Nov 1846	Samuel B. Cobb
Glass Saml.	Huldah B. Blackwell	28 Apr 1866	Deleware Hooper
Glass Willison J.	Sally Durham	20 Apr 1829	Silvanus Stokes
Glaze Ralph	Elizabeth Shelton	6 Nov 1823	Starling H. Gunn
Glenn Sampson M.	Clary Ingram	-- Feb 1803	Thomas Harrelson
Goadge William	Polly Ferguson	1 Jul 1805	Maraday Price
Godwin George W.	Sophia Shankes	13 Nov 1818	John M. Williams
Goin John	Betsey Hickman	24 Nov 1795	Burbage Going William Rainey
Going Goodrich	Betsey Matthews	6 Sep 1791	Allen Going
Going Jesse	Selley Bairding	9 Jun 1784	John Going
Going Jesse	Polly Draper	12 Nov 1807	Vincent Going
Going John	Seeley Bairding	9 Jun 1784	Jesse Going
Going Sherwood	Ruth Bennett	30 Apr 1793	James Gillaspy
Going Sherwood	Betsey Coventon	31 Dec 1804	James Gillaspy
Gold William	Mary Dameron	30 Jul 1806	Byrd G. Parker
Gomer Barzillai	Judith Beaver	29 Sep 1814	Vincent Peterson
Gomer Benjamin	Janey Tarpley	4 Nov 1789	John Ferry
Gomer James	Dicey Gomer	17 Dec 1816	William Gomer
Gomer James	Elizabeth Hall	22 Apr 1819	Sarah Hall Elijah Withers
Gomer James J.	Anne Sanders	18 Dec 1838	Iverson Harrelson
Gomer James J.	Elizabeth Mitchell	12 Aug 1845	Andrew J. Mitchell
Gomer John	Ann Beaver	20 Feb 1810	Martin Browning
Gomer John	Polley Parrish	11 Mar 1816	John Scott Jr.
Gomer Pinckney	Mary Strader	2 Oct 1847	Jethro J. Walker
Gomer Thomas	Salley Mason	17 Aug 1829	Archibald D. Hubbard
Gomer Wiley	Catharine Blackwell	28 Sep 1846	A. J. Mitchell
Gomer William	Nancey Wattson	11 Mar 1807	Jesse Beaver
Gooch David	Jenney Williams	19 Dec 1788	William Kimbro
Gooch Francis	Ailcey King	30 Dec 1837	Henry Turner
Gooch James	Elisabeth Kelley	3 Aug 1785	Edward Anderson
Gooch James	Sally Porter	29 Nov 1801	George Stovall
Gooch John	Polley Walters	25 Aug 1807	James Page
Gooch Nathl.	Patsey Tate	30 Nov 1797	William Smith
Gooch Nathaniel	Jenney Bozwell	23 Jan 1816	Thomas Bozwell
Gooch Nathaniel	Louisa A. Ferrell	19 Jul 1852	James P. Bozwell
Gooch Nathaniel	Nancy King	14 Mar 1864	Alexander McAlpin
		20 Mar 1864	md by A. G. Anderson MG
Gooch Thomas	Elizabeth Anthony	13 Aug 1799	Henry Williams
Gooch Thomas	Frances Martin	6 Oct 1834	Ephraim Turner
Gooch William	Mary Turner (wid)	2 Jun 1866	R. E. Stadler
		10 Jun 1866	md by F. L. Oakley MG
Gooch William Jr.	Mary Fanning	5 Dec 1798	Benjamin Stovall
Goodman Joseph	Elioner Brown	15 Mar 1781	Christopher Brookes
Goodson George T.	Sarah J. Burton	9 Oct 1852	William L. Fowler
Goodson George T.	M. E. Powell (wid)	22 Sep 1865	James N. Harrison
		24 Sep 1865	md by R. G. Barrett MG
Goodwin James H.	Adeline Philips	9 May 1837	William W. Price
Gorden William	Eliza Nipper	11 May 1802	William Willson
Gordon Alexander	Susannah Johnston	19 Oct 1807	Solo. Debow
Gordon James	Elizabeth Walters	19 Nov 1845	Jno. Woodie W. A. Whitfield
Gordon Robert	Crosha Trammell	11 Dec 1845	Thomas Mansfield N. J. Palmer
Gosne Benjamin H.	Martha Ware	19 Sep 1825	Talbert Ware
Gossage Danl.	Peggy Hudson	5 Jan 1801	Job Siddel

GROOM	BRIDE	DATE	BONDSMAN OR WITNESS
Gossage Richard	Rachel Greenhaw	12 Apr 1797	Greenbeary Voss
Gosset Joel	Sarah Gorden	17 Oct 1827	Sterling Willis
Gossett Thomas	Nelly Pyrant	4 Jan 1808	William Cannon
Gould Benjamin	Eliza Brady	10 Nov 1838	Augustus C. Finley
Gowin Richard	Polly Bennett	4 Jul 1807	James Rainey
Gowing Vincent	Nancy Reed	30 Dec 1806	Burch Swann
Graham Albert	Lillie J. Cooper	16 Dec 1867	H. F. Brandon
		19 Dec 1867	md by E. W. Beale
Graham James	Susan Dameron (wid)	24 Feb 1853	John C. Harvey
Graham Thomas	Emily G. Williamson	7 Jan 1857	Benjamin F. Williamson
		22 Jan 1857	md by D. R. Burton
Graham Travves	Martha Stout Rose	13 Feb 1786	William Corum
Graham William P.	Farmesia Nash	28 Sep 1819	William J. Nash
Grahams James	Martha Douglass	9 Jan 1816	David Douglass
Grant James P.	Virginia C. Dean	31 May 1862	E. E. Atkinson
			md by Jacob Doll MG
Grant John W.	Deborah Cobb	16 Jul 1812	Alex. Murphey
Grant Neely	Lucy Perkins	23 Sep 1793	Alex. Murphey
Graves Alfred	Evelina Graves	20 Jul 1867	H. F. Brandon
		22 Jul 1867	md by S. G. Mason
Graves Augustus S.	Elizabeth W. Comer	13 Nov 1849	William P. Graves
			R. Y. Graves
Graves Azariah	Penelope Simpson	16 May 1809	William Graves
Graves Azariah	Isabella S. Howard	10 Mar 1858	Philemon H. Neal
		17 Mar 1858	md by Thomas W. Tobey MG
Graves Azariah Jr.	Elizabeth Neal	20 Jun 1846	Henry A. Womack
Graves Barzillai	Ursley Wright	9 Apr 1783	Esa Wright
Graves Benjiman	Mary Ann Reid	23 Feb 1867	Franklin Roberts
		25 Feb 1867	md by S. G. Mason
Graves Calvin	Elizabeth Lea	2 Jun 1830	Paul A. Haralson
Graves Cato	Lizzie Rudd	20 Oct 1866	George Pattillo
			md by M. A. Turner JP
Graves Charles I.	Maggie R. Lea	8 Nov 1862	Calvin L. Graves
Graves David S.	Ida V. Sanders	29 Sep 1862	F. L. W. Graves
			md by W. B. Bowe JP
Graves Elijah Jr.	Eliza A. Gunn	21 Oct 1828	John H. Graves Jr.
			Richard H. L. Bennett
Graves Elijah Jr.	Mary J. Crump	26 Nov 1849	William P. Watlington
Graves Geo.	----------------	20 Sep 1866	Squire Graves
Graves George A.	Isabella M. Williamson	4 Apr 1865	Sidney S. Lea
			md by R. G. Barrett MG
Graves Henry L.	Rebecca W. Graves	2 Feb 1836	Algernon S. Yancey
Graves Isaac (Col- son of Robin & Graves)	Mary Hunley (Col)	21 Sep 1867	H. F. Brandon clk
		25 Sep 1867	md by Jasn. J. Clendening JP
Graves Iverson L.	Elizabeth B. Payne	2 Oct 1828	Calvin Graves
			md by Danl. A. Penick MG
Graves Jacob M. Jr.	Polly Eubank	13 Sep 1827	Miles Kimbrough
Graves James	Polley Slade	15 Apr 1800	Alex. Murphey
Graves James	Elizabeth Pleasant	18 Nov 1824	Azariah G. Kimbro
Graves James L.	Elizabeth G. Womack	12 Mar 1840	Thomas W. Graves
Graves James L.	Francis A. Kerr (wid)	7 Nov 1849	Thomas W. Graves
			R. Graves
Graves Jeremiah	Delilah Lea	14 Mar 1816	William B. Graves
			Azariah Graves
Graves Jeremiah Jr.	D. R. Thornton	11 Jun 1860	Robert W. Lawson Jr.
		13 Jun 1860	md by Saml. G. Mason
Graves John	Elizabeth Coleman	28 Nov 1808	Groves Howard
Graves John Jr.	Polly Yancey	13 Feb 1794	John Kimbrough Jr.
Graves John A.	Catherine M. Whited (wid)	31 May 1848	Jno. K. Graves
			R. Y. Graves

GROOM	BRIDE	DATE	BONDSMAN OR WITNESS
Graves Jno. K.	Laura A. Willis	20 Jan 1844	William P. Graves
Graves John L.	Martha W. Dick	20 May 1824	Paul A. Haralson
Graves John S.	Susan B. Simpson	3 Apr 1858	J. L. McKee
		4 Apr 1858	md by G. G. Walker
Graves Lewis	Elizabeth Graves	12 Nov 1818	Allen Gunn
			Azariah Graves
Graves Lewis Dixon	Nancey Willis	20 Sep 1836	Henderson House
Graves Lucien (Col	Matilda Brown (Col)	27 Oct 1865	Jno. Lee Graves
Graves Morris (Col)	Susan Adkins (Col)	26 Oct 1866	Thos. Donoho md by Thos. W. Graves JP
Graves Nathan (Col)	Adline Wommack (Col)	26 Dec 1865	Bristo Wommack md by S. G. Mason
Graves Peter (Col- son of Gabriel & Priscilla Graves)	Hettie Palmer	19 Nov 1867 21 Nov 1867	H. F. Brandon md by S. G. Mason
Graves Solomon	Nancey S. Graves	21 May 1836	George W. Graves
Graves Thomas	Polley Bennett	5 May 1801	Henry E. Williamson
Graves Thomas	Nancey Lampkin	26 Jul 1821	James Graves
Graves Thomas W.	Mary Graves	17 Jul 1828	Dr. Henry McAden Azariah Graves
Graves William	Isbell Graves	25 Nov 1805	Wm. Gooch Sr.
Graves William	Nancey Graves	25 May 1815	Barz. Graves Azariah Graves
Graves William	Eliza Hester	5 Nov 1833	James C. Dobines
Graves William B.	Sarah H. Lea	16 Jul 1863 17 Jul 1863	Tho. W. Graves clk md by S. G. Mason
Graves William G.	Anna R. Lea	11 Dec 1865	R. W. Graves
Gravett Lodwick	Susannah Moss	7 Dec 1789	William Thaxton
Gray Alexander	Lucinda R. Wiley	10 Nov 1840	Robert M. Wiley G. W. VanHook
Gray James	Elizabeth Stokes	29 Nov 1780	Woolsey Pride
Gray John	Margret Wiley	16 Dec 1800	Alexander Wiley
Gray Yancey	Jane Rose	25 Mar 1828	George Winstead
Green Burwell	Phebe Caddel	4 Jul 1789	Lewis Green
Green Joseph G.	Amanda S. Allen	12 Oct 1836	John S. Oglesby
Green Lewis	Elizabeth Caddell	26 Dec 1789	Andrew Caddel
Green Thomas C.	Jane McMullen	13 May 1844	Thomas J. Currie
Greenwood Thomas	Minerva J. Carver	4 Nov 1843	Viveldi Rowlett
Greer Samuel*	Elizabeth Graves	22 Nov 1831	Yancey G. Warren
Gregory John H.	Mary Sisson	22 May 1841	James A. Higginbottom
Gregory Samuel	Patsey Tharp	5 Dec 1807	John Wesley
Gregory Thomas J.	Cassandia Caroline Patterson	4 Apr 1825	William Patterson
Gregory Thomas J.	Polly Wynne (ward of Wm. Linn, Danville, Va)	1 Dec 1827	Thompson Bird
Gresham Henry	Mary Loot	5 Jan 1788	James Wilson
Grider Jacob (Crider?)	Recey Washburn	22 Apr 1797	Robert Martin
Griffin Alvis L.	Malinda Fitch	23 Feb 1850	Ander J. Griffin
Griffin Andre J. (or Andrew J.)	Martha Ann Sawyer	20 Sep 1851 23 Sep 1851	William A. Dameron md by Geo. F. Deshago JP
Griffin John	Elizabeth Crawley	21 Jul 1840	Henry D. Turner
Griffin Owen	Catharine Wisdom	17 Apr 1816	Thomas Tindal Isaac Rainey
Griffin Vincent	Salley Evans	12 Sep 1820	Azariah G. Kimbro
Griffin William	Lucy Pleasant	13 Apr 1812	Walter Murry
Griffins Alexander	Anness Roan	12 Sep 1809	James Roan Jeremiah Rudd
Griffith James	Susanna Roe	31 Jan 1822	Robert Roe
Griffith Jesse C.	Mary J. Vernon	15 Jan 1845	William B. Bowe
Griffith Richard H.	Judith Starkey	10 Dec 1820	Jno. C. Harvey

GROOM	BRIDE	DATE	BONDSMAN OR WITNESS
Groom Calvin	Elizabeth Martin	8 Nov 1859	James T. Mitchell
Groom Carter	Polley Butler	27 Oct 1819	Henry Miller
Groom John	Frances G. Chandler	3 Aug 1848	B. Lownes
Groom John	Sarah A. Rainey	3 Apr 1858	James G. Loyd
		4 Apr 1858	md by J. Doll
Groom Robert	Elizabeth Pinson	4 Dec 1824	Samuel Groom
Groom Samuel	Frances Scott	20 Jul 1824	John C. Harvey
			William Russell
Groom Thomas	Mildred Jeffreys	17 Oct 1821	Carter Groom
Groom Thomas	Welthy Crafton	28 Dec 1835	John Baxter Jr.
Groom William	Nancey Pierce	24 Mar 1813	Zadok Rice
			Goodwin Evans
Gude William Jr.	Vilet Mitchell	3 Nov 1850	William Gude Sr.
Guerrant Peter M. C.	Mariah L. Cobb	19 Jan 1855	Haywood H. Haizlip
Guerrant T. D. F.	Sarah J. Stanfield	25 Oct 1858	Wm. H. Badgett
Guinn James	Nannie Rew	27 Dec 1866	Thomas Wyles
			md by E. Hunt JP
Gunn Dr. Allen Jr.	Minerva Ann Henderson	7 Oct 1829	Thomas Graves
Gunn Asa	Nancey Harrelson	22 Nov 1819	Thomas Vaughan
Gunn Daniel	Nancy Burton	19 Oct 1818	Griffin Gunn
Gunn Daniel B.	Eliza H. Brandon	19 Oct 1839	Daniel L. McAlpin
Gunn George	Emily Hooper	12 Jan 1867	Arch. Corbett
Gunn Dr. Geo. W.	Jennie Hennie Burton	19 Oct 1860	R. W. Lawson Jr.
		21 Oct	md by Jno. Long MG
Gunn Griffin	Vashti Womack	18 Sep 1837	John C. Harvey
Gunn James	Barbary Walker	21 Apr 1808	Starling Gunn
Gunn James*	Elizabeth Yancey	17 May 1831	Allen Gunn
			Henderson House
Gunn James	Frances A. Henderson	7 May 1835	Owen McAleer
Gunn James M.	Mary M. Batton	13 Mar 1843	James E. Foster
Gunn John	Huldy Ware	28 Jan 1807	Elijah Graves
Gunn John (Col)	Eliza Phillips (Col)	20 Jan 1866	B. Harrelson
		4 Apr 1866	md by A. A. Pattillo JP
Gunn John Jr.	Elizabeth Palmer	5 Jul 1827	Jno. G. Womack
			Jones M. Gunn
Gunn John A.	Martha Haralson	2 Apr 1839	John A. Gunn
			Owen McAleer
Gunn Penny (Col)	Catharine Walker (Col)	24 Dec 1867	H. F. Brandon
Gunn Richard	Susannah Foster	30 Oct 1810	Thomas Gunn
Gunn Samuel (Col)	Leana Jones (Col)	24 Mar 1866	Edward Gunn
			md by S. G. Mason
Gunn Sterling (son of John W. & Martha J. Gunn)	Mary A. Jones (dau of R. H. & Martha A. Jones)	14 Jan 1868	H. F. Brandon md by Thos. J. Brown JP
Gunn Thomas	Patsey Graves	22 Sep 1792	Griffin Gunn
Gunn Thomas	Nelly Alverson	24 Oct 1797	James Burton
Gunn Thomas	Patcey Miles	20 Sep 1802	William Moore
Gunn Thomas Jr.	Anne Montgomery	22 Jan 1811	Richard Gunn
Gunn Wiley (Col)	Arrimenta Lea (Col)	3 Apr 1867	H. F. Brandon
			md by Thomas J. Brown
Gunnell John	Sally Smith	4 Jan 1838	Pleasant Waddill
			W. R. Sott
Gurnes Richard (Col)	Mary Toney (Col)	19 Feb 1855	Wm. Delauney R. A. Newbell
Gutry John D.	Elacy Manley	15 Dec 1838	Samuel Page
Guttery William	Elisabeth Sheppard	2 Oct 1782	Andrew McKnight
Guy Alvis (Colson of Willis & Sally Guy)	Lavina Mitchel (Col-dau of John & Peggy Mitchel)	24 Dec 1867	H. F. Brandon
Gwyn Augustus	Jane E. Madding	2 Jun 1838	Thomas Swift

GROOM	BRIDE	DATE	BONDSMAN OR WITNESS
Cwyn Augustus	Emily T. Corbitt	21 Jun 1854	Thomas D. Atkins md by Ed Jones JP
Gwyn Daniel	Mary N. Hatchett	30 Aug 1815	Zadok Rice
Gwyn John	Permelia Dupree	2 Aug 1839	Rice Gwyn Geo. W. VanHook
Gwyn John W.	Frances Hornbuckle	14 Sep 1856	Benjamin F. Williamson md by Thos. J. Williamson
Gwyn Jones (Col)	Phillis Watlington (Col)	31 Dec 1866	George Watlington md by Stephen Neal JP
Gwyn Rice	Elizabeth B. Rice	1 Mar 1842	Abisha Slade
Gwyn Robert Z.	Nancey Corbett	29 Nov 1859	Pinckney Gwyn Allen Harrelson DC
Gwyn Zeri	Temperence Goodson	21 Dec 1800	Ziza Rice

- H -

GROOM	BRIDE	DATE	BONDSMAN OR WITNESS
Hackney Samuel	Sarah Reynolds	23 Sep 1791	Laurence Lea
haddock Andrew	Peggy Green	21 Jun 1806	Jacob Quine
Haddock Bedford	Malinda Hughs	22 Apr 1829	James Kannon
Haddock David	Salley Roberts	13 May 1802	Josiah Boman
Haddock Henry	Mary Bruce	17 Feb 1844	Joseph M. Swift
Haddock Richard	Providence Wright	29 Jul 1796	Lawrence Richardson
Haddock Stephen	Nancey Pittard	20 Oct 1820	Edward Montgomery
Haddock Stephen	Sarah Davis	25 Dec 1834	Thomas Turner
Hagie Thomas	Luzella M. Broughton	19 Oct 1841	Lewis Love
Hague James	Martha Street	9 oct 1784	Andrew Buchannon
Hagwood James	Nancey M. Hodges	23 Nov 1836	Dudley G. Stokes
Hagwood John	Elizabeth Stephens	8 Jan 1835	Thomas W. Graves
Hagwood John	Catharine Stephens	24 Oct 1839	Benjamin F. Stephens
Hagwood Lewis	Martha Jackson	7 Apr 1819	Absolem Burton H. Smith
Hailey Henry B.	Polley Lyon	22 Jul 1812	John Stowers
Hailey Partrick C.	Bettie A. Crawford	10 Jul 1862 12 Jul	Robert E. Spaulding md by S. G. Mason
Hairston Charles (son of Ransom & Sally Paine)	Lucy Dix (dau of John & Mariah Dix)	29 Dec 1867	H. F. Brandon md by John J. Jones JP
Haithcock Allen F.	Lucinda Burch	28 Feb 1821	Thomas Overby
Haithcock John (Col-son of Williamson & Manerva)	Sarah J. Haith (Col- dau of John & Sarah)	18 Aug 1867	H. F. Brandon md by C. J. Richmond
Haithcock Martial	Martha Wilson	4 Nov 1866 7 Dec	Coleman Burch J. Smith md by C. J. Richmond JP
Haizlip Haywood H.	Martha J. Hooper	25 Sep 1856	B. Harrelson md by James P. Simpson
Halcom George	Freelove Merritt	2 Oct 1786	Solomon Marritt
Halcom George	Sarah Henderson	25 Dec 1788	Solomon Merritt
Halcomb Warren	Elizabeth Hooper	20 Jan 1824	John A. Nelson
Halcomb William	Nancy Jeffreys	16 Aug 1805	Benjamin Jones
Halcomb William	Sarah Thomas	5 Jan 1824	Alexander Montgomery
Hales Samuel	Elizabeth M. Jennings	24 Jun 1856 1 Jul	G. T. Crutcher md by J. B. Jackson
Hall Alexander	Patsey Brinsfield	25 Mar 1828	Armstead Watlington
Hall Anthony	Winney Harvell	22 Sep 1792	John Hall
Hall Benjamin P.	Mary L. Young	16 Jun 1858	J. M. Smith Jr. md by J. S. Totten JP
Hall Berry	Mary Owen	28 Mar 1856	Robert Hodges md by Geo. W.Thompson
Hall Beverly	Lucy Owen	21 Aug 1854	Asa Scott md by J. M. Allen JP

GROOM	BRIDE	DATE	BONDSMAN OR WITNESS
Hall Charles	Cintha Harrison	23 Mar 1852	B. Y. McAden
		24 Mar 1852	md by Stephen Neal JP
Hall David	Blanche Peterson	7 Mar 1825	Freeman Hubbard
Hall James	Eliza A. Ferrell	29 Dec 1856	John T. Hooper
			J. M. Allen
Hall James H. (son of Benj. & Leah)	Lucy Ann Hancock (dau of Stephen & Ann)	7 Sep 1868	H. F. Brandon md by N. M. Lewis JP
Hall John	Nancey Harwell	18 Oct 1791	Edmund Alley
Hall John	Sarah Poteat	2 Jul 1859	John F. Graves
		3 Jul 1859	md by J. S. Totten JP
Hall Lambert W.	Frances N. Bennett	13 Mar 1858	Jesse C. Griffith
		25 Mar 1858	md by S. A. Stanfield MG
Hall Pleasant	Cynthia McAden	10 Feb 1807	Geo. M. Willson
Hall Robert	Frances Scott	11 Dec 1800	William Willis
Hall Solomon	Morning Ingrom	24 Dec 1817	Merit Coats
Hall William	Peninah Robinson	18 Nov 1783	George Samuel
Hall William J.	Lydia B. Earp	1 Feb 1864	Jno. T. Russell
			md by John J. Jones JP
Halreson Calvin	Sally McDaniel	16 Feb 1867	H. F. Brandon
Hamblett Bird	Polley Simpson	4 Jan 1806	William Hamblett
Hambleton Joseph	Elizabeth W. Prather	18 Dec 1831	James Byrd
Hamlett Andrew J. (son of Lucy M. Hamlett)	Catharine Thomas (dau of Lucy Hicks)	11 May 1867 12 May	md by J. J. Jones JP
Hamlett James	Rebeccah Carrol	9 Feb 1793	Tobias Williams
Hamlett James	Patsey Taylor	7 Oct 1822	James Taylor
Hamlett John E.*	Martha R. Durham	12 Dec 1831	Henry Taylor
Hamlett Robert	Mary Glidewell	27 Dec 1843	George W. Hamlet
Hancock Farmer	Frances Taylor	17 Dec 1852	Richard A. Slaytor
			Jno. B. Barrett
Hancock John J.	Rosa Fowler	9 Oct 1858	W. Alex. Lockett
		10 Oct 1858	md by Jacob Doll MG
Hancock Stephen	Ann Warren	3 Jul 1839	James H. Thompson
Hanks Abraham	Mary Combs	12 Jan 1792	Thomas M. Hamlet
Hanner James	Mary Carter	3 Feb 1817	William Carter
Haralson Herndon	Mary Murphey	4 Oct 1791	Alex. Murphey
Haralson Major	Elizabeth Black	16 Jul 1793	Paul Haralson
Haralson Paul A.	Leannah H. Graves	30 Sep 1824	Azariah Graves
Haralson Thomas	Anne Bush	18 Nov 1787	Herndon Haralson
Haralson William	Sarah King	7 Nov 1837	John N. Henderson
Haraway William	Mary J. Walters	29 Jan 1866	John Walters
Harben William	Maryann Dill	4 Dec 1780	John Harben
Harden Henry	Elisabeth Hornbuckle	14 Aug 1795	Presley Harden
Hardicree Jonathan	Patsey Cameron	5 Jul 1797	Elijah Carman
Harding Ephraim H.	Mary D. Richmond	18 Jan 1859	Samuel H. Hines
Hardison Thomas	Sarah Hooper	2 Aug 1845	Solomon Corbett
Hardy George	Susannah Durham	25 Feb 1850	Milton Sparks
Hardy Green	Mary A. Weeden	3 Dec 1844	Isaac Cook
Hardy Robert	Manerva Brag	17 Aug 1854	Daniel W. Swann
Hardy Robert T.	Adaline W. Wright	4 Oct 1865	James H. Hardy
			md by J. J. Jones JP
Hardy Samuel	Nancy True	11 Jan 1851	William Norman
Hargess Shadrack (of Person Co.)	Sally Jones (of Caswell Co.)	18 Dec 1817	William Hargiss Isaac Rainey
Hargis James O.	Martha T. West	10 Sep 1825	Stairling H. Gunn
Hargis John	Jane Pyron (dau of Will. Pyron)	3 Jun 1778	James Smith
Hargis Thomas	Bridget Vanhook (dau of Laurence Vanhook)	3 Jun 1778	Archibald Murphey
Hargis William	Hanner Howel	3 Feb 1791	William Hargis Sr.
Harley Hiram	Betsey Stafford	27 Dec 1815	John Morgain
Harper Jesse	Anne Cox	9 Jun 1813	Robert Carter
			Thomas Bouldin

GROOM	BRIDE	DATE	BONDSMAN OR WITNESS
Harper Thomas	Nancey Nunn	25 Dec 1824	James Murphey
Harralson Henderson	Mary F. Morton	28 Mar 1853	Thomas B. Adkins
		31 Mar 1853	md by P. Hodnett JP
Harralson Jonathan	Jane Huston	12 Mar 1782	Geo. Huston
Harralson Sidney	Lucy A. Mitchell	9 Apr 1866	
Harraway Daniel (Col)	Betty Haskins (Col)	4 Oct 1867	H. F. Brandon
Harraway Richard (Col)	Minerva Clark (Col)	4 Oct 1867	H. F. Brandon
Harrelson Bennatt	Ammy Vershear	14 Aug 1815	Thomas Harrelson
Harrelson Forbes	France Bush	24 Nov 1790	Thomas Harrelson
Harrelson Forbes	Betsey Henderson	19 Nov 1793	Nathan Harrelson
Harrelson James	Polly Powell	6 Jan 1834	John P. Harrison
Harrelson James C.	Ibby Manley	2 Feb 1858	Jesse C. Griffith
		10 Feb 1858	md by Stephen Neal JP
Harrelson James M.	Betsey Gunn	23 May 1832	Thomas D. Connally
Harrelson Jeremiah	Patcey Brackin	29 Nov 1803	Henry Atkinson
Harrelson Madison	Harriet Slade	29 Oct 1866	Stephen Slade
Harrelson Nathaniel	Polly Tabor	9 Aug 1821	Henry Hooper
Harrelson Thomas	Martha Williamson	10 Jul 1802	Jeremiah Harrelson
Harrelson Thomas W.	Euphrasia Collins	23 Jan 1826	Dr. Henry McAden
Harrelson Thomas W.	Martha Collins	29 Jul 1839	Henry Willis
Harrelson William E.	Sarah V. Bowe	18 Apr 1853	Thomas Slade Jr.
		20 Apr 1853	md by Will. M. Jordan
Harrington J. B.	J. F. Burns	22 Nov 1860	Jno. F. Wrenn
Harris Christopher	Polly Payne	12 Jan 1801	Duke Williams
Harris Gustin (Col)	Mary Irvine (Col)	19 Jan 1867	Bedford Jeffreys
Harris James	Susannah Gunn	1 Nov 1819	Henry Shelton
Harris James L.	V. E. Anthony	4 Feb 1852	B. F. Whitescarver
Harris James M.	Elizabeth Hamlet	4 Dec 1848	David T. Elliott
Harris John	Elizabeth Yancey	28 May 1837	Martin Morgan
Harris Reubin	Catherine Raimey	16 Jan 1837	James Harris
Harris Robert	Elisabeth Lawson	18 Oct 1791	Pleasant Pryor
Harris Robert S.	Mary P. Williamson	31 Aug 1818	John H. Brown
Harris Tyree	Susanah Swift	18 Apr 1785	Jesse Oldham
Harrison Andrew	Nancy Williamson	18 Apr 1785	Robert Burton
Harrison Andrew W.	Matilda H. Sharpe	30 Sep 1836	Wm. W. Richardson
Harrison Calloway J.	Prudence Richardson	16 Feb 1839	Benjamin Hooper
Harrison Charles K.	Martha Stokes	5 May 1818	Jno. Smith
Harrison Charles P.	Susanna B. Price	12 Oct 1820	Wm. P. McDaniel
Harrison Edmond R.	Eliza J. Harrison	13 Sep 1844	Samuel S. Harrison
Harrison Headley	Sally Shelton	10 Dec 1803	James Shalton
Harrison James	Sarah Key	13 Jan 1825	Thomas Gibson
Harrison James R.	Susan Bolton	3 Feb 1852	A. G. Yancey
		6 Feb 1852	md by T. S. Campbell
Harrison Jesse	Eliza Bewsey	13 Jun 1822	John E. Wilkinson
Harrison John*	Mary Ann Murray	15 Dec 1846	John K. Brooks John K. Graves
Harrison Martin (son of Ruben & Matilda Harrison)	Bell Cobb (dau of Major & --- Cobb)	2 Nov 1867 15 Nov	H. F. Brandon md by Jas. J. Clendenin JP
Harrison Richard B.	Martha Emerson	12 Dec 1866	Abner R. Terry md by S. G. Mason
Harrison Robert L.	Mildred L. Harrison	19 Feb 1833	Thomas D. Connally
Harrison Samuel S.	Louisa M. McDaniel	11 Sep 1838	William M. Knight
Harrison Thomas	Mildred Johnston	4 Nov 1807	John P. Harrison

43

GROOM	BRIDE	DATE	BONDSMAN OR WITNESS
Harrison Thomas Jr. (son of Thomas)	Jenny Burton	9 Mar 1798	Andrew Harrison
Harrison Thomas D.	Virginia C. Harrison	30 Apr 1844	Geo. W. Price
Harrison Thomas P.	Mary F. Atkinson	19 Oct 1852	James M. Burton
		4 Nov 1852	md by Wm. Anderson
Harrison Thomas S.	Adeline H. Slade	22 Aug 1863	Daniel Everet
		23 Aug 1863	md by P. J. Carraway MG
Harrison William	Temperance D. Yarbrough	31 May 1833	Lancelot T. Johnston
Harrison William K.	Martha Verser	21 Oct 1839	Samuel B. Holder
Hart Ellick	Lucinda Gillispie	9 Dec 1849	Alexander Cousins
Hart Thomas	Patsey Hart	21 Mar 1792	William Haynie
Hartman Frederig	Mahael S. Crawford	9 Nov 1852	Jacob C. Mayer
Harvel Henry	Elizabeth Gillaspie	18 Nov 1814	Crafton Williams
Harvell Littleton Tazwell	Levina Harvell	11 Sep 1826	William Harvill
Harvell Pati (or Peyton)	Jamima Belew	17 Sep 1788	Robert Willson
Harvell William	Sarah Cox	10 Jun 1825	Thomas Graves
Harvey Charles L. (son of John C. & Martha Harvey)	Nora W. Gordon (dau of Robert & Martha J. Gordon)	26 Mar 1867	H. F. Brandon md by R. G. Barrett MG
Harvey David	Salley Storks	14 Nov 1809	William Fitz
Harvey John C.	Dorothy M. Gunn	21 Mar 1827	Dr. Stairling M. Gunn
Harvey John C.	Susan M. Hodges (wid)	11 Jan 1864	John Kerr
		12 Jan 1864	md by Wm. B. Bowe JP
Haskins John	Salley Brown	26 Oct 1799	Leonard Brown
Hastin Eldridge	Susannah Mitchell	2 Jan 1802	William Scoggin
Hasting James	Minerva King	25 May 1830	Thomas Jackson
Hatchett Allen L.	Elizer A. Womack	28 Mar 1859	George W. Gunn
		30 Mar 1859	md by John W. Lewis
Hatchett Jack (Col)	Milissa Johnston (Col)	26 Oct 1867 3 Nov	H. F. Brandon md by Jas. J. Clendenin JP
Hatchett John W.	Martha A. Gwyn	13 Feb 1858	Brice Harrelson
		18 Feb 1858	md by J. Doll MG
Hatchett Rufus	Sarah Foster	24 Dec 1866	Squire Foster md by R. G. Barrett
Hatchett William H.	Harriett E. Montgomery	2 Dec 1866 4 Dec 1866	James L. Goodson md by R. G. Barrett
Hatchett William S.*	Lucy Ann Tabour	24 Dec 1831	Joseph S. Totten
Hatley James R.	Margret McMullin	5 Feb 1825	Robert D. Wade
Hawker James W.	Rebecca J. Hall	1 Feb 1864	Jno. T. Russel
Hawkins Ephrem	Ann Farmer	1 May 1788	Jno. Womack Hosea Tapley
Hawkins Harbird	Nancey Webster	28 Nov 1833	James C. Dobines
Hawkins Howell	Martha Russell	4 May 1843	Lewis Love
Hawkins John	Margaret J. Malone	12 Dec 1854	Dudley Y. Murphey
		13 Dec 1854	md by Benj. Wells JP
Hawkins Robert	Mary Webster	10 Aug 1844	Samuel Love T. M. Miles
Hawkins Stephen	Martha J. Roberts	6 Jan 1857	Albert A. Malone
		7 Jan 1857	md by B. Wells JP
Hawkins Thomas	Dolly Roark	21 Dec 1852	Benjamin Roark
Hawks Randal	Lucy R. Rear	24 Dec 1827	John Westbrooks
Hayes James	Nancy Bruce	30 Dec 1788	John Bruce
Hayes Richard H.	Barbara Lea	4 Nov 1813	Gabriel B. Lea
Haymes John B.	Marthy E. Rice	12 Jul 1865	Robert T. Vernon
Haymes Richard W.	Mary M. Childes	6 Nov 1827	Josiah Rainey
Heggie Archibald	Nancey Love	24 Sep 1835	Robert Blackwell

GROOM	BRIDE	DATE	BONDSMAN OR WITNESS
Heisleep F. C.	Nici Snipes	3 Jul 1865	L. J. Anderson
Henderson Albert G.	Martha A. Hooper	16 Feb 1856	md by Jas. P. Simpson MG
Henderson Benjamin H.	Margarett Compton	14 Nov 1840	John L. Harrison
Henderson Byron	Emeline Neal	8 Sep 1866	Isham Brown md by S. G. Mason
Henderson Hiram Jr.	Martha Foster	18 Feb 1837	Solomon Corbett
Henderson Jacob	Fanney Haralson	8 Dec 1807	Joseph Henderson
Henderson Jacob	Sarah Hatchett	31 Dec 1829	Philip Hodnett
Henderson James A.	Rebecca L. Johnston	15 May 1866	Preston Roan
		23 May 1866	md by Jacob Doll MG
Henderson James S.	Hannah M. Slade	26 Nov 1832	John H. Graves
Henderson John N.	Elvira J. King	18 Jan 1839	Williamson P. Foster
Henderson Ludolphus B.	Annie Simpson	24 Jul 1862	George Gunn
		10 Aug 1862	md by T. Page Ricaud MG
Henderson Rufus	Ann Holderby	11 Aug 1866	Wm. Russell
Henderson Rufus R.	Sarah White	6 Sep 1834	William Henderson
Henderson Samuel	Rody Ware	3 Dec 1804	William Henderson
Henderson Thomas	Kitty Voss	5 Jul 1813	Allen Gunn
Henderson William	Nancey Bennatt	5 Jan 1807	Alex. Murphey
Henderson William	Elizabeth Simpson	19 Dec 1829	James Miles
Henderson William	Frances Mims	18 Sep 1844	Owen McAleer
Henderson William Jr.	Elizabeth J. Harrelson	29 Oct 1838	John N. Henderson
Hendrick A. J.	Mary R. Worsham	15 oct 1866	William Lockhart md by S. G. Mason
Hendrick C. M.	E. M. Smith	15 Oct 1866	Wm. Lockhart
Hendrick James	Lucy Worsham	23 Jul 1814	John Pass
Hendrick James	Mobsey A. Broughton	20 Dec 1836	Thomas D. Johnston
Hendrick Thomas W.	Aderlaid V. Burton	9 Dec 1859	John L. Roberts
		13 Dec 1859	md by John W. Lewis
Hendrick William H.	Susan Bennett	19 Mar 1841	Stephen L. Dodson
Hendrix John	Polly Stoner	11 Nov 1785	Elijah Hendrix
Hendrix William	Nancey Bradsher	23 Dec 1786	Richard Lea
Henry James W.	Laura A. Graves	12 Oct 1850	N. E. Graves
Henry John H.	Susan Dameron	3 Feb 1867	George Smith
Hensely Addison	Rachel Musting	25 Nov 1847	William J. Dabbs
Henslee Addison	Eliza Parks	15 Sep 1843	John Henslee
Henslee Bedford W.	Lucinda Stamps	12 Feb 1833	William W. Moore
Henslee Benjamin	Elizabeth Bruce	4 Jan 1812	Robert Bruce
Henslee Buford B.	Annis Underwood	10 Nov 1853	Rainey Massey md by John C. Pinnix
Henslee Enoch	Amy Hasten	27 Oct 1806	James Mitchell
Henslee John Jr.	Matilda Kemp	2 Apr 1816	Thomas Henslee
Henslee Mansfield	Frances Jones	22 Sep 1801	Richd. Jones
Henslee Micajah	Nancy Harrison	6 Dec 1836	Calloway J. Harrison
Henslee Thomas	Lois Bush	18 Nov 1805	Zns. Bush
Henslee William	Mary Milberey Pleasant	23 Jan 1811	Buford Pleasant
Hensley Azariah	Frances Vaughan	17 Oct 1824	John Vaughan
Hensley Henry T.	Elizabeth A. Powell	21 Feb 1866	B. Harrelson
		22 Feb 1866	md by Thomas W. Graves
Hensley John	Artilia Parks	24 Dec 1840	Solomon Corbett
Hensley Sidney	Selia Bowls	28 Apr 1855	Addison Hensley
		3 May 1855	md by Thomas Covington
Hensley Thomas	Elizabeth B. Milton	16 Mar 1842	Littleton A. Gwyn
Heritage William	Polly Willis	19 Dec 1809	James Miller
Herndon Edmund	Mary Boswell	26 Aug 1851	Jefferson M. Walker
Herndon George	Prisilla Wells	20 Dec 1805	Miles Wells Jr. Wm. Wilkinson

GROOM	BRIDE	DATE	BONDSMAN OR WITNESS
Herndon George	Martha Aldridge	16 Jan 1866	William Vaughan
		18 Jan 1866	md by F. L. Oakley MG
Herndon Larkin	Elizabeth Terrill	13 Feb 1790	Solomon Parks
Herring James A.	Elizabeth Roberts	7 Dec 1833	Thomas C. Pass
Hesse Archibald U.	Susannah Hewlet	6 May 1818	Robert McKee
Hester Elijah	Polley McMullin	30 Nov 1813	William Mitchell
			Goodwin Evans
Hester Col. Elijah	Nancey Snipes	6 Sep 1828	James McMullin
Hester Hamilton	Recey H. Badget	27 Mar 1837	Hiram Henderson
Hester J. R.	Mary N. Russel	9 Feb 1866	L. J. Anderson
		22 Feb 1866	md by F. L. Oakley MG
Hester Robert H.	Mary Collins	15 Jan 1834	Robert A. Torian
Hester Wilson	Permelia Warren	7 Jan 1833	Sieria G. Compton
Heydon John H.	Chatherine Mitchell	16 Sep 1825	John Fielder
Heydon Leachman	Henrietta Manley	1 Feb 1825	William Cobb
Heydon Samuel F.	Rebeca H. Simmons	6 Jun 1840	C. J. Harrison
Heydon Thomas*	Jemima Benton	19 Dec 1831	Samuel F. Heydon
Hickman William	Jenny Man	7 Dec 1796	Nathan Holloway
Hicks John P.	A. L. Hitower	7 Feb 1867	Jas. Martin
Hicks Larkin W.	Rebeckah Phelps	8 Oct 1818	Thomas Phelps
Hicks Luke	Betsey Rasberry	14 May 1810	John Roan
Hicks Maryland	Jane Watkins	12 Sep 1842	John Thomas
			M. P. Huntington
Hicks Simon (Col-son of Fredrick & Bettie Hicks)	Lucy Echols (Col-dau of John & Martha Echols)	27 Dec 1867	H. F. Brandon md by J. J. Jones JP
Hicks Thomas D.	Malinda Johnston	21 Oct 1837	William H. Johnston
Hicks William	Elizabeth Dunnaway	7 Feb 1825	Daniel Hicks
Hicks William T.	Virginia E. Lea	6 Sep 1865	Sandy L. Smith
			md by J. J. Jones JP
Hightower Allen	Elizabeth Hatcher	27 Jan 1808	Duke Williams
Hightower Charnel	Winneyford Corder	17 Jan 1798	Elisha Evans
Hightower Daniel	Catey Stephens	14 Oct 1806	Alexander Wiley
Hightower Devereux	Cesley Gooch	13 Jan 1816	Nathaniel Gooch
Hightower Francis	Martha Boswell	28 Sep 1850	Howell Boswell
Hightower James	Nancey Smith	14 Dec 1812	Daniel Hightower
Hightower John	Agness Matlock	22 Mar 1790	Joshua Carney
Hightower John A.	Mary Jackson	9 Nov 1843	Alanson M. Lea
Hightower John W.	Margaret Hester	27 Jan 1836	Robert Smith
Hightower Joshua	Delilah Slade	24 Nov 1792	Hearndon Lea
Hightower Joshua	Eunicey Lea	31 Mar 1800	Thomas Lea
Hightower Joshua	Jincy Wall	15 Apr 1817	William Whitlow
Hightower Joshua	Susan Jackson	18 Oct 1833	James C. Dameron
Hightower Joshua	Francis G. Chandler	17 Nov 1843	John T. Stadler
Hightower Robert	Margarett Lowell	24 Apr 1830	Thomas L. Lowell
Hightower Thomas	Polley Thomas	23 Nov 1803	Thomas Compton
Hightower Vinson (Col- son of Robert Wilson & Judah Hightower)	Margaret West (Col- dau of Jesse Gunn & Catharine West)	22 Apr 1867	H. F. Brandon md by J. J. Jones JP
Hightower William	Elizabeth Bartlett	4 May 1824	William Muzzall
Hightower William	Mary Stamps	16 Dec 1844	A. Slade
Hightower William	Vina Johnston	9 Jul 1847	Yancy Dameron
Hightower William S.	Margaret Swift	25 Sep 1848	David Rudd
Hill Anderson G.	Martha Ann Ragsdale	7 Nov 1853	Richard Yarbrough md by Lancelot Johnston
Hill Garland	Betsey Waid	14 Sep 1801	Samuel Dameron
Hill Henry	Nancy James	29 Dec 1866	J. Allen md by Jas. Malone JP
Hill John R.	Eliza F. Slaten	9 Jan 1866	Joseph T. Lindsey md by E. Hunt JP

GROOM	BRIDE	DATE	BONDSMAN OR WITNESS
Hill Joseph W.	Susan P. Shields	20 Apr 1835	Samuel B. Cobb
Hill Levi	Polly Merricks	18 Jan 1817	Durrett Richards md by Wm. Rainey JP
Hill Lewis	Lucy Hart	21 May 1851	Tazwell Cousins
Hill Richard	Betsey Royal	15 Oct 1799	William Norton
Hillyer James	Polley Hart	8 Nov 1808	Bartlett Yancey
Hines Benjamin	Sarah P. Holder	17 Mar 1834	George W. Johnson
Hines Frank (Col)	Frances Durham (Col)	19 May 1866	Dr. Witchel md by J. J. Jones JP
Hinton Alexander	Elizabeth J. Hooper	15 Jul 1848	Henry Hubbard
Hinton Allen	Mary A. Nelson	28 Nov 1843	Woodlief Thomas
Hinton Christopher	Elizabeth Overby	1 Sep 1830	Thomas Overby
Hinton Henry	Milly Wray	29 Jan 1801	Elijah Barton
Hinton James	Rebecca Overby	9 May 1833	Thomas Overby Henderson House
Hinton James N.	Margarett Lyon	1 Sep 1866 9 Sep 1866	Edward R. Stamps md by N. M. Lewis JP
Hinton John	Keziah Wilson	5 Oct 1801	Johnston Wilson
Hinton Nathaniel	Frances Hooper	11 Jun 1848	Rufus Ramey
Hinton Richard	Judith Cochran	7 Dec 1791	James Robinson
Hinton Samuel	Barbara Gunn	27 Dec 1825	Abisha Slade
Hinton Wesley	Margaret Willis	11 Aug 1866	Thomas R. Kimbro md by A. A. Patillo JP
Hinton William	Anny Wattson	14 Aug 1805	Eppy Everett
Hinton William (son of William & Elizabeth Hinton)	Virginia Smith (dau of Charles & Nancy Hubbard)	20 Nov 1867 21 Nov	H. F. Brandon md by J. J. Jones JP
Hipworth Jno.	Mary Winters	18 Feb 1782	Hugh Dobbin
Hix Reubin	Delphia Simpson	21 May 1792	John Johnston
Hix Willis	Tabitha Moore	9 Mar 1784	George Conaly
Hobbs Isaac	Mary Knighten	2 Sep 1823	Robert Perkins
Hobson William	Betsey Warrin (dau of Hedgman Warrin)	10 Jun 1788	Nathaniel Warrin
Hodge David	Nancy Wall	7 Feb 1801	Samuel Hodge
Hodge David	Betcey Kile	29 Nov 1819	Samuel Hodge
Hodge Isaac	Nancy Dameron	17 Nov 1792	Joshua Carney
Hodge John	Sally Long	28 Mar 1812	David Hodge
Hodge John	Sally Ables	10 Nov 1822	Thomas Bastin
Hodge Morton*	Jancey Hodnett	16 Jan 1831	Barz. Graves
Hodge Samuel	Mary Roberts	19 May 1790	Joshua Carney
Hodge Thomas	Jane Hightower	4 Nov 1828	David Hodge
Hodge William (Col)	Sina Hodge (Col)	10 Nov 1867 16 Nov 1867	H. F. Brandon md by Harrison Scott
Hodges Coleman	Elizabeth Chattin	16 May 1837	James Hodnett Milton Hodges
Hodges Fealding L.	Georgian Jones	1 Feb 1867	Henry E. Hodges
Hodges Fielding L.	Henrietta Harralson	4 Feb 1865	William P. Hooper
Hodges Harrison L.	Aryann Ware	15 Nov 1845	Cary W. West
Hodges Henry E.	Mary C. Gunn	10 Dec 1842	Cary W. West
Hodges Henry E.	Elvira A. McDaniel	12 Jan 1853 19 Jan 1853	Washington T. Hodge md
Hodges Henry E.	Margaret Knight	6 Jan 1863 14 Jan 1863	Samuel S. Harrison md by P. J. Carraway MG
Hodges James M.	Martha Wilson	8 Nov 1865	James H. Ferrell
Hodges John T. (son of James A. & Susan Hodges)	Virginia E. Slade (dau of ---- & ---- Crumpton)	18 Nov 1867 19 Nov	md by R. G. Barrett
Hodges Nathan (Col)	Bettie Edmonds (Col)	22 Apr 1867 24 Apr	md by H. E. Hodges
Hodges Washington T.	Sarepta W. Price	27 Jul 1858	Benjamin F. Oaks

GROOM	BRIDE	DATE	BONDSMAN OR WITNESS
Hodnett James M.	Frances A. Nowlin	23 Nov 1841	Stephen L. Dodson Jno. Daniel
Hodnett Philip	Parthena Haralson	26 Apr 1827	Nathaniel M. Roan
Hoge Henry L. (Col-son of Cabe Lawson & Gracie Hoge)	Amanda Goode (Col- dau of William & Vilett Goode)	10 Oct 1867	md by J. J. Jones JP
Hoge Winston (Col- son of Taylor & Winnie Whitlock)	Lucinda Hunt (Col-dau of Richard Cooper & Vina Hunt)	9 Nov 1867	md by J. J. Jones JP
Heith Alex	Martha Corn	6 Feb 1864	Lorenzo Baynes
		9 Feb 1864	md by C. J. Richmond JP
Holcomb Samuel	Hannah Henderson	29 Dec 1789	George Holcom
Holden E. B.	Bettie R. Currie	4 Oct 1855	Samuel Watkins
Holden James	Sally Johnston	17 Jan 1805	Jno. Stamps Jr.
Holderby James D.	Martha Knight	30 Jun 1832	John Kitchen
Holderness John (Col)	Eliza Roan (Col)	27 Dec 1865	Allen Harralson md by R. G. Barrett MG
Holderness Robert	Elizabeth Brooks	20 Feb 1819	James Watlington
Hollan James	Polley Watson	1 Aug 1816	Reubin Taylor Smith Murphey
Holland John	Patsey Runnalds	4 May 1805	Absalom Shackelford
Hollis Jesse	Frances Brown	27 Sep 1798	Hudson Brown
Holloway James	Susannah Pulliam	19 Jan 1796	Charles Boulton
Holloway Richard	Rachel Stewert	13 Feb 1792	Harrison Stanfield
Holloway Robert	Betsey Scott	6 Aug 1799	James Arven
Holt Clabin	Elizabeth Dobbin	22 May 1786	John Low
Holt Dibden	Mary Alison	3 Apr 1787	Ezekiel Alison
Holt James G.	Lucy A. Burton	4 Feb 1840	Franklin Burton
Holt Joseph R.	Manerva J. Wyatt	21 Jun 1865	Thomas Martin
Holt Pleasant A.	Emily A. Williamson	9 Sep 1850	John O. Holt
Holt Robert T.	Laura A. Lockett	22 Jul 1858	B. Y. McAden
		25 Jul 1858	md by J. S. Totten JP
Holt Washington	Lucinda Mitchell	5 Jun 1858	John Mitchell
Holycross Robert	Eliza A. Adams	18 Feb 1841	Cpt. Wm. Vernon
Hood Jesse	Polly Sawyers	18 May 1807	Henry Curtis
Hood Martin	Nancey Roan	25 Dec 1821	James Roan
Hood Stephen	Henrietta Bowers	10 Sep 1823	William Currie
Hood Thomas (Col-son of Thomas Mason & Jinnie Hood)	Adaline Thornton (Col-dau of Ret & Millie Thornton)	19 Jun 1867	md by E. Hunt
Hood Wiley	Mary Fox	10 Dec 1823	William Warren
Hooper Benjamin	Nancey Henderson	22 Sep 1800	Starling Gunn Jr.
Hooper Charles H.	Amanda Moore	10 Dec 1851	Joseph M. Russell
Hooper George J. N.	Fanny Rainy	30 Nov 1857	Madison Harralson
Hooper Henry	Elizabeth Bennett	23 Sep 1854	Samuel N. Dunn
Hooper Henry Jr.	Tabitha Kimbrough	13 Dec 1830	Richard H. L. Bennett
Hooper John C.	Mary Williamson	10 Nov 1856	Andrew J. Kimbro
		20 Nov 1856	md by John H. Pickard MG
Hooper John J.	Mildred Watlington	15 Dec 1825	Paul A. Harlason
Hooper Joseph*	Eleanor W. Mims	14 Dec 1831	Theodorick Stubblefield
Hooper N. G.	Jane McDaniels (wid)	25 Feb 1867	B. Harralson
Hooper Spencer	Mary Wiley	6 Oct 1832	Edward A. Tarwater
Hooper Squire	Rachel Crumpton	8 Sep 1866	Byron Henderson
Hooper Thomas	Polley Bennatt	28 May 1814	Ashley Davis
Hooper Thomas	Sally Hall	8 Nov 1849	Thomas Hardison
Hooper William	Delilah L. Raimey	7 Nov 1833	Owen McAleer
Hooper William	Mary Jones	13 Dec 1854	B. Harralson
		21 Dec 1854	md by John Stadler
Hooper William Y.	Elizabeth Harrelson	25 Jan 1830	Woodlief Hooper

GROOM	BRIDE	DATE	BONDSMAN OR WITNESS
Hooper Woodlief	Pirzila Henderson	12 Apr 1802	Benjamin Hoopper
Hooper Woodlieff	Virginia Foster	19 Jan 1860	Nathl. Hooper
		24 Jan 1860	md by H. F. Atkins JP
Hooper Z.	Adaline Patite	7 Jun 1854	Jas. T. Graves DC
			md by N. M. Lewis JP
Hooper Zachariah Jr.	Mary Love	12 Aug 1825	Jno. G. Womack
Hooper Zachariah Jr.	Louisa Ware	12 Jun 1836	Green Hardy
Hooper Zachariah Sr.	Elizabeth Raimey	16 May 1825	Stairling H. Gunn
Hooper Zachariah	Mary Hubbard	11 May 1860	A. A. Mitchell
Hoopper Samuel	Susanna Alford	7 Jan 1817	Maj. S. Graves
Hope George N.	Martha Taylor	18 Aug 1846	Owen McAleer
Hopper Samuel	Elizabeth Murphey	24 Mar 1801	James Murphey
Horn Abel	Nancey Wallace	7 Nov 1803	Maj. Wallis
			James Currie
Horn Edward M.	Susan C. Whittrow	6 Oct 1855	William H. Chiles
Hornbuckle Franklin	Frances Brooks	15 Jan 1825	William Simpson
Hornbuckle Richard	Elisabeth Smith	9 Jan 1792	William W. Smith
Hornbuckle Thomas	Nancey Hornbuckle	22 Jul 1800	George Harben
Horsford John Carter	Jane Cobb	17 Feb 1832	Westley Burton
Horton George	Margret Grier	8 Feb 1809	Bozzel Warren
Horton George	Susannah Gray	3 Feb 1813	Thomas Compton
Horton James G.	Elizabeth Williams	3 Nov 1826	William Jeffreys
Horton John	Milly Gilaspy	20 Nov 1797	Alexander Gilaspy
Horton John	Eliza Ann Powel	28 Jan 1835	John E. Roper
Horton Rolly	Mary Dobbin	9 Feb 1791	John Low
Horton Thomas J.	Eliza Ann Bryant	20 Aug 1859	Colman Brincefield
		21 Aug 1859	md by Wm. B. Bowe JP
Horton William J.	Mary C. Powell	26 Jan 1862	Colman Brincefield
Horton Willis	Mary Howard	13 Nov 1835	Stephen J. Chandler
Hostler Richard	Margret Brandon	2 Apr 1782	William Brandon
House Henderson	Ann C. Oliver	13 Nov 1839	George W. G. VanHook
How William	Permintia Chambers	29 Dec 1835	John McDaniel
Howard Alanson	Susan S. Shelton	10 Dec 1833	Wm. Henry Glass Jr.
Howard Alexis	---------	1 Dec 1842	Jno. K. Graves
Howard Baalam (Col-son of George Jones & Rhoda Howard)	Maria Norman (Col-dau of Thomas & Lavina Rucker)	29 Feb 1868	md by Stephen Neal JP
Howard Broadie	Nancey Howard	7 Apr 1813	Samuel Hunt
Howard Cary A.	Elizabeth S. Blackwell	25 Feb 1828	John G. Womack
Howard Charles (Col-son of Isaac & Louisiana Watlington)	Maria Williamson (Col-dau of Jerry Windsor & Maria Williamson)	6 Jul 1867	md by H. G. Anderson
Howard Daniel (Col)	Mollie Watkins (Col)	12 Jan 1867	Mat Richmond
Howard Francis	Polly Montgomery	11 Nov 1801	Groves Howard
Howard Franklin*	Martha E. Betts	17 Oct 1831	Alanson Howard
Howard George Jr.	Anna Stamps	2 Dec 1861	Lotte W. Humphrey
		3 Dec 1861	md by S. A. Stanfield MG
Howard Henry	Mary McAden	19 Dec 1787	Jno. McAden
Howard Henry	Eliza Betts	20 Mar 1820	William Badget
Howard Henry A.	Elizabeth G. Settle	22 May 1847	Jno. A. Graves
Howard Henry O. (son of Alanson & Susan)	Laura Wemple (dau of J.D. & Polly)	18 Dec 1867	H. F. Brandon
		19 Dec 1867	md by S. G. Mason
Howard Horac	July Lyon	20 Mar 1841	James Clark

GROOM	BRIDE	DATE	BONDSMAN OR WITNESS
Howard Hugh	Elizabeth Brackin	3 Nov 1815	Jno. Badgett
Howard John	Elisabeth Meredith	28 Nov 1785	Mason Foley
Howard John	Precilla Yancey	26 Dec 1814	Allen Gunn
			Azariah Graves
Howard John W.	Mary E. Keen	7 Sep 1866	David G. Womack
		8 Sep 1866	md by Jas. J. Clendenin
Howard Woodson	Abigail Finley	24 Jul 1824	Cary A. Howard
Howell Leroy	Elizabeth Nowell	29 Dec 1795	Edward King
Hubbard Archibald D.	Malinda G. Cobb	26 Nov 1837	William P. Womack
Hubbard Charles	Betsey Huston	31 Jan 1804	Jacob Wright Jr.
Hubbard Charles	Nancey Stephens	27 Sep 1819	Thomas Poteat
Hubbard Freeman	Martha Williams	9 Dec 1793	James Paul
Hubbard Freeman	Nancy Hinton	9 Jun 1803	John Hinton
Hubbard Freeman	Mary Scott	8 Jun 1844	John Henslee
Hubbard Henry	Elizabeth Ware	17 Oct 1842	Williamson P. Foster
Hubbard James	Artimesia B. Grant	2 Jan 1838	Wm. P. Womack
Hubbard James	Eveline Kennon	18 Sep 1849	Alexander McAlpin
Hubbard James	Mary E. Harris	26 Feb 1862	Henry Hubbard
			md by Wm. B. Bowe JP
Hubbard John S.	Mariah A. Petty	11 Dec 1838	Henry Taylor
Hubbard Phenias	Elizabeth Ingram	5 Apr 1839	Martin Browning
Hubbard Ralph	Patsey Gunnell	10 Aug 1809	William Hubbard
Hubbard Ralph	Frances Richardson	6 Mar 1821	Stephen Kitchen
Hubbard Rufus	Virginia Lea	5 May 1857	William G. Perkins
		29 Jun 1857	md by Wm. J. Moore JP
Hubbard Thomas	Mary J. Purkins	13 Sep 1856	David Gillaspie
			md by J. M. Allen JP
Hubbard William	Nancey Quarles	14 Sep 1807	William Randolph
Hubbard William	Elizabeth Perkins	18 Mar 1852	David A. Gillaspie
			md by Carter Powell JP
Hubbard Zebulon B.	Jane Gillgore	19 Jan 1785	Zeri Rice
Huddleston Rowland	Henrietta Dawson (dau of Wm. H.)	5 Oct 1833	Stairling S. Kent C. Stone
Hudging Thos.	Nancy Hargis	-----------	Abraham Hargis
			J. Womack
Hudson David P.	Mary P. Owen	15 Jan 1833	Layton T. Roberts
Hudson Ezekiel	Judith Coleman	27 Nov 1811	John Price Jr.
Hudson George	Milly Foster	22 Jan 1798	Ambrose Foster
Hudson J. M.	Sarah F. Winn	27 Jan 1859	William H. Puryear
			James M. Williams Jr.
Hudson Shadrach	Mary Brandon	25 Sep 1784	John Brandon
Hudson Shelton	Ann R. Wade (sister of John J. Wade)	8 Nov 1843	Barzillai Graves
Hudson William F.	Susan A. Fowlks	13 Dec 1858	Bedford A. Satterfield
Hudson William F.	Isabella C. Roper	11 Dec 1865	Edgar Stanley
Hughes Andrew	Lucinda Tate	26 Jan 1818	Alexander Wiley
Hughes B. G.	Martha Newbell	13 Jan 1851	William T. Smith
			J. S. Poore
Hughes George (Col)	Ellen Elliott (Col)	10 Jun 1867	H. F. Brandon clk md by John J. Jones JP
Hughes James (Col)	Ann Eliza Barker (Col)	15 Jan 1856	Meshac Pounds J. M. Allen
Hughes Joseph D.	Polley Woods	14 Aug 1809	Thomas Woods
Hughes Milton T.	Lucy Hughes	10 Jan 1853	Napoleon E. Graves DC
			md by Geo. W. Thompson
Hughes Thomas H.	Cornelia Mitchell	20 Jan 1844	James C. Dobins
			Thos. H. Miles
Hughes William	Catharine Fitch	21 Sep 1844	Saml. Hughes
Hughes William	Rachel Hobson	17 May 1855	Richard A. Newbell
		18 May	md by J. M. Allen JP
Hughs Henry	Sina Squire	26 Mar 1828	James Rudd

GROOM	BRIDE	DATE	BONDSMAN OR WITNESS
Hughs John	Nancey Jackson	12 Sep 1810	Richard Hamlet Stephen D. Watkins
Hugins Jacob	Susanna Ward	28 Oct 1817	John Ward Tho. Slade
Hugle John (Private in 20th Infantry)	Sally Arnett (dau of Mary Arnett, wid)	20 Jun 1814	Jno. Williams Sol. Debow
Hulgin John R.	Nancy Overby	2 Jan 1856	Daniel W. Swann Wm. A. Vernon
Humfres Alfred	Nancy Paskill	11 Jan 1825	John C. Totten
Humphreys Henry	Susanna Paschall	24 Sep 1824	Alfred M. Nash
Humphreys Henry A.	Nancy Norman	19 Jul 1841	Joseph Goodwin
Humphreys John Henson	Susannah Keen	11 Jan 1817	William Smith
Humphreys Thomas	Celia Cobb	25 Jan 1826	David Walker
Humphreys William	Polley Holloway	27 Dec 1799	Greenbury Voss
Humphry Colmore	Nelley Orr	28 Feb 1809	Joseph Roe
Hundly Henry W.	Eliza L. Hooper	14 Dec 1837	Zachariah L. Hooper
Hunt Algernon	Ellen Wilson	4 Mar 1867	Adolphus Hunt md by E. Hunt JP
Hunt Charles	Louisa Hunt	8 Dec 1866	Armstead Hunt md by E. Hunt JP
Hunt Eustace	Anna S. Watkins	26 Sep 1863	M. Hunt Jos. C. Pinnix DC
		30 Sep 1863	md by S. A. Stanfield MG
Hunt Garland	Isabella Jeffreys	25 Dec 1865	Traverse Jeffreys md by E. Hunt JP
Hunt James	Fannie Marable	23 Mar 1867	George Royal md by John J. Jones JP
Hunt L. H.	Susan J. Thornton	9 Dec 1856	N. M. Lewis
		11 Dec 1856	md by --- Jackson
Hunt Littleton T.	Mary E. Jeffreys	31 May 1854	William M. Broocks
		14 Jun 1854	md by S. A. Stanfield MG
Hunt Samuel	Precilla Hunt	12 Jan 1867	Windsor Hunt md by E. Hunt JP
Hunt Steven (Colson of Isaac Caldwell & Tildy Hunt)	Chainy Brodnax (Coldau of Daniel Farmer & Marthy Brodnax)	15 Jun 1867	md by E. Hunt JP
Hunter Solomon G.	Malinda Hubbard	16 Apr 1835	James Gunn
Huntington Martin P.	Susan Holder	30 Apr 1822	Jno. E. Lewis
Huntington Martin P.	Mary A. Donoho	29 Sep 1834	Albertis L. Watts
Hurdle B. F.	M. C. Walker	19 Jan 1866	B. Harralson
		23 Dec 1866?	md by F. M. Jordon, Elder
Hurdle Jacob O.	Eunice Boswell	27 Sep 1836	John Leachman
Hurdle James	Catherine Walker	26 Oct 1840	Nathan Brown
Hurdle James M.	Malinda Walker	22 Jan 1856	John F. Leath
Hurdle James M.	Margaret F. Walker	4 Dec 1858	Thomas S. Ector
		9 Dec 1858	md by John Stadler
Huston Jonathan	Joannah Smith	21 Oct 1817	George Hustin
Huston William	Susanah Allen	26 Jan 1785	John J. Farley
Huston William	Sarah Wallace	18 Nov 1826	John Daniel
Hutcherson Wm. W.	Rebecca Dudley	3 Apr 1821	Abner Dudley Elijah Withers
Hutson Moses	Betsey Randolph	9 Oct 1784	William Randolph
Hyde Joseph	Elizabeth H. Colley	12 Jul 1851	Granderson Warren
		15 Jul 1851	md by C. H. Richmond JP

- I -

GROOM	BRIDE	DATE	BONDSMAN OR WITNESS
Ingraham T. E.	Ann Bane (wid)	5 Nov 1851	md by C. H. Richmond JP
Ingram Benjamin	Nancey Womack	9 May 1786	William Cochran
Ingram Benjamin	Priscilla Wright	21 Apr 1814	William Peterson
Ingram Charton (son of Benjamin)	Lucy Womack	2 Nov 1778	Benjamin Ingram Wm. Campbell
Ingram Elisha	Peggy Taylor	-- --- 1808	Thomas Burton
Ingram James	Betsey Evans	18 Oct 1808	David Womack
Ingram James	Sarah C. Wynn	2 Nov 1841	John Travis
Ingram James	Mary E. Reid	11 May 1858	Dr. Allen Gunn
		13 May 1858	md by Wm. B. Bowe JP
Ingram James J.	Mary A. Lunsford	22 Jan 1858	Warner J. Lunsford
Ingram Martin	Anne Howard	6 Nov 1827	John Ware Jr.
Ingram Stephen	Mira Bush	10 Dec 1808	Elisha Ingram
Ingram Thomas E.	Frances T. Echols	13 Nov 1856	Charles B. Firesheets md by J. M. Allen JP
Ingram Vench	Mary Cammical	18 Mar 1805	Barz. Graves
Ingram William R.	Herett A. E. Neal	10 Nov 1857	Warner J. Lunsford
Ingram Yancey W. (of Pittsylvania Co. Va.)	Lettice W. Terry	28 Jul 1834	Dr. Allen Gunn
Ingrum Jordan L.	Eliza C. Sparrow	6 Feb 1860	Alexander Dodson md by N. M. Lewis JP
Inman Henry	Polly Smith	16 Dec 1836	John Smith
Irvin Robert	Nancey Sawyer	4 Apr 1822	Thomas Jackson
Irvine John (Col)	Mary Garland (Col)	1 Jan 1867	Philip Gordon
Irvine John Sr.	Anna Stanfield	11 Apr 1811	Jno. Green Murphey
Irvine Richmond (Col-son of William Irvine & Lucy Claiborne)	Jennie Irvine (Col- dau of Burrel Farmer & Silvey Irvine)	20 Apr 1867 21 Apr 1867	md by J. J. Jones JP
Irvine William Jr.	Virginia A. Jeffreys	31 Oct 1857	Jesse R. McLean
Irvine William C.	Mary Ann Lewis	14 Aug 1843	Samuel Watkins
Irwin James C.	Sarah E. Hoofman	20 Mar 1840	Parham A. Boley
Iseley Asa	Jane Sawyers	18 Dec 1849	John Pinnix Rufus Y. Graves

- J -

Jackson Abel	Emily Green Hall	4 Sep 1847	O. P. Shelton C. D. Vernon
Jackson Andrew P.	Agness Fulling	28 Mar 1821	Archibald Rice
Jackson Daniel	Patience Dameron	20 Nov 1805	John Warren
Jackson Daniel	Salley Ward	31 Aug 1807	Robert H. Jackson
Jackson Epaphroditus	Nancey Hightower	23 Aug 1834	Joshua Hightower
Jackson George	Francis Spencer	10 Oct 1785	William Henslee
Jackson J. R.	Mary Burch	16 Jun 1860	Peter Jones Allen Harralson
Jackson James	Ann M. Matthews	31 Dec 1824	William Upton
Jackson John	Ednea Evans	5 Jun 1816	Robert H. Jackson
Jackson Richard W.	Julietta W. Gregory	17 Oct 1836	Henderson House
Jackson Robert	Polley Dameron	27 Sep 1808	Daniel Jackson
Jackson Robert (Col)	Amy Gunn (Col)	1 Jan 1866 2 Jan 1866	Archy Doll md by A. McAlpin JP
Jackson Robert Jr.	Rachil Carney	1 Jun 1811	Robert H. Jackson Sr. A. B. Morton
Jackson Shadrack	Clorey Coram	1 Oct 1782	William Coram
Jackson Spencer	Rainey Brintle	20 Dec 1815	Eldridge Huston
Jackson Thomas	Jenney Smith	5 Dec 1798	William Johnson
Jackson Thomas	Marey Hunter	-- Dec 1818	James Spencer

52

GROOM	BRIDE	DATE	BONDSMAN OR WITNESS
Jackson William	Elizabeth Lewis	15 Nov 1828	Hugh Cox
Jackson William P.	Elizabeth Dameron	24 Dec 1811	Samuel Dameron
Jackson Williams	Sarah Tate	25 Mar 1786	George Jackson
Jacob Lewis	Amy Fuller	26 Dec 1866	
		27 Dec 1866	md
James David	Lucy Richardson	18 Jul 1848	Paul H. Dodson
			John Vaughan
James Henry	Susan Burton	24 Jun 1866	Solomon Falkner
			md by Jerry Smith JP
James John (Colson of Martha James)	Rutha Bohannan (Col- dau of Wm. & Philis Bohannan)	22 Apr 1867	md by John J. Jones JP
Jarnagin Jeremiah	Elizabeth Hightower	24 Dec 1808	John T. Curl
Jay James	--------------------	24 Jan 1798	Law Lea
Jay James	Sally Wisdom	4 Feb 1804	Lewis Wisdom
			William Wilkerson
Jean Jessy	Polly Wyatt	23 Nov 1789	John Low
Jean Sherwood	Rosanah Lea	20 Feb 1785	Jonathan Lea
Jeffers John	Mary Ann Crews	21 Oct 1833	Obadiah Crews
Jeffres Newell	Cyntha Jones	1 Aug 1828	Joshua Soes?
			Wm. Anderson
Jeffres Walton	Silvy Ballard	8 Aug 1818	Lewis Jeffres
Jeffres Newton B.	Elizabeth A. Hatchett	14 Mar 1855	Nathaniel C. Motley
Jeffres Wm. C.	Sallie F. Thornton	11 Jun 1866	C. H. Moseley
			md by S. G. Mason
Jeffreys Adkinson	Sarah Jane Martin	3 Feb 1862	Calvin Groom
Jeffreys	Mary W. Taylor	11 May 1858	William S. Yarbrough
Archible W.		12 May 1858	md by Jas. P. Simpson MG
Jeffreys Atkinson	Mary Gillaspie	29 Dec 1837	William H. Hendrick
Jeffreys Franklin (son of John Jeffreys & Dilsy Enocks)	Delphia Enocks (dau of Scott Walker & Martha Enocks)	26 Nov 1867 28 Nov	md by A. G. Anderson
Jeffreys Isaac	Frances Swift	10 Oct 1827	James Kerr
			John H. Graves
Jeffreys Iverson	Ann Wilson	14 Dec 1854	Elijah Heathcock
		21 Dec 1854	md by A. B. Walker JP
Jeffreys Jackson	Melissa Jeffreys	14 Dec 1848	Bazel Murphey
Jeffreys James	Louisa Harper (dau of Anna Harper of Pittsylvania Co. Va.)	23 Dec 1822	Alexander McAlpin
Jeffreys John	Jincey Edwyn	9 Mar 1795	James Burton
Jeffreys John	Nancey Moss	29 Nov 1823	John A. Pass
Jeffreys John	Ruth Taylor	18 Dec 1843	John M. O'Brian
Jeffreys Joshua	Cloe Walters	31 Jul 1804	Thomas Ware
Jeffreys Osborn	Salley Taylor	3 Jun 1778	Robert Dickson
Jeffreys Reubin	Kissiah Hawly	30 May 1808	Mial Scott
Jeffreys Thomas	Kiziah B. Watlington	22 Oct 1824	Thomas Bolton
Jeffreys Thomas Jr. (Col)	Sarah Donaldson (Col)	9 Jun 1866	Moses Donoho (Col)
Jeffreys Washington	Betsy Stephens	3 Feb 1830	Benjamin Jones
Jeffreys Washington (Col)	Sophia Tapp (Col)	17 Aug 1866	Richard Jeffreys (Col)
Jeffreys William	Bashebe Harton	24 Apr 1822	Thomas Howell
Jennings Byrd T.	Martha S. Brightwell	9 Oct 1839	Carter Collie
			B. C. West Sr.
Jennings Joseph	Patience E. Glass	27 Aug 1842	Henry Badgett
Jennings William*	Sarah W. Wilkinson	6 Oct 1831	William Saunders
Jeter Joseph H.	Araminta Harrison	10 Oct 1837	Henderson House
Jinkins Edward	Sally Williams	2 Jan 1796	James Williams
Johnson Hampton (Col)	Elizabeth Royster (Col)	25 Aug 1866	Isaac Reed (Col)
			md by J. J. Jones JP

GROOM	BRIDE	DATE	BONDSMAN OR WITNESS
Johnson Isaac	Nancy Yancey	10 Dec 1795	Allen Johnson
Johnson James	Rebeccah Poston	19 Jun 1781	Jere Poston
Johnson James	Rebeckah Ellis	3 Oct 1810	Tompson Birk
			Stephen D. Wilkins
Johnson John	Rebecah Leath	16 Sep 1796	Thomas Spencer
Johnson John Jr.	Margaret Bastin	26 Oct 1830	John Cahall
Johnson Thomas	Martha Terry	6 Nov 1827	Pleasant H. Womack
Johnson William	Nancey Brown	18 Dec 1838	John M. Walker
Johnston Caleb A. (Col)	Nancey Graves (Col)	16 Feb 1866 17 Feb 1866	Rufus Ball md by Thos. W. Graves JP
Johnston Daniel (Col)	Catharine Graves (Col)	12 Dec 1865	A. A. Pattillo JP
Johnston George	Elizabeth Cobb	11 Oct 1830	Joseph G. Carter
Johnston James	Agness Huston	4 Oct 1813	Jesse Vanhook
			Jeremiah Rudd
Johnston John	Dicey Bratcher	31 Jan 1792	Jacob Crider
Johnston John	Fanney Donoho	4 Jan 1800	William Smith
Johnston John	Sally Hodge	29 Nov 1819	Samuel Hodge
Johnston Joseph	Mary Mahan	28 May 1831	Hosea Compton
Johnston Moses (son of Moses & Kizia Johnston)	Lucinda Graham	30 Nov 1867 31 Nov 1867	H. F. Brandon md by T. S. Harrison JP
Johnston Peter	Hannah Wyatt	21 Feb 1782	John Low
Johnston Peter	Nancey Walker	21 Dec 1835	Enoch G. Davis
Johnston Pleasant	Susanah Jackson	22 Aug 1804	David Henslee
Johnston Remus	Catherine Johnston	3 Mar 1866	Alfred Johnston (Col) md by Jacob Doll MG
Johnston Thomas	Hannah Carmon	10 Sep 1783	William Corum
Johnston Thomas D.	Sarah G. McAden	23 Feb 1825	Abisha Slade
Johnston Thomas M.	Sarah Richmond	20 Nov 1839	James Malone
Johnston Warren (son of John Poteat & Hannah Johnston)	Cornelia Garland	27 Dec 1867 28 Dec	md by Jacob Doll MG
Johnston William	Elizabeth Rainey	20 Mar 1783	William Rainey
Johnston William	Catharine Chamberlin	10 Dec 1819	Robert Brown
Johnston William H.	Frances T. Hightower	29 Nov 1836	Lewis Malone
Jones Allen	Polley McNeeley	9 Aug 1811	William Mitchell
Jones Allen	Polley Kiersey	29 Jul 1818	Richard Jones
Jones Allen	Martha W. Burton	26 Jun 1833	John C. Harvey
Jones Andrew	Celly Phillips	30 Nov 1843	Fedrick Phillips
Jones Benjamin	Faithey Roberts	30 Nov 1788	Jacob Vanhook
Jones Benjamin B.	Arreminta Roper	9 Nov 1827	Maurice Vaughn
Jones Beverly	Marshaw Partee	17 Jun 1817	Phillip Jones Isaac Rainey
Jones Calvin	Mary C. Hester	9 Nov 1841	Thomas Brumet
Jones Calvin (Col)	Amy Robertson (Col)	6 Jun 1867 10 Jun	md by Thomas J. Brown JP
Jones David	Martha Dixon	23 Nov 1819	John Blackwell
Jones David (Col)	Rachael Williamson (Col)	16 Aug 1866	Rufus Neal (Col) md by Stephen Neal JP
Jones David A.	Ann Hurdle (wid)	27 Feb 1856	J. W. Mims
Jones Edward D.	Elizabeth H. Rainey	10 Oct 1811	James Rainey
Jones Edward M.	Matilda Blackwell	23 Dec 1817	John Blackwell
Jones Eli	Frances Warren	25 Sep 1837	Thomas D. Connally
Jones Erasmus K. Jr.	Lucind Lovelace	13 Sep 1827	William Weatherford
Jones Ezekiel	Rebecca Mallory	10 Jan 1799	James Mallory
Jones Henry	Susan Cox	14 Jan 1833	James Jones
Jones Henry (Col)	Ellen Jones (Col)	18 Nov 1865	John Jeffreys (Col)

GROOM	BRIDE	DATE	BONDSMAN OR WITNESS
Jones Henry (Col)	Jennett Cobb (Col)	12 Oct 1866	Henry King
		18 Oct 1866	md by T. S. Harrison JP
Jones J. Riley	Sarah Gwynn	15 Dec 1865	T. H. Boswell
Jones James	Eddy Vaughn	31 Aug 1783	Samuel Slaughter
Jones James (Col)	Jane Jones (Col)	19 Dec 1850	James S. Warren
Jones James	Susan V. Thomas	12 Feb 1867	Greensby Carter
		17 Feb 1867	md by N. M. Lewis JP
Jones James B.	Judith B. Hall	29 Sep 1814	Wm. P. Hall
Jones James M.	Elizabeth Chandler	30 Aug 1848	John P. Rainey
Jones James W.	Martha J. Mims	24 Sep 1844	James M. Neal
Jones Jeremiah	Ann Waldrope	3 Jun 1806	John Rice
Jones John E.	Mary Watlington	5 Oct 1847	Jno. W. Mims
Jones Jno. G.	Elizabeth S. McCain	10 Dec 1834	William Dismukes
Jones Keen	Mary W. Smith	13 Aug 1862	Thomas J. Hodges
Jones Lawson	Martha J. Roan	11 Oct 1842	James H. Dameron
Jones Matt	Margaret Thomas	24 Feb 1846	Willie Cousins M. P. Huntington
Jones Mintus	Susan Bowe	18 Jan 1867	Wm. Jones
		26 Jan 1867	md by S. G. Mason
Jones Moses	Elizabeth Kelley	14 Feb 1809	George Kelley Wm. Gooch Sr.
Jones Phillip	Katey Bohan	5 Dec 1815	Ambrose Bohan
Jones Randolph	Maria Jones	10 Dec 1828	Hanry Jones
Jones Reuben	Susannah Vanhook	11 Jun 1801	Cornelius Dollarhide
Jones Reuben	Susan Boswell	2 Jan 1843	R. Saunders Boswell
Jones Richard	Martha Bruce	25 Dec 1792	Solomon Parker
Jones Richard	Perry Holcomb	30 Oct 1804	Charles Shearman
Jones Richard	Polley Foster	9 Dec 1811	Thomas Foster
Jones Richard	Eliza Fuller	5 Dec 1866	H. F. Brandon
Jones Richard Jr.	Frances M. Swift	8 Dec 1844	Thomas Swift
Jones Richard H.	Martha A. Blackwell	26 Feb 1848	Milton P. Mitchell
Jones Robert	Mary C. Warren	7 Dec 1857	Sidney B. Malone
		13 Dec 1857	md by Benj. Wells JP
Jones Robert	Maria Chandler	26 Dec 1866	Titus Jones
Jones Simon (Colson of Moses & Minerva Jones)	Bell Cobb (Col-dau of Jack Robertson & Fanny Cobb)	14 Sep 1867	H. F. Brandon
		22 Sep 1867	md
Jones Thomas	Darkus Bullard	16 Oct 1819	William Garrett
Jones Thomas	Nancy Lockhart	24 Jan 1829	Thos. Jones S. T. Tillinghast
Jones Thomas J.	Margaret A. Connolly	1 Feb 1845	Thomas H. Miles
Jones Thompson	Martha Ann Dice	17 Dec 1855	Johnston Jeffreys
		3 Jan 1856	md by B. Cooper JP
Jones Wilie	Dicy Kirsey	27 May 1797	Alexander Kiersey
Jones William (of Elbert Co. Ga.)	Rachel Landers	20 Nov 1816	Larkin A. Landers Isaac Rainey
Jones William	Polley Travis	20 Jun 1820	John Travis
Jones William	Mary Day	4 Dec 1848	John W. Roan
Jones Dr. Willie	Priscilla J. Henderson	5 May 1836	N. M. Roan Wm. M. McGehee
Jones Yancey	Martha R. Miles	20 Jul 1850	Rufus Graves
Jones Zalman	Mary Bateman	20 Oct 1846	Charly H. Webster
Jordan Thomas N.	Minerva A. Gunn	22 Nov 1865	Robert H. Williamson
		23 Nov 1865	md by J. W. Wonycott MG
Jouett Thomas	Hannah Tate	26 Jan 1801	Duncan Cameron
Judkins Edmund	Zilpah Rice	19 Nov 1832	William Rice
Justice Benjamin W.	Elizabeth S. Womack	8 Nov 1824	Richard F. Moore
Justice Julas	Hannah Stuart	-- --- 178-	Robert Seymour Thos. Barnett

- K -

GROOM	BRIDE	DATE	BONDSMAN OR WITNESS
Kanon Bartlet	Janey Kennon	20 Jan 1794	William Kannon
			Joseph Hall
Kearson Charles R.	Elizabeth Curtis	21 Oct 1841	Hugh W. Gillespie
Keen John	Mary Baldin	17 Oct 1800	Joseph Payne
			John G. Murphey DC
Keen William	Elizabeth Cobb	23 Feb 1811	Joseph Windsor
Keesee Charles	Elizabeth Gatewood	26 Jul 1815	Lewis Gatewood
Keesee Jno. D.	Jane E. Johnston	21 Jan 1854	C. Strader
		26 Jan 1854	md by John H. Pickard
Keirsey Franklin	Sarah A. Curls	2 Nov 1849	Thomas S. Poore
Keirsey John (or Casey John)	Agniss Hightower	2 Dec 1794	Epaphroditus Hightower
Keirsey Wm. H.	Emiline Hadock	29 Dec 1857	R. A. Newbell
		6 Jan 1858	md by J. B. Jackson
Kelley George	Nancy Bruer	12 Aug 1805	Moses Smith
Kelley George	Salley Hunt	8 Aug 1820	Joseph N. Warren
			Mary Murphey
Kelley George	Catharine A. Warren	5 Nov 1823	Joseph N. Warren
Kelley James	Jane McCalips	23 Jan 1802	Moses Smith
Kelly Aaron (son of Jim & Clara Kelly)	Pheby Ann Lewis (dau of Jim & Nancy Bullock)	24 Aug 1867	md by N. M. Lewis JP
Kelly William (Col)	Harriet Hatchet (Col)	16 Jun 1866	Fanuel Walters
			md by J. J. Jones JP
Kemp Barnett	Mary McKee	23 Feb 1810	Robert McKee
Kennon Abel K.	Martha Morton	28 Jan 1843	John E. Jones
Kennon Elijah	Mary Bush	11 Jun 1813	William Cannon
Kennon Jackson	Sarah Childress	13 May 1843	Benjamin F. Evans
			Wm. M. Nance Jr.
Kennon James	Mary Ann Alverson	1 Dec 1821	Jesse Alverson
Kennon John	Hannah Carrol	1 Nov 1812	William Evans
Kennon John	Mahala Philips	2 Feb 1826	John C. Harvey
			Benjamin Mayo
Kennon John	Frances Pyron	28 Aug 1840	Jackson Cannon
Kennon Joseph B.	Louisa D. White	26 Feb 1851	George W. Manly
			md by John Stadler
Kennon Richard	Polley Henderson	8 May 1813	Thomas Kennon
Kennon Richard	Parthena Norwood	18 Sep 1850	W. L. Fowler
Kennon Thomas	Susanna Hooper	12 Feb 1814	Griffin Gunn
Kennon Thomas	Mary Brown	2 Mar 1839	William Graves
Kennon William	Mary Willis	31 Jan 1827	Azariah Graves
Kent S. S.	Jane Mitchell	-- --- 1843	A. McAlpin
Kent Smith F.	Sally Sadler	21 Feb 1807	Edward Sadler
Kent William S.	Elizabeth C. Epperson	11 Dec 1855	Charles C. Kent
Kerby Richard	Rachel Anderson	21 Jan 1802	Jeremiah Kerby
			William Rainey
Kernodle Richard	Mary E. Leath	11 Aug 1843	James L. Graves
Kerr Barzillai	Polley Cantrel	22 Mar 1806	Joseph Anthony
Kerr James	Frances McNiel	29 Sep 1835	John Kerr Jr.
Kerr John Jr.	Evelina B. Campbell	23 Dec 1835	Thomas D. Connally
			Wm. K. Ruffin
Kerr William	Polly Tait	14 Jul 1800	James Birk
Kerr William	Jane Kyle	19 Jan 1824	David Kyle
Kersey Alexander Jr.	Elizabeth Buckner	23 Jun 1828	Edward H. Robertson
			L. T. Johnston
Kersey Clark A.	Sarah A. Page	12 Dec 1860	S. E. Brackin
Kersey James L.	Bettie Roberts	19 May 1866	Wm. F. Lyon
		20 May 1866	md by Jacob Doll MG
Kersey Richard	Jane Frederick	29 Aug 1829	Thomas Overby
Kersey Samuel	Mary Matlock	23 Dec 1790	William Keling
Kersey William	Nancey Thomas	7 Dec 1816	James Matlock

GROOM	BRIDE	DATE	BONDSMAN OR WITNESS
Key Peyton*	Elizabeth Harrison	10 Jan 1831	John Harrison
Kidd Lewis	Frances Grant	26 Mar 1815	Davie Grant
Kiersey Drury	Polly McFarland	9 Feb 1826	James Kersey
Killgore Charles	Unice Lea	24 Sep 1796	Daniel Thomas
Killgore Thomas	Pheby Lea	2 Jan 1786	Thomas Yeats
Kimbell Thomas M.	Ann E. Pattillo	19 Nov 1837	Thomas Bigelow
Kimbro Andrew J.	Mary Hooper	15 Mar 1858	Iverson L. Oliver
		18 Mar 1858	md by John Stadler
Kimbro James	Nancy Turner	27 Dec 1787	Thomas Turner
Kimbro James B.	Susannah Kimbro	9 Jan 1823	Zephaniah T. Kerr
Kimbro Miles	Dianah Burton	20 Nov 1822	Thomas W. Graves
Kimbro Thomas	Faithey Johnagain	18 Aug 1781	Jonathan Sinard
Kimbro William	Susannah Barker	9 Nov 1797	James Yancey
Kimbro William N.	Sarah Ann Baldwin	28 Sep 1847	Jno. K. Graves
Kimbrou Thomas R.	Elizabeth A. Evans	30 Jan 1835	Elijah G. Browning
Kimbrou William	Elizabeth Miles	9 Dec 1799	James Graves
Kimbrough Elijah	Polly Fury	5 Sep 1803	George Kelly
			Wm. Wilkerson DC
Kimbrough John	Betsey Link	6 Sep 1804	William Kimbrou
Kimbrough John	Polley Warwick	19 Oct 1809	John Warrick
Kimbrough John M.	Nancy Turner	5 May 1825	John S. Kimbrough
Kimbrough John T.	Mary J. Hensley	13 Aug 1866	Brice Harralson
		19 Aug 1866	md by R. G. Barrett MG
Kimbrough M. Duke	Salley Love	30 Nov 1818	Henry Willis
Kimbrough Thomas	Elizabeth Graves	29 Mar 1792	James Yancey
Kimbrough William C.	Nancy Kimbrough	26 Aug 1852	John C. Hooper
Kimbrough Wm. T.	Lucinda Davis	31 Dec 1853	Wm. N. Kimbrough
King Daniel	Nancy Milton	19 Oct 1820	Robert Stadler
King Edmund (of Va.)	Nancy Legrant	11 Aug 1800	John Herman (of Va.) Archd. Carnall (of Person Co. N.C.)
King Harvey	Polly Nichols	25 Apr 1822	Enoch Henslee
King Henry	Delilah Campbell	8 Dec 1840	Francis Gooch
King Henry (Colson of Joseph & Winnie King)	Leana Jones (Col-dau of Moses & Minerva Jones)	7 Dec 1867	H. F. Brandon
King Isaac	Rachel Perkins	7 Nov 1808	Saml. King
King J. W.	Elizabeth Vaughan	15 Oct 1849	James Poteat
King James	Patsey Arvin	27 Jan 1817	David Davison
King James	Henrietta Roberts	17 Nov 1849	David Rudd
King James P.	Sarah Burton	27 Oct 1830	Jesse C. Page
King Joseph	Fanny Bull	19 May 1815	William King
King Joseph	Pamelia Frances Page	26 Jun 1850	George W. Manly
King Newton	Lucy King	24 Dec 1866	Saml. Blackwell
		25 Dec 1866	md by Stephen Neal JP
King Robert J.	Salley Badget	24 Dec 1821	Joseph King
King Samuel J.	Drusilla Badgett	28 Jun 1834	Azariah Foster
King William	Polley Perkins	30 Oct 1804	Joseph Brackin
King William D.	Ann Howard	14 Feb 1859	John W. Cobb
		17 Feb 1859	md by John Stadler
Kinnibrough William	Biddy Hastin	6 Nov 1822	William Mitchell
Kirk Samuel	Jane Berry	17 Jun 1822	Barzl. Graves
			Peter Hooper
Kirk William	Salley Burroughs	25 Jan 1816	Severn Beusey
Kitchen James*	Priscilla Vaughan	8 Sep 1831	Stephen Kitchen
Kitchen John	Elizabeth Montgomery	23 Dec 1820	Stephen Kitchen
Kitchen Joseph	Betsey Vaughan	8 Nov 1815	Thomas Langley
Kitchen Moses	Polley Stephens	9 Oct 1815	Thomas Langley
Kitchen Stephen	Polly Finley	23 Dec 1822	James Kitchen
Knight Evans	Sally Burton	17 Dec 1800	Joseph Jno. Knight
Knight Evans	Mary Adams	27 Dec 1841	Thos. J. Reid

GROOM	BRIDE	DATE	BONDSMAN OR WITNESS
Knight Jesse (Col-son of Richard Knight & Bettie Hatchett)	Rhoda Cobbs (Col-dau of Alx. Matthews & Rhoda Cobbs)	10 Aug 1867	md by J. J. Jones JP
Knight Joseph	Judith Dameron	8 Dec 1801	George B. Dameron
Knight Joseph D.	Magara Clempson	28 Apr 1830	Noel Burton Jr.
Knight Robert	Elizabeth Burton	15 Sep 1832	William Knight
Knight William	Rebeccah Lyon	30 Mar 1809	William Cannon
Knight William W.	Susan Harrison	8 Jan 1836	Alexander McAlpin
Knighten James	Purlina Travis	9 Aug 1841	Elzey W. Travis
Knorman Thomas*	Rachel Strader	26 Dec 1831	John N. Ford
Knott James	Mary Williamson	13 Jun 1810	Edward M. Foulkes S. D. Watkins

- L -

GROOM	BRIDE	DATE	BONDSMAN OR WITNESS
Lackey Robert	Sarah Mitchell	14 Feb 1795	Richard Henslee
Lain Beverly	Jane Dawson	30 Dec 1843	William Bass
Lamb John	Jane Rines	23 Dec 1829	Tillotson McCain
Lambert Clayton	Isabella Bricefield	14 Apr 1854	C. P. Harrison
Lambeth John	Frances Walker	2 Sep 1828 11 Sep 1828	William Walker md by Jarratt W. Cook
Lambeth John J.	Jane E. Walker	10 Dec 1855 16 Dec 1855	David Strader md by Lancelot Johnston JP
Lambeth Lovick L.	Eliza J. Windsor	25 Nov 1848	Jno. Kerr
Lamon Alexander	Sarah Grant	11 Mar 1786	James Grant Jr.
Land Williamson H.	Ann P. Anderson	29 Sep 1858	John F. Wrenn
Landers Abraham	Nancey Nelson	8 Nov 1809	Larkin Landers
Landers John	Mary Parks	15 Oct 1833	Robeson McMennamy Abr. Landers
Landrum James A.	Emaline Davis	2 Jul 1857	John W. Willis md by Joseph Jennings JP
Lane Joseph	Salley Rice	10 Oct 1809	Levy Lane
Lane William N.	Elizabeth M. Roberts (ward of Isaac Medley)	24 Dec 1834	Thomas Graves John Kerr Jr.
Langhorne Maurice M.	Eliza M. Farley (dau of James Farley of Milton, N.C.)	15 May 1837	Milton G. Scoggins
Langley Thomas	Ester Kitchen	25 Oct 1813	John Wiley
Lanier C. V.	Isabela Jeffers	14 Jan 1839	W. G. Craghead B. C. West Sr.
Lanier James	Elizabeth Johns	11 Feb 1804	Isaac Johns
Lanier James	Polly Johns	23 Oct 1809	Thomas Ragsdale
Lannom Joseph	Delila Browning	21 Sep 1799	Abner Rosson
Lashley Powell	Elizabeth Prendergast	21 Sep 1844	Tho. Hardison
Latta Jas. C. (son of James & Hannah Latta)	Jane S. Howard (dau of C. A. & Elizabeth S. Howard)	26 Oct 1867 12 Nov	H. F. Brandon md by G. W. McNeely MG
Latta James G. (son of Anderson & Elizabeth Latta)	Cattie F. Howard (dau of C. A. & Elizabeth S. Howard)	26 Oct 1867 12 Nov	H. F. Brandon md by G. W. McNeely MG
Lauson John B.	Jemima J. Whitmore	29 Sep 1827	Joel F. Motley
Law Butler	Patsey Southerland	28 Dec 1812	Thomas Henderson
Law James T.	Pocahontas A. Badgett	9 Feb 1859 24 Feb 1859	Jno. D. Badgett md by N. W. Wilson MG
Law John (Col-son of Billy & Locky)	Sylva Graves (Col-dau of Isaac & Hannah)	19 Apr 1867	H. F. Brandon
Lawrence James	Catherine Sneed	29 Dec 1836	Alexander McAlpin

GROOM	BRIDE	DATE	BONDSMAN OR WITNESS
Lawson John	Dolly Robertson	28 Dec 1866	Maj. Long
			md by R. G. Barrett
Lawson John Jr.	Elizabeth Allen	25 Mar 1790	Francis Lawson
Lawson Moses	Betsey Bradley	6 Dec 1788	John Lawson
Lawson Robert W.	Nancey Brown	20 Nov 1827	John Lawson
Layn Garret C.	Elizabeth W. Pryor	11 Dec 1834	Thomas Graves
Lea Absalom	Frances Muzle	30 Apr 1794	Samuel Evans
Lea Alanson M.	Rebecca S. Hightower	9 Dec 1834	Vincent Bradsher
Lea Alexander	Elisabeth Ferguson	24 Oct 1797	Wm. Dix
			Duke Williams
Lea Alvis	Nancey Kerr	29 Mar 1832	Maj. C. Lea
Lea Ambrose	Frances Whealer	10 Aug 1779	John Lea Z. Rice
Lea Archibald	Lucinda Hendrick	11 Jul 1821	James Gallaugher
			Wm. G. Cochran
Lea Aron V.	Sarah Currie	13 Aug 1830	Paul A. Haralson
Lea Barnett	Mourning Roan	21 Dec 1782	George Lea
Lea Barzillia G.	Elizabeth Henderson	8 Dec 1829	Noel Burton Jr.
Lea Bedford	Dianah Winstead	20 Oct 1866	Thos. J. Brown
			md by M. A. Turner JP
Lea Benjamin	Nancy Kerr	9 Feb 1796	Jeremiah Lea
Lea Carter	Patty Hubbard McNeill	26 Feb 1782	Edmund Lea
Lea Edmund	Nancy Wright	1 Oct 1794	John Lea
Lea George	Jane Douglass	24 Feb 1785	Benjamin Douglass
Lea George G.	Sarah E. Wright	5 May 1835	William A. Lea
Lea Herndon	Fanny Hightower	22 Jun 1791	Epaphroditus Hightower
Lea Henry	Fanny Coe	21 Mar 1846	Martin Morgan
Lea Henry	Virginia Roan	26 Dec 1866	Silman Graves
			md by Jacob Doll MG
Lea Isaac	Malinda Stephens	10 Nov 1866	Wm. G. Graves
			md by S. G. Mason
Lea J. A.	Mollie E. Lindsey	13 Feb 1867	H. F. Brandon
		15 Feb 1867	md by S. G. Mason
Lea Jack	Louvina Oliver	14 Dec 1866	Wm. G. Graves
		21 Dec 1867	md by R. A. Moore MG
Lea Jake	Caroline Swift	25 Nov 1865	Allen Harralson
			md by S. G. Mason
Lea James	Nancy Hightower	15 Nov 1796	Gregory Hightower
Lea James	Elizabeth Morgan	20 Dec 1819	Charles Webster
Lea James	-------------	11 Apr 1821	Romulus M. Sanders
Lea James	Elizabeth Rice	9 Mar 1841	William Hightower
(see Lee)			
Lea James Jr.	Betsey Graves	15 Apr 1815	Jno. Lea
Lea James K.	Margaret D. Sergent	16 Dec 1848	George Williamson
Lea James W.	Virginia S. Harrison	3 Feb 1858	James M. Murrie
Lea James W.	Caroline N. Durham	29 Sep 1858	William T. Smith
Lea Jeremiah	Polley Kerr	20 Dec 1797	William Kerr
Lea Jeremiah	Mary P. Kerr	9 Nov 1830	John F. Lea
Lea John	Elizabeth Bradley	23 Apr 1780	Archibald Murphey
	(dau of James		Jona. Murphey
	Bradley)		
Lea John	Mary Crider	4 Mar 1786	William Rainey
Lea John	Mary Stephens	30 Dec 1786	Elisha Evans
Lea John	Hannah Slade	22 Jan 1793	Benjamin Lea
Lea John	Elizabeth Vaughan	8 May 1809	James Lea
Lea John	Polley Swift	30 Mar 1816	Benjamin T. Fielder
Lea John (son of	Susannah Wright	10 Sep 1825	William Lea Jr.
Cpt. John)			
Lea John Bratcher	Frankey Dollarhide	24 Nov 1802	Starling Warren
Lea John W.	Isabella Williamson	15 Jun 1861	Green P. Womack
Lea Jonathan	Mary Hightower	16 Oct 1786	Charnel Hightower
Lea Larwrence	Phebe Sargent	23 Sep 1793	Samuel Evans
Lea Lemuel	Rebeca Cates	14 Nov 1839	Martin Morgan
Lea Louis (Col)	Hester Jones (Col)	25 Dec 1866	John E. Robertson
			md by J. J. Jones JP

GROOM	BRIDE	DATE	BONDSMAN OR WITNESS
Lea Major	Salley Farley	29 Aug 1790	John Burton
Lea Nelson	Mary Davis	30 Aug 1867	H. F. Brandon
		1 Sep 1867	md by J. F. Leath JP
Lea Simeon	Peggy Westbrook	28 Mar 1822	Richard Lea
Lea Thomas	Salley Lea	13 Oct 1801	Jeremiah Lea
Lea Thomas A.	Mary Ware	11 Oct 1843	Silas Ware
Lea Thomas L.	Ann B. Wright	16 Apr 1833	William Lea
Lea Tinsley	Frances Fulloe	18 Sep 1820	Jesse A. Dollarhide
Lea Westley	Caroline Cates	29 Oct 1842	Lemuel Lea
Lea William	Sarah Gold	3 Nov 1790	Hearndon Haralson
Lea William	Lea Long	31 Aug 1816	James Rudd
Lea William	Mary L. Willson	7 Oct 1834	Thomas D. Connally
			D. Knott
Lea William	Betsey B. Graves	24 Jun 1836	Thomas P. Connally
Lea William	Barbara Brooks	12 May 1848	Johnston Scoggin
Lea William A.	Jane Weastbrook	10 Nov 1824	Richard Lea
Lea William A.	Lucy Ann Hargis	1 Oct 1851	David Burch
		2 Oct 1851	md by B. Cooper JP
Lea William A.	Martha B. Carter	5 Feb 1862	Bartemas H. Warren
		13 Feb 1862	md by N. M. Lewis JP
Lea William G.	Susan J. Lea	19 Mar 1848	Henry N. Holden
			James M. Farmer
Lea William M.	Mary Cheek	11 Nov 1851	John W. Roan
Leak William Jr.	Martha Simmons	24 Mar 1782	William Leak Sr.
Leath Colman	Hannah Simmons	14 Mar 1808	Joel Leath
Leath Joel	Betsey Jones	21 Dec 1798	James Mallory
Leath John F.	Cornelia Ann Nutt	3 Apr 1847	George Herndon
Leavell Alfred R.	Phebe O. Williams	22 Apr 1839	Noel Burton
			B. C. West Sr.
Lecount John	Mildred Hubbard	6 Apr 1850	Samuel S. Harrison
Lee Alexander			
(see Lea			
Alexander)			
Lee James	Nancy Burch (wid)	17 Aug 1795	Joseph Hall
Legrand Herbert W.	Mary Merritt	4 Apr 1836	Richard Gates
Leigh David G.	Mary Wilson (dau of	16 Dec 1822	Tillotson McCain
	Elizabeth Wilson)		
Leigh William	Mary McDaniel	1 Sep 1814	Jno. G. Willson
Lemmon Alexander	Catherine Somers	12 Sep 1808	Joshua Grant
			William Carmichael
Lemmon H. S.	Missouri F. Payne	26 Jul 1846	Rob. L. Kent
(see Lamon)			Wm. P. Graves
Lesley John	Rachel Wallis	15 May 1799	John Bowes
Lester Robert	Alcey Moore	2 May 1832	Dabney Rainey
Lewis A. S.	Sarah S. Thompson	8 Dec 1846	L. D. Lipscomb
Lewis Anderson	Isabella H. Childris	26 Jan 1830	Thomas Hailey
Lewis Anderson	Martha A. Dabney	15 May 1852	Albert G. Henderson
			md by Philip
			Hodnett JP
Lewis Burrell	Fanney Turner	24 Aug 1813	Hiram Lewis
Green			
Lewis Charles	Lucy Boulton	8 Jan 1795	Phillip Thomas
Lewis Charles	Winny Williamson	22 Jun 1804	Alva Oliver
Lewis Charles	Elizabeth Murphy	2 Apr 1865	John Carter
			md by Stephen Neal JP
Lewis Charles A.	Elizabeth Lewis (wid)	15 Dec 1853	Calvin D. Vernon
Lewis Edward	Elizabeth Kendrick	9 Feb 1815	Presley Carter
Lewis Fielding	Betsey Evans	6 Oct 1810	Thomas Henshaw
Lewis Fielding B.	Samuella Jennings	5 Dec 1859	N. L. Walker
		7 Dec 1859	md by S. A. Stanfield
Lewis George W.	Nannie W. Owen	8 Dec 1863	Tho. W. Graves clk
			md by Jacob Doll MG
Lewis Henry H.	Celia Ford	28 Dec 1825	Thomas Harper
Lewis Hiram	Agness Cearney	3 Mar 1806	Thomas Henshaw

GROOM	BRIDE	DATE	BONDSMAN OR WITNESS
Lewis J. T.	Sallie A. Corbin	3 Mar 1864	Thomas S. Harrison
		5 Mar 1864	md by George T. Goodson
Lewis James	Jane Roberts	19 Dec 1853	William McNutt
			Jas. Thos. Graves
		25 Dec 1853	md by B. Cooper JP
Lewis James H.	Marry A. Roberts	17 Dec 1857	Brice Harralson
			John H. F. Graves DC
Lewis Pleasant	Sally Hightower (dau of William Hightower)	31 Dec 1816	John Bennett
Lewis Pleasant	Martha Childress	29 Jan 1848	Caloway J. Harrison
Lewis Shadrac	Elizabeth Lenox	10 Oct 1826	Charles Willson
Lewis Thomas Johns	Harriet Gunn	16 Feb 1867	Merriwether Lewis
			md by E. Hunt JP
Lewis Wade N.	Elizabeth C. Carmical	16 Apr 1860	William H. Wilkinson
			md by N. M. Lewis JP
Lewis William (of Person Co.)	Nancy Matlock	31 Jan 1805	Henry W. Howard (of Person Co.)
Lewis William	Elizabeth Shelton	6 Aug 1847	John Burton
Lewis Zachariah	Jemima Ferguson	3 Mar 1866	Minnie Lewis
			md by E. Hunt JP
Liggon John	Margaret Hughes	19 Jan 1867	Louis Lewis
			md by John J. Jones JP
Ligon Richard F.	Elizabeth C. Hayes	19 Jul 1837	Thomas S. Hayes
			Geo. W. Graves
Lillard Thomas M.	Laura V. Wright	3 Oct 1866	R. T. Blackwell
		6 Oct 1866	md by George W. McNeely MG
Lindsey A. C.	Elizabeth L. Graves	14 Jun 1843	R. W. Hughes
			Wm. M. Nance Jr.
Lindsey Geroge R.	Sallie E. Poteat	25 Jan 1861	R. H. Bledsoe
		5 Feb 1861	md by S. G. Mason
Lindsey Henry	Lucinda Stamps	20 Apr 1867	md by N. M. Lewis JP
Lindsey Isaac Newton	Hesteran Nunnally	15 Nov 1865	Joseph T. Lindsey md by E. Hunt JP
Lindsey William	Rosy Coleman	17 Sep 1800	William Florence
Link Byrd	Avey Morton	12 Mar 1799	John Morton
Link John	Betsey Morton	12 Jan 1802	Jesse Morton
Linthicum Henry	Nancy Bocock	24 Nov 1827	Obediah Gordon
Lipford John J.	Agnes Moseley	1 Nov 1855	William B. Powell
			md by J. M. Allen JP
Lipscomb J. H.	Sarah E. Drain	3 Feb 1857	J. M. Smith Jr.
			R. H. Ward
Lipscomb John	Elizabeth Gwyn	26 Jan 1807	Zeri Gwyn
Lipscomb John	Phebe Richmond	14 Dec 1808	Step Morton
Lipscomb Joseph R. E.	Eliza Harralson	11 Mar 1830	Thomas D. Connally
			John C. Harvey
Lipscomb Joseph R. E.	Margaret Graves	29 May 1833	Thomas D. Connally
			D. Knott
Lipscomb Thomas	Elizabeth Turner	14 Oct 1799	Thomas Turner
Lipscomb Thomas	Martha Eskridge	29 Apr 1828	William Day
Lipscomb Thomas	Rebecah Eskridge	13 Oct 1829	Hiram Lockard
			Chs. Willson
Lipscomb Thomas W.	Mary A. C. Dodson	30 Jan 1847	Samuel B. Holder
Little David	Sarah Sneed	2 Mar 1789	Benjamin Snead
Lloyd Thomas	Jane Mahan	23 Aug 1804	Archable Maughan
Loafman Benjamin	Nancey Perkins	7 Sep 1813	Edward Loafman
Loafman Edward	Salley Perkins	24 Jul 1810	Elisha Ingram
Locher Henry S.	Lucy A. Orrich	28 Jul 1852	James M. Lea
			md by Jacob Doll MG
Lockard Hiram	Priscilla McKissock	-- Apr 1819	John L. Hucherson
Lockett David S.	Mary A. Hawkins	27 Feb 1864	William H. Pattillo
Lockett Zachariah	Ann Mills	11 Jul 1825	Joseph McDowell

GROOM	BRIDE	DATE	BONDSMAN OR WITNESS
Lockhart William	Caroline McAlpin	12 May 1841	Archibald H. Boyd
Logan William	Martha Dicks	10 Feb 1859	James Barker md by J. S. Totten JP
London Joseph	Nancey Nunn	11 Aug 1835	William London
Long Alexander M.	Mary A. Montgomery	19 Jul 1824	John Long
Long Baszely M.	Mary Hodge	5 Jul 1828	Henry Lipscomb Lancelott T. Johnston
Long Benjamin	Rachel Moore (dau of Alexander, decd.)	24 May 1780	Robert Moore John Moore
Long Benjamin	Judith Gomer	3 Jun 1830	Dr. Allen Gunn
Long Edmond	Cilla Bowe	19 May 1866	Alex. Ferguson
Long James	Priscilla Todd	16 Feb 1782	Robert Long
Long John	Elizabeth Comer	21 Apr 1800	Samuel Hodge
Long John (Col)	Kizzia Edwell (Col)	9 Dec 1835	Tilman Snow
Long John (Col)	Sally Long (Col)	16 Feb 1866	Alfred Johnston
Long John D.	Elizabeth A. Penick	7 Feb 1854 8 Feb 1854	Thomas C. Bowe md by Thomas W. Tobey
Long Joseph	Susan Philips	31 May 1838	Tilmon Snow
Long Robin E.	Sally Harris	29 Sep 1830	Tilmon Snow
Long Samuel (Col)	Polly Featherston (Col)	22 Apr 1867 17 Jun 1867	H. F. Brandon md by R. F. Moore
Long William	Hannah Skeen	5 Nov 1788	Reubin Newton
Long William	Eady Edwell	22 Dec 1807	Isaac Wright
Long William	Sarah Johnston	20 Oct 1828	Nathaniel M. Roan
Long William (Col)	Nancy Toney (Col-dau of John & Lucy Toney)	26 Jan 1842	Tilmon Snow (Col)
Longwell David	Cornelia A. Gordon	8 Oct 1857	R. A. Newbell md by J. B. Jackson
Longwell Timothy	Polley Ruark	27 Nov 1811	John Ruark
Lorentz Joseph	Elizabeth Dix	8 Feb 1865	Richard Ward md by E. Hunt JP
Loughgin David	Lithe Going	18 Nov 1783	Jesse Going
Love John	Polly Currie	26 Mar 1793	Richard Arwin
Love John C.	Maranda R. Morton	15 May 1839	Robert Walton
Love Lewis H.	Lucy Vaughan	21 Jan 1851	Thomas L. Evans
Love Robert	Sarah Moore	12 Dec 1833	Hiram Lockard
Love Samuel	Frances Malone	3 May 1791	David Haralson
Love Samuel Jr.	Mary Love	18 Jul 1828	Anderson Snipes Lancelott T. Johnston
Love Snelson	Frances Browning	18 Dec 1823	Andrew McCulloch
Lovelace Barnett	Betsy Orr	23 May 1821	Jesse Orr
Lovelace Henry R.	Jemima Beaver	8 Apr 1858	John Smithy
Lovelace John	Nancy Carver	9 Jan 1826	John Holloway
Lovelace Joseph	Matilda Lovelace	2 Jul 1850	William M. Withers
Lovelace Nicholas	Matilda Lovelace	26 Dec 1822	Brewis Loveless
Lovelace Nicholas	Celie Walker	17 Aug 1864	Robert Sanders
Lovelace Pinckney	Lithy Southard	11 Feb 1840	William Southard
Lovelace William	Libba Lovelace	15 Dec 1828	Pryor Lovelace
Lovelace William	Selma Paschall	24 Jan 1842	William Paschall
Loveless Benjamin C.	Nancey Hall	1 Nov 1837	Thomas Brinsfield
Loveless Brewis W.	Martha Jones	6 May 1824	Richard Jones
Loveless Joseph	Martha Walker	26 Nov 1857	Daniel J. Page
Loveless Pryor	Sally Page	29 Aug 1809	Whitehead Page
Lovell Lent G.*	Priscilla Burton	19 Nov 1831	William Knight
Lowrey Henry	Saluda Overby	21 Oct 1850	Craddock Elliott
Loyd Alexander G.	Nancy Martin	2 Nov 1825	Asa Gunn
Loyd John	Nancy Walker	10 Mar 1823	James Womble
Lumpkin George	----- Gillaspie	11 Feb 1815	Richard Haddock
Lunceford William	Thursey Beviell	27 May 1833	Jonathan Smith
Lunsford Paten L.	Margaret Fuqua	29 Jul 1866 31 Jul 1866	John L. Graves md by J. Smith JP

GROOM	BRIDE	DATE	BONDSMAN OR WITNESS
Lunsford Walter H.	Lucitta Ann Campbell	1 Dec 1836	William A. Richmond
Lunsford Warner J.	Rusalinda Campbell	2 Feb 1850	Henry A. Richmond
Lunsford Weldon H.	Martha A. Foard	17 May 1866	A. L. Pleasant md by R. A. Moore
Lunsfurd Colley W.	Elizabeth Lea	17 Sep 1839	Henderson House
Lunsfurd Rushea H.	Nancey Sparrow	12 Jan 1835	Zachariah McFarling
Luster Jacob W.	Ann Stephens	14 Jul 1842	Geo. W. Jeffreys
Luster Robert	Matilda Stevens	28 Oct 1860	Turner Carter md by N. M. Lewis JP
Lynch Thomas	Mary Byrd	10 Dec 1827	James Fausett
Lynch William B.	Rebecca M. Neal	4 Apr 1861	md by Jacob Doll MG
Lynn Bayless	Lucinda Benton	10 Oct 1820	Anthony Foster
Lynn Patrick H.	Virginia Ema Neal	8 Mar 1857	James M. Williams Jr. md by J. Jennings JP
Lyon James N.	Jane Traywig	21 Nov 1866	Noel Burton md by E. Hunt JP
Lyon John	Patsey Stephens	23 Feb 1813	William Jones Goodwin Evans
Lyon Nicholas	Mildred Jones (of Pittsylvania Co. Va.)	11 Feb 1853 15 Feb 1853	N. E. Graves md by J. M. Allen JP
Lyon Noel W.	Mary Harp	26 Dec 1837	Thomas D. Conally
Lyon Noel W.	Mildred Goodson	19 Jan 1852 20 Jan 1852	James L. Roberts md by Philip Hodnett JP
Lyon Richard	Sarah Nickels	13 Oct 1791	Henry Lyon J. Womack
Lyon Robert	Elizabeth Stephens	30 Dec 1821	Azariah Graves Paulus A. Haralson DC

- Mc -

GROOM	BRIDE	DATE	BONDSMAN OR WITNESS
McAdam David	Elixena Collins	2 Mar 1839	George C. Bouldin
McAden Henry	Mary Bradley	6 Nov 1792	William McAden
McAden Henry	Frances W. Yancey	4 Nov 1829	Thomas D. Johnston
McAden James	Betsy Dowdwell	28 Dec 1815	Thomas Walton
McAden John	Betsey Murphey	30 Nov 1797	Thomas Jeffreys
McAlister John	Nancy Pike	26 Jan 1801	Forister Stainback
McAlpin Alexander	Charlotte Farley	26 Jul 1818	Stewart Farley
McAlpin Alexander	Mary M. Badgett	19 Jan 1841	Owen McAleer
McAlpin Alexander	Jane W. Jones	31 Oct 1857	Tho. W. Graves
McBride Andrew	Phebe Boran	11 Oct 1784	Isaac Boran J. Campbell
McCaden Atkinson (Col)	Ann Richmond (Col)	30 Jun 1866	Cesar Dodson (Col) J. J. Jones JP
McCain Alexander	Hannah Foster	29 Jan 1790	John McCain
McCain Alfred P.	Mary J. E. Apple	7 Sep 1864	Joseph N. McCain md by A. G. Anderson MG
McCain Benjamin C.	Caroline M. Shelton	29 Apr 1842	Sherwood Owen
McCain Edmund	Harriet Mebane	11 Jan 1867 13 Jan 1867	Ephraim Hatchett md by Thomas S. Harrison JP
McCain James A.	Julia C. Lockhart	17 Nov 1866 20 Nov 1866	Thomas D. Hubbard md by Jacob Doll MG
McCain John	Elisabeth Warrin	23 Jun 1790	John Pearson
McCain John	Nancy Morgan	20 Dec 1842	John K. Brookes
McCain John W.	Mary M. Ball	8 Nov 1849	William Thacker
McCain Joseph N.	Emily F. Boulton	15 May 1858	William P. McCain
McCain Louis (Col- son of Louis Lewis & Juda McCain)	Roxey Moore (Col-dau of Richard & Viney Moore)	20 Dec 1867	md by J. J. Jones JP
McCain Robert	Charlotte Ware	15 Mar 1842	Ansel Ware

GROOM	BRIDE	DATE	BONDSMAN OR WITNESS
McCain Samuel D.	Araminta A. Powell	25 Sep 1865	William G. Robson
McCain Tillotson	Betsy Elmore	11 Jan 1825	John McCain
McCain Tillotson (see McKeen)	Patsy Roper	19 Nov 1839	Francis Phillips
McCallam William	Martha Ware	2 Nov 1787	Isaac McCallum
McCauley John	Polly Moore	14 Sep 1796	James Moore
McCauley John W.	Nancy J. Walker	20 Dec 1845	William A. Lea
McCauly Johnston	Frances Walker	10 Jan 1843	John S. Shaw
McClain George	Polley Keen	2 Nov 1804	Henry Humphrys
McCain Joseph	Tempa Poteat	17 Mar 1806	William Lyon
McClarney Holt	Mary Tyree	30 Dec 1830	William Busey
McCord William	Peggy Barnwell	3 Mar 1801	Edward Barnwell
McCord William	Temperance A. Barnwell	25 Sep 1824	Edward Davison
McCormack Aaron F.	Ann Campbell	16 Aug 1849	James M. Farmer
McCray James	Leannah Dickey	11 Oct 1806	Thomas Shanks
McCrory David	Frances Albert	2 Jan 1838	Joseph McAdams
McCubbins William	Rachel Farebanks	17 Feb 1784	John H. Pryor
McCubins Alfred	Sarah Watson	5 Dec 1827	William B. Trigg
McCulloch Joseph	Nancey Walker	9 Apr 1814	Solomon Browning
McDade John A.	Nancy M. Woods	21 Aug 1830	A. M. Woods
McDade John M.	Elizabeth F. Murphey	5 Dec 1853	Ashel McDade
		8 Dec 1853	md by Benj. Wells JP
McDaniel Joel A.	Jane N. Chambers	10 Oct 1854	John Y. Stokes
McDaniel John	Mary M. Price	8 Apr 1828	William H. Nunnally
McDaniel William	Patsey Dameron	24 Nov 1802	Christopher Dameron JR
McDaniel William J.	Priscilla Hewbank (Eubank?)	23 May 1832	Solomon Whitlow
McDaniel William P.	Nancy Harrison	15 Jul 1817	James Richardson
McDonald Alexander	Mary Jennings	27 Dec 1818	Richard Ogilby Merryman Maynard
McDonald William R.	Virginia Y. Graves	6 Jan 1864 13 Jan 1864	Elias Dodson md by S. G. Mason
McDowel James	Polly Elliott	20 Oct 1801	Bluford Warren
McDowell Joseph M.	Margaret C. Taylor	24 Oct 1854	E. B. Holden md by J. M. Allen JP
McFarland Daniel	Mary Bazwell	10 Sep 1789	Hearndon Haralson
McFarland James H.	Cisley Womack	22 Jan 1787	James Robinson
McFarland Jno.	Dicey Lea	15 Jul 1779	George Lea A. Tatom
McFarland John	Frances Lea	24 Feb 1804	Lewis Ragsdale
McFarland Thomas	Rachel Winters	15 Mar 1797	Joseph Swann
McFarland William	Ritta Kiersey	19 Apr 1832	Christopher Hinton
McFarling Zechariah	Emsey H. Pitman	10 Dec 1835	William A. Richmond
McGehee Albert G.	Ann V. Payne	17 Oct 1834	Henderson Stanfield
McGehee Henderson (Col)	Susan Stanfield (Col)	29 Dec 1865	John Lea (Col) md by J. J. Jones JP
McGehee Jeremiah (Col-son of Jeremiah & Sallie McGehee)	Lucinda Lisberger (Col)	11 Jan 1868 15 Jan	md by J. H. Forbes
McGehee Paul (Col)	Cornelia Jeffreys (Col)	20 Apr 1867	md by J. J. Jones JP
McGehee Thomas	Elizabeth M. Jeffreys	7 Dec 1812	James Samuel
McGinnis James	Elizabeth Williams	15 Jan 1790	Mace Stokes
McGonnigil Samuel	Celia Yates	29 Dec 1832	Ellis Evans
McGruder Albert	Mary Ann Gordon	21 Nov 1860	David Longwell B. Hines
McHaney William R.	Lucy S. Blackstock	26 Dec 1860	Henry H. Hall md by N. M. Lewis JP
McIntosh Nimrod	Nancey Murphey	15 Dec 1788	Hugh Currie
McKee James L.	Frances M. Graves	15 Jun 1852	Ezekiel D. Jones md by Jno. H. Lacy

GROOM	BRIDE	DATE	BONDSMAN OR WITNESS
McKee Robert	Polly Wilkerson	23 Jul 1814	Hazelwood Wilkerson
			Isaac Rainey
McKeen Alexander	Betsey Bizwell	12 Dec 1799	William McCain
McKiney Thomas W.	Judith Chandler	2 Jan 1814	John T. Stadler
			Tho. H. Miles
McKinney Brooks	Elizabeth Sartin	4 Feb 1843	J. B. Humphreys
McKinney D. W.	Elizabeth F. Rudd	31 Oct 1860	W. Thomas Parish
McKinney Drury	Susannah Richardson	19 Sep 1820	William Cannon
McKinney George C.	Emma C. Sartin	22 Jan 1866	William Lockhart
McKinney Henry	Manerva Sanders	13 Oct 1829	Henry Turner
McKinney Isaac (Col-son of Isaac & Amy McKinney)	Bettie Carter (Col)	25 Dec 1867	H. F. Brandon
McKinney James A.	Martha F. Stadler	11 Jan 1854	Jefferson H. Walker
		12 Jan 1854	md by John Stadler
McKinney Nathaniel	Rachael Hensley	4 Jul 1833	William Sanders
McKinney Robert	Martha G. Alverson	13 Jun 1852	Wm. T. McKinney
		15 Jun 1852	md by Tho. W. Graves JP
McKinney William	Jane Pierson	20 Feb 1820	Peter McKinney
McKinney William T.	Isabella V. Reid	15 Dec 1858	Thomas J. Foster md by Wm. B. Bowe JP
McKinsey John A.	Sallie A. Penick (or Pinnix)	22 Feb 1864	James N. Blair md by W. B. Swann JP
McKinsey John W.	Martha Walters	24 Mar 1841	William C. Claiborne
McKissack John	Elisabeth Love	23 Aug 1830	Samuel Love
McKnight Andrew	Eliza Nash	7 Jan 1783	Alexander Murphey John Moore JP
McKnight Anthoney	Mary West	11 Mar 1794	Robert West
McLaughlan Rawley	Mary Philips	16 Oct 1847	Irby Philips
McLean Jesse R.	Emma J. Jennings	18 Jan 1859	Samuel H. Hines
McMenamy James	Susan Bouldin	9 Jan 1832	George Bouldin
McMullen John	Margaret Currie	11 Jan 1787	John Currie
McMullin James M.	Sarah A. Allen	6 Aug 1852	J. W. Roan
McMurrey James	Jemima Gould	22 Dec 1787	John Sarrett
McMurry Charles	Jannet Douglas	22 Dec 1789	James Hall
McMurry Samuel	Parthena Owens	7 Nov 1818	Samuel Mitchell
McNeal M. (Col)	Amy Comer (Col)	11 Jan 1866	Allen Harralson md by Jacob Doll MG
McNeeley Addom	Ann Parker	20 Dec 1791	Risdon Fisher
McNeeley George W.	Elizabeth Howard	16 Nov 1834	Stephen J. Chandler
McNeely James	Polly Yates	6 Sep 1804	Robert Samuel
McNeill Hosea	Isbell Graves	16 Mar 1807	Gabriel Lea Jr.
McNeill John H.	Ann Darby	25 Jun 1810	James Darby
McNiel Benjamin	Elizabeth Moore	18 Dec 1787	Edmond Roberts
McNiel John	Anniss Lea (dau of William Lea)	8 Sep 1780	James Roberts
McNiell George	Minerva Dillard	29 Nov 1823	Elijah Graves
McReynolds James	Lucy Fleming	2 Dec 1790	Matthew Price

- M -

Maayhon William	Sarah Grant	19 Dec 1781	Peter Fuller
Mabane David	Elizabeth Yancy	28 Oct 1817	James Yancey
Mabe William P.	Mary Love	17 Jul 1856	Jno. T. Hooper R. A. Newbell
Mabry Lewis	Judith Woodey	1 Sep 1784	Yancey Bailey
Madden Samuel Q.	Artelia S. Pleasants	30 Sep 1861	Stanly Madden
		8 Oct 1861	md by C. J. Richmond JP
Maddin Champness	Francis Duncan	17 Jan 1792	Daniel Merritt
Madding Robert	Martha Cobb	9 Oct 1818	Matthew Dodson
Madren Amos	Ellenor Hicks	9 Sep 1840	William Harbin
Mahon Henery	Patsey Eppyson	16 Dec 1808	James Dix

GROOM	BRIDE	DATE	BONDSMAN OR WITNESS
Mallery Thomas	Frances Simms	29 Dec 1789	Stephen Mallory
Mallory James	Salley Jones	16 Jan 1798	Joel Leath
Mallory Stephen	Lornah Simms	18 Dec 1790	Joseph Carter
Mallory Thomas	Rosey Fitzgerald	16 Oct 1802	Nathan Williams
Malone Alfred	Polley Smith	8 Dec 1813	Bennet Valone Goodwin Evans
Malone Bartlett Y.	Mary F. Crumpton	31 Oct 1866	Allen Harralson
		15 Nov 1866	md by F. L. Oakley MG
Malone Bennet	Nancey Chandler	10 Dec 1817	Curtis Payne
Malone Daniel Jr.	Betsey Lea	11 Dec 1801	Batt Damaron
Malone Henry	Jane Wilkerson	5 Nov 1820	John Ellis Clabourn Crisp
Malone James	Mildred A. Yancey	2 Jan 1849	Thomas W. Currie
Malone James T.	V. W. Bateman	16 Sep 1857	Lorenzo Baynes
		20 Sep 1857	md by Benj. Wells JP
Malone John	Rebecca Pittard	5 Nov 1816	Humphry Pittard
Malone Lewis	Nancy Blackwell	18 Oct 1792	Carter Blackwell
Malone Lewis	Betsy Blackwell	2 Dec 1811	Garland Blackwell
Malone Lewis	Margarett C. Richmond	11 Mar 1836	William Malone
Malone Loney	Nancey Eubank	27 Mar 1811	Philip Burch
Malone Mark	Hannah Hamblett	4 Sep 1796	John Blackwel
Malone Staples	Phebe Evans	16 Feb 1789	Lewis Evans
Malone Stephen	Celey Parks	1 Oct 1804	George Eubank
Malone Thomas	Jane Muzzle	20 Oct 1789	Lewis Malone
Malone Thomas	Elizabeth Dameron	25 Sep 1819	Daniel Malone
Malone William	Frances Johnston	2Sep 1829	John W. Richmond
Manley John	Lucy Page	14 Nov 1815	John Page
Manley Samuel	Henrietta Cobb	1 Feb 1821	John Cobb
Manly George W.	Mary Page	25 Mar 1852	Saml. M. Cobb md by John H. Pickard MG
Manly Rufus	Martha A. Thacker	5 Feb 1849	Azariah Scott
Manly Thomas M.	Malina S. Cobb	20 Dec 1860	Felix M. Neal md by Stephen Neal JP
Manly William	Martha Nunn	20 Jan 1830	Jno. Harrison
Manly William S.	Rebecca H. Moore	15 Dec 1858	Thomas M. Manly
		16 Dec 1858	md by Stephen Neal JP
Mann Forgis	Rachel Richardson	21 Feb 1797	Thomas Richardson
Mann Henry	Polly Moss	11 Jan 1826	Miles Poteet
Mann James	Betsey Warren	8 Jan 1810	William Mann
Mann Thomas	Margaret Crossett	10 Jan 1800	William Mann
Mann William Jr.	Lucy Warren	19 Apr 1800	William Mann Sr. James Heggie
Mansfield James	Eliza Gillaspie	21 Dec 1849	William T. Smith T. S. Poore
Mansfield James L.	Malinda Westbrooks	19 Dec 1845	James Burch
Mansfield James L.	Lucy C. Fergason	6 Oct 1858	Richard A. Newbell
		10 Oct 1858	md by N. M. Lewis JP
Mansfield John	Salley Terrell	16 Mar 1814	Barnett Kemp D. W. Simpson
Mansfield Thomas	Mary Morris	4 Jan 1853	Joseph J. Yarbrough md by J. M. Allen JP
Marain Thomas	Mary Hughs	20 Oct 1800	John Marain
Markes John	Paggey M. Dotson	26 Jan 1815	Joel Price Martin Wilson
Marr Ambrose R.	Judith C. Williams	14 Aug 1837	John H. Graves
Marr David J.	Mary A. Terry	4 Apr 1862	Pinkney N. Shelton md by N. M. Lewis JP
Marr George W.	Huldah Swann	3 Feb 1834	William B. Swann
Marshall Charles	Elizabeth Allen	17 Apr 1833	V. McMurry
Marshall D. P.	Martha J. Dooly	12 Sep 1865	R. J. Bayes md by J. A. Hodges JP
Marshall G. W.	Mary C. Tally	18 May 1867	H. F. Brandon
		25 May 1867	md by H. E. Hodges JP

GROOM	BRIDE	DATE	BONDSMAN OR WITNESS
Marshall Willis L.	Sarah Roberts	23 Dec 1859	Thomas P. Oakly
			Allen Harralson DC
Martin Claiborn R.	Martha A. Swain	9 Aug 1867	
		12 Aug	md by Jas. J. Clendenin JP
Martin Elijah	Salley Cantrille	19 Apr 1815	Mumford Ford
Martin George	Rachel Cantrel	26 Oct 1813	James Yancey
Martin George Jr.	Mary Murphey	27 Dec 1824	Aldridge Rudd
Martin George W.	Mary Swift	21 Oct 1845	Franklin Graves
Martin Howard*	Jane Murphey	14 Jan 1831	Henry Willis
Martin James	Sarah Cantrell	5 Feb 1816	George Martin
Martin James	Nancey Cantrill	8 Mar 1827	George A. Connally
Martin John	Lucy Burton	19 Nov 1796	Joseph Dameron
Martin John	Rebeckah Stephens	28 May 1809	Joshua Beaver
Martin Lewis	Polley Morton	2 Jan 1811	Josephsiah Morton Jr.
Martin Richard	Frances Turner	25 Oct 1783	James Turner
			Josiah Cole
Martin Richard	Sarah Brown	16 Mar 1816	Jacob Brown
Martin Robert	Susannah Richardson	30 Nov 1781	John Campbell
Martin Robert	Betsey Ballard	2 Jan 1798	Groves Howard
Martin Robert	Nancey Browning	21 Mar 1812	Solomon Browning
Martin Samuel F.	Harriett A. Jeffreys	5 Dec 1857	Davis Pittard
		6 Nov 1857?	md by A. M. Woods JP
Martin Thomas	Catharine A. Richmond	17 Oct 1842	John C. Love
Martin William	Elizabeth Sanders	18 Jul 1814	George Sanders
Martin Zenes	Kitty Love	11 Dec 1816	Elijah G. Kimbro
Mase George*	Mary Meadows	29 Nov 1831	James Rudd
(Massey?)			Creed Adams
Mason David	Hannah Mayo	-- Dec 1800	James Mayo
Mason Henry	Eliza Pettifoot	6 Aug 1859	Joseph L. Prior
Mason John	Betsey Hughes	31 Jan 1814	Andrew Hughs
Mason John	Sarah Toney	16 Oct 1843	William L. Whittemore
			Tho. H. Miles
Mason Partrick	Patsey Going	3 Dec 1790	Zachary Hill
Mason Patrick	Catherine Delaney	16 Nov 1836	John D. Cobb
Mason Stephen	Sally Poinor	29 Jul 1794	David Poyner
Mason Stephen	Frances Pittard	2 May 1820	Drury Burton
Mason Wiley	Nancey Sims	15 Dec 1825	Kenny Ford
Mason Willey	Nancey Beusey	17 Oct 1809	Nathaniel Forguson
Massey Abraham*	Sarah Hensley	24 Nov 1831	James Boswell
Massey Benjamin	Frances Hensley	10 Feb 1835	Isaac Simmons
Massey Eli	Frances Gooch	21 Jan 1833	Thomas Massey
Massey John	Nanny Hastin	18 Nov 1801	Eldridge Hastin
Massey Joseph	Betsey Nichols	30 Nov 1815	Robert Stadler
Massey Levi	Polly Stadler	23 Aug 1836	Amsey Cobb
Massey Levi P.	Sarah Boswell	9 Dec 1861	Reece E. Stadler
		12 Dec 1861	md by G. W. Prendergast
Massey Mark	Louisa Ward	28 Jun 1838	James W. Arnold
Massey Nathan	Jemima Cantrill	20 Oct 1826	James Malone
Massey Nathan	Mary Brown	10 Sep 1828	Wiley Birk
Massey Nathan T.	Artelia Gooch	9 Nov 1858	Jehu Bird
			md by John Stadler MG
Massey Nathan T.	Elizabeth Burke	24 Sep 1866	R. Miles
		25 Sep 1866	md by A. G. Anderson MG
Massey Pleasant C.	Elizabeth Boswell	31 Dec 1852	Will. H. Massey
		6 Jan 1853	md by Howell Boswell JP
Massey Rainey	Mary Hensley	2 Nov 1846	Samuel Bethel
Massey Raney	Elizabeth Henslee	12 Nov 1850	George W. Martin
Massey Thomas	Margarett Massey	29 Aug 1832	Archibald R. Birk
Massey William	Judith Collir	30 Mar 1814	Robert Stadler

GROOM	BRIDE	DATE	BONDSMAN OR WITNESS
Massey William	Jane Burch	17 Nov 1818	Richard F. Archer
Massey William Sr.	Catherine Redden	9 Jun 1835	Wiley Birk
Massey William H.	Martha A. McKinney	9 Jan 1844	James W. Arnold
Massie Albert A.	Emily L. Frederick	11 Apr 1867	md by F. L. Oakley MG
Massie Joseph W. (son of William H. & Martha Massie) (see Mase)	Margaret A. Garrison (dau of John G. & Sarah Garrison)	21 Aug 1867 29 Aug	md by A. G. Anderson MG
Mathews Christopher	Elizabeth Love	20 Jan 1814	John Love
Mathews Drury	Delilah Jackson	21 Jul 1821	Alexander M. Dameron
Mathews Ezekiel	Sarah Cumbo	7 May 1793	Allen Going
Mathews Isaac	Sarah Jackson	19 Sep 1827	Samuel Love Jr.
Mathews Joel	Patsy Mason	24 Apr 1822	Joseph McDowell
Mathews Luke	Lucy Burton	21 Oct 1822	Francis H. Burton
Mathis Charles	Sally Dameron	21 Sep 1795	Vines Mathis
Mathis John	Elizabeth D. Jackson	3 Dec 1823	William Mathis
Mathis Samuel	Susannah Horsley	2 Aug 1784	John Brandon
Mathis William (see Matthis)	Sarah Jackson	3 Dec 1823	John Mathis
Matkins Dennis	Rebecca J. Walker	29 Jan 1867	md by Stephen Neal JP
Matkins John C.	Mary Jane Bouldin	21 Feb 1861 28 Feb 1861	Martin Bouldin md by Stephen Neal JP
Matkins John H.	Elizabeth Gwyn	17 Apr 1843	Thomas Matkins
Matkins Joseph	Louisa Simpson	14 Jan 1834	James M. Garrett
Matkins Silas	Susan Bouldin	10 Jul 1862	John W. Matkins
Matkins William	Sarah A. Walker	11 Dec 1866 18 Dec 1866	James P. Hornbuckle md by John F. Leath
Matlock B. L.	Anne Richmond	18 Jan 1843	John Matlock
Matlock Benjamin	Polley Lee (Lea?)	21 Jan 1806	James Matlock
Matlock Benjamin L.	Mary Heygood	26 Aug 1850	John Matlock
Matlock James	Patsey H. Gunn	13 Jan 1810	Benjamin Matlock
Matlock John	Mary J. Burton	5 Nov 1860	B. L. Matlock md by John D. Long JP
Matlock William	Annis Pool	20 Nov 1848	H. A. Richmond
Matthews Albert M.	Sophia W. Lampkin	17 Jul 1833	James Gunn
Matthis James	Elizabeth Goldsby	30 Nov 1791	Obadiah Sanders
Matthis Thomas (see Mathis)	Betsey Childs	29 Nov 1810	Batt Jackson
Maughan James	Polley Stadler	29 Jul 1809	William Fitz
Maury Philip	Betsey Anne Cunningham (dau of Wm. Cunningham)	4 Dec 1793	Jesse Carter
Maxwell Bezl.	Agness Long	30 Jun 1798	Anderson Terpin
May W. H.	Sarah F. Barnard	19 Feb 1850	Jas. M. Watlington
Mayhan William	Mary Cox	18 Sep 1822	William Corbit
Mayhan William	Minerva Fitch	2 Dec 1847	William H. C. McNutt
Mayhoe Vernell W.	Sally Schavers	7 Jun 1858	Richard Grubbs
Maynard Richard	Margaret Moore	23 Oct 1844	Joseph Pinnix
Maynard Wagstaff	Barbara Jane Penick	4 Dec 1841	Jacob Hurdle
Maynard Wagstaff	Julia Ann Rice	18 Apr 1859 21 Apr 1859	Tho. W. Graves md by John W. Lewis MG
Mayo Richard	Nancy Beavor	23 Dec 1795	Joshua Beaver
Mays Samuel	Sarah Somers	30 Sep 1837	Joseph Crawford
Meacham Banks	Louisa Lovelass	24 Nov 1829	Edward M. Jones
Meaders Major	Amanda Vaden	5 Nov 1841	George Maze
Meados Samuel A.	Martha J. Davis	19 Nov 1841	John D. Meadors Jno. Daniel
Meadows Gabriel	Polley Morton	14 May 1818	Hezekiah Morton
Mebane Alexander	Frances Mitchell	26 Sep 1818	John Mitchell
Mebane Benjamin F.	Fannie L. Kerr	31 Aug 1857 8 Sep 1857	James W. Lea md by Thomas W. Tobey

GROOM	BRIDE	DATE	BONDSMAN OR WITNESS
Mebane Edward (Col-son of Edward & Milly Mebane)	Tempy Harris (Col-dau of Henry & Huldah Harris)	4 Dec 1867	md by John J. Jones JP
Mebane Giles	Mary C. Yancey	8 Mar 1837	James Mebane Jr.
Mebane Giles (Col)	Malissa Smith (Col)	16 Dec 1865	Robert Jackson
Mebane Henry (Col)	Malissa Willis (Col)	1 Jan 1867	Jeremiah Mebane
Mebane James	Polly Graves	17 Jan 1833	William Graves
Mebane Jno. H.	Ann S. Graves	9 Feb 1837	Azariah Graves Jr.
Mebane Lemuel H.	Caroline L. Yancey	1 Nov 1841	John Turner
Mebane William G.	Emma C. Mebane	11 Dec 1865	R. W. Graves
		14 Dec 1865	md by Jacob Doll MG
Medlin Harrison	Susan Jones	30 Dec 1819	Harvey Swift
Meeks John	Carthrin Daniel	30 Aug 1833	John McDaniel
Megonegal George W.	Mary B. Yates	21 Dec 1839	William B. Trigg
Melear John	Rachel Baggett	12 Jan 1801	Rob. Hamblett
Mellett Dr. J. Y.	Julia A. Terry	27 Mar 1865	J. W. Mims Jr.
Melton Albert	Eliza Morris	4 mar 1841	Maj. H. Graves
Melton David	Susanna Aldridg	30 Dec 1816	John Maurice
Melton James	Fanney Cock	24 Nov 1818	Iverson Graves
Merideth James	Elizabeth Patterson	31 Oct 1780	David Patterson
Merritt Daniel	Nancy Duncan	27 Jan 1784	William Ragsdale Jr.
Merritt Daniel T.	Frances Oan (Gan?)	28 May 1820	John Pass Tho. Donoho Jr.
Merritt George H.	Narcissa R. Gordon	14 Feb 1850	Napoleon B. Taylor
Merritt James	Lettie Clift	17 Nov 1795	William Clift
Merritt Levi	Jincy Harvel	21 Apr 1825	John Peterson
Merritt Solomon	Elisabeth Poteate	10 Dec 1789	Daniel Merritt
Merritt Solomon	Sarah Dunavant	9 Sep 1863	Nathaniel M. Roan
Merritt Solomon	Priscilla Stone	30 Aug 1866	Th. Alexander Lockett
Meux Thomas W.	Eliza E. Nash	1 Oct 1819	Alfred M. Nash
Middlebrooks John	Nancy Humphries	18 Jan 1781	Richard Boggass Wm. Campbell
Middlebrooks John	Mary Lyon	16 Jul 1781	Nehemah Darcy
Milam John	Martha Shepherd	20 Apr 1854	Wm. Bryant md by J. M. Allen JP
Miles Abner	Delila Wommack	24 Nov 1819	Thomas L. Slade Thomas W. Rainey
Miles Abner	Sarah Jane Smith	3 Apr 1856	Rufus A. Rudd
		10 Apr 1856	md by John Stadler
Miles Abner Jr.	Mary A. Foster	13 Apr 1849	Richard Miles
Miles Elijah H.	Mary Lunsford	14 Jan 1840	James M. Tate
Miles Henry	Polly Malone	6 May 1830	John Vaughan
Miles Jacob Jr.	Nancy Rice	7 Oct 1783	Alexander Miles
Miles James	Betsey B. Gunn	3 Feb 1807	James Gunn
Miles James Jr.	Saludia Rowlett	20 Nov 1834	Solomon Corbett
Miles James Jr.	Malinda Rudd	10 Dec 1834	Levi L. Bruce
Miles John	Martha Lunsford	30 Dec 1840	Aldridge Rudd
Miles John Jr.	Nancey Evans	8 Dec 1828	Oliver Faulks
Miles John K.	Sarah C. Murry	20 Dec 1858	John B. Browning
		23 Dec 1858	md by A. B. Walker JP
Miles John S.	Eliza Murray	25 Jan 1849	Thomas C. Miles
Miles Richard	Martha J. Hooper	9 Oct 1850	E. L. Paschal
Miles Richard	Mary C. Walker	13 Dec 1860	C. D. Donoho
		18 Dec 1860	md by A. G. Anderson MG
Miles Thomas	Elisabeth Tolbert	15 Dec 1784	John Tolbert
Miles Thomas C.	Catharine Jackson	17 Sep 1846	John S. Miles
Miles Thomas H.	Lucie L. Palmer	11 Nov 1863	J. W. Fitzgerald
		18 Nov 1863	md by E. H. Harding
Miles Uriah	Irrena Rudd	11 Sep 1834	James Miles Jr.
Miles William	Viney Warren	29 Sep 1818	George Walker
Miles William	Dolly Pleasant	10 Sep 1821	Yancey G. Warren

GROOM	BRIDE	DATE	BONDSMAN OR WITNESS
Miles William	Rebecca H. Stubblefield	10 Mar 1859	George G. Walker
Miles William W.	Sarah J. Vaughn	5 Jul 1859	William McNutt md by Calvin J. Richmond JP
Miller Charles	Penny Mitchell	7 Apr 1826	Frances Jones
Miller Henry	Nancey Groom	16 Jul 1818	William Groom
Miller James	Leanah Horton	29 Nov 1785	Shadrack Jackson
Miller James	Polley Coleman	17 May 1814	James M. Powell Jno. Coleman
Miller Jno.	Ellennor Smith	15 Oct 1823	William W. Price
Miller John	Mary Ann Davis	11 Apr 1838	Henry Rose
Miller Tho.	Polly Pane	12 May ----	Robert Paine
Miller William D.	Frances Baldwin	6 Dec 1845	William McKinnney
Mills Samuel	Ellen Smith	15 May 1847	Ferinand Crowder Thomas S. Poore
Mills Thomas J.	Sarah H. Brackin	29 May 1841	William Stubblefield
Milner Jackson C.	Susan P. Henderson	20 Dec 1837	Thomas D. Connally
Milum James L.	Virginia Burton	21 Feb 1867	Lafayette Hudson md by E. Hunt JP
Mimms Drury A.	Martha Sawyers	18 Jul 1836	Dabney Rainey
Mimms Pinkney	Caroline Hodnett	9 Jun 1866	Jno. S. Park md by R. G. Barrett MG
Mims John W. Jr.	Martha N. Hatchitt	26 Mar 1850	Thomas L. Slade
Mims John W. Jr.	Martha A. Burns	11 Jun 1852	John W. Mims Sr.
Mims Martin M.	Susannah W. Brooks	29 Jan 1824	Jno. G. Womack
Minor Richard	Huldah Miles	1 Sep 1844	Michael Brown
Mitchall. Gilliam D. (Col)	Sarah F. Franklin (Col)	13 Oct 1855	William A. Donoho
Mitchel Charles	Ann Duty	5 Jan 1829	Thomas Bolton Cha. Willson
Mitchel David	Martha Love	30 Jan 1788	John Johnston Jr.
Mitchel Robert	Esther Love	4 Feb 1787	Edward Doyle
Mitchell Alford	Eunes Badgett	12 Jul 1836	Henderson House
Mitchell Charles	Sarah Smith	8 Dec 1803	Richard Smith William Wilkerson
Mitchell Charles	Nancy Weatherford	12 Apr 1828	Thomas Graves
Mitchell Charles G.	Martha Blackwell	23 Sep 1843	John S. Blackwell
Mitchell David	Joice Hughs	20 Feb 1823	Alexander McAlpin
Mitchell David	Joice Hughs	30 Jan 1823	Isaac Watkins
Mitchell David Jr.	Ann Anderson	24 Jun 1782	John McMullan
Mitchell David Jr.	Nancy Muzzall	12 Feb 1817	Hutchens Burton
Mitchell James	Sarah Foster	3 Oct 1826	Anthony Foster
Mitchell James E.	Margaret Murphey	18 Nov 1819	L. A. Landers
Mitchell James E.	Fanny Jones	8 Feb 1833	Jonathan Murphey
Mitchell James T.	Mildred W. Jeffreys	19 Mar 1849	William C. Paxton
Mitchell Jefferson (son of George & Becky Graves)	Martha Mitchell (dau of Pleasant Carter & Julia Mitchell)	20 Jul 1867 21 Jul	md by S. G. Mason
Mitchell John	Polly Anderson	2 Jan 1796	George Sims
Mitchell John	Fanny Scott	14 May 1800	Henry Mitchell
Mitchell John	Mary A. Neal	18 Nov 1850	John Epperson
Mitchell John	Charlotte Chavos	22 Aug 1857	Meshack Pounds md by N. M. Lewis JP
Mitchell John	Menerva Moore	5 Jun 1858 9 Jun 1858	Washington Holt md by J. B. Jackson
Mitchell John B.	Eliza C. or Sary Catherine Montgomery	17 Dec 1856 18 Dec 1856	John B. Blackwell md by John Stadler
Mitchell Milton P.	Mary W. Simpson	18 Nov 1856 20 Nov 1856	J. B. Mitchell md by John Stadler
Mitchell Randolph	Margret Terrell	4 Oct 1819	Samuel Grier

GROOM	BRIDE	DATE	BONDSMAN OR WITNESS
Mitchell Richard	Arkey Brackin	18 Dec 1821	William P. Martin
Mitchell Wiley (Col-of Danville Va.)	Rachel Freeman (Col)	25 Feb 1839	William Jenkins
Mitchell William	Salley Chandler	23 Oct 1803	John Pinson
Mitchell William	Susannah Foster	2 Oct 1826	Anthony Foster
Mitchell William	Jane Epperson	3 Jan 1857	William H. Epperson
Mitchell William M.	Minerva Malone	29 Jan 1842	Elbert Murphey
Mize Thomas	Fanney Gillam	22 Dec 1812	Alex. Murphey
Monroe Federick (Col-son of Richard & Rhoda Monroe)	Frances Brandon (Col- dau of Stephen Brandon)	2 Aug 1867 10 Aug 1867	md by J. J. Jones JP
Monroe John	Salley Sheperd	8 Feb 1787	Jno. Womack
Montgomery Abraham B.	Nancy M. Hatchitt	16 Jun 1821	David Montgomery
Montgomery Alexander	Lucy Matlock	3 Dec 1801	Francis Howard
Montgomery David G.	Mary F. Davis	30 Jun 1840	Henry W. Long
Montgomery David G.	Mary F. Davis	4 Feb 1842	Stephen L. Dodson Jr.
Montgomery Edward	Tabitha F. Pinix	22 Feb 1825	John Pittard
Montgomery Frank (Col)	Patsey Sanders (Col)	11 Oct 1866	Harry Goodwin (Col) md by J. J. Jones JP
Montgomery James	Kitty Connally	27 Oct 1807	John Montgomery
Montgomery James (Col-son of Clinton & Susan McCain	Emeline Conway (Col- dau of Wm. Hopkins & Mary Conway)	18 Aug 1867	md by J. J. Jones JP
Montgomery Michael Jr.	Lucy Davis	26 Feb 1816	David Davis
Montgomery William	Sarah Matlock	28 Feb 1804	Alexander Montgomery
Montgomery William J.	Mary Ann Foster	23 Nov 1852 25 Nov 1852	Albert G. Henderson md by P. Hodnett JP
Moor Robert	Mary Foster	20 Dec 1784	Ambrose Foster
Moore Albert	Martha Ann Allen	7 Aug 1827	Alexander Winstead
Moore Armistead	Sally Turner	14 Dec 1795	Simon Adams
Moore Austin T.	Carthrin Colman	22 Apr 1837	George W. Price
Moore Britain	Isbell Tyrrell	2 Jan 1808	Henry Burch
Moore Charles W.	Martha Smith	21 Nov 1854	James Herring
Moore Charles W.	Martha Smith	30 Oct 1858	William Sanders
Moore Eps	Elizabeth Dameron	24 Sep 1811	Moses Langley Jas. Yancey
Moore Jesse	Salley Pass	7 Jan 1785	Nathaniel Pass
Moore John	Sarah Rea	11 Apr 1821	William F. Smith
Moore John	Hester A. Fuller	9 Jan 1867	Jno. D. Paylor
Moore Joseph E.	Sariah H. Evans	3 Oct 1854 5 Oct 1854	Saml. Pittard md by B. Cooper JP
Moore Lawrence H.	Cornelia F. Oakley	1 Apr 1851	H. Oakley
Moore Lawrence H.	Arrena Oakley	29 Oct 1856 30 Oct 1856	Thomas P. Oakley md by B. Cooper JP
Moore Leonadas B.	Margaret J. McNeil	21 Oct 1844	J. W. James
Moore Matthew P.	Huldah Grynn	20 Feb 1843	James Moore
Moore Robert	Mary Drurey (dau of -- Drurey, deceased)	24 May 1780	Benjamin Long
Moore Robert	Elisabeth McGehee	24 Aug 1784	Mumford McGhe John Moore JP
Moore Robert A. (see Moor)	Elizabeth B. Hines	4 May 1859	George W. Thompson
Moore Rufus (Col)	Lucinda Slade (Col)	2 Jun 1866	Caleb A. Johnston
Moore Samuel	Elisabeth Williamson	29 Sep 1783	Hugh Hemphill

GROOM	BRIDE	DATE	BONDSMAN OR WITNESS
Moore Solomon (Col-son of Sam Lyn & Edith Owen)	Frances Gwyn (Col-dau of Simon Holderness & Ritter Gwyn)	27 Dec 1867	H. F. Brandon
Moore Spencer	Sarah Clark	16 Dec 1856	Peter F. Clark
		18 Dec 1856	md by J. M. Allen JP
Moore Stephen J.	Sarah Jane Burton	13 Aug 1859	John Matlock
Moore T. Jefferson	Sina Wadleton	20 Oct 1860	L. Fels
Moore Terrell	Ann Terrell	2 Apr 1834	Madison McMury
Moore Thomas	Ann Scoggins	6 Aug 1850	Will C. Moore
Moore Thomas A.	Mary R. Stewart	15 Sep 1851	William W. Taylor
		18 Sep 1851	md by Solomon Apple MG
Moore Thomas E.	Nancy A. Evans	24 Oct 1842	William M. Badgett
Moore Thomas J.	Darthey C. Mayo	22 Aug 1837	Zorobolb Evans B. C. West Sr.
Moore Thompson	Caroline Westbrooks	7 Sep 1835	Robert Love
Moore William	Nancey Graves	25 Nov 1799	Thomas Simmons
Moore William	Patsey Roan	10 Sep 1828	Williamson Moore Barzl. Graves
Moore William (Col-son of John & Hannah Moore)	Belle Hamlett (Col-dau of Thomas Hamlett)	28 Sep 1867	md by J. J. Jones JP
Moore William C.	Mildred Jackson	2 Apr 1856	Tho. W. Graves clk
		4 Apr 1856	md by Tho. Covington JP
Moore William D.	Elizabeth Spain	22 Nov 1851	Richard Yarbrough
Moore William G.	Martha B. Nelson	29 Oct 1842	Azariah Nelson
Moore William J.	Mary E. McNeel	21 Dec 1840	James W. James
Moore William W.	Sarah McKinney	28 Oct 1826	Peter McKinney
Moorefield John H.	Elizabeth Milam	2 Mar 1865	Timothy Dodson md by J. J. Jones JP
Moorfield James	Polly Powell	13 Sep 1816	Thomas Carter
Morefield Paul H.	Eliza E. Chaney	23 May 1860	Andrew J. Strange
		24 May 1860	md by C. H. Richmond JP
Morgan Addison	Mary Richmond	2 Dec 1839	Samuel H. Smith
Morgan Benjamin F.	Mary J. Woods	28 Nov 1848	Thomas C. Green
Morgan Daniel	Nancey Wright	15 Apr 1806	Jesse Whitlow William Wilkinson
Morgan George W.	Mary A. Dillard	23 Jul 1850	Addison Morgan
Morgan John	Nancey Stenson	27 Sep 1796	Ebenezer Whitehead
Morgan John C.	Elizabeth Waterfield	27 Jun 1827	William Stephens
Morgan L. D.	Sarah A. Evans	21 Dec 1857	Benjamin Stephens
		22 Dec 1857	md by J. B. Jackson
Morgan Lafayette	Catharine Farmer	19 Jan 1848	James C. Dobbins
Morgan Warren	Mary Woods	19 Dec 1838	John Lea Richmond
Morgan William	Reliance Paschall	17 Jan 1806	John Hinton
Morgan William	Betsey Willson	7 Sep 1812	John Hinton
Morgan William H.	Sarah Wedding	11 Oct 1838	Thomas W. Chandler
Morgan William M.	Judah Matlock	14 Jul 1847	Benjamin F. Morgan
Morris Edward J.	Araminta D. Vanhook	18 Jul 1842	William P. Anderson
Morris Edwin S.	Ann E. Fowler	18 Jan 1856	Ezekiel P. Jones
		23 Jan 1856	md by Wm. Carter
Morris James	Eliza Barnwell	10 Nov 1841	Bird H. Bateman
Morris John H.	Mary Ann Eliza Freeman	9 Sep 1832	Richard G. Lampkin
Morris John R.	Nancey Bowles	15 Feb 1830	Jesse Fuller
Morris Richard A.	Caroline Blartlett (Bartlett?)	25 Sep 1836	John Blackwell
Morris Samuel	Sally Kindrick	10 Jan 1807	Abram Price
Morris William	Betsey McGinnis	12 Mar 1786	Hugh Dobbin
Morrow Benjamin M.	Margarett Love	29 Jan 1828	George T. Winstead
Morrow Daniel	Fanny Hall	8 Oct 1790	James Wallis
Morrow John	Betsey Davis	23 Dec 1835	Thomas Fitch

GROOM	BRIDE	DATE	BONDSMAN OR WITNESS
Morrow Robert	Ann Hurley	15 Oct 1782	William Morrow
Morrow William	Salley Jay	5 Jan 1789	James Jay
Morrow William	Mary Burns	10 Jul 1793	Robert Sanders
Morton Alexander B.	Henrietta Cantril	4 Nov 1819	Elijah Martin
Morton Alexander B.	----------	16 Jun 1837	Jeremiah Lea
Morton Anderson	Letty Samuel	9 Dec 1803	Payton Morton Jr. William Wilkerson
Morton Azariah G.	Hetta C. Martin	8 Jun 1837	A. B. Morton
Morton Bedford B.	Aryann Travis	30 May 1848	James A. Hodges
Morton Edward Z.	Susannah Peterson	3 Jul 1825	John Lea
Morton Elijah	Polley Lea	5 Nov 1811	Samuel Evans
Morton George	Martha McGhee	18 Feb 1788	Meshack Morton
Morton Jesse	Betsey Burton	28 Oct 1802	Richard Vaughn
Morton John	Judah Zachory	4 Apr 1804	Samuel Morton Jr.
Morton John	Nancey Poteet	3 Jan 1820	Solomon Graves
Morton John	Matilda Manly	4 Jul 1843	Abel Kennon
Morton John	Elizabeth Harrison	22 Jul 1846	David R. Murray
Morton Martin	Mary Fuller	14 Mar 1818	Elijah Morton
Morton Step	Nancy Richmond	2 Jan 1809	George Martin Jeremiah Rudd
Morton William	Milley Samuel	31 May 1803	Samuel Dameron
Morton Williamson	Rebecca Collier	23 Dec 1822	William McKinney
Moseley John R. (Col)	Frances Johnson (Col)	25 Dec 1866 26 Dec 1866	Harry Moseley (Col) md by J. J. Jones JP
Moss Daniel B.	Sarah Williamson	14 Aug 1827	Leonard D. Prather
Moss John P.	Drucilla Shelton	12 Sep 1827	Barzillai Graves Jr.
Motheral Samuel	Sarah McMinamy	26 Dec 1782	Joseph Motheral
Motley Alfred H.	Mary J. Wright	8 Jul 1856 10 Jul 1856	Rufus L. Wright md by John Stadler
Motley Booker (Col)	Ellen Hunt (Col)	13 Oct 1867	md by Eustace Hunt JP
Motley Hartwell	Martha Hooper	22 Mar 1824	John Hooper
Motley Joel	Eliza K. Whitemore	24 Oct 1823	William W. Price
Motley Nathaniel C.	Clarender F. Hatchett	22 Oct 1853 26 Oct 1853	J. A. West md by W. M. Ferguson
Motley Thomas J.	Mary S. Johnston	17 Sep 1855 27 Sep 1855	G. P. Bailey md by John H. Pickard
Motz Andrew	Frances A. Dodson	23 Sep 1840	Henry McAden
Muirhead Claud	Elisabeth Wade	13 Jun 1781	Archibald Campbell
Mullins Jerry (Col)	Ann Bethell (Col)	19 Jan 1867	Lewis Graves md by Stephen Neal JP
Mullins Thomas	Patsey Stublefield	26 Jul 1797	Robert Mullins
Mullins Thomas	Matilda B. Mims	10 Oct 1836	Jno. W. Mims
Murphey Abraham	Mary Walker	7 Mar 1839	William Kimbro Sr.
Murphey Alexander	Polley Smith	29 Aug 1815	Herndon Haralson Jr.
Murphey Alexandre	Sarah Graves	11 Sep 1822	Pleasant Rudd
Murphey Barzel	Elizabeth Fury	21 Sep 1803	William McIntosh Wm. Wilkerson DC
Murphey Bazel	Nancy Warren	23 Dec 1846	William Cooper
Murphey James	Patsey Terrell	21 Mar 1795	Gabriel Murphey
Murphey James	Ary Nunn	14 Dec 1824	John Nunnally
Murphey James	Frances Moor	11 Aug 1825	Stephen Murphey
Murphey James	Sarah Lovelace	2 Mar 1843	Samuel Page
Murphey Jno.	Polly Corder	11 Feb 1803	Joseph McCain
Murphey John	Sarah Terrell	10 Apr 1804	James Murphey
Murphey John C.	Permilia A. Murphey	12 May 1851 15 May 1851	Lorenzo Baynes md by F. L. Warren JP
Murphey Joseph	Sally Kennon	27 Oct 1800	John Cobb
Murphey Stephen	Nancy Malone	5 Nov 1827	William Malone
Murphey Thomas	Nancy Lovelace	30 Jan 1852 -- Feb 1852	Joseph Lovelace md by Lancelot Johnston

GROOM	BRIDE	DATE	BONDSMAN OR WITNESS
Murphey Wiley	Sarah Richmond	14 Oct 1866	Yancey Richmond
			md by Jerry Smith JP
Murphey William	Lucy Terel	2 Mar 1798	Gabriel Murphey Jr.
Murphey William	Mildred Kendrick	7 Oct 1830	Jonathan Murphey
Murphey William	Aartesia Pleasant	6 Feb 1839	Jonathan Murphey
Murphey William M.	Mary Southard	28 Dec 1852	Nelson Chapman
Murphy Gabriel Jr.	Clarey Hearndon	4 Feb 1788	Nimrod McIntosh
Murphy Lewis	Louisa Thorp	10 Sep 1866	Saml. P. Hill
Murphy William (of Pittsylvania Co. Va.)	Charity Wynne (ward of Wm. Linn)	17 Apr 1832	Daniel S. Price
Murphy William H.	Susan Ann L. Smith	9 Oct 1858	Albert A. Malone
		12 Oct 1858	md by John Stadler
Murray David R.	Sarah A. McCain	6 Jul 1847	F. L. Warren
Murray Eli	Nancy Oliver (wid)	28 Jul 1845	Linsey Oliver
Murray Hector M.	Francis T. Murray	7 Jan 1843	John L. Harrison
Murray Mark S.	Izabella Farley	24 Oct 1849	A. L. Ball
Murray Thomas	Rebecca Montgomery	12 Mar 1850	Clayton Lambert
Murray Walter	Francis Warrin	4 Mar 1825	William Warren Jr.
Murray William J.	Isabella P. Carter	16 Apr 1861	Thomas A. Hudson
		18 Apr 1861	md by N. M. Lewis JP
Murrey William J.	Mary A. Brooks	24 Aug 1867	md by David Burch JP
Murrie James	Tabbitha Browning	26 Sep 1818	Charles Murrie
			Isaac Rainey
Murry Walter	Elionar Bryant	18 Jul 1797	James Rainey
			John Walters
Mustain Clark	Louisa Dodd	28 Aug 1828	Peter E. Hooper
			Cornelius West
Mustain James W.	Sally Shelton	11 Mar 1814	Virgil M. Rainy
Muzzall Joseph W.	Jean Norfleet	2 May 1815	Thomas Slade
			Isaac Rainey
Muzzall William	Mary Malone	22 Aug 1789	Deloney Malone
Muzzall William A.	Sarah Anderson (wid)	4 Sep 1838	Aleander Miles

- N -

GROOM	BRIDE	DATE	BONDSMAN OR WITNESS
Nabers William J.	Elizabeth Y. Hensley	12 Feb 1867	Sidney L. Hensley
Nance Clemmons	Frances Berry	8 Dec 1819	Elisha Berry
Nance Frederick	Polley Berry	9 Jan 1809	John Paschall
Nance Joseph W.	Emeline D. Butler	4 Jun 1853	John T. Nance
Nance Thomas	Elizabeth Clark	12 Dec 1853	E. B. Holden
		20 Dec 1853	md by N. M. Lewis JP
Nance William M.	Caroline M. T. Howard	9 Jan 1844	Richard A. Pate
Nash Alfred M.	Cornelia Snipes	30 Mar 1841	Samuel J. Evans
Nash Thomas	Rebecca Erwin	6 Jul 1784	Alexander Murphey
Neal Abram T.	Mary A. E. Owen	16 Sep 1865	David N. Atkinson
			md by J. J. Jones JP
Neal James M.	Martha E. Nunnally	18 May 1846	Jno. K. Graves
			A. G. Yancey
			E. Graves
Neal John	Nancey Lawson	22 Jan 1788	John Lawson
Neal Jno. T.	Lucy A. Howard	10 Dec 1859	James H. Womack
		11 Dec 1859	md by S. G. Mason
Neal Philemon	Nancey Simpson	8 Dec 1804	John Keen
Neal Philemon H.	Zippora J. Gwyn	5 Sep 1861	John L. Williamson
			md by S. G. Mason MG
Neal Stephen	Frances A. Turner	26 Dec 1838	William R. Neal
			Jas. M. Neal
Neal Stephen (Col)	Aggy Hamlett (Col)	19 May 1866	Mack Dixon (Col)
			md by Solomon Apple MG
Neal William R.	Martha J. Hooper	11 Nov 1846	Calvin L. Graves Jr.
Neal Zachariah	Rebecah Rice	16 Dec 1811	Oliver Simpson
			Smith Murphey

GROOM	BRIDE	DATE	BONDSMAN OR WITNESS
Nealy John	Peggy Durham	6 May 1819	Rawley Kearn
			Elijah Withers
Neblett Colin	Victoria C. Garland	24 Oct 1855	James H. M. Neblett
Neeley Garnett	Anne Dollerhide	7 Jun 1801	Robert Hamlet
Nelson Ambrose	Nama Bracher	9 Sep 1817	Thomas Evans
			Isaac Rainey
Nelson Ambrose	Frances Bradsher	10 Jul 1822	Vincent Bradsher
Nelson Azariah	Eliza Evans	10 Dec 1842	Stephen C. Nelson
Nelson Barzillai	Margarett Owens	26 Aug 1822	Samuel Nelson
Nelson Iverson	Mary Hightower	12 Apr 1841	James Thomas
Nelson James	Mercy Terrel	1 Feb 1816	James Terrel
			Isaac Rainey
Nelson James (Col-son of Bird & Lucy Gunter)	Jane Stamps (Col-dau of Warner & Eliza Stamps)	18 Aug 1867	H. F. Brandon md by J. J. Jones JP
Nelson Joel H.	Tameran Cox	19 Dec 1842	James Jones
Nelson John B.	Elizabeth Marr	20 Dec 1852	William M. Sadler
Nelson John H.	Elizabeth Jones	28 Jul 1848	John J. Case
			M. J. Palmer
Nelson Samuel	Harriotte Prendergast	14 Nov 1820	Alfred Parks
New John D.	Malinda C. Perkins	13 Nov 1866	Thomas N. Carlton
			md by N. M. Lewis JP
Newbell John	Rebecca Seal	19 Sep 1828	Joseph Bohannon
Newby Asa R.	Sophia Angles	11 May 1859	Layton T. Dodson
			md by N. M. Lewis JP
Newman A. B.	Mary F. Chandler	29 Apr 1867	
		1 May	md by Jacob Doll
Newman Aaron (Col)	Susan Richmon (Col)	2 Aug 1866	Alfred Fuller (Col)
Newman Anderson B.	Elizabeth E. Moore	11 Dec 1851	John G. Woody
		17 Dec 1851	md by Solomon Apple
Newman Remus (Col)	Sarah Richmond (Col)	14 Jan 1866	Burley Richmond (Col)
Newman Robert	Adeline T. Stewart	16 Nov 1849	Joseph M. Stanfield
Newman Washington	Leticia Walker	5 Dec 1838	James Dobbins
Newman Wm.	Sarah Williams	17 Nov 1866	Hampton Johnston
Newton Henry	Mildred White	23 Mar 1791	Thomas Carver
Newton John G.	Judith Crider	14 Oct 1818	John Miles
Nicholls Isaac	Sarah London	27 Oct 1825	Samuel Walker
Nichols David A.	Martha Taylor	13 Dec 1849	E. J. Hall
			M. P. Huntington
Nichols James E.	Martha Parrish	18 Jul 1867	md by N. M. Lewis JP
Nichols John W.	Jane M. Furgerson	27 Nov 1866	Bevin D. Oliver
Nichols Wright	Sarah Burch	11 Jan 1791	John Tapley
Nicholson Joseph	Margarett Fielder	3 Feb 1829	John J. Fielder
Nickols Isaac	Anny Norman	25 Dec 1818	Westly Norman
Nightin James	Peggy Walker	7 Jan 1814	Edmund Lyon
			D. W. Simpson DC
Nighton Turner	Sarah Glaze	2 Jan 1849	John H. Pickard
Nipper James	Susanah Pleppa	5 Aug 1809	William Gordon
Nipper Samuel	Tabitha Gordon	23 Nov 1816	William Gordon
Noble Andrew	Louisa Ann E. Moore	4 Dec 1857	John H. Maynard
Noble John	Frances Payne	6 Apr 1807	William Linn
Noel Ephraim	Nancey Boman	13 Dec 1803	Joseph Richmond
Norfleet James S.	Ursula G. McNeel	11 Feb 1826	Alexander Winstead
			John H. Graves
Norfleet M. W.	M. E. Kirkpatrick	14 Dec 1864	S. Dickson
		15 Dec 1864	md by Jacob Doll MG
Norfleet Marmaduke	Mary Roan	5 Dec 1833	Thomas W. Owen
Norman Charles H.	Mary S. Norman	11 Feb 1856	George W. Thompson
			R. A. Newbell
		26 Feb 1856	md by J. B. Jackson
Norman Henry J.	Louisa S. Cahal (dau of Barney Cahal)	11 Mar 1852	James Poteat
			George C. Cahal
			Wm. H. Nance
			md by Thos S. Campbell

GROOM	BRIDE	DATE	BONDSMAN OR WITNESS
Norman James B.	Martha E. Cahal (dau of Barney Cahal)	11 Mar 1852	George C. Cahal Wm. H. Nance md by Thos S. Campbell
Norman Wesley	Elizabeth Barnett	24 May 1816	Maj. Brockman Jr.
Norman William	Milcey West	14 Jan 1812	John Norman
Norman William	Nancy Yates	3 Jul 1845	A. Slade
Norman William	Betsey Harris (wid)	9 Oct 1850	Henry Trice
Norman William (see Knorman)	Nancy Bays	1 Dec 1858	Levi C. Page
Normond William	Priscilla Cook	28 May 1825	William Cook
Norris William	Sally K. Owen	1 Oct 1840	Henry W. Long
Northern T. H.	S. Jane Smith	29 Jun 1854	R. A. Newbell md by J. M. Allen JP
Norvell Braxton	Mildred Ann Philips	28 Dec 1830	George W. Taylor Richard H. L. Bennatt
Nowel Ephraim	Sarah Siddel	27 Dec 1787	James Kimbro
Nowels William	Rebeccah Hailey	1 Jul 1812	Thomas Reed
Nowls John	Mileah Dawson	29 Sep 1807	William Noles Abraham B. Morton
Nunn Admiral N.	Anna Sartin	26 Jan 1836	James J. Gomer
Nunn Carlton (of Rockingham Co.)	Martha Stanback	25 Jan 1820	Joseph A. Taylor (Rockingham Co.)
Nunn James	Mary Jane Waters	27 Dec 1860	Alfred G. Stanley md by Stephen Neal JP
Nunn Miller	Susan B. Swann	10 Oct 1859	Philemon H. Neal md by Alfred Norman MG
Nunn William	Hannah Bastin	26 Oct 1830	John Cahall
Nunnally Archelaus	Pamelea Gatewood	4 Mar 1822	Merry Maynard
Nunnally Archelaus	Caroline Spence	14 Sep 1835	John S. Oglesby
Nunnally Hartwell (Col-son of Mericus & Maria Cobb)	Jane Pinnix (Col-dau of Stephen & Ann McNeil)	9 Nov 1867	H. F. Brandon clk
Nunnally Jas.	Lucy Farish	18 Apr 1866	Saml. Gunn
Nunnally James S.	Tabetha H. Gillaspy	21 Jan 1824	Alexander Gillaspy
Nunnally John	Sytha Anne Withers	22 Jul 1817	Elijah Withers
Nunnally John (Col)	Nancy Fitzgerald (Col)	21 Dec 1865	Thomas P. Neal md by Jas. A. Hodges JP
Nunnally John H.	Susan L. Withers	13 Jun 1854	James M. Neal
		20 Jun 1854	md by John Stadler MG
Nunnally William H.	Nancy Price	6 May 1823	Henry Cobb
Nutt Absalom	Frances Leath	4 Aug 1821	William Bruce
Nutt David D.	Agness Jackson	18 Apr 1816	Nicholas Hightower

- 0 -

Oakeley Thos.	Elizabeth Crossix	16 Nov 1820	J. W. McMurry
Oakley Alexander	Parthenia Broughton	19 Feb 1833	James W. Sadler
Oakley Archibald	Jirilla Smith	13 Mar 847	Franklin L. Warren
Oakley F. L.	Frances A. Rudd	25 Oct 1866	Thomas L. Rudd F. M. Neal md by Robt. Shreve
Oakley William	Nancey Ashley	4 Dec 1790	Millintun Blalack
Oakly Thomas P.	Susan J. Cooper	18 Dec 1856	Thomas B. Smith W. A. Vernon DC
		21 Dec 1856	md by William Burns
OBriant E. M.	Eliza Cooper	10 Dec 1866	H. F. Brandon clk
Oglesby John S.	Sarah P. Allen	7 Oct 1834	Joseph McDowell
Old William B. (son of Robert T. Old of Halifax Co. Va.)	Sallie P. Tucker (dau of Robert Tucker of Halifax Co. Va.)	21 Apr 1867	md by John Jones JP

GROOM	BRIDE	DATE	BONDSMAN OR WITNESS
Oldham George	Hennritta Stacey	6 Jan 1807	David Henslee
Oldham John	Anne Rice	26 Feb 1783	Hezekiah Rice
Oldham Richard	Ursley D. Peoples	20 Oct 1786	Jeri Poston
Oliver Alva	Betsey Holloway	13 Feb 1792	Nathan Holloway
Oliver Bivin D. (son of Bivin M. & Permelia Oliver)	Helen M. Ball (dau of Alfred L. Ball)	2 Dec 1867 5 Dec 1867	md by S. A. Stanfield
Oliver Charles J.	Amandar Jones	22 Sep 1835	John McDaniel
Oliver Creed T.	Jane D. Harrison	15 Jan 1830	Isaac O. Stanfield Chs. Willson
Oliver Douglas	Milley Kernall	18 Mar 1783	Geor Elliott
Oliver Durrett	Matilda Lea	2 Nov 1811	James Lea
Oliver Iverson L.	Mary T. Coverington	8 Nov 1859 13 Nov 1859	John G. Oliver md by Jacob Doll MG
Oliver Jerry	Silvy Williamson	22 Dec 1866	Robin Covington md by James K. Lea
Oliver John M.	Virginia H. Pamplin	15 Nov 1865	William A. Oliver md by J. J. Jones JP
Oliver Josiah	Nicey M. Phelps	12 Dec 1834	Andrew W. Stephens
Oliver Linsey	Martha Ann Willis	24 May 1842	A. Slade
Oliver Monroe	Ann L. Hooper	22 May 1860 24 May 1860	Jerry Smith md by J. Doll MG
Oliver Reuben	Nancy Lea	17 Jan 1824	Dabney Rainey
Oliver Yancy	Judith Lea	22 Dec 1826	Joel Jones
Olvis John	Addeline Cock	20 May 1833	Daniel S. Price Cary W. West Benj. C. West
O'Neill John	Hannah Ware	20 Dec 1790	William Ware
Orr Ezekiel J.	Annie J. Forrest	14 Oct 1867 15 Oct 1867	md by Jacob Doll MG
Orr Robert	Frances Swift	2 Jan 1811	William Orr
Orr Samuel	Nancey Swift	16 Mar 1813	Robert Orr
Orr William	Catharine Paschall	9 Nov 1804	James Orr
Outlaw Samuel (son of Dennis & Bettie Outlaw)	Margaret Pinnix (dau of Louisa Pinnix)	16 May 1867	H. F. Brandon clk
Overby Owen	Puritha Wilkerson	19 Apr 1825	Henry D. Fuqua
Overby Samuel	Sarah Coile	11 Oct 1830	Enoch Coyles
Overby Thomas	Levina Hicks	13 Aug 1827	Samuel Hodge
Overby Thomas	Mahaley J. West	5 Feb 1833	Benjamin C. West Jr.
Overstreet John	Mary Overstreet	1 Apr 1779	James Ingram William Overstreet
Overstreet Robert	Rhody Wilkerson	27 Oct 1801	Thomas Hightower
Owen Alfred	Perlina Tucker	25 Jun 1860	Theodore Owen M. P. Huntington
Owen Elza W.	Margaret A. Roan	1 May 1847	James N. Fuller
Owen Henry S.	Rebeccah Nelson	28 Sep 1842	John Bolton
Owen John	Nancy Martin	5 Nov 1788	Robert Martin
Owen John	Martha Owen	25 Jan 1825	William M. Terell
Owen Peter	Lucy Jones	22 Dec 1842	Henry Sawyer Geo. W. Swepson
Owen Reuben P.	Martha M. Holcomb	17 Nov 1820	John Holcomb
Owen Sharod	Martha Harris	14 Oct 1815	Henry Shelton
Owen Thomas W.	Mildred Thomas	28 Jan 1834	Maramduke Norfleet
Owen Thomas W.	Penelope M. Vanhook	28 Oct 1845	James McMullin
Owen William	Polly Rowark	11 Nov 1794	John Hargis
Owens Andrew J. (Col)	Adalaide Hinton (Col)	23 Aug 1865	John Camp md by J. J. Jones JP
Owens William T.	Martha E. A. H. Edgar (dau of Wm. Edgar of Bedford Co. Va.)	9 Jan 1842	Oliver Powell
Owin David	Polley Martin	21 Sep 1798	Robert Martin

GROOM	BRIDE	DATE	BONDSMAN OR WITNESS
Oxford Jonathan	Susanah Cannon	12 Dec 1784	William Cannon
			Josiah Cole
Oyler James T. (son of Clemens & Nancey Oyler)	Louisa J. Morgan (dau of Jubila & Irena Morgan)	24 Oct 1867	H. F. Brandon md by W. W. Duncan

- P -

Padgett Joseph M.	Mary J. Vermillion	8 Oct 1841	Alfred M. Nash
Padgett Tinsley	Elizabeth Powell	14 Jan 1833	Benjamin C. West Jr.
Page Albert M. (son of W. A. & Silvia)	Nannie L. Simpson (dau of S. Simpson)	-- --- 1867 12 Dec	md by F. L. Oakley MG
Page Azariah*	Anna Smith	19 Oct 1831	Zenith Page
Page Benjamin	Jane Scarlett	10 Apr 1832	Zenith Page
Page Bentley W.	Lucy Terrell	29 Sep 1843	William N. Kimbro Jr.
Page Daniel J.	Elizabeth Page	25 Jan 1860 26 Jan 1860	William L. Page md by Stephen Neal JP
Page Franklin B.	Milly D. McKinny	29 Jul 1859 4 Aug 1859	Nathaniel Hooper md by John Stadler MG
Page James	Betsey Adkens	22 Feb 1802	John Page
Page James	Mary Willis	24 Nov 1830	Stephen Page
Page James	Sally Herndon	20 Oct 1855 25 Oct 1855	Nathan Oakley md by Jno. C. Pinnix
Page James B.	Mary C. Gunn	15 Oct 1865	B. J. Page
Page James H.	Eady Robertson	20 Dec 1860 23 Dec 1860	H. Page md by H. F. Adkins
Page James P.	Margarett Boswell	16 Dec 1837	Deverex Hightower
Page John	Betsey Perkins	10 Nov 1806	George Stovall
Page Joseph F.	Amy Brintle	3 Feb 1832	Jesse C. Page
Page Josiah	Henritta Page	5 Apr 1827	John Moris
Page Levi C.	Marinda C. Vernon	21 jul 1841	Philip Hodnett
Page Milton	Ann R. Adkins	12 Oct 1839	Azariah Foster
Page Noah	Susan Peterson	10 Jan 1820	Benjamin Dameron
Page Samuel	Delila Page	21 Dec 1819	Jesse Foster
Page Stephen	Elizabeth Shepard	11 Jan 1832	Joseph Pinson
Page Thomas	Nancey Vaughn	19 Feb 1800	James Page
Page Whitehead	Jenny Atkins	23 Dec 1795	Thomas Page
Page Whitehead (or Coleman Joshua)	Betsey Wright	15 Dec 1809	Joshua Wright (or Coleman)
Page Whitehead	Rachel King	20 Mar 1815	James Page James Yancey
Page William	Nancey Cobb (or Nancey Whitehead)	31 Dec 1796	Whitehead Page
Page William	Mary Manley	9 Dec 1854	James P. Boswell
Page William	Lily Bowe	19 Nov 1866	Moore Williamson md by Thomas J. Brown
Page William A.	Silviah Stalcup	9 Dec 1833	Stephen Page
Page William C.	Jane E. Grant	10 Dec 1844	Addison A. Williamson T. H. Miles
Page William C.	Martha A. Pleasant	28 Dec 1848	Levi C. Page
Page William M.	Celia Foster	5 Nov 1839	Milton Page
Page Zachariah (son of James & Elizabeth Page)	Frances Pinson (dau of Joseph & Lucy Pinson)	1 Oct 1867 10 Oct	H. F. Brandon clk md by F. L. Oakley MG
Page Zenith	Martha Cobb	20 Mar 1837	John H. Faucett
Page Zenith	Mary Page	6 Apr 1858	A. L. Reid md by John H. Picken
Paisley John	Jane Crossett	25 Apr 1828	James Crosset
Palmer Clem (Colson of James Barnett & Lucy Palmer)	Mary B. Blackwell (Col)	16 Sep 1867 19 Sep 1867	md by Jacob Doll MG

GROOM	BRIDE	DATE	BONDSMAN OR WITNESS
Palmer Dabney	Fanny Barge	30 Dec 1848	William C. Adams
Palmer John	Eliza Ann Freeman	12 May 1862	B. Y. McAden
			md by S. G. Mason
Palmer Joyner	Susan Hightower	16 Feb 1850	Thomas Moore
Pamplin James	Susan J. Childress	20 Dec 1866	Nicholas P. Oliver
			md by J. J. Jones JP
Panton Scott	Amanda Hairston	27 Dec 1867	
(Col-son of	(Col-dau of Lewis		md by J. J. Jones JP
Minger & Rhoda	& Harriett		
Rhoda Cobb)	Hairston)		
Parish James	Anthy Sawyers	12 Oct 1826	Stairling H. Gunn
Parish William T.	Mary A. Totten	-- --- ----	
		28 Oct 1856	md by John H. Pickard MG
Park Jno. S.	Mary Jane Mims	4 Dec 1856	F. J. Dennis
			md by James P. Simpson
Park M. A.	Nannie L. Crutchfield	17 Dec 1866	R. J. West
		20 Dec 1866	md by W. W. Duncan
Parker Byrd G.	Elizabeth Sargent	6 Aug 1807	Thomas Trotter
Parker Jephtha	Jincey White	2 Oct 1813	William Kiersey
Parker Powel	Nancy Lumpkin	24 Dec 1787	David Parker
Parker William	Ursley Kersey	20 Oct 1798	Wila Jones
Parker William	Betsey Williams	15 Dec 1801	John Williams
Parks Alfred	Polley Nelson	11 Mar 1806	Hiram Parks
Parks Hiram	Lucy Vaughn	2 Jan 1799	Vaughn Scott
Parks James N.	Malinda Walker	20 Oct 1843	Jno. K. Brooks
Parks Jeptha	Libbie Culberson	14 Sep 1800	George Prendergast
Parks Robert	Lucinda Henslee	19 Jun 1825	James Arnold
Parks Robert G.	Polley McClary	26 Feb 1803	Richard Vaughn
Parks Samuel B.	Mary Ann Currie	2 Jun 1845	Zachariah P. Pattillo
Parks Solomon	Avey Atkinson	20 Dec 1782	Hearndon Haralson
Parks William	Hannah Corder	9 Mar 1798	Van Scott
Parr William	Elizabeth Norton	26 Dec 1788	William Norton
Parrett Thomas	Margaret Long	10 Jan 1860	J. H. Butler
Parrish A. P.	S. A. Fulks	4 Dec 1860	T. C. Oakes
			md by Jacob Doll MG
Parrish James	Zilla Blackwell	25 May 1861	
		29 May	md by Jacob Doll MG
Parrish John J.	Emily N. Ford	18 Jul 1867	md by N. M. Lewis JP
Paschael William	Nancy Paschael	14 Jan 1840	Samuel W. Bethel
Paschal Elisha	Martha F. Harrelson	12 Feb 1857	William T. Parish
		17 Feb 1857	md by J. H. Pickard MG
Paschal Ezekiel D.	Eliza E. Parrish	9 Oct 1850	Richard Miles
Paschal Jesse D.	Eliza A. Canaday	6 Mar 1861	Philemon H. Neal
			md by E. K. Withers JP
Paschal John H.	Parthena A. Totten	18 Oct 1860	John W. Justice
			md by Stephen Neal JP
Paschall Elisha	Patcey Sanders	13 Jan 1813	Forester Stainback
Paschall Jerry (Col)	Betsey Howard (Col)	29 Dec 1865	Iverson Howard (Col)
		6 Jan 1866	md by M. A. Turner JP
Paschall William D.	Susannah Davis	17 Nov 1819	Elisha Paschall
Paschell Thomas	Nancy Price	11 Feb 1789	William Paschell
Paskel John	Martha Jane Justice	-- --- ----	
		20 Nov 1854	md by John Stadler
Pass Fantelleroy	Frances Pruett	10 Mar 1837	Reubin Morgan
Pass Hollaway	Kiziah Robinson	21 Dec 1785	James Robinson
Pass James M.	Harriet A. Chambers	30 Aug 1851	George W. Gunn
Pass John	Delany Birch	28 May 1820	Danl. T. Merritt
			Tho. Donoho Jr.
Pass John A.	Judith Buckner	7 Jan 1823	Benj. Clabon West
Pass Nathaniel Jr.	Milley Tapley	9 Jul 1794	George Stephens
Pass Nathaniel W.	Frances Buckner	22 Feb 1821	James Murphy
Pass Seth W.	Elizabeth Tate	7 Oct 1840	Allen J. Cunnaway

GROOM	BRIDE	DATE	BONDSMAN OR WITNESS
Pass Thomas C.	Jane N. Roper	19 Dec 1837	Thomas Reed
Pass Thomas C.	Nancy Samuels	3 Nov 1859	Samuel Watkins md by C. H. Richmond JP
Pass Thomas Y.	Sally Rudder (dau of Jane Rudder)	26 Nov 1826	John A. Pass
Pass William H.	Elizabeth Chambers	29 Nov 1847	Andrew W. Stephens
Pate Richard A.	Susan T. Wooding	7 Jan 1848	Samuel B. Holder
Paterson John	Mary Ann Taylor	26 Jul 1838	William Mullin
Patterson Turner	Celia Tennisson	25 Jul 1808	Levy Tennisson
Patterson Turner	Sarah E. Durham	5 Jun 1866 6 Jun 1866	Robert J. Bayes md by W. B. Swann JP
Patterson William B.	Leah Powell	19 May 1843	Christian Strader
Pattillo Albert A.	Eliza Ann Dodson	21 May 1838	Thomas Bigelow
Pattillo Anderson H. W.	Mary E. Adkins	3 Sep 1866 13 Sep 1866	Thomas J. Walker md by F. M. Jordan
Pattillo Lewis A.	Lucinda Baswell	22 Jan 1839	Thomas Bigelow
Pattillo William	Margaret Gunn	29 Dec 1866	A. A. Pattillo
Pattillo Zachariah	Mary Jordon	10 Dec 1814	James Harrison Jeremiah Rudd
Pattillo Zachariah A.	Elizabeth B. Willis	22 May 1847	Yancey Jones
Patton John D.	Mary Jack McAlpin	27 Dec 1853	Wm. B. Graves md by Jno. S. Grasty
Pattoson David	Sally Chambers	27 Mar 1781	John Chambers
Paul Asa	Pembrook Anthony	27 Aug 1803	Thomas Gooch
Paul James	Lettice Hightower	13 Feb 1795	Samuel Paul
Paul James	Rebeccah Fawling	25 Sep 1797	Isekiah Farley
Paul Robert	Priscilla Burton	28 May 1781	Samuel Paul
Paul Samuel	Judith Burton	14 Jan 1784	Robert Paul J. Campbell Wm. McAden
Paul Samuel	Elizabeth Lea	22 Mar 1819	Vincent Peterson
Paxton William C.	Harriet H. Burton (wid)	19 May 1852	D. W. Wilkinson md by Thomas S. Campbell
Paylor James H.	M. V. Pattillo	14 Mar 1865	J. J. James
Paylor Moses	Laura Reid	2 Feb 1867 14 Feb 1867	Abb Morton J. Smith md by David Burch JP
Payne Daniel	Elizabeth Harrel	22 Jan 1806	William Bruce
Payne John	Ann Hensley	5 Mar 1779	John Henslee Wm. Campbell
Payne John	Priscilla Gunn	-- Sep 1802	Thomas Harrison
Payne John	Betsey Chandler	10 Nov 1811	James Page
Payne Robert	Eliz. McKenney	14 Sep 1807	James Vaughan Sr.
Payne Thomas W.	Polly Shocklee	16 Sep 1821	Robert B. Shocklee Elijah Withers
Payne William	Ann Elizabeth Dabbs	24 Nov 1853	Luther Y. Rudd md by Howell Boswell
Peale Anderson Newman	Sarah Jane Bushnell	27 Apr 1857 28 Apr 1857	James M. Bushnell md by Thomas W. Tobey
Peale Jonathan	Margaret Bushnell	7 Oct 1845	James M. Bushnell
Pearce James S.	Sarah J. Strader	6 Feb 1867 7 Feb 1867	David Strader md by Jno. D. Keesee
Pearce Obadiah	Parthena Wallace	21 Jan 1829	Allen Wallis
Pearson Thomas	Nancy Ennet	30 Dec 1815	David Watson
Pemberton William B.	Nancy Stubblefield	1 Jul 1819	Wyatt Stubblefield Elijah Withers
Penick Giles A.	A. B. McGill	21 Feb 1866	Wm. H. Pattillo md by W. S. Penick MG
Peoples Reuben	Ursly Duke Williams	1 Feb 1783	William Rice
Perkins Jesse	Susanah Ingram	19 Aug 1795	James Burton

GROOM	BRIDE	DATE	BONDSMAN OR WITNESS
Perkins John	Mary A. Powell	10 Feb 1846	Augustus Gwynn
Perkins John	Virginia Smith	27 Nov 1862	Rawley McLaughlan
		29 Nov 1862	md by Wm. W. Taylor JP
Perkins Logan	Elgy Landrum	1 Feb 1845	John Perkins
			T. H. Miles
Perkins Martin	Dicey Sawyer	21 Aug 1787	James Perkins
Perkins Martin	Elizabeth Sawyer	2 Dec 1833	Owen McAleer
			Henderson House
Perkins Nathan	Cloeyann Lovelass	5 Oct 1832	Joel Stanley
Perkins William	Polly Yates	26 Dec 1811	David Boyd
Perrow Stephen W.	Virginia Henrick	16 May 1839	Horatio Depriest
			B. C. West
			R. J. West
Perry William	Anne Johnston	19 Nov 1792	Thomas Bruce
Perryman William	Nancy Stokes	16 Jan 1782	Richd. Crook
Peryman Richard	Mary Fleeming	7 Apr 1794	Abraham Dunaway
Peterson James O.	Mary F. Murray	13 May 1858	James W. James
		30 may 1858	md by Benj. Wells JP
Peterson Joseph Jr.	Sinty Stafford	7 Sep 1790	Joseph Peterson Sr.
Peterson Thomas	Anne Brown	1805-1807	James Ingram
Peterson Vincent	Polly Peterson	19 May 1821	Noah Page
Peterson William	Patsey Nowles	20 Jan 1814	William Nowles
			D. W. Simpson
Peterson Williamson	Nancey Fergis	22 Dec 1835	Sterling S. Kent
Petterford Levi T.	Elizabeth Hart	30 Jul 1861	Alexander Hart
Pettigrue Charles Lemuel	Adeline Tate	28 Dec 1855	John A. Pettigrue
			md by Wm. B. Bowe JP
Pharoah John	-------	21 Oct 1789	John Willingham
Phelps Ambrose	Sally Dye	19 Aug 1796	Larking Phelps
Phelps Henry J. (Col-son of Robin & Lucy Lewis)	Lucy Wilson (Col-dau of Mike & Lucindy Wilson)	13 Oct 1867	md by N. M. Lewis JP
Phelps Hirum	Sarah Pass	6 Oct 1818	William Williams
Phelps James L.	Temperance Stevens	19 Nov 1866	Lawson Earp
			md by John J. Jones JP
Phelps Larking	Anna Dye	19 Aug 1796	Willis B. Smith
Phelps Levi	Leathy M. Walters	25 Jul 1866	Robert R. Wiles
			md by J. J. Jones JP
Phelps Obediah	Peggy Dye	28 Dec 1796	James Randal
Phelps Reubin	Mary M. Taylor	16 May 1848	Fleming Word
			M. P. Huntington
Phelps Robt. C.	Ann E. Foster	24 Feb 1858	Jasper Fleming
			md by J. B. Jackson
Phelps Thomas	Mary Pass	17 Dec 1791	Jesse Moore
Phelps William	Jane Warrin	10 Jan 1786	Shadrack Hudson
Philips Federick	Margaret Bass	14 Jan 1846	Thos. Hardison
Philips John	Emilea A. Campbell	8 Oct 1840	Walter H. Lunsford
Philips William (Col)	Elisabeth Hughes (Col)	25 Dec 1857	William M. Richardson
			R. A. Newbell
Phillips Ben.	J. Briggs	12 Dec 1860	D. Burch
			A. Harralson dpt
Phillips Franklin	Evelena Campbell	4 Jan 1841	Irby Phillips
			Calvin Simpson
Phillips Hugh	Cathrine Wilson	22 Jan 1814	William Wilson
Phillips Joshua	Polly Griffin	1 Nov 1802	Solomon Merritt
Phillips Paul C.	Mary C. Powell	17 Oct 1863	Weldon H. Lunsford
			md by John D. Long JP
Pickrel Henry	Elizabeth Boswell	6 Oct 1854	Wm. D. H. Norcutt
			md by J. Jennings JP

GROOM	BRIDE	DATE	BONDSMAN OR WITNESS
Pierce Gabriel (Col)	Virginia James (Col)	19 Nov 1865	King Watkins md by J. J. Jones JP
Pike Joshua	Sally Mallory	1 Mar 1805	Tho. Mallory
Pike Lewis	Mary Berry	10 Jan 1787	Stephen Dill
Pike Samuel R.	Martha Ann Barker (dau of Henrietta Barker)	1 Jan 1852	Samuel D. Crowder md by Wm. P. Graves JP
Piles Albert	Mahala Bass	8 Oct 1855	R. A. Newbell md by Geo. W. Thompson
Piles Henry (Col)	Susan Philips (Col)	1 Jul 1858	B. Harralson
Piles Henry (Col)	Emily Brannum (Col)	27 May 1861	md by N. M. Lewis JP
Piles James	Salley Ashford	23 Oct 1802	Jno. Landers
Pinchback John W.	Helen E. Jeffreys	19 Jul 1841	Samuel C. Cobb
Pinix Alexander K.	Harriet S. Harrison	28 Apr 1848	Jno. M. O'Brian
Pinnix Benjamin	Almeda Simpson	12 Feb 1840	G. J. Farish
Pinnix Frank (Col-son of Peter Garrant & Anne Pinnix)	Sally Miles (Col-dau of Amos & Eliza Miles)	5 Jul 1867	H. F. Brandon clk
Pinnix George W.	Mary U. Graves	18 Sep 1854 19 Sep 1854	Dr. Allen Gunn md by Thomas W. Tobey MG
Pinnix James (Col-son of William & Matilda Simpson)	Frances Snipes (Col-dau of John More & Hannah Snipes)	1 Feb 1868	H. F. Brandon
Pinnix Jerry (Col-son of Eli & Adam Pinnix)	Priscilla Walker (Col-dau of Wm. & Eliza Walker)	11 Oct 1867 12 Oct	md by A. G. Anderson
Pinnix John	Barbary Spencer	8 Dec 1780	George Barker
Pinnix John (son of Geo. & Phillis Gunn)	Martha Gunn (dau of Maria Gunn)	10 Jun 1867	md by R. G. Barrett MG
Pinnix John C.	Barbarah E. Davis	27 Mar 1844	James M. Brookes
Pinnix Joseph	Betsey Kerr	22 Jan 1816	Christopher W. Brookes
Pinnix Robert	Martha Pinnix	2 Sep 1866	James Smith md by Jerry Smith JP
Pinson Drury	Susanna Smith	18 Oct 1816	John McNeill Williams
Pinson Isaac	Rebeccah Pinson	15 Dec 1810	James Graves Stephen D. Watkins
Pinson Joseph	Lucey Chandler	11 Jan 1832	Stephen Page
Pinson Thomas	Patsy Smith	19 Feb 1823	Richard Smith
Piper Robert P.	Ann Kent	13 Oct 1858	James B. Jackson
Pitman John	Sarah Cook	10 Apr 1794	James Williamson
Pitman John Jr.	Eliza Marit	18 Oct 1823	Noah Page
Pitmon Moses	Eliza Hightower	13 Jan 1846	James Malone
Pittard Benjamin S.	Agness S. Richmond	7 Jan 1839	Jno. Pittard
Pittard Benjamin S.	Susan A. Richmond	5 Nov 1859	md by Az. Graves JP
Pittard Davis	Lucy Terrell	30 Nov 1840	Robert D. Mitchell
Pittard Jno.	Mary L. Stanfield	19 Dec 1851	Calvin D. Vernon
Pittard Martin (Col)	Malissa Garland (Col)	18 May 1867	md by J. J. Jones JP
Pittard Samuel	Elizabeth Samuel	21 Dec 1790	John Ragsdale
Pittard Samuel	Sarah F. Dameron (wid)	13 Mar 1866	John H. Burton md by David Burch JP
Pitts James S.	Narsissus McCulloch	26 Jan 1859	Rufus W. McCulloch
Plats Frank	Mary C. Lester	21 Apr 1864	James M. Hudson md by W. B. Swann JP
Pleasant Beauford	Elizabeth Henslee	31 Oct 1810	William Henslee
Pleasant Beaufort	Sarah Henslee	21 Jan 1822	Thomas Henslee
Pleasant John	Frances H. Florence	13 Dec 1860 14 Dec 1860	William McNutt md by G. W. Prendergast JP

GROOM	BRIDE	DATE	BONDSMAN OR WITNESS
Pleasant John H.	Martha E. Miles	5 Sep 1838	George W. Lamkin
Pleasant Micajah Jr.	Nancy Murray	7 May 1827	John Chandler
Pleasant Pinkney J.	Elizabeth Miles	6 Oct 1849	William C. Page
Pleasant Ruffin	Sarah Enocks	18 Feb 1823	John Clindinan
Pleasant Stephen W. (son of Wm. B. & Nancey)	Sarah E. Lunsford (dau of C. W. & Elizabeth)	13 Jan 1868 15 Jan 1868	H. F. Brandon clk md by S. G. Mason
Pope John	Elisabeth Parks	12 Jan 1793	Solomon Parks
Poe Jonathan	Tabitha Lannom	-- --- 1804	Obediah Florence
Pogue Daniel	Salley Tomson	10 Aug 1814	Ludwell Worsham Benj. C. West
Pogue Joshua	Jinsey Thomas	13 Jul 1804	John Roberts Jr.
Pollard Joseph B.	Catharine J. Norris	17 Nov 1865	Jarvis Friou md by J. J. Jones JP
Pond James	Elisabeth Standbury	16 Jan 1786	Caleb Carman
Pond Walter	Elleonor Hardegree	28 Jul 1795	John Carman
Ponds Benjamin	Milley Swan	19 Jan 1807	William Alford
Peel Isaac	Cindy Poteate	9 Jan 1867 12 Jan 1867	Tillman Burton md by David Burch JP
Pool Lea	Sally Swift	21 May 1866 9 Jun 1866	Saml. Currie md by D. Burch JP
Poore Thomas S.	Elizabeth McCain	21 Nov 1842	Wm. T. Smith
Poore Thomas S.	Mary E. Covington	21 Jul 1852	N. E. Graves md by N. M. Lewis JP
Pope Abraham	Elizabeth Farley	24 Jan 1820	Steuart Farley
Posey Alexander	Patsey Oliver	9 Aug 1816	Yancy Oliver
Poston Jeremiah	Elizabeth Warson	3 May 1779	Wm. Campbell
Poston William	Edy Tait	29 Jan 1803	Sol. Debow
Poteat Alex.	Mary Morgan	21 Jan 1867 25 Jan 1867	Ransom Poteat md by Jerry Smith JP
Poteat Allen	Isabella Smith	30 Aug 1866	Abner Pirant
Poteat Charles	Frances Smith	27 Dec 1866	William Poteat md by A. A. Pattillo JP
Poteat George	Fannie Richmond	26 Jan 1867	md by David Burch JP
Poteat James	Isabella G. Roberts	14 Oct 1837	Stairling S. Kent
Poteat James	Julia A. McNeill	17 Nov 1855	J. N. Montgomery
Poteat John Jr.	Elizabeth Horton	8 Feb 1859	John Hall md by Wm. B. Bowe JP
Poteat Thomas	Martha Rudd	22 Dec 1834	Solomon Corbett
Poteat Thomas	Nanny Scott	17 Dec 1855	Lewis W. Dishong
Poteat William	Subrina Pyrant	22 Mar 1856 23 Mar 1856	Joseph Cannon md by Thomas W. Tobey MG
Poteet James	Tempy Lyon	11 Nov 1801	Miles Poteet J. G. Murphey DC
Poteet Miles	Susanah Tapley	12 May 1796	Solomon Merritt
Poteet Miles Jr.	Rebecca Hunter	10 Jul 1828	Phineas Hubbard L. T. Johnston
Poteet William	Polly Christenbery	3 Mar 1796	Solomon Merritt
Poteet William	Martha Henderson	26 Jun 1828	William Hubbard John Morton
Pounds Shach	Sally Runnells	9 Aug 1847	George Wiley N. J. Palmer
Powel Thomas	Anne Kennon	4 Aug 1820	Joel Cannon
Powell Barzilai	Betsy Poteet	17 Dec 1825	Henry Hooper
Powell Barzilai	Willy Sparrow	2 Jan 1834	William Powell
Powell Edmond (Col)	Jenny Mitchel (Col)	9 Nov 1865	Christopher Smith
Powell Edward M.	Ann P. Watlington	5 Jan 1856 8 Jan 1857	J. N. Montgomery md by John H. Pickard

GROOM	BRIDE	DATE	BONDSMAN OR WITNESS
Powell George	Jamima Roberts	8 Mar 1793	Lawrence Richardson
Powell Giles	Susan Carter (of Halifax Va.)	24 Feb 1853	James Foster md by J. M. Allen JP
Powel Henry	Nancey Poteet	14 Jul 1826	Stairling H. Gunn
Powell Henry A.	Mary Sheppard	9 Jan 1840	Owen McAleer
Powell J. C.	Susan McKinny	6 Nov 1866 12 Nov 1866	Alpheus Stanly md by Stephen Neal JP
Powell James	Mary Ann Chambers	17 Aug 1864	Robert B. Bass md by J. J. Jones JP
Powell James B.	Narcesia B. Terry	6 Oct 1840	Henry L. Smith
Powell James M.	Betsey Mitchell	10 Jan 1809	William Lyon
Powell John	Margarett C. Humphreys	18 Mar 1834	John R. Griffith
Powell Josiah	Martha Hooper	26 Jun 1849	Charles Simpson
Powell Mastin J.	Susan H. Gillispie	19 Jun 1852 20 Jun 1852	David A. Gillispie md by Thomas L. Lea JP
Powell Peter	Patcey Carrol	31 Aug 1802	Vincent Roberts
Powell Peter Jr.	Frances Philips	19 Sep 1832	Vincent Roberts
Powell Richard M. (son of John B. & Nancey T. Powell)	Margarett S. Howard (dau of Thomas J. & Charlotte F. Howard)	18 Dec 1867 19 Dec	md by J. H. Forbes
Powell Thomas B.	Mary W. Carter	21 Apr 1866 22 Apr 1866	Thomas Davis md by J. J. Jones JP
Powell Thomas J.	Malinda A. Morrison	14 Oct 1863	Robert F. Oliver
Powell William B.	Martha T. Gatewood (wid)	31 Dec 1859 1 Jan 1860	Elias B. Carter md by C. H. Richmond JP
Powell William H.	Mary N. Yarbrough	5 Jan 1861	William G. Carter md by N. M. Lewis JP
Poyner Jesse	Nancey Paschall	3 Jan 1818	William D. Paschall
Prather Leonard	Frances Williamson	11 Feb 1799	George A. Swift
Prather Leonard D.	Mary S. Tait	1 Jan 1833	Adam T. Farish
Prendergast George W.	Mary Kimbrough	14 Sep 1841	Ethelbert S. Rascoe
Prendergast Thomas	Nancey Harrison	12 Mar 1799	Luke Prendergast
Presnell Gilbert	Nancey Watlington	14 Jul 1835	Thomas J. Stamps
Preston David	Rebecah Brandon	20 Aug 1787	Richard Hostler
Price Abram	Betsey Moore	18 Jul 1808	William Price
Price Brunswick	Josephine Slade	19 May 1867 20 May 1867	H. F. Brandon clk md by H. E. Hodges JP
Price Charles	Francis Wadlington	20 Feb 1792	Thomas Brookes Jr.
Price Christopher H.	Philena Sutherland	10 May 1827	Edward Watlington
Price Daniel S.	Agness R. Harrison	12 Feb 1833	Dudley G. Stokes
Price Daniel S.	Eliza F. Stokes	14 Dec 1842	James Durham
Price George	Mary Palmer	26 Sep 1823	David Traynham
Price Granville	Louisa Price	21 May 1866 27 May 1866	Alex. Bass md by W. B. Swann JP
Price Haskin	Nancy Fisher	18 Nov 1799	Bluford Warrin
Price Hiram M.	Araminta Ferrell	16 Apr 1852	John D. Keesee
Price James A.	Martha Jane Wright	26 Jun 1841	Allen Y. Stokes
Price John	Mary Brown	15 Jan 1781	Robert Moore
Price John Jr.	Susannah Garrott	4 Jan 1808	Joseph Coleman
Price John P.	Ann W. Price	10 Nov 1851	Robert M. Price
Price John S.	Mary Richardson	23 Dec 1824	John C. Harvey Thomas Payne
Price Josiah	Mary Culberson	28 Dec 1818	Hiram Culberson
Price Matthew	Elisabeth Eskridge	22 Feb 1786	Archibald Murphey
Price Meridith	Sarah McDaniel	13 Apr 1819	Thomas Penick
Price O. D.	Ellen Morton	20 Jan 1864	H. M. Raine md by W. B. Swann JP
Price Peter	Nancey Arnett	1 Sep 1804	Edward Ruark
Price Robert M.	Susan W. McDaniel	10 Nov 1851	John P. Price

GROOM	BRIDE	DATE	BONDSMAN OR WITNESS
Price Robert M.	Mary E. Stamps	11 Dec 1854	Jno. R. Knight
		13 Dec 1854	md by J. H. Lacy MG Danville Va.
Price Robt. M.	L. Knight	7 Dec 1860	Dr. Geo. W. Gunn
		12 Dec 1860	md by John Long MG
Price Thomas L.	Lydia Bolton	21 Sep 1830	Thomas Bolton
Price William	Edney Culberson	12 Jan 1807	Jepthah Parks
Price Wm.	Martha Jones	23 Jun 1866	Nathan Yancey
Price William	Matilda Price	18 Dec 1866	John Price
			md by W. B. Swann JP
Price William W.	Susannah B. Stokes	24 Sep 1814	Thomas Penick
Pride Burton	Sally Biswell	29 Oct 1780	William Smith
Prior Joseph	Eliza Mangram	17 Jun 1859	David Walker
			md by Jno. D. Keesee JP
Prior Pinkney C.	Margaret Marr	19 Feb 1859	David Durham
Pritchett Edward	Kesiah Powell	9 Jun 1805	Thomas Windsor
Proctor Daniel R.	Elizabeth Hawkins	4 Aug 1852	Joshua J. Wood
			md by Benj. Wells JP
Pruett Nathaniel	Laura L. Driskill (dau of Sarah W. Driskill)	30 Dec 1864	Robert Pruett md by John J. Jones JP
Pruit Griffin P. (son of Joseph & Sarah Pruit)	Jemima A. P. Lovlace (dau of Umphrey & J. Beavers)	21 May 1867 22 May	H. F. Brandon clk md by Stephen Neal JP
Pruit John	Rachel Ray	10 Oct 1850	David Allen Henry P. Harrison
Pryor William	Heaty Going	19 Jul 1803	Jesse Going Nathl. Pass
Pucket Goselin	Mary Reid	25 Jan 1808	Zachariah Hooper
Pucket Thomas	Susan Sotherland	24 Dec 1832	Robert W. Mason
Puckett James	Nancy Alderdice	27 Dec 1833	David Walker
Pugh Alfred M.	Mary E. Pugh	1 Mar 1857	A. A. Mitchell
			md by Jacob Doll MG
Pugh E. L.	Nancy A. Fowler	28 Nov 1861	John A. Bowden
			md by N. M. Lewis JP
Pulliam Calvin	Caroline Elliott	10 Mar 1867	Thomas Elliott
			md by John J. Jones JP
Pulliam James (Col)	Manda Paylor (Col)	16 Dec 1867	md by David Burch JP
Pilliam Thomas (Col)	Mary Currie (Col)	26 Dec 1866 19 Jan 1867	Sam. Currie (Col) md by David Burch JP
Pullium Jack (son of Fountain & Sarah Pullium)	Martha Currie (dau of Jobe Tate)	16 Oct 1867 19 Oct	md by Jerry Smith JP
Purkins Robert	Edy Hobbs	26 Jul 1820	Richard Foster
Purkins Wm. M.	Mary A. Marshall	24 Oct 1857	Stephen Travis Jno. F. Graves DC
Putnam Jeremiah	Susannah Dean	4 Apr 1823	William Ware
Pyron Charles	Nancy Childers	22 Sep 1836	Allen Scott
Pyron John	Sarah Leath	26 Nov 1799	Joel Leath
Pyron Westley	Polly Manly	2 Jul 1839	John Kennon

- Q -

Quine Benjamin	Esther Coram	2 Sep 1780	William Coram
Quine Goolsby	Patsey Hubbird	7 Jan 1823	David Montgomery
Quine Jacob	Elinor Gunn	9 Nov 1801	Benjamin Quine
Quine William	Frances Baxter	12 Nov 1808	Henry Quine

- R -

| Regan Wm. S.* | Denishia McClarney | 17 Apr 1831 | Jos. Stone |

GROOM	BRIDE	DATE	BONDSMAN OR WITNESS
Raggan John C.	Fanny McFarland	24 Jan 1861	William B. Graves
Ragin William T.	Julia McFarlin	31 Dec 1858	Jno. Rozes
			md by James McMullin
Ragsdale Benjamin	Mary Duncan	-- --- 1792	James Merritt
Ragsdale Clement	Nancy M. Hamblett	12 Nov 1817	Benjamin Johnston
Ragsdale John	Nancy Douglass	14 Oct 1783	William Ragsdale Jr.
Ragsdale Peter	Mary Hamlett	9 Dec 1788	Samuel Pittard
Ragsdale William	Fanney Moore Hamlett	2 Oct 1788	Robert Moore
Railey C. H.	Mary J. Tanner	9 Nov 1849	Thomas E. Madison
Rainey Dabney	Nancy C. Cheles	5 May 1821	Munford Stanfield
Rainey Heared*	Nancy House	29 Oct 1831	James Rudd
Rainey James G.	Sophia Hendrick	20 Aug 1823	Archibald Lea
Rainey John	Nelley Neeley	14 Sep 1798	Henry Thomas
Rainey Jno. P.	Martha Durham	14 Jan 1836	Tarlton W. Brown
Rainey John P. Jr.	Elizabeth Richmond	12 May 1855	Rufus Wright
Rainey Sanford H.	Sarah L. Furgis	19 Oct 1859	John T. Brown
			N. W. Norfleet
			md by Wm. B. Bowe JP
Rainey Thomas	Jenny Samuel	17 Sep 1792	Daniel McFarland
Rainey William	Elisabeth Ekels	22 Jan 1782	James Rainey
Rainey William	Molley Wright	1 Oct 1784	Jno. Wright
Rainey William	Chloe Malone	28 Sep 1789	William Dollarhide
Rainey William T.	Mary J. Carter	24 Dec 1851	Thomas R. Hatchett
		25 Dec 1851	md by Wm. Anderson
Ralph Thomas	Jane Coram	12 Apr 1791	Travis Graham
Ramey Albert W.	Liewvinia E. Riffetoe	11 Apr 1848	H. N. Ramey
	(dau of David)		James M. Graham
Ramey Edward	Susan Ramey	5 Dec 1846	George W. Dodson
Ramey George	Lucy Pass	29 Dec 1866	Nelson Hodges
		30 Dec 1866	md by H. E. Hodges JP
Ramseur S. Dodson	Ellen Richmond	27 Oct 1863	Charles R. Dodson
			R. W. Graves DC
			md by E. H. Harding
Ramsey Ambrose K.	Nancey Yancey	7 Oct 1817	Barzillai Graves
			Azariah Graves
Ramsour Jacob A.	Lucy M. Dodson	3 Oct 1833	Caleb Phifer
Randolph George	Elioner Harp	6 Jul 1813	Willm. Taylor
Randolph James	Mary Dye	12 Dec 1781	David Shelton
Randolph James	Mamima Harp	11 Oct 1813	Wesley Irp
Randolph John	Sally Curls	4 Mar 1806	James Randolph Jr.
Randolph William	Sally White	15 Nov 1783	James Ranndolph
Randolph William	Mary Hinton	21 Aug 1808	Freeman Hubbard
Ransom Charles (Col)	Elizabeth Marshall (Col)	3 Jan 1867	King Watkins (Col) md by John J. Jones JP
Rasco Henry T.	Elizabeth Loyd	19 Jan 1855	Daniel B. Renolds
Rasco John	Sarah E. Coleman	24 Sep 1859	Smith Rasco
Rasco William	Herry Pleasant	5 Jul 1815	Daniel Gunn
			Smith Murphey
Rasco W. M. (son of Arthur & Mary Rasco)	Mrs. Nancy Rasco (dau of James & Mary Walker)	19 Oct 1867 20 Oct	md by J. F. Leath JP
Rascoe Ethelbert	Nancey Kimbrough	20 Oct 1840	James Florence
Rascoe John	Martha Pleasant	5 Dec 1816	William Rascoe
Ravens James	Nancey Allren	19 Oct 1791	Jessey Watson
Rawlins James M.	Mary A. Gatewood	8 Jan 1855	Joel A. McDaniel
		10 Jan 1855	md by Jno. H. Lacy MG
Rawlins James M.	Martha G. Simpson (wid)	3 May 1865	William H. Pattillo
Ray Charles	Jinsey Fisher	14 Dec 1804	James Randolph Jr.
Ray Darling	Mary Reid	12 Nov 1794	Edmd. Alley
Ray David	Nancey Orr	9 Dec 1820	Samuel Orr
Ray James	Ellionar Hensley	28 Oct 1794	James Currie
Ray Joseph	Kessiah Henslee	24 Oct 1798	Robert Kimbrough
Ray Robert	Elizabeth Jones	1 Oct 1840	William Fuller

GROOM	BRIDE	DATE	BONDSMAN OR WITNESS
Ray Robert	Mary Warner	24 Jan 1843	James Warner
Rayner Willie	Orphie Ragland (wid)	11 Aug 1850	Napoleon Graves N. J. Palmer
Read Jackson	Amanda Scott	30 Apr 1845	Samuel W. Bethell
Read James W.	Susan B. Thomas	10 May 1839	Pleasant Chandler
Read Noel	Nancy Hubbard	15 Apr 1815	Elijah Carman
Read Thomas	Lucy Roberts	22 Jan 1823	Warren Halcomb
Read Thomas	Mary Smith	11 Oct 1841	Samuel W. Bethell
Reagan John C.	Lou F. Royester	9 Nov 1865	Brice Harralson
Reagin John C.	Francis McFarland	27 Mar 1861	Franklin Graves
Reany Isaac	Sarah Melone	6 Mar 1786	Nathaniel Malone
Reddin William	Milley Burk	25 Nov 1812	Thomas Bradford
Redmun William (of Charlotte Co. Va.)	Sarah Allin	27 Dec 1791	Tobias Williams
Reece John	Maryann Stringer	29 Jul 1780	Nathan Jean
Reed A.	Sallie J. Richmond	21 Aug 1860	Wm. E. Bevill md by J. P. Simpson MG
Reed Anthony	Tabitha Owen	30 Nov 1824	Reubin P. Owen
Reed Blewford	Nancy Nowles	25 Jun 1793	William Rainey
Reed James W.	Margaret Locket	10 Oct 1844	John W. C. McMullin
Reed John	Nancey Ballard	26 Jun 1807	James Barker
Reed John	Nancey Vaughan	1 Jul 1825	Alexander McAlpin
Reed Thomas	Mary M. Roper	6 Nov 1838	William Herring
Reese Josias	Nancy Shaw	19 Jun 1779	Thomas Whrey Wm. Campbell
Reeves Asa (son of George K. & Sarah R. Reeves)	Nancy J. Nichols (dau of David & Susan Nichols)	9 Oct 1867	md by J. J. Jones JP
Reid Anthony	Martha Owen	9 Mar 1833	John Poteet Jr.
Reid Hugh K.	Caroline H. Graves	22 May 1857	Jno. A. Graves J. R. Graves
		27 May 1857	md by Thomas W. Tobey MG
Reid James	Polly Wilson	12 Feb 1800	Thomas Reid
Reid John	Keziah Buchanan	20 Mar 1784	David Burton Richd. Simpson
Reid Jno. W.	Martha W. Richmond	21 Nov 1865	William E. Bevill
Reid William B.	Edey H. Brown	15 Nov 1825	James Rice
Reno Dr. John P. T.	Susan E. Watson	27 Oct 1838	E. W. Mason Benj. C. West Sr.
Rhoades John	Amey Burch	18 Jun 1822	John Chamberlain
Rhodes Noah	Sidney Medlin	6 Apr 1827	George Claughton
Rice Archabal	Zibba Bush	2 Feb 1803	James Yancey
Rice Archabal	Salley Yancey	6 Jul 1811	Jno. Yancey
Rice Archibald	Sarah Richmond	22 Jul 1813	Goodwin Evans
Rice Edmond	Henrietta Rice	5 Dec 1795	Williamson Rice
Rice Edmund	Martha Brown	30 Nov 1814	James Collier Jeremiah Rudd
Rice Edmond B.	Margaret Simmons	19 Oct 1844	Iveson Foulks
Rice Henry	Margret Shelton	20 Dec 1798	Booker Shapard
Rice Ibzan	Dolly G. Carloss	27 Feb 1796	Carter Blackwell
Rice Ibzan	Polley Brooks	8 Dec 1818	William Graves
Rice Ibzan	Ursley Brooks	5 May 1824	Thomas W. Graves
Rice Ibzan	Emeline Totten	13 Dec 1849	Pinckney Gwyn
Rice Iverson	Nancy Gomer	23 Oct 1845	William R. McKinny
Rice James	Nancey Bruce	3 Nov 1825	James Malone
Rice Jephthah	Nancey Jouet	19 Aug 1784	Anthony Swift
Rice Jeremiah	Elizabeth Harden	14 Oct 1816	William H. Rice
Rice Jeremiah	Nancy Harrison	20 Oct 1843	Hugh E. Cobb
Rice Jeremiah	Mary A. Perkins (wid)	3 Jun 1851	Samuel Cobb
Rice John	Elizabeth Starkey	21 Dec 1805	William Clemson
Rice John	-------	23 Dec 1806	John Keen

GROOM	BRIDE	DATE	BONDSMAN OR WITNESS
Rice John	Mary Cobb	19 Nov 1844	John R. Brooks
Rice John H.	Jane Page	30 Dec 1845	Hugh E. Cobb
Rice Joshua Morris	Susannah Gunn	1 Oct 1806	Abraham Miles
Rice Nathan*	Minerva Foster	17 Oct 1831	Ezekiel Sawyer
Rice Nathan	Polley King	19 Jan 1825	Edward M. Jones
Rice Nathan Jr.	Sally Poyner	23 Dec 1801	Christopher Brookes
Rice Nathaniel	Susanah Butler	29 Jan 1781	William Rice
Rice Nathaniel L.	Henrietta Rice	23 Dec 1812	Henry Williams
Rice Solomon	Sarah S. Swift	18 Nov 1826	Stephen Rice
Rice Thomas	Harriott Parish	22 Dec 1828	William Manly
Rice Thomas B.	Isabella Hightower	20 Feb 1847	Stephen C. Stadler
Rice William	Susanah Brooks	20 Dec 1784	Nathaniel Rice
Rice William	Esther Chounan	21 Dec 1793	Joshua Boyd
Rice William H.	Sarah Gooch	7 Sep 1795	John Windsor Jr.
Rice William H.	Eliza Walker	23 Nov 1841	Abner Walker Jr.
Rice William H.	Sally Moore	9 Nov 1852	Rufus Graves
		11 Nov 1852	md by John H. Lacy
Rice Williamson	Zuriah Simms	9 Jan 1797	Edmond Rice
Rice Zadok	Celah Lynch	27 Feb 1821	James Slade
Rice Zeri	Mary Mitchell	3 Sep 1782	Hearndon Harralson
Rice Ziba	Fanny Browning	17 May 1806	Nathaniel Browning
Richards Durritt	Polly Moore	12 Jul 1802	Josiah Samuell
Richardson George (Col)	Fannie Mimms (Col)	12 Feb 1866	Jno. S. Park md by Jas. J. Clendenin
Richardson James	Elizabeth Pass	4 Apr 1803	Holloway Pass
Richardson James N.	Elizabeth A. Standfield	1 Apr 1856	Jno. W. Lewis
Richardson Josiah	Elizabeth A. Hewell	31 Dec 1834	Henry W. Farley
Richardson Robert P.	Mary E. Watlington	30 Dec 1850	John M. Richmond
Richardson Thomas	Obediance Gates	10 Jan 1819	Henry Roper C. Willson
Richardson William	Polly Burton	28 Aug 1802	Thomas Harrison Jr.
Richmond Archibald D.	Elizabeth Currie	27 Nov 1832	Nathaniel M. Roan
Richmond Bethel	Caroline Lea	25 Dec 1866	Levi Hensley
		27 Dec 1866	md by S. G. Mason MG
Richmond Caleb H.	Ann S. Rainey	11 Apr 1830	George W. Clibourn
Richmond Caleb H.	Mary R. Dodson	28 Sep 1838	John K. Graves
Richmond Calvin J.	Frances Collins	23 Dec 1837	John L. Richmond
Richmond Daniel	Nancy Comer	16 Dec 1805	George Willson
Richmond David	Elizabeth McNeil	9 Dec 1834	Marcus A. Vanhook
Richmond David (Col-son of Green Brown & Mary Richmond)	Sarah Flintoff (Col-dau of G. Murray & Violet Malone)	3 Oct 1867 2 Nov 1867	md by C. J. Richmond JP
Richmond Franklin (Col)	Charlotte Freeman (Col)	31 Jan 1867 6 Feb 1867	Cesar Dodson (Col) md
Richmond George T.	Martha Moore	15 Mar 1840	Thomas Burton
Richmond Henry A.	Elizabeth Evans	1 Apr 1851	John W. Roan
Richmond James	Betsey Boman	10 Nov 1802	John Richmond
Richmond James D.	Susan T. Richmond (wid)	1 Jun 1865	A. Morgan
Richmond James L.	Mary Dameron	19 Jan 1860	James R. Aldridge md by H. F. Adkins JP
Richmond James M.*	Judith M. Dameron	26 Oct 1830	Alexander Gray
Richmond Jesse	Elizabeth Hughston	29 Dec 1817	Elijah G. Kimbro
Richmond John	Sarah Lea	21 Dec 1799	Robert Donaldson
Richmond John	Mary Currie	15 Feb 1802	Joseph Currie
Richmond John	Nancey Morton	21 Dec 1805	Joel Richmond
Richmond John Jr.	Elizabeth Anderson Rose	10 Oct 1827	Joseph Langley

GROOM	BRIDE	DATE	BONDSMAN OR WITNESS
Richmond John Currie	Betsey Stephens	31 Jul 1821	Jno. Chandler
Richmond John L.	Mary A. Davis	28 Jul 1839	Robert M. Wiley
Richmond Joseph	Anna Connally	6 Feb 1804	James Bolling
Richmond Joshua	Pheby Roberts	4 Jan 1800	John Richmond
Richmond Leonidas	Annis Lea	31 Mar 1859	John D. Long
		4 Apr 1859	md by M. C. Thomas MG
Richmond Thomas B.	Susan Burton	18 Nov 1833	James C. Dameron
Richmond Tinsley (Col)	Violet Richmond (Col)	12 Jan 1866	A. A. Pattillo md by E. H. Harding
Richmond William	Margret Woods	1 Oct 1802	John Richmond
Richmond William A.	Mary Gold	8 Oct 1829	Andy M. Woods
Richmond William D.	Sue F. Martin	15 May 1862	M. W. Norfleet md by F. A. Wiley JP
Richmond Willis M.	Miranda Richmond	6 Oct 1846	John M. Richmond
Richmond Yancey	Harriet A. Murphey	8 Jul 1866	Squire Walker md by Jerry Smith JP
Rickman John	Agniss Rickman	13 Nov 1794	Partrick Mason
Riggs Aderson	Susin Morgan	25 Nov 185-	Dr. N. M. Roan
Riggs Drusis	Mary Long	4 Feb 1812	John Whitlow Smith Murphey
Riggs George W.	Louisa Richardson	3 Dec 1846	John W. Dameron
Riggs George W.	Fanny G. Burke	18 Aug 1862	John L. Graves
		19 Aug 1862	md by Wm. B. Bowe JP
Riggs John	Ann Philips	1 Apr 1840	John A. Swann
Riggs John	Rebecca Stephens	19 Dec 1866	A. Riggs md by R. A. Moore MG
Riggs Thomas	Polly Riggs	22 Dec 1812	Drusis Riggs
Riggs Thomas	Martha A. Bradsher	20 Dec 1838	Richard H. Bradsher
Riggs Thomas	Eliza W. Reid	26 Nov 1849	Algernon D. Stephens
Riley Thomas W.	Nancy Ward	27 Dec 1855	John W. Riley md by B. Cooper JP
Rimare James W.	Malinda Holmes	19 Feb 1822	John Hagwood
Roach William (Col)	Leanna Hill (Col)	26 Apr 1860	James Warren md by N. M. Lewis JP
Roaling William P.	Sarah F. Hill	22 Mar 1860	James K. Davis md by J. S. Totten JP
Roan George	Delphia Phelps	29 Mar 1788	Reubin Phelps
Roan James	Writta Burch	1 Jul 1809	James Sargent
Roan James	Caroline McAden	22 Apr 1867	md by Jacob Doll MG
Roan James P.	Sarah Roan	27 Aug 1825	James Roan (son of Thomas)
Roan James T.	Elizabeth Fullington	31 Aug 1826	William Chandler
Roan John	Fanny Comer	14 Dec 1802	Thomas Comer
Roan Justin	Elizabeth G. Long	26 Oct 1836	John W. Roan
Roan Nathaniel M.	Mary B. Henderson	18 Nov 1835	Thomas D. Connally
Roan Thomas	Nancy Phelps	14 Nov 1782	Barnett Lea
Roan Weldon (son of Harrison Wiley & Dorca Roan)	Fannie Evans	5 Nov 1867 9 Nov	md by J. Doll
Roark Benjamin	Sarah C. Hester	1 May 1854	B. Harralson
		3 May 1854	md by Benj. Wells JP
Robbins Thomas J.	Frances E. Muse	19 Apr 1850	Smith L. Morris
Robenhiser Robert R.	Rose E. Annmonett	4 Jul 1866	S. T. Wilkinson md by James K. Lea JP
Roberds David	Nancey Ann Hawkins	14 Dec 1858	Bartlet Y. Malone
		16 Dec 1858	md by A. M. Woods JP
Roberson Christopher	Polly Miles	15 Apr 1830	Woodson Morris
Roberson Christopher	Caty Payne	17 Dec 1835	Thomas Roberson
Roberson Pinckney	Lucy McKinney	31 Jan 1839	Maj. H. Graves

GROOM	BRIDE	DATE	BONDSMAN OR WITNESS
Roberson Pleasant	Lucinda Dudly	4 Jan 1825	James Wilson
Roberson Thomas	Fanny Miles	20 Nov 1832	John Browning
			Henry F. Smith
Roberson William	Lydia Marget Strader	29 Dec 1824	Henry Strader
Roberts Arthur	Nancy Hargis	25 Mar 1789	David Roberts
Roberts David	Anne Moore	20 Jul 1790	Osborn Jeffreys Jr.
Roberts Elijah	Rebecca B. Davis	4 Nov 1826	Alexander McAlpin
Roberts George	Betsey Warren	13 Jan 1811	George Smith
Roberts George	Martha Blackwell	1 Mar 1827	Richard Jones
Roberts Geo. W.	Arrenia M. Allen	2 Jan 1840	John McMullin
			W. C. Page
Roberts Henry	Eliza Piles	22 Dec 1836	Henry Hughs
Roberts Humphrey	Elizabeth Browning	23 Jan 1793	Francis Smith
Roberts James	Salley Wisdom	2 Nov 1818	Larkin A. Landers
Roberts James L.	Elizabeth F. Lyon	19 Aug 1857	William A. Roberts
Roberts John	Salley Tapley	28 Dec 1802	Thomas Roberts
Roberts John	Martha Griffin	30 Apr 1843	P. Turner
Roberts John	Polly Benton	19 Jan 1846	Zachariah Lockett
Roberts John R. L.	Mary J. Parish	7 Dec 1849	Ezekiel D. Paschal
Roberts Joshua	Nancy Stephens	29 Jan 1820	Lemuel H. Carroll
Roberts Laton T.	Susan S. Harris	17 Dec 1833	Owen McAleer
Roberts Levin	Nancy Carrell	14 Nov 1798	George Carrell
Roberts Roland	Polly Brintle	6 Apr 1829	Robert Zachary
Roberts Roland W.	Mary Gomer	24 Dec 1818	William Tarpley
Roberts Simon	Betsey Hudson	1 Sep 1798	Joshay Hutson
Roberts Stephen	Ellioner Mitchel	13 Aug 1791	James Simmons
Roberts Step.	Ellenor Burgess	22 Jan 1814	Joseph Richmond
Roberts Thomas	Peggy Swann	14 Oct 1812	William Tarpley
Roberts Thomas	Sophia Cantrel	1 Jan 1859	William H. Rice
			md by W. Maynard JP
Roberts William A.	Mary C. Watlington	28 Jan 1859	M. W. Norfleet
		1 Feb 1859	md by Jno. W. Lewis MG
Roberts William H.	Nancy E. Willis	15 Dec 1865	Allen Harralson
		17 Dec 1865	md by Jacob Doll MG
Roberts William R.	Elizabeth Jane Ward	19 May 1852	James C. Halsamback
			md by B. Cooper JP
Roberts Zephaniah	Betsy Smith	29 Aug 1822	Thomas Warren
Robertson Aaron P.	Ann Browning	15 Nov 1838	John Jones
Robertson	Sarah J. Rudd	30 Jun 1866	B. Harralson
Albert G.		1 Jul 1866	md by Tho. W.
			Graves JP
Robertson Alex.	Hannah Hunt	10 Nov 1866	Jesse Stokes
		12 Nov 1866	md by Thomas S.
			Harrison
Robertson Edward	Sarah Irby	12 Jul 1856	Daniel S. Price
			W. A. Vernon
Robertson	Susan A. Young	10 Dec 1844	Paschal Voss
Edward S.			
Robertson George	Sarah S. Allen	2 Aug 1826	Charles Willson
W. B.			
Robertson Green	Margaret Rudd	2 Jan 1849	James Tate
Robertson Green	Mary J. McKinney	30 Sep 1857	James C. Rudd
Robertson James	Amanda Smith	27 Jul 1854	Luther Y. Rudd
			md by H. Boswell JP
Robertson Jessee	Mahala Ann Boyles	10 Jun 1867	md by John J. Jones JP
(Col)	(Col)		
Robertson John	Mary Moore	3 Apr 1782	Solomon Parks
Robertson John	Glasshey Bailey	25 Dec 1794	Robert Black
Robertson John	Nannie Stokes	4 Dec 1866	Joseph Thornton
		25 Dec 1866	md by John D. Keesee
Robertson John	Henrietta Virginia	11 Jun 1867	
Edward	Mebane	12 Jun	md by S. A. Stanfield
Robertson John M.	Nancey Burk	24 Nov 1866	S. T. Simmons
		29 Nov 1866	md by F. L. Oakley MG

GROOM	BRIDE	DATE	BONDSMAN OR WITNESS
Robertson Joseph	Margret Darby (dau of George Darby)	2 Sep 1780	George Darby
Robertson Thompson G.	Martha A. Patterson	4 Nov 1854 9 Nov 1854	John M. Swann md by William Anderson
Robertson William	Silvey Reid	20 Apr 1867	md by John J. Jones JP
Robertson William A.	Frances Tolloh	5 May 1821	Richard Dismukes
Roberttson Christopher	Mildred Rudder	5 Feb 1830	Nathaniel Harrelson
Robesonn John	Fanny Bazwell	12 Oct 1784	Frederic Debo
Robinson Jesse	Ann Griffy	19 Apr 1785	Lancelot Johnston
Robinson John	Nancey Cavanis	8 Oct 1816	John Goodson
Robirson John H.	Susanna Scott	30 Dec 1853	Ransom B. Austin md by J. M. Allen JP
Robson J. W.	M. C. Word	13 Nov 1863	W. M. Shelton
Robson William	Nancey McCain	25 Aug 1817	Joseph McCain
Robson William G.	America L. McCain	14 Sep 1865	Tillotson McCain
Rodden James W.	Ann T. Hughes	27 Sep 1853	Henry Kirby md by J. M. Allen JP
Rodden Spencer	Elizabeth Hill	27 Dec 1821	James Holden
Rodgers R. S.	Permelia A. Gwynn	29 Nov 1865 5 Dec 1865	J. W. Justice md by R. G. Barrett MG
Rodgers William M.	Lucinda B. Hill	19 Nov 1856 20 Nov 1856	R. A. Newbell Felix F. Thornton md by J. B. Jackson
Roe Robert	Polley Hooper	1 Jan 1817	Allen Gunn
Roe Robert	Kitty F. Bozwell	8 May 1822	Robert Singleton
Rogers Armistead	Susannah D. Jouit	11 Jun 1781	Isaac Johnson
Rogers Byrd	Sarah Clay	4 Feb 1785	Edward Clay
Rogers John Jr.	Jane Haralson	2 Jan 1785	John Chambers
Rogers John C.	Patsey Samuel	9 Mar 1810	Thos. Gatewood
Rogers William A.	Sarah Jane Adams	29 Apr 1842	Jesse Owen
Rohr William M.	Judeth West	26 May 1830	Daniel S. Price
Roland Fendul	Rachel Walker	18 Jan 1790	Saml. Paul
Roland Fendul	Elizabeth Adams	16 Jan 1815	Elijah Duncan
Roper David	Nancy Lewis	13 Jul 1801	Giden Robertson
Roper Henry	Rachel Farley	4 Oct 1810	Abner Burton
Roper Henry	Polly Elmore	9 Nov 1832	Owen McAleer
Roper James	Mary ONeill	27 Mar 1792	John Peterson
Roper William	Kiziah Yates	31 Aug 1781	John Yeats
Roper William F.	Emily M. Gunn	15 Aug 1836	William P. Gunn
Rose Alexander Jr.	Polly Vanhook	3 Apr 1805	John Vanhook
Rose Duncan Jr.	Sally M. McAden	19 Aug 1799	John McAden Thos. Kendrick
Rose Howel S.	Mary Durham	19 Nov 1829	John W. Roan
Rosson Abner	Fanny Pogue	20 Feb 1790	Rhodan Pogue
Rowark Elisha	Elizabeth Barnett	18 Sep 1804	John Stafford
Rowark John	Elizabeth Compton	26 Sep 1817	Thomas Malone Jr.
Rowark Larkin	Frances Eubank	3 Mar 1816	Thomas Tindil Isaac Rainey
Rowland Micajah	Anne Lee	19 Nov 1812	Jessy Rolen Thomas Bouldin
Royester Thomas	Louisa Rivers Hughs	5 Feb 1833	Archelaus Nunnally
Ruark Edward	Margret Arnett	3 Nov 1802	William Robertson Wm. S. Webb
Ruark Henry	Jane Walker	24 Feb 1816	James Walker
Ruark John	Mimy Smith	22 Jul 1811	Martin Clark
Ruark Samuel	Mary Rhoades	3 Aug 1815	Timothy Langwell
Rucker George G.	Mary R. Pope	30 Dec 1850	William W. Womack
Rudd Aldridge	Nancey Murphey	28 Aug 1824	Oliver Foulks
Rudd Alexander	Zibby Sawyer	31 Aug 1842	Ezekiel Sawyer
Rudd Bethel	Dicys Love	31 Jan 1867	John Fuller md by Jas. Malone JP
Rudd David	Nancy F. Jackson	26 Jan 1846	George A. Swift

GROOM	BRIDE	DATE	BONDSMAN OR WITNESS
Rudd David	Teby Smith	21 Dec 1853	Archable Baynes
		25 Dec 1853	md by Thomas Covington JP
Rudd Franklin G.	Mary Evans	21 Nov 1838	Thomas Henslee
Rudd Hezekiah	Mary Sartin	25 Jul 1848	Thomas L. Rudd
Rudd James	Nancy Ball	27 Mar 1812	William Wilson
Rudd James	Sarah Swift	30 Apr 1845	James M. Brooks
Rudd James C.	Mary Ann Massey	12 Feb 1857	Green Robertson W. A. Vernon DC
Rudd Jeremiah	Susanna Evans	2 Jan 1811	Stephen D. Watkins
Rudd Jeremiah Jr.	Sarah Sawyers	10 Jul 1837	George Simmons
Rudd Jessee	Judy Rudd	18 Aug 1866	David Rudd md by J. Smith JP
Rudd John S.	Cornelia A. Cheek	25 Dec 1866	W. L. Saunders md by M. A. Turner JP
Rudd Joseph	Tabbitha Culberson	19 Jan 1824	Joshua Rudd
Rudd Joshua	Susannah Culberson	24 Feb 1819	Robert Singleton
Rudd Lorenzo D.	Arabella C. Chambers	3 Feb 1854	Jerry Smith
Rudd Luther	Sarah Stephens	7 Jun 1855	Anderson R. Smith
		21 Jun 1855	md by Wm. B. Bowe JP
Rudd Pleasant	Annise Browning	21 Feb 1822	Elisha Rudd
Rudd Rufus A.	Frances Page	11 Jun 1856	Robert W. Graves
		15 Jun 1846?	md by E. M. Jones
Rudd Thomas	Elvira Montgomery	19 Nov 1844	Hezekiah Rudd
Rudd Thomas H.	Louisa E. Alred	6 Jan 1866	J. L. McKee clk
		16 Jan 1866	md by F. L. Oakley MG
Rudd William	Susannah Manning	10 Jun 1805	Jacob Ahart
Rudd William	Rebecah Goodson	8 Mar 1809	Jeremiah Rudd
Rudd William H.	Isabella Williamson	2 Sep 1866	Azariah Williamson md by Stephen Neal JP
Rudder Edward V.	Martha J. Farley	2 Apr 1866	William H. Rudder md by N. M. Lewis JP
Ruling William T.	Sally E. Davis	21 Nov 1867	md by E. Hunt JP
Runnels William	Susan Elliot	17 Jun 1848	Robert J. West
Russel Edward	Polly Blair	9 Jan 1808	Henry Roper
Russel Joseph	Caty Payne	7 Apr 1815	William Russell Jeremiah Rudd
Russell James	Mandy Torian	14 Dec 1866	James M. Walker
		19 Dec 1866	md by David Burch JP
Russell John	Rebecca Bohannon (dau of Nancy Bohannon)	5 Jan 1815	Bosten Bohannon
Russell John A.	Sarah J. Stanfield	21 Sep 1844	Charles G. Russell
Russell John P.	Nancey A. Watson	10 Aug 1863	Yuel F. Hodges md by J. A. Hodges JP
Russell Joseph M.	Louisa Hodge	5 Apr 1854	Andrew J. Kimbrough md by P. Hodnett JP
Russell William	Isbella Slade	29 May 1828	Thomas W. Graves
Russell William	Cynthia A. Neal	29 Mar 1859	Jesse F. Slade md by Stinceon Ivey
Russell William	Martha Jane Womack	27 Jul 1861	Alex. McAlpin md by S. G. Mason
Russell William F.	Tabitha T. Carrel	24 Nov 1825	Robert White
Rutherford John	Polley Hubbard	16 Feb 1782	Dudley Y. Runnels
Ryan Charles J.	Mary E. Harrison (dau of Lewis of Lynchburg Va.)	29 Jul 1843	Wm. P. Graves

- S -

Sadler Benjamin	Lucy Dunaway	2 Mar 1811	William Tate
St. John Abraham	Franky Murry	26 Sep 1806	Samuel Grier
Salman William T.	Eliza F. Roberts	21 Dec 1865	M. V. Craft
		24 Dec 1865	md by F. L. Oakley MG

GROOM	BRIDE	DATE	BONDSMAN OR WITNESS
Salmon Henry	Elizabeth Winters	23 Aug 1824	Ozza True
Samman John	Suckey Colmon	11 Feb 1815	Marthus Forguson
Sammons Branch	Susan A. Womack	4 Jun 1842	Jesse Owen
Samuel Anthony	Anna Waters	25 Dec 1786	Benj. Merritt
			William Moore
Samuel James Jr.	Polly Fisher (dau of Thomas Fisher)	15 Nov 1803	Randolph Buckley
Samuel Jeremiah	Sally Samuel	30 Dec 1782	Archd. Samuel
Samuel Walker	Lucy Samuel	29 Dec 1829	Maurice Vaughan
Samuell Archibald	Mary Samuel	13 Mar 1782	Anthony Samuell
Samuell Benjamin	Aggy Sanders	24 Jan 1785	George Samuell
Samuell Harnden	Jane F. Roper	4 Nov 1815	Samuel Brandon
Samuell Josiah	Ann P. Sanders	27 Feb 1804	George Willson
Samuell Walker	Judith Samuell	10 Jan 1811	Harnden Samuell
Sanders Alves	Susan Somers	6 Jan 1845	Wiley Gomer
Sanders Alves	Susan Sanders	3 Nov 1856	William Apple
		4 Nov 1856	md by Lancelot Johnston JP
Sanders Andrew	Nancey Humphreys	22 Mar 1830	Elisha Sertain
Sanders James	Polly Dix	22 Sep 1809	Josiah Samuell
Sanders James	Priscilla Ballad	19 Nov 1822	Richard Estes
Sanders James	Elizabeth A. Burges	23 Sep 1860	John A. Turner
			md by N. M. Lewis JP
Sanders James M.	Nancy Poteat (wid)	20 Nov 1865	Thos. R. Gwyn
		23 Nov 1865	md by M. A. Turner JP
Sanders Jesse	Omah Sanders	13 Jan 1838	William Sanders
			John C. Totten
Sanders Leroy	Polly Sanders	5 Sep 1832	John Somers
Sanders Leroy	Lucy Ann Roberts	25 Oct 1858	William Sanders
Sanders Obadiah	Elisabeth Farley	24 Jan 1786	Thomas Rainey
Sanders Ransom P.	Dilila Beaver	8 Mar 1832	Elisha Sertain
Sanders Richard P.	Mary J. Chandler	30 Jan 1847	Thos. W. Davis
Sanders Robert	Verlinchey W. Elam	6 Jul 1801	John Richmond
Sanders Robert	Susan Murphy	23 Dec 1861	Nathan Canaday
			md by E. K. Withers JP
Sanders Romolus M.	Rebeccah Carter	21 Dec 1812	Josiah Samuell
Sanders William	Nancy Cuningham	13 Jan 1795	William Cunningham
Sanders William	Elizabeth Bouland	24 Oct 1863	John A. Pettigru
Sanders Zephaniah	Eleanor Paynor	25 Aug 1822	Colmore Humphreys
Sanders Zephaniah	Susannah Roe	28 Dec 1821	Thomas Gibson
Sargent Daniel	Delphy Carny	3 Jan 1780	Joseph Carny
			Ze. Rice
Sargent Demsy	---------	-- --- 1815	Moses Langley
Sargent Ephraim	Elisabeth Hodge	25 Jul 1792	John McFarland
Sargent James	Rachael Phelps	4 Aug 1791	Samuel Evans
Sargent James	Jane Love	2 Oct 1792	John Love
Sargent Stephen	Fanny Long	11 Nov 1786	Elijah Reynolds
Sartin Anslum	Frances Beaver	22 Oct 1834	Humphrey Browning
Sartin Anslum E.	Elizabeth Gipson	30 Jul 1855	Chordy Whiteheart
			md by Stephen Neal JP
Sartin Ellis	Susan H. Roland	26 Aug 1864	Thomas J. Sartin
		30 Aug 1864	md by Stephen Neal JP
Sartin Moses R.	Mary C. Page	11 Oct 1865	M. H. Cobb
			md by S. G. Mason
Saterfield Isaac	Sarah Yarbrough	3 Sep 1782	Jno. Saterfield
Saterfield William	Susannah Wheeler	1 Oct 1791	William Morrow
Satterfield Amos	Susannah Samuell	4 Feb 1805	Isaac Kirk
			Sol. Debow
Satterfield Anthony	Martha Peterson	27 Dec 1825	David Hall
Satterfield Jesse	Elizabeth Allin	16 May 1789	John Saterfield
Satterfield R. A.	Elisabeth F. Turner	13 Aug 1859	Philip P. Voss
		17 Aug 1859	md by Robt. B. Jones MG

GROOM	BRIDE	DATE	BONDSMAN OR WITNESS
Saunders Charles W.	Sarah E. Underwood	27 Dec 1866	Robert H. Cheek md by M. A. Turner JP
Saunders Drewry W.	Louisa Turner	22 Dec 1864	John T. Russel md by John J. Jones JP
Saunders John	Sally P. Roe	23 Oct 1820	Thomas Pinson
Saunders Reason C.	Mary Ann Womack	18 Mar 1842	Lewis P. Womack
Saunders Robert D.	Missouri A. Carter	17 Aug 1841	Edmund R. Harrison Jno. Daniel
Saunders William	Frances Martin	15 Jan 1825	William Smith
Saunders William F.	Nancey J. Foster	17 Dec 1855 20 Dec 1855	Abner Miles md by P. Hodnett JP
Sawyars Isaac O.	Nancey D. Rickettes (dau of James Rickettes)	20 Nov 1839	John J. Crawley
Sawyer Cary	Agness Cox	26 Jun 1805	William Needham
Sawyer John	Mary Purry Carter	8 Feb 1799	Theoderick Carter
Sawyer John	Nancy Michel	15 Dec 1807	Ald. Murphey CCC
Sawyer John	Nancey Malory	30 Apr 1820	James Sawyer
Sawyer John	Lucy Ann Palmer	12 May 1845	Henry Piles W. A. Whitfield
Sawyer Levi	Martha Faucett	14 Dec 1842	George Smith
Sawyer Robert	Alletha Simms	23 Jan 1798	James Sawyer
Sawyer Stephen	Elizabeth Parrish	9 Jan 1816	Robert Singleton
Sawyer Stephen	Luisia Weeden	1 Dec 1818	John Sawyer
Sawyer Thomas	Fanny Faucett	26 Dec 1832	William Hughs
Sawyer William	Lucy Bennatt	8 Oct 1804	William Tarpley
Sawyer William	Salley Mallory	2 Jan 1805	Ezekiel Jones
Sawyers Absalom	Anne Loafman	8 Feb 1808	Edward Loafman
Sawyers Henry	Meriah A. Powell	22 Feb 1843	A. Slade
Sawyers John	Sally Allen	31 Dec 1825	Moses Sawyers
Sawyers Solomon	Nancy Farler	19 Jul 1823	Henry McAden
Sawyers William	Elizabeth Kitchen	11 Jan 1814	Alex. Murphey
Sawyers William	Mirine Mitchell	6 Dec 1824	David Mitchell
Scales Joseph A.	Louisa A. Swann	7 Jan 1850	John M. Swann
Scarlett William	Sarah Siddle	7 Sep 1829	John Siddall
Scoggin Johnson	Mary Fuller	7 Apr 1827	Stephen Fuller
Scoggin William	Patcey Rice	20 Jun 1804	Wylie Yancey
Scoggin William D.	Frances Fuller	25 Jan 1830	Aron V. Lea
Scoggins Milton G.	Martha J. Stevens	11 Jan 1837	Henry W. Farley Abner Miles
Scoggins William H.	Martha A. Dameron	17 Sep 1852 18 Sep 1852	md by B. Cooper JP
Scott Allen	America Bennett	30 Mar 1823	Francis Watlington
Scott Asa	Patsey Shelton	-- Dec 1812	Barton Terry Jr. Tho. Bouldin
Scott Azariah	Deborah Page	3 May 1837	John Scott
Scott Bartlett	Bashaba Roberts	14 Jan 1824	John Scott
Scott Daniel	Darcass Cannon	21 Dec 1811	Reubin Kennon
Scott David	Emily Dodson	9 Jun 1853	md by J. M. Allen JP
Scott German	Sally Holloway	8 Jun 1799	Whitefield Holloway
Scott Harry	Sarah Harrison	23 May 1798	John Barnwell
Scott James	Polley Rice	2 Jul 1806	Wm. Wilkinson
Scott James M.	Syntha Cobb	7 Dec 1840	James E. Cobb
Scott Jesse M.	Senia Malone	25 Jul 1833	John Vaughan
Scott John	Mary Beaver	22 Dec 1789	Thomas Smith
Scott John	Mary Jeffreys	28 Oct 1816	James Scott
Scott John	Mary Watlington	17 Dec 1823	Bartlett Scott
Scott John H.	Malinda Martin	8 Jul 1836	James Anthony Dr. Allen Gunn
Scott John J.	Martha J. McKinney	29 Jun 1860 5 Jul 1860	Iverson McKinney md by J. S. Totten JP
Scott John W.	Mary A. Watlington	21 Jul 1849	Rufus Y. Graves
Scott John W.	Ann Burnett	30 Apr 1855 1 May 1855	Thomas B. Adkins md by P. Hodnett JP

GROOM	BRIDE	DATE	BONDSMAN OR WITNESS
Scott Miles	Rhody Miles	8 Jun 1808	Harbert Scott
Scott Pleasant	Susan McKinney	5 Jun 1851	John Scott
			md by Wm. P. Graves JP
Scott Richard	Fanney Corder	10 Dec 1797	Hirem Parks
Scott Robert	Patsey Vaughn	15 Feb 1800	John Murrey
Scott Robert	Susan Vowell	25 Jan 1832	John Vaughan
			John Miles
Scott William	Rachal Scott	11 Mar 1786	John J. Farley
Scott William	Rebecca Harper	22 Jun 1814	Daniel Scott
Scott William	Elizabeth Mason	8 Nov 1824	John C. Harvey
Scott William	Polly Puckett	30 Sep 1826	Bartlett Scott
			Drury A. Mims
Scott William	Betsy Mason	2 May 1827	Henry Badgett
Seamore Singleton	Susy Seamore	27 Jan 1820	John C. Rogers
Searcy Alexander M.	Elizabeth L. Cook	13 Jun 1848	Saml. Moore
Seed Thomas	Nancey Jones	9 Dec 1818	Sanders Donoho
Seewell Robert W.	Carnelia A. Donoho	8 Jan 1838	William T. Smith
Sellears William	Nancey Swift	19 Aug 1836	William Holt
Sergant Stephen	Nancy P. Richardson	1 Jan 1828	John P. Harrison
Sertain Elisha	Frances Paschael	8 Dec 1840	A. Nelson Nunn
Sertain Johnston	Nancey Berry	20 Jul 1830	William Sanders
Settle Josiah	Frances L. Graves	3 Jun 1826	Tho. Graves
Settle Thomas	Henrietta Graves	18 Sep 1820	Azariah Graves
Seymour Robert (see Seamore)	Amy Duty	28 Jan 1784	Reuben Newton John Moore JP
Shackelford Armstead	Nancey Halcomb	24 Oct 1786	William Halcomb
Shackleford Abram (Col)	Lucinda Garland (Col)	25 Aug 1866	Charles H. Walters md by J. J. Jones JP
Shackleford Francis	Anna Davis	10 Dec 1819	Garland Shackleford Thomas Gunter
Shackleford Francis A.	Elisabeth A. Harris	28 Sep 1857 30 Sep 1857	Robert T. Vernon md by J. M. Allen JP
Shackleford John	Nancey Keen	8 Dec 1815	John H. Humphreys
Shackleford William (son of William & Ann Shackleford)	Mary E. Edwards (dau of James M. & Mariah Edwards)	21 Sep 1867 24 Sep	md by C. C. Chaplin
Shaman Charles	Milley Edwyn	31 Oct 1794	Edmund Alley
Shaman William	Fanny Edwards	8 Mar 1791	William Willson
Shanks Charles	Salley Street	5 Jan 1798	Hirem Parks
Shanks Joseph	Mary Roberson	18 Jan 1832	Woodson Foulks
Shanks Thomas	Polley Means	9 Jan 1799	Robert Shanks
Shanks Thomas Jr.	Hannah Roberson	2 Aug 1828	Israel Barker
Shannon William R.	Sarah E. Ingram	15 Jul 1858	William A. Ferguson md by N. M. Lewis JP
Shanon Marcus	Letta Shaw	2 Jan 1837	Stephen Dodson
Shapard James	Frances Brooks	30 Aug 1797	Alex. Murphey Anne Smith
Shapard John J.	Martha S. Watts	11 Feb 1867	James T. Carr md by John J. Jones JP
Shapard Lewis	Martha Nicholson	22 Nov 1796	James Shepard
Sharman William	Polly Edwyn	14 Aug 1799	Abner Qualls
Sharp George	Polly Hamleton	25 Nov 1811	John Chilton
Sharp Granderson M.*	Martha G. Slade	9 May 1831	Allen Gunn Sr.
Sharp William T.	Ann S. Harrison	7 Nov 1837	Abishai Slade
Shaw James	Elizabeth Gibson	28 May 1783	Edwd. Upton
Shaw James	Mary Pendergrass	9 Jan 1786	Edd. Upton
Shaw John S.	Martha Woods	15 Feb 1848	Rufus W. McCulley
Shaw John W.	Nancy Vaughan	16 Nov 1847	Thomas Burton
Shaw Joseph M.	Elizabeth Ann Hughs	4 Dec 1857	George Herndon
Shaw Nathaniell	Sookey Cox	11 Oct 1800	Philip Cox

GROOM	BRIDE	DATE	BONDSMAN OR WITNESS
Shaw Saml. (Colson of Saml. Faucett & Sally Shaw)	Sarah Walker (Coldau of Stephen Walker & Mariah Anderson)	23 Sep 1867 24 Sep	md by A. G. Anderson
Shearman Thomas (see Shaman)	Sarah Burch	11 Dec 1800	Jacob Burch
Shelton David	Susanah Vaughn	3 Jun 1784	Alexander Miles
Shelton F. L. R.	Martha A. E. Thomas	17 Nov 1849	William C. Shelton T. S. Poore
Shelton Henry	Temperence Harris	2 Aug 1815	Edwin Reany
Shelton James F. (of Pittsylvania Co. Va.)	Mary Ann Mariah Shelton (dau of Wesley of Pittsylvania Co. Va)	24 Apr 1843	Thompson Robertson
Shelton James W.	Mary Ann Jones	9 Feb 1841	Thomas Swift
Shelton James W.	Martha C. Martin	4 Apr 1848	Wesley Swift
Shelton John	Susannah Bradley (dau of James Bradley)	31 May 1780	Alexander Miles
Shelton Peter	Sena Murphey	5 Jun 1838	Lewis W. Withers
Shelton Samuel E.	Mary McCain	4 Aug 1846	Dabney Terry W. A. Whitfield
Shelton W. N.	Fannie Johnston	20 Jan 1863	J. L. McKee md by Jacob Doll MG
Shelton William	Betsey Swift	25 Dec 1809	Alfred Bethell
Shelton William H.	Frances Gatewood	27 Nov 1812	Lewis Gatewood
Shields Dr. P.	Eliza E. Tally	29 Aug 1864	Robt. T. Bernon md by J. J. Jones JP
Shields John	Christiana Duprey	12 Jan 1820	Henry Glass
Shields Johnson	Mary Sikes	10 Oct 1826	Jno. C. Womack
Shields Thomas R.	Martha Hubbard	27 Feb 1867 28 Feb	md by Thomas J. Brown JP
Short James	Creasy Tennesson	25 Dec 1800	John Short
Shreve Robert	Elizabeth Summers	14 Feb 1854	Ralph Glaze md by E. K. Withers JP
Shreve Robert D.	Sally Cox	19 Dec 1866	W. T. Dallas md by F. L. Oakley MG
Shryer Jacob	Nancey Bennatt	13 Jan 1810	James Yancey
Sibley James W.	Ann M. Stanfield	28 May 1862	Cornelius E. Woods md by N. M. Lewis JP
Siddall Ira	Polly Smith	2 Nov 1805	John Montgomery
Siddall Job	Sarah Hudson	17 Aug 1791	Adams Sanders
Sidebottom James H.*	Mary Ann Mims	26 Sep 1831	Maj. C. Lea
Sidebottom James H.	Julia Ann Henderson	2 Jul 1832	Nathaniel W. Pass
Sidebottom James H.	Mary Ann Mims	4 Oct 1832	Edward A. Tarwater
Simmons Abram.	Salley Barton	6 Mar 1813	Elisha Barton
Simmons Elisha	Frances Birke	25 Nov 1845	Birrel Corbett
Simmons George	Ann Barton	16 Dec 1797	Elisha Barton
Simmons James	Stacia Roberts	5 Sep 1791	Arthur Mitchel
Simmons James	Avicey Bush	8 Mar 1812	Bennet Bush
Simmons John	Rhody Bush	15 Nov 1809	Zenas Bush
Simmons John	Martha Thomas	19 Dec 1835	Isaac Simmons
Simmons John	Nancey Simmons	15 Dec 1840	Colemon L. Mitchell
Simmons John Jr.*	Nancey Simmons	18 Dec 1831	Thomas Massey
Simmons Joseph B.	Elizabeth L. McNutt	16 Oct 1854	Rufus L. Wright
Simmons Levi	Elisa Jackson	16 Dec 1832	Archibald R. Birk
Simms Buckner	Nancey Whitlock	20 Oct 1784	Thos. Palmer Jos. Willson
Simpson Alvis	Nancy V. Rich	20 Dec 1859	Edward O. Jones

GROOM	BRIDE	DATE	BONDSMAN OR WITNESS
Simpson Benjamin F.	Martha P. Hightower	13 Oct 1843	John T. Stadler
Simpson Charles	Jemima Cannon	15 Jul 1841	Thomas C. Harderson
Simpson Dennis	Jane Boulden	3 Aug 1866	Solomon Corbett
		18 Aug 1866	md by F. L. Oakley MG
Simpson Enoch	Elizabeth Carter	29 Dec 1818	Francis L. Simpson
Simpson Francis L.	Priscilla Simpson	16 Dec 1815	Thomas Garrett
Simpson George	Elizabeth Barker	11 Dec 1830	George Barker
Simpson James M.	Martha Ann Smith	25 May 1858	Brice Harralson md by G. G. Walker
Simpson John Calvin	Martha G. Gatwood	3 Oct 1849	Vinson S. Garrett Samuel F. Heydon
Simpson John H.	Elizabeth L. Snipes	5 Nov 1853	Wm. F. Davis
		8 Nov 1853	md by Howell Boswell JP
Simpson Joseph	Susan B. Anderson	12 Dec 1843	Sandford M. Simpson
Simpson Moses	Jenney M. Tracey	23 Nov 1809	Azariah Graves Jr.
Simpson Moses	Jane Smith	4 Nov 1833	Joseph Matkins
Simpson Moses S.	Delphey Florence	22 Oct 1804	Hugh Walker
Simpson Oliver	Betsey Rice	10 Mar 1810	John Cooper
Simpson Richard	Jane Durham	19 Dec 1860	Nathaniel Durham md by W. B. Swann JP
Simpson Richard Jr.	Susannah Simpson	2 Feb 1807	Green L. Brown
Simpson Roger	Peggy Williamson	27 Dec 1808	Oliver Simpson
Simpson Silas	A. M. F. P. Boley	8 May 1844	Christian Strader
Simpson Solomon	Elizabeth Hunter	17 Nov 1813	Joshua Hightower D. W. Simpson
Simpson Thomas T.	Martha W. Hodges	21 Nov 1848	Isaac Simmons
Simpson Vinson	Mary Huskins	16 Feb 1826	George W. Garrett
Sims John	Polly Wright	18 Oct 1791	Thomas Rice
Sims William B.	Sallie L. Richmond	20 May 1858	W. G. Stephens
Simson William	Nancy Dowell	17 Jul 1788	John Hall
Singleton Jerre	Cary Benton	11 Apr 1801	Stephen Roberts
Singleton Joseph	Elizabeth Kitchen	23 Dec 1824	John C. Harvey Peter Hooper
Singleton Robert	Kittey Roberts	11 Dec 1816	Thomas Graves
Singleton William A.	Nancy Cates	24 Mar 1855	Hiram A. Watlington
		26 Mar 1855	md by J. Jennings JP
Skeen Jonathan	Elizabeth Sargent	14 Jan 1792	Wm. Long
Skeen Peter	Sarah Sargant	15 Oct 1782	George Lea John Moore JP
Slade Abisha	Polly K. Harrison	5 Jan 1826	James Miles
Slade Abisha	Mary Graves	23 Apr 1846	---------
Slade Elias	Elizabeth Turner	11 Apr 1825	John J. Hooper
Slade Ezekiel	Mary Hubbard	17 Jan 1798	Thomas Lea
Slade James M.	Pricila Jones	16 Jan 1866	Jas. J. Clendenin
Slade John R.	Bettie A. McCain	27 May 1863	Elias D. Slade md by S. S. Harrison JP
Slade John T.	Martha A. Walters (Col)	26 May 1866	md by Jas. J. Clendinin JP
Slade Josiah	Jane Gomer	22 Jul 1815	William Gomer
Slade Lemuel	Betsy Smith	26 Feb 1867	Henry W. Cobb
		2 Apr 1867	md by Q. A. Ward MG
Slade Nathan	Elizabeth Yancey	26 Jun 1792	John Graves
Slade Robt. (son of Luke Womack & Fanny Ingram)	Margaret Slade (dau of Daniel & Phebe Slade)	30 Nov 1867 22 Dec 1867	md by Thomas S. Harrison JP
Slade Thomas	Elizabeth Taber	30 Jan 1823	Thomas Turner Jr.
Slade Thomas Jr.	Mary Williams (dau of Henry Williams)	22 Nov 1779	Thos. Slade Sr. A. Tatom
Slade Thomas Jr.	Isabella Graves	12 Dec 1782	Robert Morrow
Slade Thomas T.	Emeline Cobb	9 May 1849	W. H. Alexander

GROOM	BRIDE	DATE	BONDSMAN OR WITNESS
Slade William	Martha Kerr	22 Dec 1786	Thomas Slade
Slade William	Mary Turner	22 Nov 1820	Jno. Chandler
Slade William	Sarah Reid	23 Dec 1856	md by Wm. B. Bowe JP
Slade William G.	Adelade R. Hendrick	18 Nov 1854	Samuel N. Dunn
		22 Nov 1854	md by Tho. L. Lea JP
Slate Richard J.	Parthena E. Newbell	3 Nov 1841	Robert M. Ferrell
			Jno. Daniel
Slaydon William W.	Mary R. Rowland	2 Dec 1833	Henry Rowland
Slayte James H.	Marthany Weldon (dau of Johnathan)	5 Aug 1829	William Headspeth Richard H. L. Bennatt
Slayton James	Mary Parsons	20 Oct 1849	James N. Montgomery
Slayton Richard	Rebecca Russell	10 Dec 1853	E. B. Holden
Sledge Crawford D. (son of Littleton & Susan Sledge)	Mary P. Neal (dau of Wm. D. & Sebilla Neal)	3 Feb 1868 5 Feb	md by S. G. Mason
Sledge John P.	Elizabeth Clay	17 Nov 1823	Jno. E. Lewis
Sledge Littleton	Susannah Ray	24 Nov 1821	Maj. L. Graves
Smales Thomas	Mary Deane	6 Nov 1841	Edward Townes
Smith Abednego (Col-son of Benjn. & Jennie)	Matilda Yarbrough (dau of David & Mendah)	22 Apr 1867	md by John J. Jones JP
Smith Amasa	Susanah Bazwell	2 Apr 1811	Thomas Burch
Smith Andrew H.	Lucinda Murphy	19 Dec 1846	Dudley Y. Murphy
Smith Clement	Sarah Cobb	11 Jan 1850	Mastin H. Cobb
Smith Daniel	Elizabeth Polston	8 Dec 1804	Henry Robinson
Smith Daniel	Sally Hubbard	9 Jan 1810	Stephen Smith
Smith Daniel	Polly Hinton	12 Dec 1842	Woodlief Thomas
Smith Edmond (Col)	Viney Wilson (Col)	28 Dec 1866	Solomon Connally
Smith Eligah R.	Frances Thomas	11 Dec 1854 14 Dec 1854	William P. Browning md by B. Cooper JP
Smith Ewell	Elizabeth Cruise	6 Nov 1826	Edward G. Stuart
Smith Francis	Betsey Willis	21 Oct 1802	William Carmikel
Smith Gardner	Milly Jones	2 Nov 1822	John Gamble
Smith Garnett	Betsey Sawyers	20 Apr 1810	Phillip Baynes
Smith George	Jenney Tait	20 Dec 1800	Zaccheus Tate
Smith George	Salley Jackson	14 Aug 1807	Thomas Jackson Jr.
Smith Green	Parthenia Burch	8 Jan 1820	Kindle Baswell
Smith Green (Col)	Fannie Thornton (Col)	22 Sep 1866	Martin Lucas
Smith Green D.	Leony Bolton	1 Sep 1819	Stephen Dodson Tho. Donoho Jr.
Smith Henderson	Polly C. Chandler	24 Nov 1828	James D. Chandler
Smith Henry	Martha Carter	13 Dec 1818	Jno. J. Oliver
Smith Henry	Mary Jane Powell	17 Mar 1840	Daniel Smith
Smith James	Sarah Culberson	6 Oct 1778	David Michell William Moore
Smith James	Salley Whitmore	8 Jun 1825	Charles Whitmore
Smith James	Anne Faucett	18 Feb 1833	George Smith
Smith James G.	Sarah J. Hawkins	22 Jul 1867 25 Jul	md by Jerry Smith JP
Smith James M.	Mary Jane Farmer	30 Sep 1848	Bentley W. Page
Smith James M.	Liley A. Poteat	6 Aug 1859 7 Aug 1859	Jas. H. Owen md by Wm. B. Bowe JP
Smith James T.	Elizabeth Herndon	21 Dec 1832	Elijah G. Browning
Smith James T.	Mehala Warren	23 May 1850	Robert S. Barnett
Smith Jeremiah	Mary Rowe (Roe?)	13 Nov 1835	Isaac Simmons
Smith Jerry	Mary A. Rudd	25 Dec 1855 27 Dec 1855	Thomas Covington md by Thos. Covington JP
Smith Jesse S.	Margaret J. Graves	15 Mar 1853	William B. Graves md by A. McDowell MG
Smith John	Rebeckah Starky	9 Nov 1803	Jonathan Starky Wm. Wilkerson DC
Smith John	Susannah Merritt	2 Jan 1824	William J. Connally

GROOM	BRIDE	DATE	BONDSMAN OR WITNESS
Smith John	Helena Persons	7 Oct 1826	James Harrison
Smith John	Virginia Hubbard	7 Dec 1854	James Wallace Stephen T. Voss
Smith John C.	Ava P. Browning	26 Apr 1845	Thomas R. Kimbro
Smith John H.	Nancy Dameron	22 Apr 1862 24 Apr 1862	Joseph F. Dillard md by G. W. Prendergast
Smith John R.	Priscilla H. Connally	22 Dec 1852	Henry N. Holden md by John H. Lacy
Smith John W.	Elizabeth W. Wade	21 Feb 1866	Augustus Atkinson md by C. H. Richmond JP
Smith Jonathan	Nancey Willis	9 Feb 1822	Martin Mims
Smith Joseph	Celia Parks	8 Nov 1827	Young Browning
Smith Lea A.	Sarah F. Cole	10 Aug 1866	Robert H. Cheek
Smith Mace	Margaret Coleston	18 Nov 1780	James Randolph Jr.
Smith Mace	Constant Brown	12 Aug 1782	James Reylye
Smith Maurice	Clarissa H. Reed	27 Apr 1830	Elijah Graves Jr.
Smith Moses	Margret Kelly	30 Jul 1794	Edmd. Browning
Smith Nicholas C.	Anna Sanders	2 Nov 1832	John Somers
Smith Peter	Mary F. Apple	6 Mar 1865 8 Mar 1865	Alexander R. Paschal md by Stephen Neal JP
Smith Reubin	Elizabeth Kemp	1 Mar 1818	Claybourn Crisp Tho. Slade
Smith Richard	Salley Anglin	26 Oct 1804	William Browning
Smith Richard	Sophia Gibson	3 Nov 1815	Robert Swift
Smith Richard Jr.*	Frances Sheppard	30 Mar 1831	Wm. Sanders
Smith Richard S.	Blanche A. Moore	26 Dec 1866	Jas. M. Evans md by Monroe Oliver JP
Smith Robert	Mary Whitworth Cole	6 Aug 1783	Josiah Cole
Smith Robert	Martha Daniel	29 May 1815	John Mansfield
Smith Robert	Leathy Matlock	17 Nov 1846	Iverson G. Warren
Smith Robt. H.	Charlotte Dickson	4 Mar 1862	Bird G. Sutherlin md by S. S. Harrison JP
Smith Robert J.	Cornelia A. Williamson	15 Apr 1840	James H. Atkinson
Smith Sam P.	Kate Lawson	22 Oct 1860	md by Sam. F. Mason MG
Smith Samuel	Elizabeth Williamson	9 Nov 1812	James Graves
Smith Samuel	Francis Browning	13 Nov 1826	Josiah Page
Smith Samuel Jr.	Elisabeth Harrison	23 Apr 1792	James Hall
Smith Samuel R. Jr.	Louisania C. Tuck	20 Oct 1836	Cary W. West
Smith Starkey	Sarah Brinsfield	19 Dec 1814	Dennard Brinsfield Jeremiah Rudd
Smith Stephen	Fanny Johnston	2 Sep 1812	George Oldham Connally
Smith Stephen	Martha Payne	16 Oct 1827	Thomas W. Harrelson
Smith Solomon	Peggy Hastin	4 Jan 1816	Richard C. Overton
Smith Thomas	Mildred Atkins	27 Nov 1804	Francis Smith
Smith Thomas	Catherine Jopling	4 Apr 1815	John Fitch Jr.
Smith Thomas B.	Hulday A. Richmond	2 Jun 1860	B. Harralson
Smith Thomas H.	Martha J. Burnette	20 Jan 1841	Robert A. Crowder
Smith Vincen M.	Elizabeth Davis	1 Jan 1856	John W. Willis md by J. M. Allen JP
Smith William	Sarah Hightower	4 Jan 1800	John Johnston
Smith William	Betsey Poston	28 Jun 1800	William Poston
Smith William	Phebe Ford	27 Jan 1814	Mumford Ford Duke W. Simpson
Smith William	Elizabeth Walker	20 Oct 1816	George Walker
Smith William	Tempy Malone	7 Sep 1819	Curtis Payne Thomas M. Rainey

GROOM	BRIDE	DATE	BONDSMAN OR WITNESS
Smith William	Betsy Ann Wilson	28 Jun 1832	Josiah Rainey
Smith William A.	Isabella Smith	6 Feb 1833	Henry F. Smith
Smith William B.	Nancey Miles	21 Dec 1859	Richard Miles
		22 Dec 1859	md by John Stadler
Smith William H.	Mary Dameron	14 Feb 1856	Rufus A. Rudd
		15 Feb 1856	md by Thomas Covington JP
Smith William P.	Fanie M. Barnes	7 Nov 1865	Birket Lownes
			md by S. G. Mason
Smith Willis Buchanham	Lucy Phelps	11 Nov 1794	Larking Phelps
Smith Zion	Mary Douglas	15 Dec 1840	Andrew Ferguson
Smithey John	Sarah Kermichael	18 Nov 1798	Thomas Browning
Smithey John	Betsey Payne	13 Aug 1805	Samuel Smyth J. Yancey
Smithey Reuben	Elizabeth Walker	4 Feb 1840	Samuel Maze
Smithey Reubin	Polley Roberts	19 May 1802	Daniel McGilvery
Smithey Samuel	Martha Groom	14 Jan 1841	Robert Scott Jr.
Smithey Thomas	Polly Paschall	3 Aug 1837	Admiral N. Nunn
Smithey Thomas	Amey Gomer	30 Oct 1838	Jethro J. Walker
Smithy John	Sarah Paschall	5 Feb 1842	William Paschall
Smythe Samuel	Nancey Warrin	17 Mar 1787	Thomas Vaughn
Snead Benjamin	Martha A. Hall	24 Feb 1853	Alexander Snead
Snead Micajah	Judith Brandon	24 Oct 1792	John Brandon
Snead Wm. L.	Mary S. Richardson	8 Dec 1849	Wm. M. Nance M. P. Huntington
Sneed Archibel	Frances Covington	23 Dec 1846	Robert Singleton
Sneed John	Elizabeth Langhorn	26 Apr 1841	Edward Hailey Jno. Daniel
Sneed William H.	Belvederrie F. Calloway	17 Oct 1832	Dr. Allen Gunn
Sneed William M.	Louisa M. Bethel	28 Jun 1842	Jno. K. Graves
Snipes Cato	Jane Walker	30 Jan 1867	Barzillai Graves
Snipes James C.	Emeline Swift	27 May 1847	Thomas B. Broach
Snipes James L.	Margarett McMullin	20 Dec 1837	Joseph M. Pearce
Snipes Nathaniel	Tabitha Kimbrough	16 Jun 1801	James Sargent
Snow Richard (Col)	Carolina Adkins (Col)	11 Aug 1845	Henry Roland
Snow Stephen T.	Nancy F. Lovelace	13 Feb 1866	William G. Snow
		15 Feb 1866	md by W. B. Swann JP
Somers Alfred	Sarah F. Mims	3 May 1858	P. W. Parker
		5 May 1858	md by J. W. Lewis JP
Somers Henry (Col)	Susann Powell (Col)	20 Oct 1866	Felix Windsor
		21 Oct 1866	md by R. G. Barrett MG
Somers James	Viney Gillaspey	30 Jan 1806	Azariah Graves
Somers James	Elizabeth Smithey	17 Dec 1846	John Smithey
Somers John	Rebecah Wright	25 Jul 1804	Isaac Wright
Somers John	Mildred Beavers	11 Nov 1843	Henry F. Adkins
Somers Reubun T. (son of James & Elizabeth Somers)	Martha E. Smithy (dau of John & Sarah Smithy)	8 Apr 1867 10 Apr 1867	md by Azariah Graves JP
Somers William	Mary A. Sartin	12 Nov 1852	William A. Somers
Somers Zeary	Nancy Berrey	20 Jul 1844	John Somers
Somers Zera	Sarah Paskell	22 Feb 1837	John Somer
Sommers William	Frances Butler	11 Jan 1853	Absalom Canaday
Southard John	Nelly Lovelace	22 Dec 1840	Pleasant L. Ford
Southard William	Malinda Fuller	24 Oct 1840	Pleasant L. Ford
Southard William	Susan Durham	14 Apr 1845	William Chapman
Southard William	Mary Carter (wid)	8 Feb 1848	William Carver
Southard William	Elizabeth Durham	26 Feb 1857	Nelson Chapman
Sowell Thomas L.	Fnces Muzzal	21 Jan 1819	Mumford Stanfield
Sowell Thomas L.	Nancy S. Mitchell	1 Jun 1830	Azariah Graves
Sparks Milton	Martha Cook	28 Sep 1847	E. D. Cook

GROOM	BRIDE	DATE	BONDSMAN OR WITNESS
Sparks Thomas	Nancy McCulley	8 Jul 1817	Isaac Gardner Philip Day
Spencer Daniel	Susannah Davis	31 Dec 1804	Bond V. Brown
Spencer John	Anne Kerr	26 Jul 1781	William Henslee
Spencer Thomas	Polly Mitchell	21 Feb 1796	John Mitchel
Spruce George	Molly A. White	7 May 1858	A. L. Bagby
		8 May 1858	md by Jno. W. Lewis MG
Stace Malon	Mary Spencer	9 Apr 1787	William Henslee
Stacey Eli	Elizabeth Spencer	23 Dec 1789	Martin Wiseman
Stacy John	Frances Hightower	19 May 1828	Robert Hightower
Stacy Thomas	Deborah Benton	30 Jul 1816	David Douglas
Stadler John	Nancey Arnold	13 Dec 1812	William Massey
Stadler John J.	Susan A. Caldnond	26 Oct 1860	R. E. Stadler
		28 Oct 1860	md by G. W. Prendergast JP
Stadler John T.	Arrena Gooch	2 Jan 1844	Thomas W. McKinney Thos. H. Miles
Stadler Robert D.	Lydia F. Arnold	3 Dec 1838	James W. Arnold
Stadler Robert D.	Nancey M. Browning	6 Aug 1862	Franklin Graves
		10 Aug 1862	md by William Burns
Stadler William B.	Artilia Aldridge	20 Oct 1840	John T. Stadler
Stafford Adam	Nancy Peterson	7 Sep 1790	Joseph Peterson
Stafford Adam	Boza Rudd	25 Dec 1809	Jere Rudd
Stafford Eli	Nancy Morgan	26 Dec 1807	Abner Wilson
Stafford James	Polly Eskridge	8 May 1799	William Stafford
Stafford James	Salley Lea	30 Dec 1817	Henry W. Wilson
Stafford John	Betsey Quine	13 Jun 1791	Tho. Stafford
Stafford John	Ann Johnston	29 Jul 1800	William Rainey
Stafford Joseph	Nancy Whitlow	9 Jun 1809	Adam Stafford
Stafford Samuel	Mary Carman	2 Aug 1796	Elijah Carman
Stafford Thomas	Fanny Whitlow	23 Feb 1791	Starritt Dobbins
Stafford William	Sally Johnston	15 Aug 1793	John Ellmore
Stainback William H.	Parthena Siddle	20 Aug 1841	John H. Farcett
Stalcup William	Cornelia K. Lea	6 Jul 1847	Louis W. Dishough
Stallcup Austin	Betsey Pleasant	24 Sep 1802	James Milton
Stallcup John	Silviah Pleasant	30 Jan 1801	Rease Enochs
Stamps James (Col-son of Warner & Lizy)	Milly Lewis (Col-dau of Burl Donoho & Lethy Lewis)	18 May 1867	md by E. Hunt JP
Stamps Jno.	Nancy Slade	13 Jan 1808	Barzalai Graves
Stamps Rufus	Martha F. Moore	17 Jun 1845	William Hightower
Stamps Samuel	Dafney Wilson	1 Dec 1866	Henry Lindsey md by J. J. Jones JP
Stamps Thomas	Eliza A. Walker	16 Mar 1842	Charles R. Dodson
Stamps William	Sarah Pinix	20 Nov 1825	Jno. Stamps
Stamps William (son of James & Matilda Stamps)	Dorcas Lindsey (dau of Coleman Johnson & Mary Lindsey)	27 Dec 1867	md by John J. Jones JP
Standfield Harrison	Sarah McGhee	31 Mar 1789	Robert Moore
Standley Allin	Salley Jones	24 Jul 1838	James Burton
Standley Will R.	Eliza A. Travis	4 Jul 1844	James E. Foster
Stanfield Benjamin F.	Sarah P. Johnston	5 Sep 1825	Willis L. Taylor
Stanfield David V.	Frances C. Bradsher	1 Aug 1850	E. S. Wilkinson
Stanfield Durrett	Lucy Warren	18 Dec 1797	Partrick Carnell
Stanfield Jno.	Patsey Robinson	24 Mar 1800	John Thomas
Stanfield Joseph M.	Ann Barnett	26 May 1836	George A. Smith
Stanfield Mark M.	Martha M. Carter	24 Apr 1849	Alexander Moore
Stanfield Marmaduke	Anne Samuel	26 Aug 1795	John Dyson Durrett Stanfield

GROOM	BRIDE	DATE	BONDSMAN OR WITNESS
Stanfield William	Elisabeth Beadler	14 Dec 1789	Josias Chambers
Stanfield William A.	Mary Read	4 May 1854	Marion P. Stanfield
Stanley Alfred M.	Emily Donoho	18 Sep 1843	Pinckney C. Bethell
Stanley Alpheus	Mary F. McKinney	18 Nov 1858	Ezekiel Orr md by J. W. Lewis MG
Stanley James	Delila Scott	9 Jun 1840	James Ingram
Stanley James	Tabitha J. Brown	31 May 1852	William R. Stanley
Stanley Joel	Lucy Duncan	13 Mar 1824	Richard Standley
Stansbery Samuel	Hannah Hix	7 Oct 1786	Calab Carman
Stansbury Luke	Comfort Roberts	16 May 1788	Saml. Stansbury
Stansbury Luke	Nancey Haddock	30 Jan 1791	Byrd Wall
Starkes Chesley	Euphranier Harrison	24 Nov 1846	William J. Murray
Starkey John	Nancey Sawyers	27 Sep 1790	William Sawyer
Starkey Thomas	Frances Roberts	22 Jan 1829	Richard H. Griffith
Staulcup Levi	Catharine L. Jones	12 Jun 1843	John T. Stadler
Stegall Durell	Harriet Nelson	18 Dec 1850	Craddock Elliott
Step Joshua	Nice Dollerhide	6 Feb 1789	Enus Jurdin
Stephens Alfred	Hannah Long	10 Nov 1866	Wm. G. Graves md by S. G. Mason MG
Stephens Andrew W.	Ann Chambers	27 Feb 1840	Williamson M. Stephens
Stephens Anthony Jr.	Dianna Thomas	22 Sep 1837	James Jones
Stephens Armstead	Lucy Kiersey	24 Dec 1835	John Stephens
Stephens Benjamin	Polley Roberts	25 Jan 1803	William Stephens
Stephens Benjamin	Sally Malone	19 Jun 1822	Stephen Rucker
Stephens Benjamin A.	Mary Brandon	18 Dec 1858	Wm. R. Fullington md by Jas. P. Simpson MG
Stephens C.	Bettie J. Weire	6 Jan 1866	James M. Williams md by Thomas S. Harrison
Stephens George	Rhoda Going	28 Jul 1806	Joseph Flippa
Stephens George	Ann Evans	8 Sep 1866	Matt Stephens md by Jerry Smith JP
Stephens Henry	Dicey Thomas	3 Aug 1835	Zachariah Lockett
Stephens Isaac	Eliza Harville	12 Apr 1838	John Perkins
Stephens Isaac	Sinai Mustion	22 Feb 1849	Henry Lea
Stephens Iverson G.	Jane Frasier	21 Aug 1834	Andrew Stephens
Stephens James	Joanna Drummond	31 Jan 1817	Henry M. Clay John Scott
Stephens John	Nancey Stanley	22 Apr 1830	Elisha Stanley
Stephens John Q.	Mary A. Melone	13 Dec 1837	George W. Willis
Stephens Matt	Jennett Comer	8 Sep 1866	George Stephens md by Jerry Smith JP
Stephens Peter	Eliza Ann Garland	7 Jul 1846	Richard Bennett
Stephens Peter	Frances Scott	18 Mar 1850	John Stephens
Stephens Thomas	Elizabeth Warwick	4 Feb 1788	Charles Stephens
Stephens Thomas	Mary Legrand	7 Sep 1838	Thomas C. Pass
Stephens William	Polley Watterfield	9 Oct 1816	William Stevens
Stephens William	Nancy Slade	1 Dec 1866	Jno. Miles Johnston md by R. G. Barrett
Stephens Williamson M.	Barbarah Stephens	16 Nov 1844	Alginon D. Stephens
Stevens George	Susan Richardson	19 Aug 1830	John P. Harrison
Stevens Henry (Col)	Caroline Hamlett (Col)	6 Apr 1867	H. F. Brandon clk
Stevens Thomas L.	Martha J. Farley	23 Jul 1832	William M. McGehee
Stevens William	Mary Nowel	4 Jan 1789	Charles Stephens
Stevens William	Jane Evens	26 Jul 1855	Bartlett Y. McAden md by Stephen Neal JP
Stevens William (Col)	Rosetta Hughs (Col)	11 Jun 1859	John Freeman

GROOM	BRIDE	DATE	BONDSMAN OR WITNESS
Steward Littleton	Betsey Steward	11 Dec 1838	Abel Foulks
Stewart Anderson (Col)	Martha Farmer (Col)	23 Dec 1865 26 Feb 1865?	Samuel Farmer (Col) md by Solomon Apple MG
Stewart Barzillai	Nancy Roan	4 Nov 1833	Justin Roan
Stewart Mack (Col)	Candis Bolton (Col)	25 Dec 1866 26 Dec 1866	Stephen Lea (Col) md by Solomon Apple
Stoane Thomas	Elizabeth Greer	19 Aug 1793	William Mann
Stockes Moore	Nancey Baxdale	22 Oct 1817	William Williams
Stokes Allen	Mary Stokes	23 Feb 1829	William Y. Stokes
Stokes Jesse	Bettie Meadows	10 Nov 1866 12 Nov 1866	Alex. Robertson md by Thomas S. Harrison JP
Stokes Joel A.	Elizabeth C. Payne	7 OCt 1836	William W. Richardson
Stokes John Y.	Susan A. C. Stone	31 Mar 1855 5 Apr 1855	James A. D. Burnes md by William Anderson
Stokes Silvanus	Nancey Gatewood	25 Dec 1809	Caleb Anglin
Stokes William Y.	Louisa T. Keesee	18 Dec 1829	Jacob Henderson
Stokes William Y.	Lucy W. Hatchett	28 Oct 1836	Green P. Womack
Stone Eli C.	Sarah A. Burns	30 May 1849	Grief G. Mason
Stone John F.	Mary E. Furguson	28 Feb 1853 10 Mar 1853	Thomas R. Stone md by Wm. Anderson
Stone Thomas R.	Priscilla M. Henderson	24 Apr 1849	William Alverson
Stone William M.	Mary F. Estes	23 Nov 1855	Wm. B. Green md by J. M. Allen
Stow Henry C.	Mildred A. Hart	20 Sep 1855	Jno. J. Peak md by S. S. Harrison JP
Stowers John	Cathrine Beaver	29 Jan 1810	John Arnold
Strader Christian	Eveline Burns	20 Feb 1844	John A. Withers
Strader David	Lucy Ann Elizabeth Walf	14 Dec 1856	Thomas P. Harvy md by J. Jennings JP
Strader Henry	Polly Scott	16 Mar 1784	Jno. Collins
Strader James	Ann Stone	27 May 1849	John Strader
Strader Jeremiah	Ann Chapman	30 Jan 1845	Nelson Chapman
Strader John	Mary Ann Scarlet	5 Jun 1863	David Strader md by Stephen Neal JP
Strader Lewis	Polly Weatherford	26 Aug 1822	William Weatherford
Strador Christian Jr.	Lucinda Lovelace	19 Dep 1827	Jesse C. Kendall
Strador David	Hannah Dill	31 May 1841	Noah Cobb
Strador John	Martha Rolley	23 Dec 1822	Christian Strador
Strador Obediah	Mary Fuller	29 Jan 1838	Eli Ford
Straten William	Deliah Bawldin	23 Dec 1823	Richard R. Kennon
Straten William	Polly Kennon	21 Jan 1824	Zachariah Hooper Sr.
Straten William	Delila Balden	31 Jan 1825	Thomas L. Slade
Stratton John C.	Lenora E. Burns	27 Jun 1855	Wm. H. Burn
Stratton John D.	Ann West	4 Dec 1829	Robert Townley Daniel S. Price
Street Anthony	Polly Gray	18 Jun 1803	Henry Gray
Street John	Anne Vincent	15 Dec 1798	Alexander Vincent
Strickland Edwin C.	C. G. Sparrow	19 Oct 1856	William W. Dodson md by Thomas W. Tobey
Strother Peter	Maryann Baxter	11 Jun 1788	Conrod Strother
Stuart Edward G.	Sarah Cruise	6 Nov 1826	Ewell Smith
Stuart John	Asanath Roan	15 Jul 1817	Barnet Kemp
Stuart Stephen	Anna Hughston	12 Sep 1812	Samuel Woods
Stuart William	Rachel Wisdom	23 Jul 1802	James Stuart
Stubblefield Beverly	Rebecca Willson	7 Oct 1826	Benjamin W. Justice
Stubblefield George W.	Salley Lawson	12 Aug 1817	David Lawson
Stubblefield Nathan	Elisabeth Todd	6 Nov 1794	Richard Bethell Benjamin Stephens

GROOM	BRIDE	DATE	BONDSMAN OR WITNESS
Stubblefield Peyton T.	Mary P. Nunnally	27 Oct 1832	George H. Holderby
Stubblefield Richard C.	Eliza Rice	8 Jun 1832	Henry W. Brooks
Stubblefield Theodorick*	Eliza Jones	24 Sep 1831	Henry W. Brooks
Stubblefield William	Mary Mabrey	18 Dec 1778	William Hubbard
Stubblefield Wm. L.*	Dorothy Brooks	14 Dec 1831	Theo Stubblefield
Stublefield Barnett (Col)	Emily Brown (Col)	27 Nov 1866	Anderson Brown md by Azariah Graves JP
Stublefield Solomon (Col-son & Manda Stublefield)	Caty Mitchell (Col)	25 Dec 1867 18 Jan 1868	md by Stephen of Ned Neal JP
Suit John	Sarah Bowls	22 Dec 1789	Joseph Atkinson
Suit William	Rebecke Wilson	28 May 1787	William Glen
Sullivent Jordan	Polley Gomer	23 Dec 1805	William Beaver
Sumers John	Mary Gimboe	2 Jul 1783	James Stringer
Sumers John	Jimima Walker	2 Sep 1824	John Cannaday
Sumers Pharo	Eliza Paschall	5 Nov 1841	Zeri Sumers
Summers Andrew	Mary H. Swift	18 Mar 1833	Thomas Swift
Summers George	Manerva Smith	12 Sep 1855	Thomas J. Walker md by Lancelot Johnston
Suthen Zachariah	Nancey Chapman	18 Dec 1847	William Chapman
Swan Daniel W.	Nancey Marlow	14 Dec 1826	John Duncan
Swann Burch	Dolley Yates	9 Apr 1808	Benjamin Ponds
Swann Edward	Joycey Yates	20 Apr 1782	John Moore
Swann Geo.	Adaline Swann	8 Nov 1866	Benj. Swann
Swann James	Elizabeth Darby	17 Aug 1816	Isaac Vanhook
Swann James	Salley Marler	8 Apr 1820	William D. Johnson
Swann John	Polly Walker	25 Nov 1803	Walker Dowell
Swann John M.	Sarah E. Voss	21 Feb 1852 22 Feb 1852	Spillby Coleman md by Wm. Anderson
Swann Joseph	Agness Willson	3 Jan 1787	James Willson
Swann Joseph	Fanney Patterson	17 Jan 1811	Isaac West
Swann Joseph	Betsey Hightower	20 Oct 1818	John Chandler
Swann William	Peggy Atwell	24 Dec 1807	Benjamin Humphrey
Swann William W.	Cassanda Patterson	20 Oct 1843	John Wilson
Swayney James	Judith Burford	2 Oct 1780	Daniel Ball
Swepson Elijah (Col)	Narcissa Vernon (Col)	24 Feb 1866	George Bigelow (Col)
Swepson George W.	Virginia B. Yancey	23 Nov 1842	Abisha Slade
Swift Alex. (Col)	Bell Gunn (Col)	21 Sep 1867 23 Sep 1867	md
Swift Anthony	Elisabeth Brown	19 Aug 1784	Jephthah Rice
Swift Anthony*	Sarah Tait	28 Mar 1831	John J. Fielder
Swift George A.	Elizabeth Rudd	14 Dec 1847	F. A. Wiley
Swift George R.	Elizabeth Hooper	15 Mar 1852 18 Mar 1852	Thos. B. Atkins md by Tho. W. Graves JP
Swift Harvey	Polley Elmore	9 Oct 1819	Robert Holderness
Swift John	Lydia Haggard	26 Jun 1792	William Cannon
Swift John	Phebe M. Mott	4 May 1815	George Williamson
Swift Joseph M.	Isabella C. Lowns	17 Nov 1856 18 Nov 1856	James R. Warren md by Thomas W. Tobey MG
Swift Richard	Catherine Moss	2 Nov 1787	Nathan Williamson
Swift Robert	Nancy Siddle	17 Dec 1825	Ira Siddall
Swift Robert*	Jane Garrott	12 Jan 1831	John Stacy
Swift Thomas	Lucinda Cox	9 Aug 1847	James Rudd

GROOM	BRIDE	DATE	BONDSMAN OR WITNESS
Swift Washinngton	Huldah Harrison	12 Jun 1866	Selman Graves md by Thomas W. Graves
Swift William	Nancey Childress	11 Apr 1813	Guilford Childress Goodwin Evans
Swift William B.	Nancey Stokes	1 Oct 1821	Jno. L. Graves

- T -

Tait James M.	Peggy Miles	29 Oct 1834	Oliver Foulks
Taite Robert J.	Nancy McFarland	31 Mar 1859	Joseph B. Kennon md by Wm. B. Bowe JP
Talley Orren	Barbara M. Fuller	15 Oct 1827	Aaron Fuller
Talley Peyton S.	Jane Batton	4 Dec 1850	Franklin Phillips
Talley William S.	Sarah J. Self	19 Jan 1858 20 Jan 1858	Willie J. Palmer md by J. B. Jackson
Talley William S.	Mary J. Nunn (wid)	2 Jan 1867	W. O. Gillespie
Tallman James	Mary A. Gooch	4 Mar 1835	Crawford West
Tally D. H. (son of G. G. & Frances Tally)	Sally A. Shields (dau of Johnston & Mary Shields)	27 Jan 1868 30 Jan 1868	md by S. G. Mason
Tally P. F.	Martha F. Walker	18 Jan 1866 23 Jan 1866	J. M. Wilson md by F. H. Jones MG
Tankersley James M.	Amandy Adams	13 Dec 1866	Richard Clark md by E. Hunt JP
Tankersley Pleasant	Nicy L. Peterson	5 Aug 1852	md by Tho. L. Lea JP
Tanner Matthew	Alcey Langley	20 Jan 1800	Joseph Langley
Tapscott Edney	Sarah Windsor	23 May 1797	William Tate
Tapscott John	Frances T. Swift	29 Jan 1827	James Simpson
Tapscott Wesley (Col)	Martha Graves (Col)	6 Dec 1866	Alfred Williamson
Tarpley James	Nancy Hix	3 Jul 1786	Thos. Tarpley
Tarpley James A.	Sarah V. Austin	16 Nov 1840	Thomas O. Tarpley
Tate A. J. (son James & Emily Tate)	Lucy F. Martin (dau of Wesley & Lucindy Martin)	19 Feb 1868 20 Feb 1868	md by A. G. Anderson MG
Tate Caswell	Martha Williamson	24 Feb 1819	Iverson Graves
Tate Caswill	Polly Swift	29 Dec 1806	Harvey Swift
Tate James	Emily Robertson	1 Sep 1842	Franklin Graves
Tate Joseph	Rebecca Kimbrough	11 Jan 1828	Andrew Kimbrough
Tate R. T.	Sarah Bird	25 Sep 1821	Wm. Jones
Tate Robert	Elizabeth Harvell	9 Sep 1814	Thomas Gossett
Tate Samuel S.	Julia W. Jackson (wid)	19 Nov 1849	Allen Tate
Tate William S.	Mary F. Corbett	15 Jan 1857 18 Jan 1857	Thomas L. Slade md by B. Wells JP
Taylor Abel	Fanny Pass	22 Dec 1795	George Taylor
Taylor Alfred G.	Geneva C. Foster	21 Nov 1866 28 Nov 1866	W. H. Taylor md by J. J. Jones JP
Taylor Dorman	Sally Kent	21 Mar 1808	George Taylor
Taylor George	Ellis Pass	22 Dec 1795	Abel Taylor
Taylor Hiram	Martha Hughs	23 Dec 1837	George W. Taylor
Taylor Harrison (Col)	Henrietta Lewis (Col)	15 Jan 1867 16 Jan 1867	Moses Garland md by N. M. Lewis JP
Taylor James	Rebeccah Brown	27 Nov 1802	Edmond Browning
Taylor James	Polly Moore	18 Feb 1807	Moses Taylor
Taylor James A.	Martha Buckingham	11 Dec 1845	Robert Taylor
Taylor John	Lucy Reed	1 Nov 1802	Thomas Reid
Taylor John W.	Lelia S. Raynolds	29 May 1861	Jas. H. Owen md by S. G. Mason MG
Taylor Joshua	Presilla Simmons	6 Sep 1785	John Yancey
Taylor Napoleon B.	Martha Austin	7 Sep 1845	Byrd Buckingham

105

GROOM	BRIDE	DATE	BONDSMAN OR WITNESS
Taylor Nathaniel M.	Sarah L. Taylor	25 Mar 1843	Henry H. Gordon
Taylor Phillip	Sally Lewis	6 Aug 1780	Jno. Lewis
Taylor Reuben	Sally Woff	12 Aug 1806	George Taylor
Taylor Robert	Elizabeth Campbell	12 Dec 1857	Wm. H. Taylor R. W. Newbell
		15 Dec 1857	md by C. H. Richmond JP
Taylor Samuel	Sarah C. Brown	30 Jan 1841	John Word
Taylor Samuel	Sally Harvey	19 Oct 1841	Thos. J. Cullins
Taylor Septimus	Elisabeth Brandon	13 Feb 1786	Francis Brandon
Taylor Shadrack	Jammimah Moore	24 Apr 1841	James Taylor
Taylor Thomas*	Rebekah Dill	26 Dec 1831	Elisha Sartain
Taylor Thomas H.	Lucy Gates	27 Oct 1831	Henry Taylor
Taylor William	Prudence Lea	7 Jan 1791	Thomas Brandon
Taylor William	Polley Hart	3 Nov 1808	Samuel Fielder
Taylor William W.	Frances A. Stewart	8 Jun 1846	Jno. R. Brookes
Taylor William W.	Sally B. Bradsher	22 Nov 1856	Tho. W. Graves
Teague Josiah (Col)	Mary Burton (Col)	18 May 1867 22 May 1867	md by Jas. J. Clendenin JP
Tennison John	Betsey Cheatwood	3 Mar 1798	Thomas Bouldin
Terill Thomas J.	S. C. Jackson	31 Jan 1866	Charles J. Fowler
Terrel William	Susannah Owen	31 Oct 1814	Benja. B. Nelson
Terrell Harrison A.	Elizabeth Austin	20 Oct 1843	Robert H. Cheek
Terrell James	Elizabeth Crisp	19 Mar 1816	Paul Terrell
Terrell James	Eliza Hanshaw	27 Sep 1852 30 Sep	md by A. M. Woods JP
Terrell John H.	Letetie Brincefield	29 Jun 1861	B. Y. Brincefield
Terrell Jonathan H.	Susan L. Mathews	8 Dec 1851 11 Dec 1851	William J. Aldrege md by Tho. W. Graves JP
Terrell Joseph J.	Catherine Piper	18 Sep 1860	Albert Fergason
Terrell Julius B.	Mary Davis (wid)	26 Dec 1818	Eaton Baynes
Terrell Lewis	Hannah Graves	31 Oct 1816	James Currie Isaac Rainey
Terrell William E.	Lucinda Burch	13 Nov 1852 16 Nov 1852	R. A. Newbell md by Geo. W. Thompson JP
Terry Abner R.	Sally B. Yarbrough	4 Jul 1850	Lafayett Bennett T. S. Poore
Terry Christopher G.	Louisa G. Burns	8 Jun 1840	Grief G. Mason
Terry Christopher G.	Julia F. Burns	20 May 1844	William H. Burns
Terry Dabney	Betsy Jeffreys	13 Oct 1825	Alexander McAlpin
Terry Dabney	Martha Yarbrough	20 Jun 1846	Geo. A. Smith
Terry Enock	Edey Wilkerson	7 Dec 1832	Robert Walters
Terry John	Betsey Carrol	14 Apr 1804	Leavin Roberts
Terry Mathew	Chaney Robinson	7 Apr 1800	James Heggie
Terry Wm. E.	Elizabeth Yates	9 Dec 1867	md by E. Hunt JP
Thacker Charles	Polley Hays	12 Aug 1808	Joseph Scott
Thacker Isaac	Mary F. Rice	29 Aug 1849	Jas. M. Neal
Thaxton Henry S.	Eugenia F. Currie	2 Sep 1865 5 Sep 1865	J. L. McKee clk md by H. G. Hill MG
Thaxton Thomas	Jamima Cobb	4 Feb 1782	Francis Robertson
Thaxton William	Sarah Gravitt	16 Aug 1783	Thos. Thaxton
Thomas A. W.	Nancy W. Harraway	24 May 1865	Jas. P. Sykes md by E. Hunt JP
Thomas Andrew	Elizabeth Dickey	27 Sep 1825	George Thomas
Thomas Archibald W.	Susan Ann Williams	3 Apr 1850	John W. Armes
Thomas Christopher	Patcey Bartlett	19 Nov 1808	Richard Vaughan

GROOM	BRIDE	DATE	BONDSMAN OR WITNESS
Thomas Daniel	Zilly Atkins	12 Jan 1808	David Thomas
Thomas Daniel C.	Nancy Smith	6 Aug 1827	David Thomas
Thomas David	Patsey Kimbrough	14 Apr 1799	Henry Thomas
Thomas David	Patience Elam	21 Apr 1807	William Tarpley
Thomas David*	Elmira Kimbrough	17 May 1831	Daniel C. Thomas
Thomas Henry	Sally Chandler	3 Jan 1803	Danl. Thomas
Thomas Henry*	Susan Stephens	30 Dec 1831	John Lenox
Thomas Henry Jr.	Ritta Simmons	10 Dec 1839	Isaac Simmons
Thomas Hurt (Col)	Jane Mebane (Col)	16 Jun 1866	Dennis Phelps
Thomas Jacob	Fanny Roan	29 Jan 1805	Lawrence Lea
Thomas Jacob	Mary Hickman	16 Oct 1819	Hugh Campbell
Thomas James W.	Rebecca C. Hicks	14 Mar 1857	A. L. Ball
			md by N. M. Lewis JP
Thomas Jesse H.	Lethe E. Dobbins	18 Apr 1821	Joel P. Thomas
Thomas Joel P.	Mary Williams	16 Dec 1837	Isaac B. Siddall
Thomas John	Salley Nelson	15 Aug 1803	Robert H. Jackson
Thomas John	---------	31 Dec 1811	Alexander Wiley
Thomas Marcus C.	Henrietta Lea	10 Jun 1858	Jas. P. Simpson
		15 Jun 1858	md by Jas. P. Simpson MG
Thomas Nelson	Sarah Warren	13 May 1834	William Hightower
Thomas Phillip	Judith Boulton	13 Jun 1781	Chas. Bolton
Thomas Richard W.	Anne W. Ragland	30 Jun 1832	Nathl. M. Roan
Thomas Robert	Marguret Warwick	26 Dec 1787	John Warrick
Thomas Thomas	Margaret Thomas (wid)	26 May 1857	Thomas J. Thomas
		29 Jun 1857	md by Wm. J. Moore JP
Thomas William (Col)	Rebecca Boswell (Col)	29 Dec 1865	George Brown
Thomas William (Col)	Matilda McCain (Col)	16 Jan 1867	Jacob Garland
			md by J. J. Jones JP
Thomas William A.	Hannah S. Graves	1 Oct 1844	John M. Richmond
			T. H. Miles
Thomas Woodlief	Frances Reid	8 Nov 1834	Noel Reed
Thomason Flemming	Sarah Gomer	25 Dec 1799	Thos. Robinson
Thompson Andrus J.	Martha C. Boswell	16 Nov 1859	James C. Thompson
			md by G. W. Prendergast
Thompson George (Col-son of Ben Thompson & Eureka Carter)	Milly Stamps (Col-dau of Jacob Simpson & Claracy Stamps)	19 Dec 1867	md by Eustace Hunt JP
Thompson George W.	Elizabeth J. Harrison	20 Feb 1838	Wm. Herring
Thompson James	Vina Morton	15 Sep 1866	Joseph Long
			md by Jerry Smith JP
Thompson James H.	Delilah Lea	17 Mar 1822	John Thompson
Thompson John	Nancy Lea	19 Feb 1823	James H. Thompson
Thompson John	Elizabeth W. Davis	1 Feb 1837	Henry Rose
			Daniel McLaughlan
Thompson Robert	Amandy Thaxton	13 Dec 1866	H. F. Brandon clk
Thompson Thomas (Col)	Sarah J. Glass (Col)	9 Aug 1867	md by Jno. D. Keesee
Thompson Thomas A.	Nancey S. Murphey	3 Nov 1820	William Smith Sr.
Thompson Thomas M.	Arrela S. Smith	2 Nov 1857	P. A. McKinny
Thornton Francis F.	Huldah M. Gunn	22 Oct 1834	Allen M. Gunn
Thornton Joseph	Easter Jane Wright	4 Dec 1866	John Robertson
		25 Dec 1866	md by Jno. D. Keesee
Thornton Presley L. W.	Eveline Thompson	7 Oct 1859	John R. Hill
			md by Saml. S. Harrison
Thornton Robert B.	Susan F. Smith	2 Nov 1833	James F. Calloway
Thorp John	Milly Tery	3 Jul 1802	James Rice
			David Tery
			Daniel Everett

GROOM	BRIDE	DATE	BONDSMAN OR WITNESS
Thorp Richard	Ann R. Smith	30 Oct 1838	Charles M. K. Taylor
Tillington Barrington	Sarah Hanshaw	10 Dec 132	Ephraim Burch
Toller John	Viney Nash	11 Jul 1854	Wiley P. Stallings
		11 Jul 1854	md by Thomas Covington
Tomson Robert	Usley Brown	28 Sep 1781	James Barker
Toney Arthur Jr.	Polly Edwell	16 Oct 1833	Tilmon Snow
Toney Charles	Martha Dyson	2 Jul 1835	Moses Bass
Toney John	Lucy Edwin	19 Dec 1832	Tilmon Snow
Toney Monroe (Col)	Susann Robards (Col)	25 Sep 1865	John Freeman (Col)
		26 Dec 1865	md by J. J. Jones JP
Toney Nat	Polly Philips	23 Nov 1837	Tilmon Snow
Torian Thomas	Agness G. Bethell	17 Jun 1836	Thomas D. Connally
Tosh Thomas	Lucy J. McClenehan	6 Apr 1833	Benjamin C. West Jr.
Totten John C.	Dorcas Haralson	5 Jun 1826	Jno. G. Womack
Totten Joseph H.	Nancy A. Sartin	15 Oct 1859	W. W. Rayl
		20 Oct 1859	md by Stephen Neal JP
Totten Joseph S.	C. A. McAlpin	24 Sep 1840	Samuel R. Browning
Totten Richard W.	Nancey Foster	13 Sep 1826	Stairling H. Gunn
Totten Thomas R.	Sarah L. Watlington	20 Dec 1853	Joseph M. Russell
		21 Dec 1853	md by John H. Pickard MG
Totton Sidney	Virginia Motley	19 May 1866	Isaac Motley
		15 May 1866?	md by E. Hunt JP
Towler H. A.	Margrett E. Knight	7 May 1858	Jn. T. Hatchett
Towlerman Phillip	Catherine Shemcy	15 Aug 1820	Thornton Carter
Towles James M.	Mary Ann Callum	19 Feb 1838	James R. Callum
Townley Alvah R.	Emily Worsham	26 May 1830	Daniel S. Price
Towns William M.	Mary C. Lipscombe	29 Jul 1851	Augustine Timberlake
		6 Aug 1851	md by A. B. Brown MG
Trammel Elisha B.	Elizabeth F. Gordon	24 Dec 1856	Saml. B. Jennings
			md by J. M. Allen JP
Trasco Hennery (see Rasco Henry T.)	Elizabeth Loyd	-- --- ---- 21 Jan 1855	md by John Staler
Travis Alfred R.	Sarah C. Swann	5 Jul 1851	Jno. W. P. Travis
		10 Aug 1851	md by Wm. Anderson
Travis Ellis	Priscilla Ingram	27 Feb 1836	Isaac Travis
Travis Ellis	Mary White	10 Apr 1843	John Travis
Travis Elzey W.	Arey A. Fugerson	28 Sep 1841	William J. Dameron
Travis George A.	Susanah C. Hodges	3 Jul 1861	James S. Travis
Travis Isaac	Mary N. Ingram	30 Dec 1836	Ellis Travis
Travis James	Nancey Ware	19 Jul 1841	William Dunkin
Travis James F. M.	Ann E. Gatewood	20 Oct 1866	R. James West
		25 Oct 1866	md by W. B. Swann JP
Travis James J.	Martha J. Stanley	23 Oct 1844	William R. Stanley
Travis John	Elizabeth B. Coleman	14 Jan 1836	Isaac H. Travis
Travis John	Mary B. West	26 Jun 1843	C. W. West
Travis John C.	Elizabeth M. Ford	16 Dec 1854	John Y. Stokes
		21 Dec 1854	md by Wm. Anderson
Travis John W. P.	Mary A. Burton	11 Apr 1854	Geo. A. Travis
Travis Stephen	Tirzah Ingram	21 Nov 1836	Isaac H. Travis
Travis Thomas	Jane M. Pinick	2 Aug 1830	John Travis
Travis William	Rachel Chilton	18 Nov 1816	James Travis
Travise David	Judith Moore	4 Feb 1782	Daniel Meritt
Traynham David	Mary Warsham	28 Dec 1825	James O. Harris
Trew Ozza	Polley Winters	11 Sep 1815	William B. Graves
Trigg William B.	Salley Busey	31 Dec 1822	John Busey
True Benjamin H.	Emily Pruitt	19 Jan 1853	John True
True Lewis J.	Levina A. Bayes	12 Apr 1864	Robert J. Bayes
			md by W. B. Swann JP
Tuder Landon	Mary Fuller	21 Jan 1832	William Sharp
Tulloch David	Betsey Bruce	26 Mar 1796	John Bruce
Tulloch James M.	Anne Singleton	29 Feb 1808	John Martin

GROOM	BRIDE	DATE	BONDSMAN OR WITNESS
Tulloch Thomas	Jane Taylor	30 Apr 1822	Robt. Singleton
Tulloh William	Mary Price	5 Mar 1800	Jno. Stanfield
Tulloh William	Alsey Going	3 Jan 1809	John Going
Tunstall Green (son of Patrick & Susan Tunstall)	Mary E. Pinnix (dau of Stephen Pinnix & Lettice Stokes)	7 Jun 1867	md by H. E. Hodges JP
Turbeville Fountain M.	Fanny Graves	10 Dec 1851	William H. Chiles
Turbiville Charles P.	Mary E. Holden	22 Oct 1853 24 Oct 1853	Napoleon E. Graves md by S. A. Stanfield
Turbeville Lewis W.	Cornelia W. Graves	30 Aug 1852 14 Sep 1852	A. Slade clk md by Jno. H. Lacy
Turner Abraham Rogers	Sarah Black	20 Oct 1784	Thomas Black
Turner Berry	Susannah Strador	18 Nov 1828	Christian Strador Jr.
Turner C. F.	Bettie Hodges	16 Oct 1866	Wm. G. Clendenin md by Tho. S. Harrison JP
Turner Charles	Polly Rudd	10 Apr 1805	Samuel French
Turner Chesley	Mildred R. Hatchett	19 Apr 1821	David Montgomery Archimedes Donoho
Turner Daniel	Susanah Fisher	23 Sep 1805	James Samuel
Turner Dennis	Julia Rudd	25 Aug 1866 26 Aug 1866	John Gunn md by Stephen Neal JP
Turner Edmund	Mary Ann Slade	12 Oct 1824	Abisha Slade
Turner Ephraim*	Saloma Gooch	2 Nov 1831	James C. Turner
Turner Ephraim	Frances Davis	3 Dec 1857 4 Dec 1857	John Turner md by James K. Lea JP
Turner George W.	Isabella Carter	16 Dec 1866	John S. Murray md by J. J. Jones JP
Turner Gideon B.	Permelia Dodson	27 Feb 1826	Chesley Turner
Turner Green	Harriett E. Powell	27 Dec 1849	John W. White
Turner Henry	Patsy McKinney	23 Nov 1826	Stephen Page
Turner Henry (Col)	Lethe Williamson (Col)	2 Nov 1866	Dick Williamson
Turner Isham	Mary Arnold	2 May 1832	Henry Turner
Turner James	Lucy Pleasant	5 Aug 1793	John Pleasant
Turner James B.	Adeline Arrington	10 Jun 1862	Wm. V. B. Moore md by N. M. Lewis JP
Turner James C.	Mary Bigelow	17 Dec 1823	Pleasant Corbet
Turner James H.	Margaret Kimbro	10 Apr 1847	Isham Turner
Turner James H.	Mary Gipson	7 Feb 1855 8 Feb 1855	James P. Boswell md by Stephen Neal JP
Turner James R.	Lucinda Roberts	21 Oct 1854	William Burch
Turner James R.	Lucinda Roberts	13 Oct 1854	William Burch
Turner John	Sarah Kimbro	14 Feb 1787	James Kimbrough
Turner John	Polley Atkinson	22 Nov 1796	James Turner
Turner John	Mildred Moore	3 Aug 1854 27 Aug 1854	Thomas M. Warren md by Thos. Covington JP
Turner John P.	Elizabeth Trammell	11 Apr 1867	md by John J. Jones JP
Turner Jordon (son of Billy Baily & Patience Rowlet)	Matilda Turner	6 May 1867 30 May 1867	md by M. A. Turner JP
Turner Lewis	Patsy Wilkins	27 Sep 1825	Henry Turner
Turner Lewis P.	Emily Moore	15 Sep 1855 21 Sep 1855	James H. Turner md by B. Cooper JP
Turner Marcus A.	Milissa V. McNeil	25 Sep 1851	William P. Watlington
Turner Moses	Martha Moore (dau of Alexr. Moore)	22 Feb 1780	Robt. Moore
Turner Stephen D.	Henritta M. Hinton	20 Mar 1854	Archibald W. Jeffreys md by Tho. L. Lea JP

GROOM	BRIDE	DATE	BONDSMAN OR WITNESS
Turner Stephen H.	Mary A. Turner	1 Jan 1850	Stephen Neal
Turner Thomas	Betsey Haralson	28 Oct 1794	Solomon Parks
Turner Thomas	Elizabeth Fisher	8 Nov 1815	George Turner
Turner Thomas	Celia Ware	21 Oct 1819	Azariah Graves
Turner Thomas	Agnes Pucket	25 Oct 1856	George W. Wright R. A. Newbell
		18 Dec 1856	md by James K. Lea JP
Turner Thomas	Mary Pyrant	17 Nov 1862	Tho. W. Graves md by Wm. W. Taylor JP
Turner Walter (Col-son of Walter Brown & Maria Turner)	Lucy Everett (Col)	20 Feb 1868	H. F. Brandon clk
Turner William	Ann Bartlett	4 Dec 1802	William S. Webb
Turner William A.	Sallie Ann Evans	8 Nov 1858	Philemon M. Neal
		10 Nov 1858	md by Jno. W. Lewis MG
Turner William B.	Sarah Holycross	4 Aug 1864	John A. Whitt md by J. J. Jones JP
Turner William W.	Seignara M. Dodson	26 Jun 1824	Elias Slade
Turner William W.	Sarah Yates	9 Oct 1860	Daniel H. Hodnett md by N. M. Lewis JP
Tyler Zachariah	Edey Parker	8 Apr 1822	Jephtha Parker
Tyree David	Hanner Obrion	6 Apr 1830	Nathan Duncan

- U -

GROOM	BRIDE	DATE	BONDSMAN OR WITNESS
Underwood Henry (Col)	Caroline Easley (Col)	23 Mar 1866 26 Mar 1866	Edmund Stubblefield md by W. B. Swann JP
Underwood James	Elizabeth Sawyer	14 Dec 1816	John Mdk. Williams
Underwood James	Sally Sawyer	13 Sep 1851 14 Sep 1851	Wm. Sawyer md by Geo. F. Deshong JP
Underwood John	Sarah Roberts	6 Oct 1841	Maj. H. Graves
Underwood Jonathan B.	Nancy Brincefield	21 Dec 1860	John E. Moore
Underwood William	Sarah A. Pleasant	5 Dec 1843	James Miles Jr.
Upton Edward	Jane Long	19 Dec 1781	Robert Long
Upton William	Mildred Dameron	20 Jan 1820	Azariah Graves
Upton William	Susannah Mathis	3 Nov 1823	John Mathis
Ussery James G.	Mary A. Fleet	25 Oct 1838	Nathaniel Holloway B. C. West Sr.

- V -

GROOM	BRIDE	DATE	BONDSMAN OR WITNESS
Valentine Thos. J.	Narcissa G. McAlpin	24 Dec 1842	W. P. Graves
Valentine Thomas J.	Martha A. Willis	21 Oct 1850	Joseph J. Lawson
VanHook Aaron	Elizabeth Leonard	1808 - 1810	Wm. Harvill
VanHook Francis M.	Elizabeth J. Carter	16 Jan 1860 18 Jan 1860	Jacob T. VanHook md by N. M. Lewis JP
VanHook Isaac	Peggy Comer	27 Jan 1817	Robt. Malone
VanHook Isaac D.	Elizabeth McMullin	2 Dec 1817	Robert D. Wade
VanHook Jacob T.	Nancy W. Totton	19 Jul 1865	John E. Robertson
VanHook John	Betsey Gordon	14 Dec 1807	Vincent Lea
VanHook John C.	Phebe Lea	24 Nov 1819	Wm. F. Smith
VanHook Kindal	Diannah Burton	22 May 1813	Drury Burton Goodwin Evans
VanHook Kindle	Anne Dobbin	25 Nov 1800	James Hamlett
VanHook Lawrence Jr.	Rachal Sargent	17 Sep 1785	Stephen Sargent Jr.
VanHook Lawrence Sr.	Vittory Rankin	1 Nov 1787	John Womack
VanHook Loyd Jr.	Salley Austin	9 Nov 1804	Daniel Darby

GROOM	BRIDE	DATE	BONDSMAN OR WITNESS
VanHook Reuben (Col)	Mariah Robertson (Col)	20 Apr 1867	md by J. J. Jones JP
VanHook Robert	Rachel Dobbin	10 Dec 1793	John Dobbin
VanHook Solomon	Mary A. Richmond	29 Apr 1839	Jacob G. Walker
VanHook Thomas	Sarah Palmer	21 Jun 1779	William White
Vass Thomas Jr.	Elizabeth Badgett	19 Nov 1838	Owen McAleer
Vaughan Bailey	Polley McClarney	18 Dec 1827	Elijah Yates
Vaughan Drury M.	Martha M. Turner	11 Mar 1830	Elias D. Slade
Vaughan James	Henrietta Malone	11 Dec 1803	Thomas Vaughan
Vaughan James Jr.	Betsy Page	14 Feb 1826	Stephen Page
Vaughan John	Betsy Curls	15 Jan 1825	John McCane
Vaughan John	Tabitha Graves	30 Oct 1832	George W. Lamkin
Vaughan John	Elizabeth Miles	18 Nov 1847	John S. Miles
Vaughan John Jr.	Leah Miles	20 Mar 1827	Henry Miles
Vaughan Lewis	Polly Wilson	1 Aug 1801	George Wilson
Vaughan Nicholas	Polly Pleasant	6 Mar 1804	John Vaughan
Vaughan Thomas Thomas J.*	Sally Francis	11 Aug 1831	Philip Roberts
Vaughan William	Susan Aldridge	30 Oct 1851	Thomas L. Evans
Vaughn A. B.	Carolin Mils	21 Dec 1860	Wm. Burch
Vaughn Maurice	Ann Jones	10 Sep 1825	Alexr. Kiersey
Vaughn Richard	Nancey Turner	28 Sep 1803	William S. Webb
Vaughn Thomas	Polly French	31 Aug 1808	James Culberson
Vaughn Warren T.	Dolly Miles	6 Oct 1859	Wm. McNutt
Vaughn Wiatt (Colson of Stephen Walker & Jinnie Walker)	Anice Simpson (Col- dau of Charles Lea & Massay Simpson)	28 Mar 1868	md by Stephen Neal JP
Vaughn William	Susan Lamkin	18 Aug 1820	James Rice
Vaughon Gidon	Sarah Lay	9 Feb 1780	George Lay
Venable Joseph	Janie Price	17 Feb 1866	Jesse C. Griffith
		22 Feb 1866	md by Jacob Doll MG
Vernon Calvin D.	Penelope Watlington	3 Mar 1855	James N. Montgomery
		8 Mar 1855	md by Thomas W. Tobey
Vernon Robert T.	Elizabeth Rice	18 Dec 1854	F. A. Shackleford
		21 Dec 1854	md by J. M. Allen JP
Vernon Thomas	Martha A. Simpson	3 Jan 1855	Thomas S. Hawken
		5 Jan 1855	md by J. M. Allen JP
Verser Daniel	Elizabeth Ponsonby	30 Sep 1837	Nicholas M. Lewis
Vertres James C.	Susan C. V. Lea	28 Jul 1849	Franklin Graves
Vincent James	Mary Martin	14 Aug 1841	Owen McAleer
Vinson Henry	Sina Richmond	17 Jan 1867	George Richmond
			md by David Burch JP
Virmillion Wilson	Nancy McNeil	18 Jul 1778	Absalom Tatom
			Reuben Estes
			W. Moore
Visage Thomas	Polly Shy	1 Oct 1792	Samuel Shy
Voss Greenbery	Betsey Swann	30 Oct 1793	Wynn Dixon
Voss Milton	Mary L. Stone	14 Dec 1858	R. T. Carter
Voss O'Kelly	Elizabeth E. Carter	5 Dec 1825	Thomas Swann Jr.
Voss Paschal	Mahaley Swan	16 Dec 1833	Dudly G. Stokes
Voss Pleasant	Unity Cook	4 Feb 1829	William Cook

- W -

Waddill Branch	Martha Elmore	8 Feb 1834	Tillitson McCain
Waddill John C.	Nancey Wimbus	27 Oct 1817	Richard Dismukes
			William Moore
Wade Charles D.	Dready Sargent	18 Apr 1816	Nathaniel Torian
			Isaac Rainey
Wade Lawson	Nannie Dixon	28 Dec 1866	Harrison Dixon
			md by Jacob Doll MG
Wade Robert Jr.	Ann Wade	16 Sep 1788	David Allin
Wade Robert D.	Mary Currie	1 Feb 1828	Azariah Graves

GROOM	BRIDE	DATE	BONDSMAN OR WITNESS
Wade William	Jane Hamlet	22 Jan 1864	Robert C. Phelps md by John J. Jones JP
Wadkins Isaac	Jenny Jones	23 Feb 1816	Charles Mathis
Wagstaff John F.	Caroline Oliver	25 Jan 1851	William Sergeant
Waid Hampton	Ann Durham	12 Nov 1796	George Elliot
Waite William	Tabitha Pryor	11 Dec 1778	Wm. Waite Absalom Tatom
Walker Abraham	Elizabeth Smith	2 Nov 1833	Dennis Matkins
Walker Abraham	Martha J. Jones	14 Dec 1857	Yancey Jones
		17 Dec 1857	md by John Stadler
Walker Ajax J.	Lucy M. Lewis	18 May 1820	John E. Lewis
Walker Alexander J.	Mary Ann Dill	26 Dec 1832	John H. Dill
Walker Archibald J.	Celia Strader	13 Oct 1859	Joseph Dill
Walker Azariah	Jane Walker	18 Dec 1837	John M. Walker
Walker Benjamin	Sally Hightower	9 Dec 1800	William McAden
Walker Benjamin	Susan Rice	1 Mar 1833	James Loveless
Walker Charles H. (Col)	Mary E. Walker (Col)	29 Apr 1867	H. F. Brandon clk
Walker Daniel	Willy Walker	23 Jun 1866	Woodey Hooper
Walker David	Patsey Dolton	30 Jan 1806	John Humphreys
Walker David	Suffy Carver	24 Dec 1825	John Holloway
Walker David	Frances Baldwin	17 Mar 1827	Mason Sanders
Walker David	Satiry Groom	30 Sep 1845	John M. Walker T. H. Miles
Walker Empson	Martha Currie	11 Sep 1825	George Currie
Walker Fielding L.	Pensy C. Wilson	28 Nov 1866	Henry A. Walker
Walker Freeman	Perthena Baynes	25 Nov 1842	Lorenzo Baynes
Walker Garrison	Lucinda Walker	12 Oct 1840	Abner Walker
Walker George	Catherine Currie	16 Feb 1811	Abner Walker
Walker George	Mary Walker	17 Dec 1822	Levi Walker
Walker James	Elizabeth Elliot	21 Nov 1781	James Elliot
Walker James	Ann Mason	16 Dec 1820	Joah Cobb Sr.
Walker James	Luscinda Tapscott	21 Dec 1820	Jesse Sanders
Walker James	Milly Parks	22 Nov 1843	George Herndon
Walker James M.	Martha Ann Lea	30 Mar 1835	Thomas W. Graves
Walker James M.	Letitia F. Williams	10 May 1853	Allen Gunn
		11 May 1853	md by J. S. Totten JP
Walker Jefferson M.	Mary F. Cooper	20 Oct 1854	George W. Florence
		22 Oct 1854	md by John Stadler
Walker Jere.	Rutha Cross	2 Dec 1805	Joshua Pike Wm. Wilkinson
Walker Jethro J.	Anne Gomer	26 Dec 1839	Samuel M. Cobb
Walker John	Betsey Beaver	18 Dec 1813	Mason Sanders
Walker John	Margaret Loyed	22 Nov 1858	Henry T. Rasco
		23 Nov 1858	md by A. B. Walker JP
Walker John G.	Partheane Currie	8 Mar 1824	George Currie
Walker John H.	Susan New	24 Aug 1838	George C. Rogers
Walker John H.	Sarah F. Brown	24 Feb 1862	Quinton A. Anderson
		26 Feb 1862	md by G. G. Walker
Walker John M.	Polly Rice	17 Oct 1828	James Walker
Walker John M.	Martha McKinney	24 Oct 1840	John C. Totten
Walker Jones H.	Catharine Summers	23 Oct 1854	David Strader
		23 Oct 1854	md by Lancelot Johnston JP
Walker Joseph	Priscilla Zachary	17 Mar 1800	John Carr
Walker Landay	Matilda J. Loveless	17 Sep 1855	Joel A. McDaniel md by J. Jennings JP
Walker Mitchell	Martha P. Davis	24 Nov 1846	Jas. M. Brookes
Walker Monroe	Minerva Briggs	8 Oct 1866	Randy Williamson
Walker Nash (Col)	Hannoh Williamson (Col)	22 Dec 1865	B. F. Hurdle

GROOM	BRIDE	DATE	BONDSMAN OR WITNESS
Walker Nicholas L.	Emily F. Hart	20 Nov 1849	Geo. W. Thompson
Walker Philip	Francis Martin	27 Dec 1833	William Walker
Walker Robert T.	Mary Montgomery	13 Jan 1858	Wm. A. Walker
		17 Jan 1858	md by John H. Pickard MG
Walker Samuel	Jean Mason	16 Dec 1820	Henry Ruark
Walker Samuel	Barbara Walker	19 May 1834	William V. Wilder
Walker Thomas	Peggy Swan	28 Oct 1811	James Gunn
Walker Thomas J.	Mary Somers	19 Aug 1845	Larkin Smith
Walker Washington	Nicy Smithey	28 Sep 1846	Jethro J. Walker
Walker William	Jane Walker	28 Oct 1830	Philip Walker
Walker William	Levicy Ford	22 Oct 1834	James Swann
Walker William A.	Sarah T. Parks	14 Nov 1843	James M. Brookes
Walker William F.	Phebe Boswell	16 Mar 1850	Martin Browning
Walker William L.	Salina Simmons	14 Sep 1850	Thomas J. Walker
Walker William T.	Celestia F. Rudd	19 Dec 1865	Robert Z. Gwyn
		28 Dec 1865	md by A. G. Anderson MG
Wall Byrd	Elisabeth Muirhead	4 Dec 1782	Mason Foley
Wall George W.	Delilah Ann Juda Strador	12 Sep 1846	Francis M. Burns
Wall Robert	Catherine Wall	15 Feb 1830	David Hodge
Wall William D.	Mary C. Hightower	28 Nov 1854	John L. Peterson
Wallas Benjamon	Sarah Sargent	5 Jun 1782	William Sargent
Waller John	Frances Woody	6 Jan 1819	Ch. Willson
Waller John S.	Ann E. Walters	21 Mar 1839	Iverson B. Walters
Waller William (Pittsylvania Co. Va.)	Frances Ghatty	7 Jun 1832	Joab Medors
Wallers Robert H.	Nancey Waddell	20 Oct 1817	Asa Fitzgerald
Walles William	Tempi Shearman	26 Jun 1795	Robert Motheral
Wallis Allen	Anne Sargent	5 Jul 1826	Moses Bradsher
Wallis James	Eddy Hall	30 Dec 1786	William Hall
Wallis James	Polley Robinson	21 Sep 1796	Thomas Burch
Wallis James J.	Elvira P. Davis	22 Dec 1853	Joshua J. Wood md by J. M. Allen JP
Wallis John	Elizabeth Fullar	7 Jan 1790	James Wallis
Wallis Major	Susannah Burton	9 Apr 1802	Drury Burton
Walters Alexander J.	Mary F. Vinson	1 Feb 1840	Azariah G. Walters
Walters Berry	Jane Shelton	28 Dec 1866	Davy Walters
		28 Dec 1866	md by E. Hunt JP
Walters Davy	Harriet Lindsey	28 Dec 1866	Berry Walters md by E. Hunt JP
Walters Ezra	Elizabeth Shackelford	24 Dec 1795	Alexander Glaspy William Rainey
Walters George) (Col)	Bell Wier (Col-dau of Thomas Wier & Huldy Harris)	4 May 1867	md by E. Hunt JP
Walters Jackson	Rebecca Chandler	1 Sep 1852	Abram M. Wright
Walters John	Cathrine Newton	29 Nov 1789	Paul Walters
Walters Thomas	Sarah Dodson	11 Occt 1837	William Simpson
Walters Thomas	Rebecca Stokes	5 Jan 1867	Henry Wilson
Walters Thornton	Margit Bohannan (dau of Nancy)	2 Jan 1816	Lodwell Buchannan
Walters William H. (see Wolters)	Talley Ingram	26 Dec 1816	George W. Jeffreys James Daniel
Walton Benjamin W.	Sarah C. Edwards	10 Feb 1863	James Edwards
Walton John	Susan Matlock	17 May 1832	Owen McAleer
Walton John H.	Mary Ann Bass	21 Feb 1860	Henry C. Bass md by N. J. Lewis JP
Walton Lewis	Fanny Richmond	23 Mar 1867	Thomas Wood
		25 Mar 1867	md by F. L. Warren JP
Walton Mazor (Col)	Betty Averett (Col)	27 Jul 1867	md by E. Hunt JP

GROOM	BRIDE	DATE	BONDSMAN OR WITNESS
Walton Thomas	Polly Johnston	28 Dec 1813	Loftin Walton
Walton William T.	Elizabeth D. Echels	30 Dec 1858	Thomas E. Ingram md by N. M. Lewis JP
Ward Alfred	Elizabeth Debrower	22 Dec 1857	William J. Ward
Ward George	Cloey Chatham	8 Dec 1801	Wilie King
Ward James L.	Phebe Roberts	8 Sep 1864	A. R. Paschal
Ward John L. (son of Stephen & Faney)	Mary Roberts (dau of Lidy)	9 Nov 1867 10 Nov 1867	md by C. J. Richmond JP
Ward Richard	Lucey Hedgcock	29 May 1787	Solomon Duty
Ward Richard C.	Mary Ann Murphey	16 Nov 1806	Willis Ashford
Ward T. F. (son of W. J. & Mary J.)	Susan A. Stainback (dau of W. H. & Parthenia)	2 Nov 1867 6 Nov 1867	md by F. L. Oakley MG
Ward Thomas	Betsy Paul	3 Sep 1815	John Ward
Ward Thomas	Permelia Hightower	12 Mar 1827	Daniel Hightower
Ward William	Mary A. Foster	13 Oct 1845	Freeman Leath Jr.
Ware Ansel	Elizabeth Matlock	10 Sep 1825	Stairling H. Gunn
Ware James	Rebecah Gitton	12 Jun 1812	Samuel Henderson
Ware James T.	Celestia A. Gunn	6 Jun 1861	S. A. Rice md by Fr. Stanly MG
Ware John	Nancy Tolbert	28 Sep 1782	Wm. Ware
Ware John	Mary M. Halcomb	9 Oct 1820	Henry N. Burton
Ware Jno. P.	Elizabeth Sanders	15 Apr 1818	Jno. Daniel
Ware Joseph T.	Susan T. Chandler	9 Nov 1832	Joseph Henderson
Ware Nathaniel	Susan Boyles	17 Apr 1849	George W. Hamblett
Ware Sidney G.	Fanny Burton	9 Jun 1857 10 Jun 1857	Dr. George W. Gunn md by Jas. P. Simpson MG
Ware Silas T.	Sarah Cannon	4 Sep 1837	Stephen Ware
Ware Silas T.	Elizabeth Ann Williams	19 Sep 1850	Thomas A. Lea
Ware Stephen T.	Eliza Shelton	10 Oct 1837	John Baxter
Ware Thomas	Sarah Talbert	17 Oct 1788	Joseph Talbert
Ware Thomas	Kesiah Durham	9 Jun 1805	Joshua Jeffreys
Ware Thomas	Jenny Holloway	28 Apr 1806	William Holloway
Ware Thomas Jr.	Nancey Ware	8 Aug 1818	Matthew Dodson
Ware William M.	Nancy Hubbard	13 Sep 1863 (or 12 Sep 1863)	L. L. Walker md by W. B. Swann JP
Ware William	Francis Perkins	2 Oct 1781	Isaac Midlebrook
Ware William G.	Mildred A. Williams	19 Feb 1859	Alexander W. Fergerson
Warf Berry	Nancy Moore	22 Jun 1808	Robert Randolph
Warf James	Sally Glaspy	23 Dec 1801	Alexander Glaspy Joseph McCain Martin Duncan
Warf James F.	Margarett Mason	20 Mar 1836	John Warf
Warf John	Julia Ann Lindsay	22 Sep 1837	Charles Hendrick
Warf Noel	Milly Bennett	29 Oct 1845	Atkinson Warf Geo. A. Smith
Warf Roger	Betsy Gilaspy	5 Jan 1802	Jesse Going
Warf Tandy F.	Elizabeth Burnett	7 Dec 1847	William Shackleford
Warf Thomas	Jane Cox (dau of Gabriel Cox)	8 Dec 1846	Francis Shackleford
Warf Thomas	Elizabeth Cox	1 Feb 1865	Lodrick E. Tally md by W. B. Swann JP
Wariner Robert H.	Agness J. Nunnally	4 Nov 1843	Robert Blackwell
Warmick Abner (Col-son of Joe & Aggy)	Latitia Alice Jimison (Col-dau of Wiley Jimison & Ann Cray)	25 Dec 1867	md by Eustace Hunt
Warren Alexander	Elizabeth Hooper	13 Apr 1846	Allen Gunn
Warren B. H.	E. C. Lea	16 Feb 1860	Jas. R. Warren md by J. L. Compton JP
Warren Benjamin	Louisa Pleasant	12 Aug 1833	Richard Whitmore
Warren Bozzel	Elizabeth Melone	21 Dec 1798	Cornelius Dollarhide

GROOM	BRIDE	DATE	BONDSMAN OR WITNESS
Warren Burwell	Frances C. Barnwell	6 Aug 1852	Samuel P. Hill
Warren Burwell	Rebecca F. Hall	17 Sep 1863	Stephen H. C. Oliver md by N. M. Lewis JP
Warren Drewry	Sallie Turner	20 Nov 1858	Thos. Covington
		25 Nov 1858	md by A. B. Walker JP
Warren Edmond	Martha Dameron	30 Oct 1829	Bird Bateman
Warren Franklin L.	Mary Wells	24 Apr 1851	Solomon Corbett md by John Stadler
Warren George N.	----------------	12 May 1818	Richard Aldridge Joseph McCulloch James Yancey
Warren George W.	Mary A. Mitchell	3 Nov 1857	Henry Warren md by Wm. J. Bowe JP
Warren Goodloe	Elizabeth Virloins	8 Oct 1816	Thos. Evans Isaac Rainey
Warren Granderson	Martha Terrell	6 May 1851	James Hutchison
		8 May 1851	md by C. H. Richmond JP
Warren Henry	Elisabeth Smith	25 Nov 1812	Samuel Garrard
Warren Hiram	Mary Brooks	26 Jul 1848	Augustus Gwyn
Warren Iverson G.	Olive Moore	12 Dec 1846	Mitchell Currie
Warren James S.	Teletha Snipes	6 Jan 1847	Mitchell Currie
Warren John	Anne Smithey	26 Jan 1810	John Smithey
Warren John	Huldah Haralson	30 Nov 1850	Warren Cooper
Warren John B.	Rachel Hunt	15 Jun 1817	James Kelley
Warren Jno. Goodloe	Isabella Melone	8 Nov 1791	Jeremiah Warrin
Warren Joseph N.	Nancey Kelley	-- Oct 1814	Robert Stadler
Warren Madison	Nancy Roberts	12 Dec 1842	Warren Cooper
Warren Martin	Ann Miles	6 Feb 1836	Alexander Miles
Warren Mason	Naomi Campbell	22 Oct 1860	John T. Russell md by C. H. Richmond JP
Warren Micajah	Sarah Mason	19 Apr 1859	Thomas Evans
Warren Micajah	Leatha Pleasant	23 Apr 1859	Thomas Evans
		24 Apr 1859	md by Calvin J. Richmond
Warren Samuel	Prescilla Fuller	31 Dec 1799	John Warren
Warren Samuel	Liddy Holsonback	5 Jan 1805	Benjamin Warren
Warren Thomas	Salley Smith	27 Jan 1810	Allin Cooper
Warren Thomas	Ann Eliza Browning	4 Oct 1853	William Cooper
		6 Oct 1853	md by Benj. Wells JP
Warren Thomas J.	Adalade Saterfield	10 Feb 1859	Lawson Earp md by N. M. Lewis JP
Warren Vinson	Nicey Neeley	15 Feb 1800	William Owen
Warren William	Polley Riddle	14 Oct 1807	Samuel Smithey
Warren William	Nancey Wisdom	26 Aug 1809	Saml. Warren Jr.
Warren William	Anny Lewis	28 Nov 1823	Ephraim Burch
Warren William Jr.	Frances Terrell	5 Jul 1825	Jonathan Murphey
Warren William Jr.	Catherine Hanshaw	24 Mar 1826	Samuel Grier
Warren William H.	Susan A. Stadler	20 Dec 1867	md by L. Oakley MG
Warren Yancy G.	Mary C. Ellison	16 Dec 1842	Joseph Murphey
Warren Yearbey	Sarah Hester	21 Apr 1828	Robert H. Hester
Warrin Benjamin	Rachael Culbertson	4 May 1791	Samuel Smythe
Warrin Bluford	Sally Yates	14 Feb 1803	John McCain
Warrin Ezekiel	Mary Wisdom	15 Apr 1816	William Currie Isaac Rainey
Warrin James	Nancey Murphey	26 Aug 1800	Gabriel Murphey
Warrin Stuart	Catherine Olliver	22 Feb 1791	William Phelps
Warrin Tho.	Margret Cook	4 Jul 1820	Ephraim Burch
Warrin Timothy	Elizabeth Tindal	13 Mar 1817	William Southard
Warrin William (see Waurren)	Sally Malone	26 Nov 1801	John Warrin
Washburn Joseph	Elizabeth Corbet	14 Sep 1848	Abner Miles

GROOM	BRIDE	DATE	BONDSMAN OR WITNESS
Washburn Willis	Nancey Evans	2 May 1825	Robert Dixon
Wasley Robert	Delilah Dye	22 Mar 1799	William Dye
Watkins James (Col-son of Harry Beverly & Polly Young)	Milly Hunt (Col-dau of Richard Barnett & Viney Hunt)	18 Nov 1867	md by E. Hunt JP
Watkins John	Mary Ray	19 Aug 1807	William Parker
Watkins Joseph V. B.	Logan S. Watkins	17 May 1857 19 May 1857	W. E. Watson md by J. Jennings JP
Watkins King (Col)	Oney McGehee (Col)	23 Dec 1865	Fed Smith J. J. Jones
Watkins Martin (Col)	Mary Lee (Col)	30 Nov 1865 9 Dec	md by A. A. Pattillo JP
Watkins Mathew W.	Urcillia P. Shaw	8 Apr 1859	Thos. A. Hudson
Watkins Philip	Jean Pickel	23 Dec 1790	Shadrack Roberts
Watkins Thomas	Elisabeth Chappel	10 Feb 1783	Mason Foley J. Cole
Watkins Thos. J.	Sarah A. Gunn	10 Aug 1843	Allen Gunn
Watkins William	Jane Terrell	6 Nov 1834	Paul Terrell
Watlington Armistead	Mary Brooks	14 Apr 1790	Thomas Brookes
Watlington Armistead	Rebecca Watlington	2 Jan 1833	Drury A. Mimms
Watlington Carter (Col-son of Carter & Patsey)	Eda Lea (Col-dau of Nathan Yancey & Eda Lea)	19 Oct 1867	md by J. J. Jones JP
Watlington David (son of Stephen & Ruthy)	Sallie Jones (dau of Daniel & Rebecca)	31 Aug 1867	md by Stephen Neal JP
Watlington Edward	Jane Brooks	15 Apr 1820	Robert Holderness
Watlington Edward Jr.	Mary Ann Mims	25 Feb 1841	Ibzan Rice Jr.
Watlington Francis	Lydia Harper	4 Nov 1823	Francis Smith
Watlington Hiram S.	Mary B. Bennett	23 Nov 1823	Thomas Jeffreys
Watlington James	Jane Scott	21 Mar 1826	Paul Watlington
Watlington James J. B.	Martha A. Watlington	8 Jul 1858	Samuel P. Hill md by Tho. W. Tobey MG
Watlington James M.	Sarah E. West	1 Mar 1850	John M. Richmond Charles R. Rice
Watlington Jas. W. (son of Edward & Mary)	Laura A. Jones (dau of John E. & Mary)	26 Mar 1867	H. F. Brandon clk
Watlington John	Betsey Donoho	4 Sep 1792	Willmun Dixon
Watlington Jonathan B.	Darothey C. Rice	7 Jun 1823	John C. Harvey
Watlington Paul	Jane P. Brackwell	21 Feb 1838	Robert Blackwell
Watlington Reid	Catherine Singleton	17 Jun 1828	Elijah Roberts
Watlington Shepperd (son of John Brown & Clara Watlington)	Celia King (dau of Moses & Clara Carter)	7 Sep 1867	H. F. Brandon
Watlington Sidney (Col-son of Ned & Eliza)	Ester Page (Col-dau of Jennie Page)	27 Dec 1867	H. F. Brandon
Watlington Thomas	Dorothy B. Brackin	2 Nov 1824	James Watlington
Watlington Thompson T.	Martha W. Lyon	19 May 1849	John D. Keesee
Watlington William	Titia Mannen	9 Nov 1816	Benjamin Willis
Watlington William P.	Mary J. Slade	20 Jul 1850	William P. Graves

GROOM	BRIDE	DATE	BONDSMAN OR WITNESS
Watson Anderson	Susan Mallory	29 Oct 1832	Ezekiel Sawyers
Watt Absalom	Elizabeth Henderson	16 Dec 1815	John Stamps
Watt James	Polley Blackwell	-- Nov 1809	Alex. Murphey
Watt Jno.	Margaret A. Price	24 Apr 1857	Robt. A. Montgomery
		29 Apr 1857	md by Jas. P. Simpson MG
Watt Russell (Col)	Becky Neal (Col)	3 Nov 1867	md by E. Hunt JP
Watt Samuel Jr.	Kiturah Blackwell	1 Nov 1808	Alex. Murphey
Watts Samuel	Marey Rice	25 Jan 1808	Garland Blackwell
Waurrin John	Patsey Harndon	14 Feb 1794	Larkin Warrin
Wealsh Samual	Susanah Jeffers	18 Feb 1789	William Glasby / William Moore
Weatherford Barten	Jane King	30 Nov 1824	John Weatherford
Weatherford Hiram	Nancey Harrelson	23 Sep 1818	John Weatherford
Weatherford Warren	Susanna Blackwell	27 Nov 1815	Henry Cobb
Weatherford William	Frances G. Hooper	3 Feb 1830	David J. Rawley
Web Anderson	Caroline Snipes	25 Dec 1866	Edward Hightower md by Jerry Smith JP
Webb Daniel D.	Martha F. Bucey	19 Dec 1831	Jesse Harrison
Webb Johnston	Grussey McCarver	12 Feb 1781	William Smith / John H. Pryor
Webb Lewis	Mary A. Crowder	16 Dec 1837	Daniel D. Winstead
Webb William R.	Elizabeth L. VanHook	14 Nov 1829	Jacob G. Walker
Webb William S.	Milly Turner	4 Apr 1804	Wm. Wilkerson
Webster Charles	Betsey Stafford	20 May 1812	Johnston Wilson
Webster Charles Henderson	Mary C. Stephens	30 May 1849	Malbon C. Webster
Webster James	Frances Westbrooks	29 Oct 1828	John Webster
Webster John	Mary Whitlow	24 Nov 1817	Charles Webster
Webster M. C. A.	Soriah Jackson	22 Feb 1854	H. A. Richmond
Webster Micajah	Nancy Hawkins	1 Feb 1843	Barnet Stafford
Webster Thomas	Elizabeth Morgan	1 Mar 1837	Samuel Love
Webster Thomas H.	Louiser Childress	7 Dec 1853	Algernon D. Stephens
		8 Dec 1853	md by Wm. J. Moore
Weeks Henry	Lovely Crowder	11 Nov 1822	Benjamin Stephens
Weeks Richard	Nancey Kiersey	27 Feb 1826	Hugh Campbell
Weiford Perie W.	Rebecca J. Kelly	12 Jun 1855	James B. Harris
		17 Jun 1855	md by J. Jennings JP
Weir David P.	Hannah L. Humeston	20 Nov 1838	D. A. Gillaspie
Weir Thomas	Happy Johns	10 Nov 1866	Newton Tanner md by E. Hunt JP
Welch Samuel (see Wealsh)	Nancy Baxter	4 Jan 1782	Elijah Duncan
Wells Ezariah	Matilda Harrison	23 Feb 1832	Miles Wells
Wells Benjamin	Eliza Crisp	20 Dec 1826	Ephraim Burch
Wells Hardey	Elisabeth Parker	20 Oct 1784	Thomas Palmer
Wells James M.	Sarah Florence	24 Oct 1840	John C. Smith
Wells John	Nancey Smith	22 Aug 1822	Jeremiah Childers
Wells Justian	Martha Gulipin	19 Jan 1836	Cary W. West / B. C. West Sr.
Wells Laborn C.	Lydia A. Barnes	8 Feb 1861	Robert C. Phelps md by N. M. Lewis JP
Wells Miles Jr.	Duppe Wells	26 Mar 1828	James Farquhar
Wells Stephen H.	Sarah J. Snipes	11 Nov 1859	James M. Wells
Wells Stephen M.	Martha J. Mitchell	11 Dec 1854	William S. Tate md by Jno. S. Grasty
Wells Thomas	Polley Rainey	11 Mar 1809	Miles Wells Jr.
Wells Thomas	Mary Foster	26 Sep 1823	Thomas Jackson
Wemple Jno.D.	Dorothy Gwyn	17 Mar 1841	Alexander McAlpin
Wesley John	Nancy Randal	22 Jan 1806	James Randal Jr.
West Benjamin C.	Mary C. Hatchett	21 Feb 1824	Paul A. Haralson
West Cary W.	Mary Hodges	10 May 1834	Dudley G. Stokes

GROOM	BRIDE	DATE	BONDSMAN OR WITNESS
West Edward	Ann Garrett	27 Aug 1866	Wm. Hatchett
			md by H. E. Hodges JP
West Joseph	Nancey Wilmouth	20 Oct 1819	William Cannon
West R. J.	Mary F. Bradshaw	21 Dec 1866	A. L. Bagby
			md by W. W. Duncan
Westbrook John	Elizabeth Stafford	21 Dec 1841	Jese B. Stafford
Westbrook Paschall	Mary Smith	17 Feb 1829	Thomas Smith
Westbrook Thomas	Ann Russel	27 Oct 1841	Thompson Moore
			Jno. Daniel
Westbrook Yancey	Jane Coil	31 Dec 1823	William Coile
			John H. Graves DC
Westbrook Yancey	Jemima Chamberlain	6 Jan 1825	Thomas Warren
Westbrooks Joseph B.	Rosa Ann Johnson	30 Jan 1854	Robert F. Furguson
			md by J. M. Allen JP
Wheelan William	Ellioner Furguson	17 Jan 1804	Rowland Lawson
Wheeler Vincent H. (son of Saml. H. Wheeler)	Louisa Shelton	19 Mar 1839	John J. Chandler
			Jas. L. Conklin
White A. W. (son of James & Nancy)	Sallie Watlington (dau of Paul & Jane)	1 Aug 1867	md by Jacob Doll MG
White Daniel H.	Eliza O. Dodson	17 Oct 1854	William Corbin
			md by Tho. L. Lea JP
White David	Salley Ponds	19 Nov 1804	Elijah Carman
White Epa.	Lydia Waller	24 Jul 1806	John Woody
			Jno. Burton
White Henry (Col)	Betsy Norman (Col)	26 Dec 1866	Pinkney Robertson
		12 Jun 1867	md by Jno. D. Keesee
White James	Nancey Ware	30 Aug 1813	Charles Beusey
White James B.	Theodotia Reynolds	12 Mar 1833	Thomas D. Johnston
White John	Elisabeth Williamson	26 Oct 1796	William Dickins
White John	Elizabeth Fuqua	10 Jan 1834	Daniel S. Price
			Benj. C. West
			C. W. West
White John W.	Frances M. Hamlett	28 Mar 1854	John R. Smith
		30 Mar 1854	md by Solomon Apple MG
White Paton (Col-son of Nelson Harrison)	Lucinda Williamson (Col-dau of Leath & Mintus)	22 Jun 1867	md by S. G. Mason
Wiles Luke	Lucy Reynolds	22 Nov 1814	William Shackelford
Wiles Samuel (Col)	Julia Howard (Col)	16 Dec 1865	Lorenzo Lewis
			md by E. Hunt JP
Wiles Thomas	Dolly Bohannan	6 Jun 1809	Eaton Banes
Wiles Thomas	Fanny Banes	27 Apr 1819	Jephtha Parker
Wiles Thomas	Melvira Guinn	15 Mar 1860	George C. Motley
			md by N. M. Lewis JP
Wiley Albert G.	Francis E. Chandler	27 Aug 1842	Robert W. Wiley
Wiley Alexander	Marthy Nowell	20 Mar 1779	Joshua Kearney
Wiley Alexander	Fanney Yancey	2 Oct 1804	Samuel Morton Jr.
Wiley Alexander	Polly Kerr	28 Dec 1807	John Wiley
Wiley Franklin A.	Sally L. Currie	8 Aug 1851	T. S. Poore
		24 Aug 1851	md by Jacob Doll MG
Wiley George (Col)	Letsy Legans (Col)	27 Apr 1847	Woody Wiley (Col)
Wiley Green (son of Elijah Moore & Matilda Currie)	Eliza Murray	30 Nov 1867 8 Dec 1867	H. F. Brandon clk md by Jerry Smith JP
Wiley Iverson	Emily Rudd	22 Sep 1866	Robert Cousins
			md by Jerry Smith JP
Wiley John	Jinney Mitchell	6 Sep 1815	Alexander Wiley
Wiley John (Col)	Bettie Martin (Col)	30 Mar 1867	George Poteate
			md by David Burch JP
Wiley John H.	Adaline W. Wiley	27 Mar 1839	Thomas W. Chandler
Wiley Thomas	Tabitha Noel	12 Apr 1805	John Richmond

GROOM	BRIDE	DATE	BONDSMAN OR WITNESS
Wiley Yancey	Ann Eliza Thompson	17 Dec 1831	Wm. Chandler
Wiley Yancey	Anniss Lea	30 Apr 1855	Franklin A. Wiley
Wilkerson Jno.C.	Justina L. Thompson	23 Mar 1852	Josiah A. Stanfield
Wilkerson Wager	Patience Duncan	27 May 1780	John Moore
Wilkerson Walter S.	Agness R. Barker	9 Sep 1862	Josiah Barker md by N. M. Lewis JP
Wilkins Joseph	Eliza Jane Perry	21 May 1858	John Pleasant md by A. B. Walker JP
Wilkinson Egbert S.	Mary Ann McCain	23 Jan 1849	Willoughby N. Shelton
Wilkinson Henry E.	Patsey Harrison	8 Dec 1819	John P. Harrison
Wilkinson John E.	Mary W. Harrison	10 Sep 1821	Jesse Harrison
Wilkinson Robert W.	Elizabeth F. Dodson	14 Dec 1855 15 Dec 1865?	Minyard Barker md by E. H. Hunt JP
Wilkinson Simon T.	Sarah A. Jenkins	10 Jul 1859	John J. Baugh md by S. G. Mason
Wilks Thomas U.	Mirah L. Graves	31 Oct 1837	Tho. D. Connally
Williams Alexander (son of Edmond & Priscilla)	Catharine Mitchel (dau of Vilette)	7 Sep 1867	md by J. J. Jones JP
Williams Alfred	Mary Perry	12 Dec 1836	Patrick Turner
Williams Daniel	Ann Rice	5 Jan 1786	Anthony Thompson
Williams Craftin	Betsey Yates	3 Mar 1798	Patin Harvill
Williams Dawson M.	Lucy T. Mansfield	2 Jan 1856 3 Jan 1856	Thomas Mansfield md by J. M. Allen JP
Williams Duke	Edey Harriss	19 Oct 1790	Robert Williams
Williams George W.	Martha R. Spain	15 Apr 1850	Pinckney J. Wray
Williams Gilbert (Col)	Lizzy Ann Foster (Col)	10 Feb 1867	Glenn Watkins md by John J. Jones
Williams Henry	Polley Gooch	31 Dec 1799	Thomas Turner
Williams Dr. J. M.	Mary E. Glass	27 Nov 1865	James K. Lea md by S. G. Mason
Williams James	Elizabeth Sawyers	18 Jun 1806	William Sawyer
Williams James M.	Francis Purkins	30 Mar 1858	Saml. B. Blackwell md by H. W. Cobb JP
Williams John	Fanny Dunnavant	13 Nov 1822	Richard Gates
Williams John Jr.	Susannah Dixon	10 Jan 1800	Duke Williams
Williams John A.	Sarah E. Miller (dau of Robert Miller, Bedford Co. Va.)	10 Aug 1835	John C. Harvey
Williams John D.	Frances Ware	9 Sep 1861	Alexander Fergerson
Williams John D. (or Williamson John D.)	Sarah J. Mattox	6 Jul 1866	A. A. Mitchell md by S. G. Mason
Williams John W.	Frances J. Allen	24 Jan 1863 29 Jan 1863	Robert D. Boyles md by Stephen Neal JP
Williams Maderson	Ester Wagstaff	8 Feb 1867	Joseph Allen
Williams Marmaduke	Agness Harris	26 Oct 1798	Alex. Murphey
Williams Nathaniel	---- Stone (wid)	17 Jan 1832	Owen McAleer
Williams Nathaniel Jr.	Elizabeth Dixon	26 Jun 1792	Robert Harris
Williams Nathaniel R.	Jemima Ann Somers	9 Apr 1859 13 Apr 1859	Geo. R. Bowman md by Stephen Neal JP
Williams Paul	Lucy Donoho	18 Oct 1791	Thos. Donoho
Williams Ralph D.	Nannie W. Powell	27 Mar 1863 9 Apr 1863	Jno. L. Stanfield md by P. J. Carraway MG
Williams Robert	Nancey Elam	6 Feb 1825	Craftin Williams Jr.
Williams Robert H.	Catharine A. Sledge	4 Sep 1851 25 Sep 1851	Cranford Sledge md by Wm. Anderson
Williams Robert W.	Martha W. Dotson	20 Feb 1850	John A. Verser
Williams Stephen E.	Emma L. McNeill	26 Feb 1850	Wm. A. Shaw

GROOM	BRIDE	DATE	BONDSMAN OR WITNESS
Williams Thomas Nesbit	Mary Fullar	7 Nov 1789	John Fuller
Williams Warner	Elizabeth M. Lewis	16 Mar 1813	Tho. Bouldin Stith Bouldin
Williams William	Penciselia Swann	22 Dec 1778	Mathew Willson Absalom Tatom
Williams William	Jemima Pass	3 Dec 1788	Nathaniel Pass
Williams Winstead	Annis Childress	16 Aug 1834	Thomas Groom
Williams Winston	Sarah Perkins	24 Sep 1842	Anderson Lewis
Williamson Addison A.	Margaret E. Butler	6 Jan 1849	James M. Bushnell
Williamson Anthony	Eliza K. Lea	27 Nov 1818	Allen Gunn
Williamson Anthony S.	Sarah A. Moore	12 Nov 1849	John M. Johnston
Williamson Benjamin	Eliza A. Hinton	15 Nov 1848	David S. Johnston
Williamson Calvin	Marth Williamson	2 Mar 1867	H. F. Brandon
Williamson Charles (Col)	Mary Hill (Col)	25 Feb 1866	Mack McNeil (Col) md by Jacob Doll MG
Williamson Edmond	Emiline Dodson	29 Jul 1866	Armsteard Hunt md by D. Hunt JP
Williamson Elisha	Luzeta Shackelford	16 Aug 1867	md by Jas. K. Lea JP
Williamson Emmanuel (Col)	Sophia Brown (Col)	2 Mar 1867	md by Azariah Graves
Williamson Felix (Col)	Mary Bushnell (Col)	1 Dec 1866	Abram Williamson md by Stephen Neal JP
Williamson George	Rebecca S. Lea	13 Nov 1815	Wm. McBride
Williamson George	Harriett E. Easly	31 Oct 1838	N. M. Roan
Williamson Green	Candice Cobb	16 Dec 1867 24 Dec 1867	H. F. Brandon md by S. G. Mason
Williamson Hall	Nancey Smith	19 Oct 1791	Nathan Rice
Williamson Henry (Col-son of Wm. & Sally)	Dilly Ann Lea (Col-dau of Spencer Lea & Gracy Pinchback)	28 Nov 1867 30 Nov 1867	H. F. Brandon md by Jacob Doll MG
Williamson John D. (or Williams John D.)	Sarah J. Mattox	6 Jul 1866	A. A. Mitchell
Williamson Jno. W.	Virginia F. Williamson	29 Jul 1863 30 Jul 1863	John Dickenson md by J. W. Montgomery
Williamson Johnston (Col-son of William & Sally)	Maranda Johnston (Col-dau of Alfred & Eliza)	22 Feb 1868 28 Feb	md by Jacob Doll MG
Williamson Lemon	Louisa Bethel	14 Apr 1866	Caleb A. Johnston md by S. G. Mason
Williamson Mark (Col-son of Abram & Amy)	Martha Slade (Col-dau of Cherry)	28 Aug 1867 31 Aug	md by Azariah Graves JP
Williamson Mintus	Leatha Williamson	3 Oct 1866 5 Oct 1867	Ben Shaw md by Jas. J. Clendenin JP
Williamson Monroe (Col)	Minerva Crutchfield (Col)	20 Apr 1867	md by Jacob Doll
Williamson Pulliam	Lucy Adkison	12 Mar 1782	James Pulliam John Womack JP
Williamson Robert H.	Harriet E. Gunn	16 May 1865 17 May 1865	George Williamson md by R. G. Barrett MG
Williamson Simon (Col)	Victoria Watlington (Col)	25 Dec 1865 26 Dec 1865	Orin Graves md by M. A. Turner JP
Williamson Simon (Col)	Caroline Bethel (Col)	13 Dec 1866	md by Jacob Doll MG
Williamson Swift	Mary Lea	12 Dec 1819	Robert R. Prather
Williamson Theoderick L.	Mary Sneed (dau of Susan Sneed	2 Apr 1828 3 Apr 1828	Levin Downs md by Danl. A. Penick

GROOM	BRIDE	DATE	BONDSMAN OR WITNESS
Williamson Thomas (Col)	Ella Gunn (Col)	9 Dec 1865	C. Brinsfield
		10 Dec 1865	md by A. A. Pattillo JP
Williamson Thomas J.	Mary P. Spencer	19 Oct 1840	Joseph F. Cornwell
Williamson Thompson (Col)	Harriet Rice (Col)	12 Jan 1867	Granderson Graves md by Stephen Neal JP
Williamson Walter S.	Aderline W. Johnston	3 Dec 1860 4 Dec 1860	E. B. Withhers md by J. Doll MG
Williamson Weldon E.	Nannie M. Johnston	25 Nov 1856	Brice Harralson md by J. Doll MG
Willingham John	Mary Burch	13 Mar 1788	Thomas Killgore
Willis Anderson	Frances B. Rice	24 May 1825	John C. Harvey
Willis Barzillai	Sarah Canor	15 Jun 1849	Zachariah Page
Willis Benjamin	Susannah Chandler	20 Nov 1811	William Willis
Willis Benjamin Jr.	Lucinda Campbell	23 Dec 1846	William N. Kimbro
Willis George	Sally J. Smith	14 Oct 1	Geo. A. Smith
Willis George W.	Malinda Stephens	14 Jan 1834	Stairling S. Kent
Willis Henry	Mary Haddock	21 May 1783	Joseph Willis
Willis Henry	Darcas Haralson	21 Feb 1821	Wm. Willis
Willis Henry Jr.	Betsy Evans	20 Jan 1830	James T. Willis
Willis James	Nancey Williams	20 Sep 1834	Thomas Willis
Willis James M. (Col)	Eliza Blackwell (Col)	20 Dec 1867	md by Thos. J. Brown
Willis James T.	Ann Williams	19 Nov 1832	Iverson G. Stephens
Willis Jerry (Col)	Adaline Pinchback (Col)	15 Apr 1867	md by J. Doll MG
Willis John	Betsy Ward	28 Feb 1827	Maj. Denny
Willis John William	Sarah A. Landrum	7 Oct 1852	Granderson F. Westbrooks A. G. Stevens
Willis Joseph	Lydia Chaney	23 Jan 1842	William H. Watts
Willis Marshall (Col)	Ibby Graves (Col)	23 Nov 1866	md by T. W. Graves JP
Willis N. W.	C. E. Ware	10 Dec 1857	Wm. Y. Hooper md by J. M. Allen JP
Willis Nicholas	Nancy Turner	29 Oct 1804	Ziba Rice
Willis Peter Jr. (son of Peter Sr.)	Rachel Jones	16 Dec 1867 19 Dec 1867	md by S. G. Mason
Willis Pinkney (son of Peter & Hannah)	Eliza Leath (dau of Chany & Ephraim	19 Nov 1867 24 Nov 1867	md by S. G. Mason
Willis Thomas H.	Harriet R. Mitchell	26 Sep 1844	John Fuqua T. H. Miles
Willis Thomas J.	Sopha A. Lea	1 Mar 1841	James M. Neal
Willis William	Elisabeth Miller	5 Dec 1785	Joseph Willis
Willis William	Charlotte McCain	1 Aug 1850	Anderson Willis
Willis William S.	Frances P. Thompson	5 Dec 1863 6 Dec 1863	J. B. Kennon md by Geo. W. Griffin elder
Willson George M.	Polly Lea	12 Apr 1810	Charles Willson
Willson James	Mildred Burgess	10 Dec 1792	William Willson
Willson John	Rebecca Boulding	29 Nov 1818	John Everett
Willson Lorenzo J.	Elizabeth Hix	28 Aug 1858 2 Sep 1858	Zachariah McFarling md by N. M. Lewis JP
Willson Robert	Abarilla Stephens	28 Dec 1782	William Willson
Willson Robert	Elisabeth M. Bryan	21 Mar 1797	William Rainey
Willson Samuel	Lucy Bows	17 Sep 1860	Thomas K. Kimbro
Willson Thaddus	Francis Bass	28 Dec 1844	A. A. Pattillo
Willson Wilem (William)	Patsy Farley	2 Jan 1793	James Willson
Wilmoth George	Sally Hall	25 Mar 1822	John Gomer
Wilmoth Miles	Adelethia Hall	11 Sep 1820	Woodlief Hooper

GROOM	BRIDE	DATE	BONDSMAN OR WITNESS
Wilson Abel	Lucy Grant	1 Nov 1800	Walter Ingram
Wilson Abner	Sally Morgan	23 Jan 1800	Lewis Evans
Wilson Dennis	Martha G. Rice	10 Aug 1818	William D. Paschall
Wilson George L.	Katharine Pass	11 Sep 1820	Elijah Withers
Wilson Giles	Patcey Ware	24 Apr 1804	John B. Johnston
Wilson Henry	Betsy Wilson	5 Jan 1867	Thos. Walters
Wilson Henry W.	Nancy Fuller	22 Apr 1818	Allen Gunn
Wilson Isaac	Mildred Walden	23 Aug 1842	John Allen
			M. P. Huntington
Wilson James	Margaret Crisp	15 Mar 1790	George Burch
Wilson James	Betsy Stanback	4 Jan 1825	Pleasant Roberson
Wilson James H.	Ann R. Kirby	8 Jan 1855	Robert W. Graves
		23 Jan 1855	md by Thomas W. Tobey MG
Wilson John	Anne Smith	4 Dec 1821	William G. Cochran
			Ch. Willson
Wilson John	Kizziah W. Willis	2 Jul 1833	Thomas D. Connally
Wilson John W.	Abigal Davis	2 Feb 1848	Saml. Davis
Wilson John W.	Eliza Jackson (wid)	16 May 1859	Thompson H. Boswell
Wilson Johnston	Ursley Whitloe	3 Dec 1788	Jeremiah Samuel
Wilson Joseph	Sarah Wells	29 Jun 1799	Robert Malone
Wilson Mike (Col-son of Moses & Nancy)	Juda McCadden (Col-dau of Bristor & Bridget Rainey)	27 Jul 1867 28 Jul 1867	md by N. M. Lewis
Wilson Robert	Elisabeth Johnston	28 Dec 1795	Thomas Johnston
Wilson Robert	Polly Walker	26 Sep 1831	Warren Weatherford
Wilson Rufus (Col)	Fannie Jones (Col)	13 Oct 1865	Robert Smith
		18 Oct 1865	md by C. J. Richmond JP
Wilson Thomas (Col)	Minerva A. Nash (Col)	21 Mar 1853	William Whitlow md by Tho. Covington
Wilson William	Mary Currie	2 Jul 1809	James Currie
Wilson William	Nancy Rudd (or Reed)	-- Jan 1812	John Hinton
Wilson William	Rebecca Bery	29 Dec 1815	John Berry
Wilson William L.	Martha S. Young	26 Aug 1862	James H. Talley md by W. B. Bowe JP
Windsor Edward (Col-son of Phenix)	Adaline Powell (Col-dau of Welton Garland)	19 Jun 1867 23 Jun 1867	md by John J. Jones JP
Windsor Felix (Col)	Sabry Bushnell (Col)	20 Oct 1866	Henry Somers md by Stephen Neal
Windsor John Jr.	Susanah Hornbuckle	7 Sep 1795	Wm. H. Rice
Windsor Joseph	Elizabeth Haralson	21 Oct 1811	Daniel Payne
			Stephen D. Watkins
Windsor Newman	Frances Windsor	7 Aug 1813	Joseph Windsor
Windsor Thomas	Milley Hornbuckle	31 Dec 1797	Edney Tapscott
Windsor William (Col-son of Alfred & Mary)	Rachel Simpson (Col-dau of John & Deby)	13 Apr 1868	md by Stephen Neal JP
Wingfield Nelson D.	Sarah A. Franklin	20 Nov 1833	Daniel S. Price Cary W. West B. C. West
Winingham Sharp	Polly Morgan	20 Jul 1793	Zachariah Evans
Winne Obadiah	Oney Boulton	4 Mar 1786	William Rainey
Winstead Charles	Sarah Moore	15 Jun ----	Contance Winstead
Winstead Stephen	Elizabeth Hays	19 Nov 1832	Daniel Sergent
Winstead William	Martha Wright	5 Dec 1844	William Royster
Winston Jno. R.	Marian Long	13 Nov 1866	Jas. M. Morehead md by S. A. Stanfield
Winston Thos.	Patsey Coleman	29 Dec 1796	Noel Coleman
Winter William	Mary Belew	30 Sep 1795	John Hipworth
Winters Walter	Betsey Draper	20 Dec 1797	William Jones
Winters Watson	Nancey Womack	5 Feb 1815	Josiah Slade
Wire Josiah	Mary Irby	7 Nov 1829	Thomas Y. Pass

GROOM	BRIDE	DATE	BONDSMAN OR WITNESS
Wisdom Abner	Mary Fuller	20 Jan 1790	James Sargent
Wisdom Barzillai	Phoebe Dameron	29 Nov 1827	Levi Fuller
Wisdom John	Sarah Fuller	10 Feb 1792	Samuel Evans
Wisdom William	Elizabeth Roan	15 Feb 1830	James C. Dameron
Wiseman John	Mary A. Downs	11 Jun 1842	Roland D. Downes
Witcher Daniel P.	Martha A. Millner	16 Aug 1852	William J. Blair
Withers Elijah	Catharine Stubblefield	23 May 1817	Wyatt Stubblefield
Withers Elijah B.	Mary A. Price	23 Mar 1863	Wm. L. Barnard
		25 Mar 1863	md by P. J. Carraway MG
Withers Elijah K.	Nancey B. Lawson	8 Apr 1826	Joel F. Motley
Withers Lewis H.	Mary A. Richardson	20 Feb 1844	Wm. H. Duprey
Withers Warren (son of Nick & Sopha)	Jane Blackwell (dau of Moses & Minerva)	27 Jul 1867	H. F. Brandon clk
Wolters Henry	Sarah Hargis	31 Jan 1792	Jobe Blackard
Womack Abraham	Louisa M. Cobb	29 Nov 1838	Wm. P. Womack
Womack Algernon S.	Fannie W. Graves	6 Aug 1855	Jas. N. Montgomery
		8 Aug 1855	md by L. L. Hendren
Womack Cato (son of Jerry Holderness & Hester Womack)	Polly Hooper	20 Nov 1867	H. F. Brandon
		30 Nov 1867	md by Jno. D. Keesee
Womack David	Dilila Graves	24 Mar 1800	Francis Howard
Womack Green P.	Elizabeth C. Hatchett	17 Oct 1831	Thomas D. Connally
Womack Joseph B.	Elizabeth Blackwell	14 Dec 1847	James S. Blackwell
Womack Lewis P.	Sarah F. Williamson	20 Feb 1846	Joseph B. Womack
Womack Pleasant H.	Sarah Haralson	4 Dec 1828	John Hooper
Womack Rufus Y.	Bettie M. Stone	18 Nov 1865	James F. White
		23 Nov 1865	md by R. G. Barrett MG
Womack Thomas J.	Ann E. Yancey	9 Jul 1855	Thomas W. Graves md by Thomas W. Tobey MG
Womack William P.	Matilda Oliver	27 Jan 1841	Henry F. Adkins
Womble James	Catharine Bouldin	1 Dec 1823	Isaac R. Currie
Wood John	Polly Anderson	11 Mar 1797	Joseph Wilson
Wood John	Margarett Fuller	22 Oct 1829	Nathan Oakley
Woodey John	Nancy Walters	27 Dec 1845	George Franklin Connally M. P. Huntington
Wooding John E.	Lucy Ann Owen	29 Feb 1834	George W. Johnson
Woods A. S. G.	Martha A. Laftis (may be Loftis)	4 Apr 1849	J. W. Roan
Woods Andy M.	Minerva Richmond	18 Jul 1834	John W. Roan
Woods Archey S. G.	Frances Richmond	20 Nov 1838	James Malone Geo. W. VanHook
Woods J. G.	Mary W. Bolton	10 Aug 1841	Henry A. Richmond
Woods James	Martha Berry	10 Dec 1822	James Rudd
Woods John	Betsey Roberts	5 Aug 1801	Eppy Everett
Woods John	Cathrine Farley	9 Nov 1801	William Willson
Woods Lewis (son of Randall Burnett)	Jane James (dau of Granville James)	15 May 1867 19 May 1867	md by David Burch JP
Woods William	Mary Farley	20 Dec 1800	Henry Burton
Woods William	Letitia Watlington	21 Oct 1845	Owen McAleer
Woody Frank	Frankie Long	4 Jul 1866	Isaac Long
Woody James	Sarah Fergerson	4 Sep 1842	Joseph M. Hightower N. J. Palmer
Woody Thomas (see Woodey)	Sally Carter	25 Mar 1808	George Spratton
Woollen Minor	Margaret Hatchett	3 Jan 1867	Jesse C. Griffith
Word Fleming	Mary C. McCain	31 Jan 1851	Thos. S. Poore

GROOM	BRIDE	DATE	BONDSMAN OR WITNESS
Workman Isaac	Susannah Sullivant	11 Oct 1799	Russell Sullivant
Worsham Beary	Elizabeth West	26 Jan 1809	Benjamin C. West
Worsham Ludwell	Elizabeth Cox (dau of Elizabeth Cox)	3 Sep 1807	Gabriel Cox
Worsham Ludwell	Nancy Bennatt	3 Jul 1813	John Bennatt Thomas Bouldin
Worsham Robert W.	Sarrah Bucey	17 Aug 1833	Benj. C. West Sr. Crawford West
Worsham Thomas J.	Julia A. Blackwell	22 Nov 1850	S. E. Brackin
Worsham William R.	Frances Durham	12 Dec 1836	Thomas C. Pass
Wosham Robert	Patsey Pistole	10 Jun 181-	Wm. R. Pistole Robert West
Wray Thomas	Amy Powell	26 Feb 1825	Noles Reed
Wray Thomas Jr.	Rebeccah Fowler	4 Nov 1790	Thomas Wray Sr.
Wray William	Salley Adams	30 Oct 1801	William Kimbro
Wrenn Hillmon W.	Sina E. Mitchell	10 Dec 1866	Wm. Wrenn md by S. G. Mason
Wrenn John F.	Lenorah H. Stratton	29 Nov 1858	William H. Land
Wright Abraham	Nancey Lea	9 Jan 1826	James Ingram
Wright Abram M.	Adaline W. Chandler	25 Jun 1850	David Ball M. P. Huntington
Wright Calib	Betsey Thomas	31 Dec 1792	Calib Carman
Wright Edward	Sina B. Lawson	7 Dec 1821	William B. Lawson
Wright Elisha	Nancy Pound	28 May 1812	Joseph Dooley
Wright George W.	Sarah A. Holcomb	5 Jan 1847	William Hinton Jno. K. Graves
Wright Hiram A.	Jane B. Lawson	6 Oct 1828	James A. Durham
Wright Isaac	Abijah Somers	12 Jan 1804	John Somers
Wright Isaac	Dolly McCubbins	28 Apr 1833	Benjamin Ingram
Wright Jacob Jr.	Polly Donoho	14 Jan 1794	Zacharias Wright
Wright Jacob Jr.	Nancey Warren	8 Nov 1815	Benjamin Ingram
Wright James B. (son of G. W. & Nancy)	Mary E. Hawkins (dau of Ephraim & Ellen)	9 Sep 1867 12 Sep 1867	md by Jerry Smith JP
Wright John C.	Paulina F. Meachum (wid)	25 Oct 1863	David Strader md by W. B. Swann JP
Wright John L.	Alice Withers	2 Oct 1863	John M. Blackwell md by William Burns MG
Wright Sidney R.	Sarah T. Lockard	31 Aug 1858 5 Sep 1858	George L. Torian md by A. N. Hall elder
Wright William B.	A. E. King	19 Sep 1865	R. L. Wright
Wright William G.	Nancy Murphey	1 Nov 1841	William B. Mann John K. Brooks
Wright Zacharias	Polly Hayes	24 Dec 1793	Robert Dixon
Wright Zera	Lyda Sanders	29 Oct 1839	John C. Totten
Wyatt Royall	Sarah Jones	3 May 1828	Barzl. Graves Williamson Holt
Wynn Robert S.	Julia F. Feigus	25 Jul 1865	John W. Ramey md by A. McAlpin JP
Wynn Stith (of Virginia)	Margaret L. Ramey (dau of Daniel of Danville Va.)	29 Sep 1847	H. N. Ramey
Wynne William B. (see Winne)	Elizabeth A. Henderson	9 May 1865 10 May 1865	John F. Charlton md by R. G. Barrett MG

- Y -

Yancey Algernon S.	Henrietta W. Graves	21 May 1838	Geo. W. Graves John K. Graves
Yancey Felix (Col)	Pathena Robertson (Col)	16 Nov 1865	Daniel Johnston md by S. G. Mason
Yancey James	Lucy Kerr	14 Jan 1794	Tryon Yancey
Yancey James	Zelphah Johnston	24 Jun 1811	Alex. Murphey

GROOM	BRIDE	DATE	BONDSMAN OR WITNESS
Yancey James M.	Ann Shuemaker	5 Jun 1833	Daniel S. Price
			Cary W. West
			B. C. West
Yancey Nathan	Fannie Glass	19 Jan 1867	Saml. Yancey
		26 Jan 1867	md by S. G. Mason
Yancey Ransom	Henrietta Foster	23 Dec 1867	
(son of Peter	(dau of Ed. Everett	24 Dec 1867	md by S. G. Mason
& Delphia)	& Sarah Foster)		
Yancey Spivy	Fanny Taylor	17 Jun 1849	James C. Dobbins
Yancey Thomas	Kesiah Simmons	24 Feb 1789	James Yancy
Yancey Thomas	Elizabeth Tait	10 Feb 1802	James Yancey
Yancey William	Damaris R. Oliver	16 Dec 1839	Ansel Ware
Yancey Wylie	Susannah Rice	12 May 1804	James Yancey
Yancy Bartlett	Nancy Graves	20 Dec 1808	Azariah Graves
Yancy John	Elizabeth Lightfoot Moore	24 Feb 1789	Thomas Yancey
Yarborough Samuel	Ailse Winsted	10 Nov 1787	Saml. Harrison
Yarbrough	Sally Ann Roberts	11 Nov 1856	Brice Harralson
Augustine J.		20 Nov 1856	md by J. B. Jackson
Yarbrough David	Miranda Yarbrough	7 Jul 1866	Jacob Harris (Col)
(Col)	(Col)		md by J. J. Jones JP
Yarbrough Joseph	Mary Herring	20 Aug 1825	Richard Yarbrough
Yarbrough	Rachel M. Pass	23 Aug 1858	Joseph J. Yarbrough
Richard L.		24 Aug 1858	md by J. W. Lewis MG
Yarbrough Thomas S.	Elizabeth A. Terry	12 Feb 1850	Jno. H. Lacy
Yates Alexander	Betsey Bayes	18 May 1850	Lawson Yates
Yates George	Pricilla Durham	20 May 1822	Westly R. Cook
Yates George W.	Mary C. Bays	29 Jan 1853	David Marshall
Yates Grief	Harriett A. Loveless	19 Apr 1860	Alexander Dodson
			md by N. M. Lewis JP
Yates Jackson	Ann Durham	30 Oct 1844	Israel Dickins
Yates James	Lydia Gillgore (Kilgore)	21 Jul 1784	Thomas Yates
Yates John M.	Harriet Durham	7 Aug 1848	Samuel McGonnigil
Yates John M. Jr.	Louisa F. Gatewood	19 Nov 1866	L. W. Yates
Yates Joseph M.	Lucinda A. Hodnett	6 May 1849	Henry Yates
Yates Joseph M.	Lucinda A. Hodnett	6 May 1849	Henry Yates
Yealock Lewis	Salley L. Mathews	13 Nov 1815	Thomas Mathews
Yealock Robert	Catharine Hodge	22 Oct 1824	Isaac Vanhook
Yearby Charles	Patsey Lay	12 Oct 1808	John Gomer
			Sol. Debow
Yeats John	Jemima Ropper	8 Mar 1779	James Ropper
			W. Campbell
Yeats John	Cathrine Caldwell	13 Oct 1780	George Samuel
Yelock James	Anne Pittard	26 Oct 1813	William Johnston
Young Jesse C.	Sarah Bennett	28 Apr 1857	John D. Meadors
		30 Apr 1857	md by J. M. Allen JP
Young Smith	Ann Eliza Harrison	11 May 1824	Robert K. Smith
Younger John C.	Emma Baugh	21 Aug 1866	C. C. McCarty
			md by Jacob Doll MG

- Z -

Zachary Bartholomew	Polly Bruce	22 May 1797	David Bruce
Zachary William	Nancy Lea	21 Nov 1780	James Lea
Zimmerman George J.	Susan S. Kimbrogh	24 Jan 1853	W. C. Rudd

INDEX

(?), Ann 30
Ables, Sally 47
Adams, Amandy 105
  Creed 67
  Eliza A. 48
  Elizabeth 91
  John 29
  M. F. 14
  Martha Ann 11
  Mary 3, 57
  Mary J. 9
  Salley 124
  Samuel 25
  Sarah Jane 91
  Simon 71
  Sylvester P. 29
  William 2
  William C. 79
Addington, William 21
Adkens, Betsey 78
Adkerson, Susannah 18
Adkins, Ann R. 78
  Carolina 100
  H. F. 17, 29, 78, 88
  Henry F. 100, 123
  James 1
  Jno. K. 1
  Mary E. 80
  Polley 33
  Susan 39
  Susanna 9
  Thomas B. 43, 94
Adkison, Lucy 120
Ahart, Betsey 11
  Jacob 12, 22, 92
Akin, Betsy 6
  Polly 31
Albert, Frances 64
Alderdice, Nancy 85
Alderson, Poindexter 1
  Rebecca (Mrs.) 1
Aldrege, William J. 106
Aldridg, Susanna 69
Aldridge, Artilia 101
  Hannah 1
  James H. 1
  James R. 10, 32, 88
  Jane 12
  Martha 46
  Nancy 15
  Richard 115
  Susan 111
Aldrige, William J. 12
Alexander, Lee 60
  W. H. 97
Alford, Susanna 49
  William 83
Alison, Ezekiel 48
  Mary 48
Allen, Amanda S. 39
  Arrenia M. 90
  David 85
  Elizabeth 59, 66
  Frances J. 119
  J. 46

Allen (cont.)
  J. J. 19
  J. M. 12, 16, 17, 23,
    28, 36, 41, 42, 50,
    52, 61, 63, 64, 66,
    69, 72, 76, 84, 91,
    94, 95, 99, 103,
    108, 111, 113, 118,
    119, 121, 125
  James M. 19
  John 122
  Joseph 119
  Martha Ann 71
  Mary 11
  Sally 94
  Sarah 10
  Sarah A. 65
  Sarah P. 28, 76
  Sarah S. 90
  Susanah 51
Alley, Edmd. 86
  Edmund 42, 95
Allin, David 111
  Elizabeth 10, 93
  Sarah 87
Allren, Nancey 86
Alred, Louisa E. 92
Alverson, Henson 2
  Jesse 56
  Martha G. 65
  Mary Ann 56
  Nelly 40
  William 1, 103
Ames, John W. 36
Anderson, A. G. 26, 32,
    37, 53, 63, 67, 69,
    82, 96, 105, 113
  Ann 70
  Ann P. 58
  Caty 28
  Edward 37
  Elizabeth 88
  H. G. 49
  James 28
  Jenny 28
  John Q. 32
  L. J. 45, 46
  Mariah 96
  Minerva M. 35
  Patsey 9
  Polly 70, 123
  Q. 27
  Q. T. 20
  Quinton A. 112
  Rachel 56
  Sarah (wid) 74
  Susan B. 97
  William 15, 91, 103
  William A. 2
  William P. 1, 72
  Wm. 14, 34, 44, 53,
    86, 103, 104, 108,
    119
Angles, Sophia 75
Anglin, Caleb 103

Anglin (cont.)
  Cathrine 10
  John 2
  Salley 99
  Wright 2
Annmonett, Rose E. 89
Anthony, Elizabeth 37
  James 94
  Jane 20
  Joseph 36, 56
  Pembrook 80
  V. E. 43
Apple, Mary F. 99
  Mary J. E. 63
  Saml. 13
  Solomon 28, 31, 34,
    72, 74, 75, 103, 118
  William 93
Archdeacon, Alsey 34
Archer, Richard F. 68
Armes, John W. 106
Arnett, Margret 91
  Mary (wid) 51
  Mary A. (Mrs.) 35
  Mary L. 35
  Nancey 84
  Sally 51
Arnold, James 79
  James W. 67, 68, 101
  John 103
  Lydia F. 101
  Mary 109
  Nancey 101
Arrington, Adeline 109
Arven, James 48
Arvin, Patsey 57
Arwin, Richard 3, 62
Ashford, Salley 82
  Willis 114
Ashley, Nancey 76
Askey, William 27
Aslum, Betsey 24
Astin, Margarett 11
Atkins, H. F. 49
  James 9
  Jenny 78
  Mildred 99
  Thomas D. 41
  Thos. B. 104
  Zilly 107
Atkinson, Augustus 99
  Avey 79
  David N. 16, 74
  E. E. 38
  Henry 43
  James H. 30, 99
  Joseph 104
  Lucey Ann 4
  Mary F. 44
  Phebe R. 30
  Polley 109
  Susan W. 32
Atwell, Peggy 104
Austen, Mary 24
Austin, Elizabeth 106

Austin (cont.)
　Fannie 2
　Martha 105
　Mary F. 36
　Ransom B. 91
　Salley 110
　Sarah V. 105
Averett, Betty 113
Ayard, Jacob 11
Badget, Recey H. 46
　Salley 57
　William 49
Badgett, A. Sidney 6
　Drusilla 57
　Elizabeth 111
　Eunes 70
　Henry 53, 95
　Jno. 50
　Jno. D. 58
　Mary M. 63
　Mary W. 36
　Pocahontas A. 58
　William M. 72
　Wm. H. 40
Bagby, A. L. 101, 118
Baggett, Rachel 69
Bagley, Lewis G. 23
Bailey, G. P. 73
　Glasshey 90
　Yancey 65
Baily, Billy 109
Baines, Marth A. 1
Bains, Elizabeth 6
Bairding, Seeley 37
　Selley 37
Balden, Delila 103
Baldin, Mary 56
Baldwin, A. C. 35
　Frances 70, 112
　Henry 29
　Nancey 5
　Salley 29
　Sarah Ann 57
Ball, A. L. 15, 74, 107
　Alfred L. 77
　Cartre 3
　Cary 19
　Daniel 104
　David 124
　Helen M. 77
　Mary M. 63
　Nancy 92
　Polly 19
　Rufus 54
Ballad, Priscilla 93
Ballard, Betsey 67
　Mary 20
　Nancey 87
　Patsey 10
　Silvy 53
Bane, Ann (wid) 52
Banes, Eaton 118
　Fanny 118
Barge, Fanny 79
Barker, Agness R. 119
　Ann Eliza 50
　Burnley 4
　Elizabeth 97
　George 82, 97
　Henrietta 82
　Isaac 17
　Israel 95
　James 62, 87, 108
　Josiah 119
　Louisa 17
　Martha Ann 82
　Mary 10
　Minyard 119

Barker (cont.)
　Sarah J. 20
　Susannah 57
Barnard, Sarah F. 68
　Wm. L. 123
Barnes, Fanie M. 100
　Lydia A. 117
Barnet, Mary 25
Barnett, Ann 101
　Anthony 3
　Elizabeth 76, 91
　Rebecca 24
　Richard 116
　Robert S. 98
　Thomas 3
　Thos. 24, 55
Barnhill, Mary 4
Barnwell, Edward 64
　Eliza 72
　Frances C. 115
　John 94
　Peggy 64
　Robert 3
　Temperance A. 64
　William 3
Barr, William 27
Barrett, Jno. B. 42
　R. G. 12, 26, 37, 38,
　　44, 47, 48, 57, 59,
　　70, 82, 91, 100,
　　102, 120, 123, 124
Barricks, Mary J. 4
Barsdale, Kesiah 27
Bartlett, Ann 110
　Caroline 72
　Elizabeth 46
　Patcey 106
Barton, Ann 96
　Aquila 3
　Chesley L. 4
　Elijah 47
　Elisha 96
　Kezia 3
　Lewis 3, 24
　Margaret E. 34
　Polly 24
　Salley 96
　Simeon C. 15
　Thomas 4
Basdall, David 6
　Frances 6
Basdell, Mary 11
Basdil, Thomas 27
Bass, Alex. 84
　Francis 121
　Henry C. 113
　Mahala 82
　Margaret 81
　Mary Ann 113
　Moses 108
　Robert B. 84
　William 58
Bastin, Ann W. 14
　Hannah 76
　Henry 4
　Margaret 54
　Thomas 14, 47
Baswell, Kindle 98
　Lucinda 80
Bateman, Barsheba 22
　Bird 115
　Bird H. 3, 4, 30, 72
　Martha B. 18
　Mary 55
　Susan 23
　V. W. 66
Batten, Sarah M. 21
Batton, Jane 105

Batton (cont.)
　Mary M. 40
Baugh, Emma 125
　John J. 119
　Louisa F. 16
Bauldin, Catherine 32
Bawldin, Deliah 103
Baxdale, Nancey 103
Baxter, Catherine 11
　Delilah 14
　Frances 85
　John 114
　John (Jr.) 40
　Maryann 103
　Nancy 117
　William 4
Bayes, Betsey 125
　Levina A. 108
　R. J. 66
　Robert J. 80, 108
Baynes, Archable 92
　Eaton 106
　Isabella 25
　Jane 12
　Lorenzo 48, 66, 73,
　　112
　Nancy 7
　Permelia 19
　Perthena 112
　Philip 4
　Phillip 98
　Polly 24
　Sally 12
Bays, Lucy 33
　Mary C. 125
　Nancy 76
Bazwell, Fanny 91
　Mary 64
　Susanah 98
Beadler, Elisabeth 102
Beale, E. W. 20, 38
Beaucey, Charles 31
　Polley 31
Beaver, Ann 37
　Betsey 112
　Cathrine 103
　Dilila 93
　Frances 93
　Jemima 62
　Jesse 37
　John 4
　Joshua 67, 68
　Judith 37
　Mary 94
　William 104
Beavers, J. (Mrs.) 85
　Mildred 100
　Umphrey 85
Beavor, Nancy 68
Belew, Jamima 44
　Mary 122
Bell, Sarah 9
Bennatt, John 124
　Lucy 94
　Nancey 45, 96
　Nancy 124
　Polley 48
　Richard H. L. 76, 98
Bennett, Adeline 14
　Ambrose L. 2, 6, 28
　America 94
　Betsey 13
　Elizabeth 48
　Frances N. 42
　John 5, 61
　Julia 5
　Lafayett 106
　Martha T. 36

Bennett (cont.)
  Mary B. 116
  Milly 114
  Polley 39
  Polly 38
  Richard 102
  Richard H. L. 38, 48
  Ruth 37
  Sarah 17, 125
  Susan 45
  Thomas 24, 25
Bennette, Lafayett 14
Benton, Abram 5
  Cary 97
  Deborah 101
  Epaphroditus 5
  Jemima 46
  Louisa 2
  Lucinda 63
  Mary 26
  Polly 90
  William 20
Bernon, Robt. T. 96
Berrey, Nancy 100
Berry, Elisha 74
  Frances 74
  Hudson 2
  Jane 57
  John 122
  Martha 123
  Mary 82
  Nancey 95
  Polley 74
  Rebecca 2
Bery, Rebecca 122
Bethel, Caroline 120
  Louisa 120
  Louisa M. 100
  Samuel 3, 17, 67
  Samuel W. 79
Bethell, Agness G. 108
  Alfred 96
  Ann 73
  Pinckney C. 102
  Richard 103
  Samuel W. 87
Betts, Eliza 49
  Maria H. 32
  Martha E. 49
Beusey, Charles 5, 118
  Nancey 67
  Severn 57
Beverly, Harry 116
Beviell, Thursey 62
Bevill, Lucy 3
  William E. 87
  Wm. E. 87
Bewsey, Eliza 43
  Severn 5
Bigelow, Geo. 5
  George 104
  Harriet 5
  Mary 109
  Thomas 7, 57, 80
Bingam, Parmela 26
Birch, Delany 79
  Sarah 18
Bird, Caty 9
  Eliza Ann 7
  Elizabeth Ann 32
  Isham 21
  Jehu 8, 67
  Lucinda 7
  Mary 12
  Mary E. 1
  Sarah 105
  Thompson 39
Birk, Archibald 12

Birk (cont.)
  Archibald R. 67, 96
  James 5, 56
  Maddison 6
  Mildred 21
  Tompson 54
  Wiley 67, 68
Birke, Archibald R. 10
  Frances 96
Biswell, Sally 85
Bizwell, Betsey 65
Black, Elizabeth 42
  Robert 90
  Sarah 109
  Thomas 109
Blackard, Jobe 123
  William 6
Blackstock, Lucy S. 64
Blackwel, John 66
Blackwell, Agnes (Mrs.) 6
  Betsy 66
  Carter 66, 87
  Catharine 37
  Chas. 6
  Cindy (Mrs.) 6
  Eliza 121
  Elizabeth 123
  Elizabeth S. 49
  Garland 66, 117
  Huldah B. 37
  James S. 123
  Jane 123
  Jno. 10
  John 6, 54, 72
  John B. 70
  John M. 124
  John S. 70
  Joseph S. 10
  Julia A. 124
  Kiturah 117
  Martha 35, 70, 90
  Martha A. 55
  Mary B. 78
  Matilda 54
  Minerva (Mrs.) 123
  Moses 123
  N. L. 14
  Nancy 33, 66
  Nickolas 6
  Polley 117
  R. T. 61
  Robert 44, 114, 116
  Saml. 57
  Saml. B. 119
  Susanna 117
  Thomas J. 8
  Zilla 79
Blair, James N. 65
  Polly 92
  Sallie 33
  William J. 123
Blalack, Millintun 76
Blalock, Millinton 15
Blartlett, Caroline 72
Bledsoe, R. H. 61
Bocock, Nancy 61
Boggass, Richard 69
Bohan, Ambrose 55
  Katey 55
Bohannan, Dolly 118
  Mainyard 6
  Margit 113
  Nancy 113
  Philis (Mrs.) 53
  Rutha 53
  Wm. 53
Bohannon, Ambrose 34

Bohannon (cont.)
  Bosten 92
  Joseph 75
  Nancy 24
  Nancy (Mrs.) 92
  Rebecca 92
Boldin, Elizabeth 5
Boley, A. M. F. P. 97
  Elvira B. 28
  Parham A. 28, 52
Bolling, James 89
Bolton, Amanda 22
  Candis 103
  Chas. 107
  Joel 5
  John 77
  Leony 98
  Lydia 85
  Mary W. 123
  Susan 43
  Thomas 53, 70, 85
  Waller 25
Boman, Betsey 88
  Josiah 41
  Nancey 75
  Parthenia 16
  Robert 7
  Samuel 7
Bomar, Ann W. 19
  Booker 19
Boran, Isaac 13, 63
  Isac 21
  Phebe 63
Boswell, Antichus 34
  Caroline 26
  Craven 7
  Eliza 20, 32
  Elizabeth 13, 15, 67, 81
  Ella 10
  Eunice 51
  Francis 9
  H. 90
  H. J. 8
  Howell 18, 46, 67, 80, 97
  James 25, 67
  James M. 13, 15
  James P. 13, 78, 109
  John 7
  John R. 7
  Judy 15
  Margaret 36
  Margarett 78
  Martha 46
  Martha C. 107
  Mary 17, 45
  Maryann 8
  Nancey 12
  Nancy 7
  Phebe 113
  R. Saunders 55
  Rebecca 107
  Sarah 67
  Sarah A. 34
  Sinthy 9
  Susan 55
  T. H. 55
  Thomas 32
  Thompson H. 7, 122
Bouland, Elizabeth 93
Boulden, Jane 97
Bouldin, Catharine 123
  Geo. T. 7
  George 65
  George C. 63
  Joseph 6
  Julia 6

129

Bouldin (cont.)
　Martin 68
　Mary 13
　Mary Jane 68
　Sarah S. 32
　Stith 120
　Susan 65, 68
　Tho. 94, 120
　Thomas 42, 91, 106, 124
　Thos. 6
Boulding, George 32
　Rebecca 121
Boulton, Charles 48
　Emily F. 63
　Judith 107
　Lucy 60
　Nancy 25
　Oney 122
　Sarah W. 25
Bours, Joseph 17
Bowden, Benjamin 26
　John A. 85
Bowe, Cely 7
　Cilla 62
　Elizabeth J. 31
　Harriet A. 30
　Lily 78
　Saml. 7
　Sarah V. 43
　Susan 55
　Thomas C. 62
　W. B. 38, 122
　William B. 24, 39
　Wm. B. 21, 30, 44, 49, 50, 52, 65, 81, 83, 86, 89, 92, 98, 105
　Wm. J. 115
Bowers, Henrietta 48
　William 34
Bowes, Frances 10
　John 60
Bowles, Nancey 72
Bowls, Sarah 104
　Selia 45
Bowman, Geo. R. 119
Bows, Lucy 121
Boyd, Archibald H. 62
　David 81
　Joshua 88
Boyles, Mahala Ann 90
　Robert D. 119
　Susan 114
Bozwell, Frances 5
　James P. 37
　Jenney 37
　Kitty F. 91
　Richard 8
　Salley 16
　Thomas 37
Brabdon, H. F. 21
Bracher, Nama 75
Brackin, Agripina 34
　Arkey 71
　Dorothy B. 116
　Elizabeth 50
　Isabella 6
　Jane 17
　John O. 17
　Joseph 57
　Patcey 43
　S. E. 56, 124
　Samuel 8
　Sarah H. 70
　Sina 20
　Sinah 25
Brackwell, Jane P. 116
Bradford, Thomas 87

Bradley, Betsey 59
　Elizabeth 59
　James 59, 96
　Mary 63
　Susannah 96
　Thomas 8
Bradshaw, Mary F. 118
Bradshear, Mattie E. 8
Bradsher, Frances 75
　Frances C. 101
　Jinny 8
　Martha A. 89
　Martha B. 36
　Moses 113
　Nancey 45
　Nancy E. 13
　Richard H. 89
　Sally B. 106
　Vincent 8, 36, 59, 75
Brady, Eliza 38
Brag, Manerva 42
Brandon, Amanda 17
　Benja. 8
　Cathern A. 11
　D. G. 25
　David 7
　Edward 17
　Elisabeth 106
　Eliza H. 40
　Elizabeth 33
　Frances 71
　Francis 106
　Francis (Jr.) 9
　H. F. 1, 2, 3, 5, 6, 7, 8, 11, 12, 14, 15, 17, 18, 20, 22, 23, 25, 26, 28, 29, 30, 31, 32, 33, 34, 35, 36, 38, 39, 40, 41, 42, 43, 44, 46, 47, 49, 50, 54, 55, 57, 58, 59, 60, 62, 65, 66, 72, 75, 76, 77, 78, 82, 83, 84, 85, 102, 107, 110, 112, 116, 118, 120, 123
　Isabella 23
　Jefferson 8
　Jenney 13
　John 9, 50, 68, 100
　Judith 100
　Margret 49
　Martha (Mrs.) 17
　Mary 50, 102
　Mary E. 19
　Peter 8
　Rebecah 84
　Samuel 93
　Smith 24
　Stephen 71
　Thomas 106
　Thomas (Sr.) 9
　William 49
　William L. 9
Brann, Peter D. 9
　Thomas 9
Brannock, Julia 7
Brannum, Emily 82
Bratcher, Dicey 54
Braughton, Jeremiah 13
　Missouri S. 19
Brechen, William 9
Breeze, Jane 3
Brewer, Hardy 9
Bricefield, Isabella 58
Briggs, J. 81
　Minerva 112

Brightwell, Martha S. 53
Brincefield, Anderson 9
　B. Y. 106
　Colman 49
　Letetie 106
　Nancy 110
Brinckle, Nancey 3
Brinsfield, Betsy 20
　C. 121
　Dennard 99
　Patsey 41
　Sarah 99
　Thomas 62
Brintle, Amy 78
　Betsy 13
　Jesse 9, 25
　Nancey 3
　Nancy 25
　Partheny 10
　Polly 90
　Rainey 52
　William 31
Broach, Jenny 9
　Nathaniel 34
　Thomas B. 100
Broache, James 9
Brockman, (?) (Maj.) (Jr.) 76
　John 36
Brodnax, Chainy 51
　Marthy 51
Broocks, William M. 51
Brookes, Christopher 37, 88
　Christopher W. 20, 82
　Hames M. 32
　James M. 7, 82, 113
　Jas. M. 112
　Jno. R. 106
　John K. 63
　Mary 13
　Mary G. 7
　Polly 1
　Thomas 116
　Thomas (Jr.) 84
　W. L. 9
Brooks, Barbara 60
　Dorothy 104
　Elizabeth 48
　Frances 49, 95
　Henritta 11
　Henry W. 104
　James M. 9, 92
　Jane 116
　Jenney 25
　Jno. K. 79
　John K. 43, 124
　John R. 88
　Logan 6
　Mary 115, 116
　Mary A. 74
　Patsey 13
　Polley 87
　Samuel 31
　Sarah 6
　Susanah 88
　Susannah W. 70
　Thomas 9
　Ursley 87
Broughton, Luzella M. 41
　Mobsey A. 45
　Parthenia 76
Brown, A. B. 108
　Albert 5
　Anderson 10, 104
　Anne 81
　Bond V. 101
　China 2

Brown (cont.)
Constant 99
Edey H. 87
Elioner 37
Elisabeth 104
Elizabeth 2
Elizabeth A. 5
Emily 104
Frances 48
George 107
Gerly G. 31
Green L. 97
Hudson 48
Isham 45
Jacob 67
John H. 43
John M. 12
John T. 86
Leonard 44
Margaret 5
Martha 33, 87
Mary 10, 19, 56, 67, 84
Matilda 39
Michael 70
Nancey 54, 59
Nancy 29
Nathan 51
Polly 11
Rebeccah 105
Robert 54
Salley 9, 44
Sally 14
Sarah 67
Sarah C. 106
Sarah F. 112
Sophia 120
Susanna 10
Tabitha J. 102
Tarlton W. 86
Thomas J. 15, 16, 40, 54, 78, 96
Thos. J. 17, 26, 40, 59, 121
Usley 108
Walter 110
William 12
William C. 35
William F. 31
Browning, Ann 90
Ann Eliza 115
Anne 13
Annise 92
Ava P. 99
Clary 21
Delila 58
Edmd. 99
Edmond 10, 105
Elijah G. 57, 98
Elizabeth 90
Fanny 88
Frances 62
Francis 99
Hannah 10
Humphrey 93
John 90
John B. 69
Manerva E. 13
Martin 20, 37, 50, 113
Mary 21
Maryan 22
Nancey 4, 67
Nancey M. 101
Nathan 4
Nathaniel 88
Nelly 11
Samuel R. 108
Sarah F. 23

Browning (cont.)
Solomon 10, 64, 67
Tabbitha 74
Thomas 100
William 16, 99
William P. 5, 98
Young 99
Bruce, Betsey 108
David 125
Elizabeth 45
James 11
John 44, 108
Levi L. 69
Martha 55
Mary 41
Nancey 87
Nancy 44
Polly 125
Robert 18, 45
Sarah 14
Thomas 81
William 33, 76, 80
Bruer, Nancy 56
Brumet, Thomas 54
Bryan, Elisabeth M. 121
Bryant, Elionar 74
Eliza Ann 49
James 11, 16
Mary 16
Sarah 14
Wm. 69
Bucey, John 33
Martha F. 117
Sarrah 124
Buchanan, John 10
Keziah 87
Buchannan, Lodwell 113
Buchanon, Andrew 41
Buckingham, Byrd 105
Byrd W. 29
Elizabeth 5
Martha 105
Buckley, Randolph 93
Buckner, Elizabeth 56
Frances 79
Judith 79
Bull, Fanny 57
Bullard, Darkus 55
Bullock, Jim 56
Nancy (Mrs.) 56
Bumpass, Lucy 18
Burch, Amey 87
Coleman 41
D. 22, 81, 83
David 22, 60, 74, 80, 82, 83, 85, 92, 111, 118, 123
Elizabeth 4, 16
Ephraim 108, 115, 117
Frances 4, 21
George 11, 13, 21, 122
Henry 9, 71
Jacob 96
James 66
Jane 8
Janney 21
Jenny 9
Laney 12
Lucinda 41, 106
Lucretia 22
Mary 4, 11, 52, 121
Nancy (wid) 60
Parthenia 98
Philip 66
Phillip 11
Polley 15
Richard 8
Richd. 14

Burch (cont.)
Sarah 75, 96
Thomas 5, 98, 113
William 29, 109
Wm. 111
Writta 89
Burford, Judith 104
Burges, Elizabeth A. 93
Burgess, Ellenor 90
Mildred 121
Burk, Milley 87
Nancey 90
Polly 28
Burke, Elizabeth 67
Fanny G. 89
James A. 20
Burks, Benjamin H. 12
Burn, Wm. H. 103
Burnes, James A. D. 103
Burnett, Ann 94
Elizabeth 114
Polly 25
Burnette, Martha J. 99
Burns, Eveline 103
Francis M. 113
J. F. 43
Julia F. 106
Lenora E. 103
Louisa G. 106
Martha A. 70
Mary 73
Sarah A. 103
Thomas 2
William 76, 101, 124
William H. 106
Burrings, F. H. 32
Burroughs, Salley 57
Burt, Nancey 19
Rebecka 19
Burton, Abner 91
Aderlaid V. 45
Allen 30
Allin 17
Ann 5
Benjamin G. 34
Betsey 33, 73
D. R. 38
Daniel 12
David 87
Dianah 57
Diannah 110
Dorrithy 8
Drury 12, 13, 67, 110, 113
Elizabeth 58
Elizabeth C. 18
Fanny 114
Francis A. 13
Francis H. 68
Franklin 48
Harriet H. (wid) 80
Henry 30, 123
Henry A. 4
Henry N. 114
Hutchens 70
Hutchins 13
Isaac 12
James 1, 5, 40, 53, 80, 101
James M. 44
Jane 5
Jas. 2
Jennie Hennie 40
Jenny 44
Jno. 118
John 12, 27, 60, 61
John H. 82
Judith 80

Burton (cont.)
  Louisa 12
  Lucy 67, 68
  Lucy A. 48
  Martha 30
  Martha W. 54
  Mary 2, 23, 106
  Mary (Mrs.) 2
  Mary A. 108
  Mary E. 34
  Mary J. 68
  Nancey 13
  Nancy 40
  Nancy J. 12
  Noel 9, 60, 63
  Noel (Jr.) 58, 59
  Polly 88
  Priscilla 62, 80
  Robert 43
  Sally 57
  Sarah 57
  Sarah J. 37
  Sarah Jane 72
  Susan 53, 89
  Susannah 113
  Thomas 12, 52, 88, 95
  Thomas W. 12
  Tillman 83
  Virginia 70
  Westley 49
Busey, Eliza 27
  John 108
  Salley 108
  William 13, 27, 64
Bush, Anne 42
  Avicey 96
  Bennet 16, 96
  Betsey 32
  Dilley 3
  France 43
  Lois 45
  Mary 56
  Mira 52
  Rhody 96
  Susannah 16
  Zenas 96
  Zibba 87
  Zns. 45
Bushnell, James M. 80, 120
  Margaret 80
  Mary 120
  Sabry 122
  Sarah Jane 80
Butler, Eliza 10
  Emeline D. 74
  Frances 100
  J. H. 79
  Malvina F. 17
  Margaret E. 120
  Polley 40
  Susanah 88
Buttery, Elizabeth 9
  Salley 11
Byrd, Baylor 9
  James 42
  Mary 63
Bysor, Peter 13
Cabell, A. S. 13
Cadal, Margret 2
Caddel, Andrew 2, 39
  Phebe 39
Caddell, Elizabeth 39
Cahal, Barney 75, 76
  George C. 75, 76
  Louisa S. 75
  Martha E. 76
Cahall, John 31, 54, 76

Caldnond, Susan A. 101
Caldwell, Appy 36
  Cathrine 125
  Isaac 51
  W. M. 36
Calloway, Belvederrie F. 100
  James F. 107
Callum, James R. 108
  Jas. R. 9
  Mary Ann 108
Cambell, Thomas 10
Cameron, Duncan 55
  John 14
  Patsey 42
Cammical, Mary 52
Camp, John 77
Campbell, Ann 64
  Archibald 73
  Delilah 57
  Elizabeth 106
  Emilea A. 81
  Evelena 81
  Evelina B. 25, 56
  Hugh 7, 107, 117
  J. 63, 80
  John 26, 67
  John G. 1
  Letecia 20
  Lucinda 121
  Lucitta Ann 63
  Margaret 15
  Meranda 34
  Naomi 115
  Rusalinda 63
  T. S. 43
  Thomas 12
  Thomas S. 80
  Thos S. 75, 76
  W. 125
  William 9, 12
  Wm. 36, 52, 69, 80, 83, 87
Camron, Martha A. 22
Canaday, Absalom 19, 100
  Eliza A. 79
  Nathan 93
Cannaday, James W. 7
  John 104
  Joseph H. 17
Cannady, Rebecca F. 17
Cannon, Darcass 94
  Jackson 56
  Jemima 97
  Joel 83
  John 13
  Joseph 83
  Sarah 114
  Susanah 78
  William 15, 38, 56, 58, 65, 78, 104, 118
Canon, William 3
Canor, Sarah 121
Cantrel, Catherine 36
  Hannah 2
  Polley 56
  Rachel 67
  Sophia 90
  Sophiah 10
Cantrell, Elizabeth 9
  Sarah 67
  William 24
Cantril, Henrietta 73
Cantrill, Benjamin 10
  Jemima 67
  Nancey 67
Cantrille, Salley 67
Carden, Leroy 20

Cardwell, Nancy 14
Carlen, Sarah 2
Carloss, Betsey 7
  Dolly G. 87
  Nancy 3
Carlton, Thomas N. 75
Carman, Calab 102
  Caleb 83
  Calib 124
  Elijah 42, 87, 101, 118
  John 83
  Mary 101
Carmical, Elizabeth C. 61
Carmichael, William 60
Carmikel, William 98
Carmon, Abagail 20
  Hannah 54
Carnal, Flemman 6
Carnall, Archd. 57
Carnell, Partrick 101
Carney, Joseph 30
  Joshua 46, 47
  Rachil 52
Carny, Delphy 93
  Joseph 93
Carr, James T. 95
  John 112
Carraway, P. J. 16, 44, 47, 119, 123
Carrel, Edward 28
  James 11
  Tabitha T. 92
Carrell, George 90
  Nancy 90
  Sally 11
Carrol, Betsey 106
  Betsy 28
  Hannah 56
  Patcey 84
  Rebeccah 42
  Starling 11
Carroll, Lemuel H. 90
  Polly 4
  Sterling 4
Carter, Agness 14
  B. H. 14
  Bettie 65
  Carnelia A. 23
  Elias B. 84
  Elizabeth 97
  Elizabeth B. 10
  Elizabeth E. 111
  Elizabeth J. 110
  Eureka 107
  George 9
  Greensby 55
  Isabella 109
  Isabella P. 74
  James W. 32
  Jesse 68
  John 23, 60
  John B. 21
  Joseph 66
  Joseph G. 54
  Martha 98
  Martha B. 60
  Martha M. 101
  Mary 42
  Mary (wid) 100
  Mary A. C. 10
  Mary J. 86
  Mary Purry 94
  Mary W. 84
  Missouri A. 94
  Pleasant 70
  Presley 60

Carter (cont.)
  R. T. 111
  Rebeccah 93
  Robert 42
  Sally 123
  Sarah Frances 20
  Sinai 14
  Susan 84
  Theoderick 94
  Thomas 72
  Thornton 108
  Turner 63
  William 14, 42
  William G. 84
  Wm. 72
Carver, Minerva J. 39
  Nancy 62
  Suffy 112
  Thomas 75
  William 14, 100
Case, John J. 75
Casort, John H. 15
Cate, Elizabeth 18
  John 24
  Margery 24
  Nancey 5
Cates, Caroline 60
  D. S. 23
  Martha E. 16
  Mary 5
  Nancy 97
  Rebeca 59
  Richard 15, 33
Cavanis, Nancey 91
Cearney, Agness 60
Chamberlain, Jemima 118
  John 87
Chamberlin, Catharine 54
  Jane 4
Chambers, Ann 102
  Arabella C. 92
  Elizabeth 80
  Harriet A. 79
  James 11
  Jane N. 64
  Jno. 15
  John 11, 15, 80, 91
  Josias 102
  Judith 11
  Mary Ann 84
  Nancey 15
  Permintia 49
  Sally 80
  Sina 16
  William 11
  Wm. F. 4
Chance, Yancey 1
Chancy, Rebecca 28
Chandler, Adaline W. 124
  Betsey 80
  Elizabeth 55
  Frances G. 40
  Francis E. 118
  Francis G. 46
  James D. 1, 15, 98
  Jno. 89, 98
  John 13, 83, 104
  John J. 118
  Judith 22, 65
  Lucey 82
  Margarett 22
  Maria 55
  Mary 1
  Mary F. 75
  Mary J. 93
  Nancey 66
  Nanny J. 22
  Pleasant 87

Chandler (cont.)
  Polly C. 98
  Rebecca 113
  Salley 71
  Sally 107
  Stephen J. 49, 65
  Susan T. 114
  Susannah 121
  Thomas W. 72, 118
  Wilkins 15
  William 89
  William G. 29
  William J. 27
  Wm. 119
Chaney, Eliza E. 72
  Lydia 121
Chaplin, C. C. 95
Chapman, Ann 103
  Elizabeth 19
  Nancey 104
  Nelson 19, 74, 100, 103
  William 16, 100, 104
Chappel, Elisabeth 116
Charlton, John F. 124
Chatham, Cloey 114
  Isaac 16
  Jno. 9
  John C. 9
Chattin, Elizabeth 47
Chavos, Charlotte 70
Cheatham, Thomas 9
  Thos. 13
Cheatwood, Betsey 106
Cheek, Cornelia A. 92
  Mary 60
  Robert H. 94, 99, 106
Cheles, Nancy C. 86
Childers, Jeremiah 117
  Nancy 85
Childes, Mary M. 44
Childirs, Isabella H. 60
Childres, Jane 26
Childress, Annis 120
  Guilford 105
  James A. 11
  Louiser 117
  Martha 61
  Nancey 105
  Nancy 9
  Pleasant 3
  Sarah 56
  Susan J. 79
Childs, Betsey 68
  Salley 5
  Thomas 5
Chiles, William H. 49, 109
Chilton, John 95
  Mary A. 23
  Rachel 108
Chittelton, Agnes 21
Chittington, Nancy 26
Chounan, Esther 88
Christenberry, Polly 83
Christenbury, Elizabeth 31
  Nancy 8
Christopher, Thomas 16
Claiborne, Lucy 52
  Sarah Ann 25
  William C. 65
Clark, Amy 17
  Elizabeth 74
  Frances L. 3
  James 49
  Martha M. 6
  Martin 91

Clark (cont.)
  Minerva 35, 43
  Peter F. 72
  Richard 105
  Sarah 72
Clarke, A. H. 19
Claughton, George 87
Clay, America F. 34
  Anna 35
  Edward 91
  Elizabeth 98
  Henry M. 102
  Sarah 91
Clayton, Rebeccah 17
  Susannah 34
Clempson, Magara 58
  Rachael 15
Clemson, William 87
Clendenin, Jas. J. 29, 43, 44, 50, 67, 88, 97, 106, 120
  Wm. G. 109
Clendening, Jasn. J. 38
  Mary 32
Clendennin, John 7
Clendinin, Jas. J. 97
Cleton, Nancey 12
Clibourn, George W. 88
Clift, Lettie 69
  William 69
Climer, Thomas 14
Climpson, Nancey 35
Clindinan, John 83
Coats, Merit 42
  Sally 5
Cobb, (?) (Mrs.) 43
  Almedia A. 14
  Amsey 67
  Ann E. 6
  Archey 25
  Bartlett Y. 18
  Bell 43, 55
  Candice 120
  Celia 51
  Deborah 38
  Ebenezar 17
  Elizabeth 17, 54, 56
  Emeline 97
  Fanny 55
  Frances 36
  H. W. 119
  Henrietta 66
  Henry 17, 28, 76, 117
  Henry W. 97
  Hugh E. 17, 87, 88
  James 17
  James E. 94
  Jamima 106
  Jane 49
  Jemima 15
  Jennett 55
  Jesse E. 18, 21, 22
  Jessey E. 18
  Joah (Sr.) 112
  John 66, 73
  John (Jr.) 17, 25
  John D. 67
  John W. 57
  Joseph K. 18
  Levi 18
  Louisa M. 123
  M. H. 93
  Major 43
  Malina S. 66
  Malinda G. 50
  Maria (Mrs.) 76
  Mariah L. 40
  Martha 65, 78

Cobb (cont.)
 Martha A. 18
 Martha H. 35
 Mary 28, 88
 Mastin H. 98
 Mericus 76
 Milger 79
 Nancey 78
 Noah 103
 Peggy 11
 Rebecca 21
 Rhoda (Mrs.) 79
 Saml. M. 66
 Samuel 87
 Samuel B. 35, 37, 47
 Samuel C. 82
 Samuel M. 18, 112
 Sarah 98
 Syntha 94
 William 17, 18, 46
 William M. 17
Cobbs, John Wilson 18
 Rhoda 58
Cochran, Judith 47
 Polley 4
 Reuben 4, 6, 11
 Sarah 3
 Tabitha 11
 William 3, 52
 William 6. 122
 Wm. G. 59
Cock, Addeline 77
 Fanney 69
 Garland 18
 Patsy 2
Coe, Fanny 59
Coil, Jane 118
Coile, Sarah 77
 William 118
Cole, B. L. 18
 Frances 20
 J. 116
 Josiah 67, 78, 99
 Leaner 28
 Mary Whitworth 99
 Sarah F. 99
 Wm. D. 18
Coleman, Elizabeth 38
 Elizabeth B. 108
 Henry E. 15
 James 32
 James M. 34
 Jno. 70
 John 18
 Joseph 84
 Joshua 78
 Judith 50
 Minerva 34
 Noel 122
 Patsey 122
 Polley 70
 Rosy 61
 Sarah E. 86
 Spillby 104
 William 1
Colemon, Nancey 11
Coleston, Anne 21
 Lattis 27
 Margaret 99
Colley, Elizabeth H. 51
 Sally 26
Collie, Carter 53
Collier, James 18, 87
 Rebecca 73
Collilns, Allen T. 35
Collins, Elixena 63
 Euphrasia 43
 Frances 88

Collins (cont.)
 Jno. 103
 Jones W. 2
 Martha 43
 Mary 46
 Syrena 7
Collir, Judith 67
Colly, Mary F. 36
Colman, Carthrin 71
Colmon, Suckey 93
Combs, James 13
 Mary 42
Comer, Amy 65
 Elizabeth 62
 Elizabeth W. 38
 Fanny 89
 Jennett 102
 John 22
 Nancy 88
 Nathaniel 25
 Peggy 110
 Thomas 19, 25, 89
Compton, Aquilla 19
 Elizabeth 6, 91
 Hosea 54
 J. L. 114
 J. S. 20
 Margarett 45
 Sieria G. 19, 46
 Thomas 46, 49
Conally, Sally 7
 Sarah L. 28
 Susan 23
 Thomas D. 63
Conaly, George 47
Conklin, Jas. L. 118
Conley, Rebecca 8
Connally, Anna 89
 Caroline 13
 Charles 19
 Elizabeth 22
 Emily 19
 Frances 7
 George 35
 George A. 19, 22, 67
 George F. 3
 George Franklin 123
 George Oldham 99
 John S. 19
 Kitty 71
 Mary A. 9
 Priscilla H. 99
 Solomon 98
 Spencer 9
 Tho. D. 119
 Thomas 8
 Thomas D. 26, 32, 43,
  54, 56, 60, 61, 70,
  89, 108, 122, 123
 Thomas P. 60
 William J. 11, 98
Connelly, Angelico 35
Connolly, Margaret A. 55
Conoley, George 19
Conway, Emeline 71
 Mary 71
Cook, Betsey 11
 E. D. 100
 E. S. 16
 Elizabeth 25, 27
 Elizabeth L. 95
 Isaac 42
 Jarratt W. 58
 Margret 115
 Martha 100
 Owen 26
 Patsy 2
 Philip 27

Cook (cont.)
 Priscilla 76
 Prisciller 7
 Sarah 82
 Unity 111
 Westly R. 125
 William 19, 76, 111
Cooper, Allin 11, 115
 B. 22, 23, 55, 60, 61,
  71, 89, 90, 94, 98,
  109
 Eliza 76
 Fannie 20
 James 4
 John 11, 97
 Lavinia 19
 Lillie J. 38
 Mary F. 112
 Nancey 34
 Richard 48
 Salenia 19
 Salley 7
 Susan J. 76
 Warren 115
 William 73, 115
Coram, Clorey 52
 Esther 85
 Jane 86
 William 52, 85
Corbet, Elizabeth 115
 Pleasant 109
 Solomon 20, 35
Corbett, Arch. 40
 B. 20
 Birrel 96
 Henry 7
 Lewis 2, 5
 Mary F. 105
 Nancey 41
 S. P. 30
 Solomon 20, 42, 45,
  69, 83, 97, 115
Corbin, Catherine C. 6
 Sallie A. 61
 William 118
Corbit, Elizabeth A. 19
 William 68
Corbitt, Emily T. 41
Corder, Elizabeth 2
 Fanney 95
 Hannah 79
 James 29
 Polly 73
 Winneyford 46
Corn, Martha 48
Cornwell, Joseph F. 10,
  20, 29, 35, 121
 Silas C. 5
Corum, William 38, 54
Cotton, Henry 5, 15
Cousins, Alexander 44
 Lewis 28
 Robert 118
 Susan 30
 Tazwell 47
 Willie 55
Coventon, Betsey 37
Coverington, Mary T. 77
Covington, Frances 100
 James 31
 John 13
 John E. 2
 Mary E. 83
 Robin 20, 77
 Tho. 26, 72, 122
 Thomas 16, 19, 45, 92,
  98, 100, 108
 Thos. 12, 27, 98, 109,

Covington (cont.)
  115
  Virginia 16
Cox, Agness 94
  Ann 24
  Anne 42
  Elizabeth 114, 124
  Frances 17
  Gabriel 14, 114, 124
  Hugh 53
  Jane 114
  Lucinda 104
  Lucy 21
  Malinda 14
  Martha 7
  Mary 68
  Mary (Mrs.) 7
  Philip 7, 95
  Phillip (Jr.) 21
  Polly 12
  Sally 12, 96
  Sarah 20, 44
  Sookey 95
  Susan 54
  Tameran 75
  Willson 20
Coyle, Enoch 18
Coyles, Enoch 77
Craft, M. V. 92
Crafton, Welthy 40
Craghead, W. G. 58
Crane, Nancy T. 18
Crawford, Bettie A. 41
  Caroline 21
  Joseph 68
  Mahael S. 44
Crawley, Barthus J. 33
  Elizabeth 39
  John J. 35, 94
Cray, Ann 114
Crenshaw, John 24
  Salley 24
Crews, Martha 33
  Mary Ann 53
  Obadiah 53
Crider, Jacob 54
  Judith 75
  Mary 59
Crisp, Betsy 11
  Clabourn 66
  Claybourn 99
  Eliza 117
  Elizabeth 106
  John 11
  John (Jr.) 11
  Lucy 11
  Margaret 122
  Maryan 11
  Richd. 34
Critington, George 25
Crittenton, George 25
  Lucy (Mrs.) 25
  Nancey 25
Crook, Richd. 81
Cross, Rutha 112
Crosset, James 78
Crossett, Jane 78
  Margaret 66
Crossix, Elizabeth 76
Crowder, Ferinand 70
  Lovely 117
  Mary A. 117
  Robert A. 99
  Salley 14
  Samuel D. 82
Cruise, Elizabeth 98
  Obadiah 33
  Sarah 103

Crump, Mary J. 38
Crumpton), (?) 47
Crumpton, Mary F. 66
  Rachel 48
Crutcher, G. T. 41
Crutchfield, Minerva 120
  Nannie L. 79
  Stapleton 21
Culberson, Edney 85
  Hiram 23, 84
  James 111
  Libbie 79
  Mary 84
  Sarah 98
  Susannah 92
  Tabbitha 92
  William 10
Culbertson, Rachael 115
Cullins, Thos. J. 106
Cumbo, Sarah 68
Cuningham, Harriett 8
  Nancy 93
  Sarah 22
Cunnaway, Allen J. 79
Cunningham, Betsey Anne 68
  Pattie 22
  William 93
  Wm. 68
Curl, John T. 13, 53
Curles, Sophia 13
Curls, Betsy 111
  Sally 86
  Sarah A. 56
Currie, Archibald 31
  Betsey (Mrs.) 22
  Bettie R. 48
  Catharine 22
  Catherine 112
  Cornelia D. 8
  Elizabeth 88
  Eugenia F. 106
  Frances 22
  Frances G. 30
  George 112
  Hugh 64
  Isaac R. 22, 123
  James 7, 49, 86, 106, 122
  John 22, 65
  John (Jr.) 21
  Joseph 88
  Margaret 65
  Martha 85, 112
  Mary 85, 88, 111, 122
  Mary Ann 79
  Matilda (Mrs.) 118
  Mitchell 115
  Nepthalin 22
  Partheane 112
  Polly 62
  Sally L. 118
  Sam. 85
  Saml. 83
  Sarah 59
  Shelby 22
  Thomas J. 39
  Thomas W. 66
  William 3, 48, 115
Curris, N. N. (Jr.) 28
Curtis, Elizabeth 56
  Henry 48
Dabbs, Ann Elizabeth 80
  William J. 45
Dabney, Martha A. 60
Dallas, W. T. 96
Dalton, Annie 3
  Patience 34

Damaron, Batt 66
Dameron, Alexander M. 68
  Alexander W. 23
  Azariah 20
  Benjamin 78
  Cathrine 23
  Christopher (Jr.) 64
  E. H. 1
  Elizabeth 53, 66, 71
  Frances 12
  Frances H. 32
  George B. 23, 58
  Geroge 23
  James C. 46, 89, 123
  James H. 55
  John 22
  John W. 3, 89
  Joseph 23, 29, 67
  Judith 58
  Judith M. 88
  Martha 12, 115
  Martha A. 94
  Martha P. 22
  Mary 37, 88, 100
  Mildred 110
  Nancy 47, 99
  Patience 52
  Patsey 64
  Phoebe 123
  Phoebe W. 29
  Polley 52
  S. W. 10
  Salinda 23
  Sally 68
  Samuel 22, 46, 53, 73
  Sarah 25
  Sarah F. 82
  Susan 45
  Susan (wid) 38
  William A. 39
  William J. 108
  Williamson 23
  Yancy 46
  Zachariah E. 22
Daniel, Carthrin 69
  Elizabeth F. 21
  Fleming 23
  James 113
  Jno. 48, 68, 94, 98, 100, 114, 118
  John 51
  Martha 99
  Martin 23
  William H. 29
  William J. 26
Darby, Ann 65
  Daniel 4, 110
  Elizabeth 104
  George 23, 91
  James 4, 65
  John 23
  Margret 91
Darcy, Nehemah 69
Darnald, Will 25
Darnell, William 13
Davey, Elisabeth 36
Davidson, Richard O. 23
Davis, Abigal 122
  Anna 95
  Anna (Mrs.) 21
  Ashley 48
  Barbarah E. 82
  Basel 24
  Betsey 72
  Caroline 25
  Cathrine 30
  David 71
  Elizabeth 99

Davis (cont.)
    Elizabeth W. 107
    Elvira P. 113
    Emaline 58
    Emily 21
    Enoch G. 54
    Fanny (Mrs.) 25
    Frances 109
    James 21
    James K. 89
    Jane 36
    John 12
    Letitia 18
    Lucinda 16, 57
    Lucy 71
    Martha A. 16
    Martha J. 68
    Martha P. 112
    Mary 60
    Mary (wid) 106
    Mary A. 89
    Mary Ann 70
    Mary F. 71
    Rebecca B. 90
    Sally E. 92
    Saml. 122
    Samuel 15
    Sarah 41
    Susannah 79, 101
    Thomas 1, 16, 84
    Thomas N. 13
    Thos. W. 93
    William 24
    Wm. F. 97
Davison, David 57
    Edward 64
Dawson, Henrietta 50
    Jane 58
    Mileah 76
    Wm. H. 50
Day, Archabel 29
    Martha 23
    Mary 55
    Mary A. 16
    Philip 24, 101
    Thomas 16
    William 61
Dean, Susannah 85
    Virginia C. 38
Deane, Mary 98
Debo, Frederic 91
Deboe, Lucy 13
Debow, Sol 20
    Sol. 27, 28, 51, 83, 93, 125
    Solo. 37
Debrower, Elizabeth 114
Deens, Mary Ann 19
Delaney, Catherine 67
Delauney, Wm. 40
Delgs, Polley 17
Delone, Frances 6
Denevant, Virginia 27
Denney, Azariah 24
    Lewis 4
    Rebecca 21
    William 21
Dennis, F. J. 79
    Jenny 4
Denny, America 1
    Azariah 17
    Maj. 121
    Nancy 17
Depriest, Horatio 81
Deshago, Geo. F. 39
Deshazo, Clem 14
Deshong, Geo. F. 110
Dewees, Elisha 24

Dice, Martha Ann 55
Dick, Martha W. 39
Dicken, Emily 27
Dickens, Albert 27
Dickenson, John 120
Dickerson, Nathaniel 25
Dickey, Elizabeth 106
    Leannah 64
    Nancey 8
Dickie, William 8
Dickins, Eaton P. 25
    Elisabeth 6
    Israel 27, 125
    Jesse 6
    Polly 25
    Rebecah 13
    Rebeccah 25
    William 118
Dicks, Martha 62
Dickson, Charlotte 99
    Robert 53
    S. 75
    Thos. 36
Dill, Archy 3
    Hannah 103
    James 17, 25
    Jane 18
    Joanna 26
    John H. 112
    Joseph 112
    Mary Ann 112
    Maryann 42
    Rebekah 106
    Stephen 82
Dillard, Joseph F. 99
    Martha 16
    Mary A. 72
    Minerva 65
Dilworth, George 9
Dishong, Lewis W. 83
Dishough, Louis W. 101
Dismuke, James 16
Dismukes, Richard 91, 111
    William 25, 55
Dix, Elizabeth 62
    Humphrey 24
    James 19, 65
    John 41
    John P. 25
    Lucinda 25
    Lucy 41
    Mariah (Mrs.) 41
    Polly 93
    Wm. 59
Dixon, Elisabeth 14
    Elizabeth 7, 119
    Harrison 111
    Jenny 8
    Jeremiah 8
    Mack 74
    Martha 54
    Nannie 111
    Polly 7, 13
    Robert 116, 124
    Susannah 119
    William 25
    Willmun 116
    Wynn 111
Dobbin, Anne 110
    Elizabeth 29, 48
    Hugh 14, 47, 72
    John 11, 29, 111
    Mary 49
    Nancy 12
    Peggy 30
    Rachel 111
Dobbins, James 75

Dobbins (cont.)
    James C. 72, 125
    John 27
    Lethe E. 107
    Nancey 12
    Sarah 29
    Starritt 101
Dobbs, Mary 14
Dobines, James C. 39, 44
Dobins, James C. 50
Dodd, Louisa 74
Dodson, Alcy 25
    Alexander 52, 125
    Cesar 63, 88
    Charles R. 86, 101
    Elias 64
    Eliza Ann 80
    Eliza O. 118
    Elizabeth F. 119
    Elizabeth W. 27
    Emiline 120
    Emily 94
    Frances A. 73
    Francis 17
    George 17
    George W. 86
    John B. 26
    Joseph 25
    Layton T. 75
    Lucy M. 86
    Marthy (Mrs.) 17
    Mary A. C. 61
    Mary F. 3
    Mary R. 88
    Matthew 2, 65, 114
    Paul H. 53
    Permelia 109
    Rebeca H. 4
    Sarah 32, 113
    Seignara M. 110
    Stephen 19, 95, 98
    Stephen L. 45, 48
    Stephen L. (Jr.) 71
    Timothy 72
    William 26
    William W. 103
Doll, Archy 52
    J. 13, 15, 24, 26, 28, 36, 40, 44, 77, 121
    Jacob 20, 31, 33, 35, 36, 38, 42, 45, 54, 56, 59, 60, 61, 63, 65, 69, 75, 77, 78, 79, 85, 89, 90, 96, 111, 118, 120, 125
Dollarhide, Cornelius 55, 114
    Frankey 59
    Jesse A. 60
    Mary 26
    Sarah 35
    William 86
Dollerhide, Anne 75
    Nice 102
Dolton, Patsey 112
    William 26
Donaldson, Robert 88
    Sarah 53
Donoho, Archimedes 109
    Betsey 116
    Burl 101
    C. D. 69
    Carnelia A. 95
    Elizabeth 1
    Emily 102
    Fanney 54
    Lucy 119
    Mary A. 51

Donoho (cont.)
  Moses 53
  Polly 28, 124
  Sanders 95
  Susannah 5
  Tho. (Jr.) 69, 79, 98
  Thomas 7
  Thomas (Jr.) 7
  Thos. 39, 119
  William 22
  William A. 70
  Wm. 28
Dooley, Joseph 124
Dooly, Martha J. 66
Doowns, Fanny 15
Doson, Phillisse B. 12
Dotson, Elmina 33
  Martha W. 119
  Paggey M. 66
Douglas, David 101
  Jannet 65
  Mary 100
  Thos. 19
Douglass, Benjamin 59
  Benjn. 29
  David 38
  Elizabeth 31
  Jane 59
  Martha 38
  Nancy 86
Dove, Thomas 26
Dowdwell, Betsy 63
Dowell, Nancy 97
  Walker 16, 104
Downes, Roland D. 123
Downs, Levin 120
  Margarett 19
  Mary A. 123
Doyle, Edward 70
  Edwd. 26
Drain, Sarah E. 61
Draper, Betsey 122
  Polly 37
  William 26
Driskill, Laura L. 85
  Sarah W. 85
Drummond, Joanna 102
Drurey, (?) 71
  Mary 71
Dudley, Abner 26, 51
  Ibby 26
  Rebecca 51
Dudly, Lucinda 90
Duffy, James 20
Duke, Betsey 27
  Buckner 13
  Eliza Jane 31
Dunavant, Sarah 69
Dunaway, Abraham 81
  Enoch 26, 27
  Lucy 92
  Mary 22
Duncan, Danl. 27
  Elijah 91, 117
  Francis 65
  John 27, 104
  Lucy 102
  Martin 114
  Mary 86
  Nancy 69
  Nathan 110
  Patience 119
  W. W. 78, 79, 118
Duncible, Kinchen 4
Dunervent, Abraham 19
  Jane 19
Dunevant, A. 27
Dunivant, Hodge 26

Dunivant (cont.)
  Nancy 26
Dunkin, William 108
Dunkly, Lucy 32
Dunn, Ellin 14
  Jarrett 24
  Samuel N. 48, 98
Dunnavan, Nancey 18
Dunnavant, Fanny 119
Dunnaway, Elizabeth 46
  Samuel 27
Dupree, Permelia 41
Duprey, Christiana 96
  Wm. H. 123
Durham, Ann 112, 125
  Caroline N. 59
  David 85
  Elizabeth 100
  Frances 47, 124
  Harriet 125
  James 84
  James A. 124
  Jane 97
  Kesiah 114
  Martha 86
  Martha R. 42
  Mary 91
  Nancey 33
  Nancy J. 25
  Nathaniel 97
  Newman 12
  Peggy 75
  Pricilla 125
  Richard 27, 28
  Sally 37
  Sarah E. 80
  Susan 100
  Susannah 42
  Wm. F. 8
Duty, Amy 95
  Ann 70
  Solomon 114
Dye, Anna 81
  Delilah 116
  Francis 9
  Mary 86
  Peggy 81
  Sally 81
  William 27, 116
Dyson, John 101
  Martha 108
Earley, Charles 3, 10
Earp, Druzey 30
  Lawson 11, 28, 81, 115
  Lydia B. 42
  Matthew 25
Easely, Beverly 28
Easley, Caroline 110
Easly, Harriett E. 120
Eaton, Will S. 8
Echels, Elizabeth D. 114
Echols, Frances T. 52
  John 46
  Lucy 46
  Martha (Mrs.) 46
Ector, Thomas S. 51
  W. S. 17
Edes, Betsy 26
Edgar, Martha E. A. H. 77
  Wm. 77
Edmonds, Bettie 47
Edwards, Fanny 95
  James 113
  James M. 95
  Mariah (Mrs.) 95
  Mary E. 95
  Sarah C. 113

Edwell, Eady 62
  Kizzia 62
  Polly 108
Edwin, Lucy 108
Edwyn, Jincey 53
  Milley 95
  Polly 95
Ekels, Elisabeth 86
Elam, Frances 11
  Nancey 119
  Patience 107
  Verlinchey W. 93
Elington, F. 10
Ellington, John P. 20
  Rachel T. 20
Elliot, Elizabeth 112
  George 112
  James 112
  Susan 92
Elliott, Caroline 85
  Craddock 62, 102
  David T. 19, 43
  Ellen 50
  Frances 21
  Geor 77
  Polly 64
  Thomas 85
Ellis, Darky 18
  Dolly 6
  John 66
  Rebeckah 54
Ellison, Mary C. 115
Ellmore, John 28, 101
Elmore, Betsy 64
  John A. 28
  Lucy Ann 28
  Martha 111
  Mary A. 18
  Polley 104
  Polly 91
  Rebecah 17
  Sally 32
  Thomas 32
Emerson, Martha 43
Emons, Hannah 17
English, John R. 23
Ennet, Nancy 80
Enoch, John 29
  Rees 29
Enochs, David 20
  Elizabeth 4
  Rease 101
  Susan 13
Enock, Susan F. 5
Enocks, Delphia 53
  Dilsy 53
  Martha 53
  Nancy A. 20
  Sarah 83
Epperson, Elizabeth C. 56
  Jane 71
  John 70
  William H. 71
Eppyson, Patsey 65
Erwin, Rebecca 74
Eskridge, Elisabeth 84
  Martha 61
  Polly 101
  Rebecah 61
  Richard 18
  Sally 18
  Walker 29
Estes, Bartlett 29
  Jane 10
  Jonathan 30
  Mary F. 103
  Reuben 111

Estes (cont.)
  Richard 3, 93
Estridge, Alley 25
Eubaley, Sarah 9
Eubank, Betsey 12
  Frances 91
  George 66
  George W. 2
  Lucretia 28
  Mary 8
  Nancey 66
  Polly 38
  Priscilla 64
Eubanks, Elisabeth 29
Eudaily, James 25
Eudaley, Thomas 14
Eudaly, Elizabeth 14
Eudeleyse, Thomas 9
Evans, Amanda A. 28
  Ann 102
  Barzillai A. 23
  Benjamin 14
  Benjamin F. 56
  Betsey 52, 60
  Betsy 121
  Catharine 23
  Ednea 52
  Elijah 8
  Elisha 46, 59
  Eliza 75
  Eliza O. 11
  Elizabeth 88
  Elizabeth A. 57
  Ellis 64
  Fannie 89
  Goodwin 33, 40, 46,
    63, 66, 87, 105, 110
  James H. 9
  Jas. M. 99
  John 11, 17
  L. B. 34
  Lewis 66, 122
  Mariann 8
  Mary 92
  Mary C. 24
  Mary P. 2
  Nancey 69, 116
  Nancy A. 72
  Phebe 66
  Pherebe 29
  Polley 23
  Robert H. 28
  Salley 39
  Sallie Ann 110
  Samuel 59, 73, 93, 123
  Samuel J. 74
  Sarah A. 72
  Sariah H. 71
  Susana 92
  Susannah 4
  Thomas 75, 115
  Thomas L. 62, 111
  Thos. 115
  William 19, 56
  Zachariah 122
  Zorobolb 72
Evens, Jane 102
Everet, Daniel 44
  Rachel 29
Everett, Daniel 107
  Ed. 125
  Eppy 47, 123
  John 121
  Lucy 110
  Mildred A. 29
Fair, Catherine 27
  Esther D. 7
Falkner, Solomon 53

Fanin, Jehu 30
Fanning, Judah 8
  Letty 6
  Mary 37
  Midleton 6
Farcett, John H. 101
Farebanks, Rachel 64
Farish, Adam T. 84
  G. J. 82
  Lucy 76
Farl, Cathrine 27
Farler, Nancy 94
Farley, Cathrine 123
  Charlotte 63
  Daniel S. 8, 25
  Elisabeth 93
  Eliza M. 58
  Elizabeth 7, 83
  George 23
  Henry W. 88, 94
  Isekiah 80
  Izabella 74
  James 28, 58
  John J. 30, 51, 95
  Keziah 12
  Martha J. 92, 102
  Mary 123
  Mary C. 3
  Pamilia 36
  Patsy 121
  Perthena 10
  Polly H. 32
  Rachel 91
  Rebeccah 11
  Salley 60
  Sarah 31
  Steuart 83
  Stewart 63
  W. T. 3
Farmer, Ann 44
  Burrel 52
  Catharine 72
  Coleman 8
  Daniel 51
  Elisabeth H. 31
  George 31
  James M. 60, 64
  Jincy 13
  Martha 103
  Mary Jane 98
  Moses 31
  Ricey (Mrs.) 8
  Sally 8
  Samuel 103
Farquhar, James 117
Farrar, Joseph 10
Faucet, Elinor 8
Faucett, Anne 98
  Fanny 94
  John H. 78
  Martha 94
  Will D. 31
Faulks, Abel 29
  Lucy Ann 10
  Oliver 69
Fausett, James 63
Fawcett, John H. 28
Fawling, Rebeccah 80
Feagins, Elizabeth 1
Featherston, Polly 62
Feigus, Julia F. 124
Fels, L. 72
Fergason, Albert 106
  Lucy C. 66
Fergerson, Alexander 119
  Alexander W. 114
  Sarah 123
Fergis, Nancey 81

Ferguson, Alex. 62
  Andrew 21, 100
  Elisabeth 59
  Jemima 61
  Polly 37
  Robert D. 30
  Sarah J. 20
  W. M. 73
  William A. 95
Fernor, James M. 8
Ferrel, Nancy 30
Ferrell, Araminta 84
  Cathrine 27
  Eliza A. 42
  Elizabeth 35
  James A. 29
  James H. 47
  Louisa A. 37
  Mary R. 34
  Piety 26
  Polly 3, 14
  Robert M. 98
Ferry, John 37
Field, Margarett 75
Fielder, Benjamin T. 59
  Jane 28
  John 46
  John J. 6, 104
  Samuel 106
  Sarah 1
Finch, Adam 21
  M. L. 32
Finley, A. C. 23
  Abigail 50
  Augustus C. 38
  Polly 57
Firesheets, Charles B.
    52
Fisher, Elizabeth 110
  Jas. L. 31
  Jinsey 86
  Nancy 84
  Polly 93
  Risdon 65
  Susanah 109
  Thomas 93
Fitch, Artilia 29
  Catharine 50
  John (Jr.) 99
  Malinda 39
  Minerva 68
  Polly 27
  Thomas 72
  William 13
Fitz, William 44, 68
Fitzgerald, Ann 31
  Asa 113
  J. W. 69
  Nancy 76
  Richard 33
  Rosey 66
Fleeming, Mary 81
Fleet, Mary A. 110
Fleming, Jasper 81
  Lucy 65
  Nancy 30
Flinn, Susannah 10
Flintoff, Sally A. 4
  Sarah 88
Flippa, Joseph 102
Flipping, Jane 9
Flood, Martha M. 2
Florence, Delphey 97
  Elizabeth 18
  Frances H. 82
  George W. 112
  James 86
  John P. 32

Florence (cont.)
  Lettice 13
  Obediah 83
  Sarah 117
  Tolifer 13
  William 61
Foard, Martha A. 63
Foley, Mason 50, 113, 116
  Narcissia 13
  Parrizetta 9
Forbes, J. H. 64, 84
Ford, Celia 60
  Eli 103
  Elizabeth 21
  Elizabeth M. 108
  Emily N. 79
  John N. 58
  Kenny 67
  Laban 33
  Lemuel 33
  Levicy 113
  Mary Ann 1
  Mumford 33, 67, 99
  Phebe 99
  Pleasant L. 100
Forguson, Marthus 93
  Nathaniel 67
Forrest, Annie J. 77
  William 3
Foster, Ambrose 50, 71
  Ann E. 81
  Anthony 3, 63, 70, 71
  Azariah 57, 78
  Celia 78
  Elizabeth 15
  Geneva C. 105
  Hannah 63
  Henrietta 125
  James 84
  James E. 33, 40, 101
  James P. 34
  Jesse 78
  John W. 32
  Julia Fannie 16
  Lewis 5
  Lizzy Ann 119
  Martha 45
  Mary 71, 117
  Mary A. 69, 114
  Mary Ann 71
  Milly 50
  Minerva 88
  Nancey 1, 108
  Nancey J. 94
  Nancy 13
  Patsey 9
  Peggy 8
  Polley 55
  Richard 85
  Sarah 5, 27, 44, 70, 125
  Squire 44
  Susannah 40, 71
  Thomas 33, 55
  Thomas J. 65
  Virginia 49
  William A. 22
  William L. 5
  Williamson P. 33, 45, 50
Foulkes, Edward M. 58
Foulks, Abel 103
  Iverson 12
  Iveson 87
  Oliver 27, 33, 91, 105
  Woodson 95
Fourd, Wyeney B. 10

Fowler, Ann E. 72
  Charles J. 106
  Elizabeth C. 20
  Maseniah 15
  Nancy 34
  Nancy A. 85
  Rebecca 36
  Rebeccah 124
  Rosa 42
  W. L. 56
  William L. 27, 37
Fowlks, Susan A. 50
Fox, Mary 48
Frailey, George 34
Francis, Sally 111
Franklin, Sarah A. 122
  Sarah F. 70
Frasier, Jane 102
Frasure, William 11
Frazer, Ann 36
Frederick, Emily L. 68
  Jane 56
Freeland, Wm. J. 34
Freeman, Charlotte 88
  Eliza Ann 79
  Elizabeth 27
  John 102, 108
  Mary Ann Eliza 72
  Rachel 71
Freman, Martha Ann 16
French, Polly 111
  Samuel 109
Fretwell, M. J. 31
Friou, Jarvis 9, 83
Fugerson, Arey A. 108
Fulks, S. A. 79
Fullar, Elizabeth 113
  Mary 120
Fuller, Aaron 105
  Alfred 75
  Amy 53
  Barbara M. 105
  Eliza 55
  Frances 94
  Hester A. 71
  James N. 77
  Jesse 2, 72
  John 91, 120
  John N. 8
  Levi 123
  Malinda 100
  Margarett 123
  Mary 73, 94, 103, 108, 123
  Mary L. 4
  Nancey 13
  Nancy 122
  Nicey 30
  Nisey L. 7
  Peter 26, 65
  Pheby 33
  Polley 1, 14
  Prescilla 115
  Sallie M. 37
  Sarah 26, 123
  Stephen 94
  William 34, 86
Fulling, Agness 52
Fullington, Elizabeth 89
  Wm. R. 102
Fullinton, Susan J. 16
Fulloe, Frances 60
Fuqua, Elizabeth 27, 118
  Henry D. 11, 77
  John 121
  Margaret 62
Furgerson, Jane M. 75
  John 35

Furgis, Sarah L. 86
Furguson, Ellioner 118
  Mary E. 103
  Robert F. 118
Fury, Elizabeth 73
  Polly 57
Futrell, William A. 24
Gaddiss, Thomas 11
Gallaugher, James 59
Gallion, Mary J. 4
Gamble, John 98
Gan, Frances 69
Gannon, W. C. 32
Gardner, Isaac 101
Garland, Amanda 3
  Cornelia 54
  Eliza Ann 102
  Isabella 26
  Jacob 35, 107
  Lucinda 95
  Malissa 82
  Mary 52
  Moses 105
  Neldenna 35
  Pheby Ann 35
  Victoria C. 75
  Welton 122
Garner, Catherine 7
Garrant, Peter 82
Garrard, Samuel 115
Garrett, Ann 118
  George W. 97
  James M. 68
  Nancey 19
  Susan 32
  Thomas 97
  Vinson S. 97
  William 55
Garrison, John G. 68
  Margaret A. 68
  Sarah (Mrs.) 68
Garrott, Eliza A. 21
  Jane 104
  Mary 33
  Susannah 84
  William 16
Gates, Lucy 106
  Obediance 88
  Richard 15, 60, 119
Gatewood, (?) 36
  Ann E. 31, 108
  Dudley 19
  Elizabeth 56
  Frances 96
  Lewis 31, 56, 96
  Louisa F. 125
  Martha T. (wid) 84
  Mary A. 86
  Nancey 103
  Pamelea 76
  Patsey 19
  Susan 14
  Thos. 91
Gattis, William 19
Gatwood, Martha G. 97
Gennings, Nancy 17
George, Bonds 7
Ghatty, Frances 113
Gibbs, John 29
Gibson, Anne 30
  Elizabeth 23, 95
  Margarett 13
  Mary 19
  Sophia 99
  Thomas 43, 93
Gilaspy, Alexander 49
  Betsy 114
  Milly 49

Gildewell, Lewis F. 30
Gill, Elizabeth 33
  Lucy 6
Gillam, Fanney 71
Gillaspe, Alexander 5
Gillaspey, Viney 100
Gillaspie, (?) 62
  D. A. 117
  David 50
  David A. 50
  Eliza 66
  Elizabeth 44
  Mary 53
  William O. 36
Gillaspy, Alexander 7, 36, 76
  James 37
  Tabetha H. 76
Gillespie, Hugh W. 56
  W. O. 105
Gillgore, Jane 50
  Lydia 125
Gillispie, David A. 20, 84
  Lucinda 44
  Susan H. 84
Gillyon, Mary 21
Gimboe, Mary 104
Gipson, Catharine 9
  Elizabeth 93
  Jemis A. 1
  Mary 109
Gitton, Rebecah 114
Givings, Mildred 5
Glasby, William 117
Glasco, Harriet 15
Glasgow, Eliza 33
Glaspy, Alexander 113, 114
  Sally 114
Glass, Fannie 125
  Henry 96
  John D. 3
  Martha S. 3
  Mary E. 119
  Patience E. 53
  Sarah J. 107
  Wm. Henry (Jr.) 49
Glaze, Ralph 23, 96
  Samuel 6
  Sarah 75
Glen, William 104
Glenn, Christine J. 35
  Mary 9
Glidewell, Archabald B. 29
  Mary 42
Going, Allen 37, 68
  Alsey 109
  Burbage 37
  Heaty 85
  Jesse 37, 62, 85, 114
  John 37, 109
  Lithe 62
  Patsey 67
  Rhoda 102
  Sally 16
  Vincent 37
Gold, Mary 89
  Sarah 60
Goldsby, Elizabeth 68
Gomer, Amey 100
  Anne 112
  Dicey 37
  James J. 76
  Jane 97
  John 121, 125
  Judith 62

Gomer (cont.)
  Mary 90
  Nancy 87
  Polley 10, 104
  Sarah 107
  Wiley 93
  William 37, 97
Gooch, Arrena 101
  Artelia 67
  Cesley 46
  Cisley 6
  Eliza 28
  Frances 67
  Francis 57
  Franklin 31
  John 7
  Mary A. 105
  Nathaniel 8, 18, 46
  Polley 119
  Saloma 109
  Sarah 88
  Susannah 7
  Thomas 2, 80
  William 12
  Wm. (Sr.) 39, 55
Good, Betsey 34
  Elizabeth 34
  Harriett 20
  Thomas 34
  Vilet 34
Goode, Amanda 48
  Vilett (Mrs.) 48
  William 48
Goodson, George T. 61
  James L. 44
  John 91
  Mildred 63
  Rebecah 92
  Sarah J. 15
  Temperence 41
Goodwin, Harry 71
  Joseph 51
  Mary Ann 4
Gorden, Sarah 38
Gordon, Altena J. 24
  Betsey 110
  Cornelia A. 62
  Elizabeth 30
  Elizabeth F. 108
  Henry H. 11, 106
  Jane P. 4
  John 4
  Martha J. (Mrs.) 44
  Mary Ann 64
  Narcissa R. 69
  Nora W. 44
  Obediah 61
  Philip 52
  Robert 44
  Sally 27
  Tabitha 75
  William 75
Gosney, Nannie J. 11
Gossett, Joel 24
  Thomas 21, 105
Gould, Jemima 65
Graham, James M. 86
  Lucinda 54
  Travis 14, 86
Grant, Artimesia B. 50
  Davie 57
  Elizabeth 33
  Frances 57
  James (Jr.) 58
  James (Sr.) 24
  Jane E. 78
  Joshua 60
  Lucy 15, 122

Grant (cont.)
  Pamelia D. 17
  Rachel 24
  Sarah 58, 65
Grasty, Jno. S. 21, 34, 80, 117
  John S. 36
Graves, Amos 31
  Ann S. 69
  Az. 82
  Azariah 3, 12, 17, 22, 27, 38, 39, 42, 50, 56, 63, 86, 95, 100, 104, 110, 111, 120, 125
  Azariah (Jr.) 69, 97
  Barz. 39, 47, 52
  Barzalai 101
  Barzilla 5
  Barzillai 5, 33, 50, 86, 100
  Barzillai (Jr.) 73
  Barzl. 18, 57, 72, 124
  Becky (Mrs.) 70
  Betsey 59
  Betsey B. 60
  Calvin 38
  Calvin L. 38
  Calvin L. (Jr.) 74
  Caroline H. 87
  Catharine 54
  Cornelia W. 109
  Dilila 123
  E. 74
  Edy 10
  Elijah 12, 40, 65
  Elijah (Jr.) 99
  Elizabeth 39, 57
  Elizabeth L. 61
  Evelina 38
  F. L. W. 38
  Fannie W. 123
  Fanny 109
  Frances L. 95
  Frances M. 64
  Franklin 1, 21, 67, 87, 101, 105, 111
  Geo. W. 27, 61, 124
  George 70
  George W. 39
  Granderson 121
  H. (Maj.) 18, 69, 89, 110
  Hannah 106
  Hannah (Mrs.) 58
  Hannah S. 107
  Henrietta 95
  Henrietta W. 124
  Ibby 121
  Isaac 58
  Isabella 97
  Isabella L. 5, 26
  Isbell 39, 65
  Iverson 13, 21, 69, 105
  J. H. F. 12, 28
  J. H. G. 13
  J. R. 87
  James 9, 39, 57, 82, 99
  James L. 56
  James T. 18
  James W. 1
  Jas. 1
  Jas. T. 35, 49
  Jas. Thos. 61
  Jeremiah 13
  Jerry (Jr.) 33

Graves (cont.)
 Jno. A. 49, 87
 Jno. F. 17, 20, 85
 Jno. K. 24, 38, 49,
   57, 74, 100, 124
 Jno. L. 105
 Jno. Lee 39
 John 97
 John F. 42
 John H. 18, 45, 53,
   66, 75, 118
 John H. (Jr.) 38
 John H. F. 61
 John K. 29, 43, 88,
   124
 John L. 62, 89
 L. (Maj.) 98
 Laura A. 45
 Leannah H. 42
 Lewis 1, 73
 Manilla 7
 Margaret 61
 Margaret J. 98
 Martha 105
 Martha W. 24
 Mary 39, 97
 Mary B. 29
 Mary U. 82
 Mirah L. 119
 N. E. 45, 63, 83
 Nancey 29, 39, 54, 72
 Nancey S. 39
 Nancy 125
 Napoleon 87
 Napoleon E. 50, 109
 Nathl. S. 25
 Orin 120
 Patsey 1, 40
 Polly 69
 R. 38
 R. W. 39, 69, 86
 R. Y. 15, 26, 38
 Rebecca W. 38
 Robert W. 19, 36, 92,
   122
 Rufus 55, 88
 Rufus Y. 2, 22, 52, 94
 S. (Maj.) 49
 Sarah 73
 Selman 105
 Silman 59
 Solomon 73
 Squire 38
 Sylva 58
 T. W. 121
 Tabitha 111
 Tho. 95
 Tho. (Col.) 7
 Tho. W. 8, 15, 16, 28,
   32, 35, 39, 60, 63,
   65, 68, 72, 90, 104,
   106, 110
 Thomas 2, 36, 40, 44,
   58, 59, 70, 97
 Thomas W. 1, 7, 23,
   30, 31, 38, 41, 45,
   57, 87, 92, 105,
   112, 123
 Thos W. 7
 Thos. W. 39, 54
 Virginia Y. 64
 W. P. 110
 William 30, 38, 56,
   69, 87
 William B. 38, 86, 98,
   108
 William P. 8, 15, 38,
   39, 116

Graves (cont.)
 Wm. B. 80
 Wm. G. 59, 102
 Wm. P. 35, 82, 92, 95
 Gravett, Elizabeth J. 8
 Gravitt, Sarah 106
 Gray, Alexander 88
   Henry 103
   Polly 103
   Susannah 49
 Green, Lewis 39
   Mary Ann 35
   Nancey 21
   Peggy 41
   Richard 27
   Thomas C. 2, 72
   Wm. B. 103
 Greenhaw, Rachel 38
 Greenwood, James 15, 27
 Greer, Elizabeth 103
   Nancey 19
 Gregory, Julietta W. 52
   Mary 34
 Grier, Margret 49
   Samuel 70, 92, 115
 Griffin, Ander J. 39
   Geo. W. 21, 121
   Martha 90
   Patsey 33
   Polly 81
 Griffis, Sally 28
 Griffith, Jesse C. 42,
   43, 111, 123
   John R. 20, 84
   Richard H. 102
 Griffy, Ann 91
 Grogan, Lucinda 9
 Groom, Bestey 5
   Calvin 53
   Carter 5, 40
   Dolpha 18
   Eliza 16
   Isabella 5
   Martha 100
   Nancey 70
   Polley 15
   Samuel 40
   Satiry 112
   Thomas 5, 120
   William 70
   Zachariah 14
 Grubbs, Richard 68
 Grynn, Huldah 71
 Gude, William (Sr.) 40
 Guinn, Melvira 118
 Gulipin, Martha 117
 Gunn, A. 10
   Adaline A. 1
   Allen L. 31, 39, 40,
     45, 50, 91, 112,
     114, 116, 120, 122
   Allen (Dr.) 2, 6, 8,
     52, 62, 82, 94, 100
   Allen (Sr.) 95
   Allen M. 107
   Amy 52
   Asa 62
   Barbara 47
   Bell 104
   Betsey 43
   Betsey B. 69
   Celestia A. 114
   Daniel 86
   Dorothy M. 44
   Edward 40
   Elinor 85
   Eliza A. 38
   Ella 121

Gunn (cont.)
   Emily M. 91
   Geo. 82
   Geo. W. (Dr.) 85
   George 45
   George W. 44, 79
   George W. (Dr.) 114
   Griffin 9, 40, 56
   Harriet 61
   Harriet E. 120
   Huldah M. 107
   James 5, 51, 68, 69,
     113
   Jesse 46
   Jinny 10
   John 109
   John A. 40
   Jones M. 40
   Margaret 80
   Maria 82
   Martha 82
   Mary C. 47, 78
   Minerva A. 55
   Patsey H. 68
   Phillis (Mrs.) 82
   Priscilla 80
   Rebecca 12
   Richard 33, 40
   Richard B. 33
   S. H. 12
   Saml. 76
   Sarah 12
   Sarah A. 116
   Stairling H. 42, 49,
     79, 84, 108, 114
   Stairling M. (Dr.) 44
   Starling 40
   Starling (Jr.) 48
   Starling H. 5, 37
   Susannah 43, 88
   Thomas 40
   William P. 91
 Gunnell, Patsey 50
 Gunter, Bird 75
   Lucy (Mrs.) 75
   Thomas 95
 Guttery, Joshua 24
 Guy, Rhoda 35
   Vilet (Mrs.) 35
   Washington 35
 Gwyn, Augustus 9, 30,
   115
   Dorothy 117
   Elizabeth 61, 68
   Frances 72
   Jane 9
   John W. 8
   L. A. 2
   Littleton A. 45
   Martha A. 44
   Pinckney 41, 87
   Rice 41
   Ritter 72
   Robert Z. 113
   Susan Y. 8
   Thos. R. 93
   Zeri 61
   Zippora J. 74
 Gwynn, Augustus 81
   Jane 8
   Permelia A. 91
   Sarah 55
 Hackson, Jeremiah 25
 Haddock, Elizabeth 16
   Mary 121
   Nancey 102
   Richard 62
 Hadock, Emiline 56

141

Hagewood, Sarah F. 18
Haggard, Lydia 104
Hagood, Thomas 18
Hagwood, John 89
Hailey, Edward 100
  Mary 35
  Rebeccah 76
  Sarah 10
  Thomas 60
Hairston, Amanda 79
  Harriett (Mrs.) 79
  Lewis 79
Haith, John 41
  Sarah (Mrs.) 41
  Sarah J. 41
Haizlip, Haywood H. 40
Halcom, Jno. 21
Halcomb, Allen 11
  Elizabeth A. 16
  Mary M. 114
  Nancey 95
  Warren 87
  William 21, 95
Hall, A. N. 124
  Adelethia 121
  Anny 17
  David 93
  E. J. 75
  Eddy 113
  Elizabeth 30, 37
  Emily Green 52
  Fanny 72
  Henry H. 64
  James 65, 99
  Jane 1
  Jno. 36
  John 9, 41, 83, 97
  John H. 4
  Joseph 56, 60
  Judith B. 55
  Martha A. 100
  Marthy Jane 12
  Nancey 62
  Rebecca F. 115
  Rebecca J. 44
  Sally 4, 48, 121
  Sarah 37
  William 113
  Wm. P. 55
Halsamback, James C. 90
Hamblett, George W. 114
  Hannah 66
  Nancy M. 86
  Rob. 69
  William 42
Hamilton, Salley 16
Hamlet, Elizabeth 43
  George W. 42
  Jane 112
  Julia 28
  Richard 51
  Robert 29, 75
  Thomas M. 28, 42
Hamleton, Polly 95
Hamlett, Aggy 74
  Belle 72
  Bird 3
  Caroline 102
  Elizabeth 2
  Fanney Moore 86
  Frances M. 118
  James 13, 110
  Mary 86
  Rebecca Ann 1
  Richard 2
  Thomas 72
Hamner, Nancey 5
Hancock, Ann (Mrs.) 42

Hancock (cont.)
  Lucy Ann 42
  Stephen 42
  Susanna 13
Hanshaw, Catherine 115
  Eliza 106
  Sarah 108
Haralson, Agness 3
  Betsey 110
  Darcas 121
  David 62
  Dorcas 108
  Dorcass 26
  Elizabeth 122
  Fanney 45
  H. 17
  Hearndon 23, 33, 60, 64, 79
  Herndon 24, 25, 42
  Herndon (Jr.) 73
  Huldah 115
  Jane 91
  Leannah 13, 14
  Leannah H. 16
  Martha 40
  Parthena 48
  Paul 42
  Paul A. 8, 22, 24, 38, 39, 59, 117
  Paulus A. 63
  Sarah 123
Harben, George 49
  John 42
Harbin, William 65
Hardegree, Elleonor 83
Harden, Deborah 34
  Elizabeth 87
  Nancey 33
  Presley 42
Harderson, Thomas C. 97
Hardige, Nancy 23
Harding, E. H. 69, 86, 89
Hardison, Tho. 58
  Thomas 48
  Thos. 81
Hardy, Green 49
  James H. 42
  Lucy 19
Hargass, Fanny 3
Hargis, Abraham 50
  John 77
  Lucy Ann 60
  Nancy 50, 90
  Sarah 123
  William (Sr.) 42
Hargiss, Jean 6
  William 42
Hargrave, Betsey 24
  Thomas 24
Hargreave, Lucy 24
Harlason, Paul A. 48
Harndon, Patsey 117
Harp, Elioner 86
  Mamima 86
  Mary 63
Harper, Anna 53
  Judy 31
  Louisa 53
  Lydia 116
  Rebecca 95
  Thomas 60
Harralson, A. 81
  Allen 48, 52, 59, 65, 66, 67, 90
  B. 2, 30, 48, 51, 82, 89, 90, 99
  Brice 57, 61, 87, 97,

Harralson (cont.)
  121, 125
  Eliza 61
  Hearndon 88
  Henrietta 47
  Madison 48
  W. Allen 36
Harraway, Nancy W. 106
Harrel, Elizabeth 80
Harrelson, Allen 41
  B. 1, 13, 40, 41, 45
  Benj. W. 14
  Brice 22, 44
  Elizabeth 48
  Elizabeth J. 45
  Iverson 37
  Jeremiah 26, 43
  Martha F. 79
  Nancey 40, 117
  Nathan 43
  Nathaniel 91
  Polley 33
  Sarah 4
  Thomas 10, 13, 26, 32, 37, 43
  Thomas W. 27, 99
  Wm. E. 18
Harris, Agness 119
  Betsey (wid) 76
  Elisabeth A. 95
  Gracie 30
  Henry 69
  Huldah (Mrs.) 69
  Huldy 113
  Jacob 125
  James 12, 43
  James B. 117
  James O. 108
  Kitty 17
  Lydia 10
  Martha 77
  Mary E. 50
  Robert 119
  Sally 62
  Sarah 18
  Susan S. 90
  Temperence 96
  Tempy 69
  Tyree 12
Harrison, Agness R. 84
  Agness W. 18
  Andrew 44
  Ann Eliza 125
  Ann S. 95
  Araminta 53
  C. J. 46
  C. P. 58
  Calloway J. 45
  Caloway J. 61
  Cintha 42
  Edmund R. 94
  Elisabeth 99
  Eliza J. 43
  Elizabeth 57, 73
  Elizabeth J. 107
  Euphranier 102
  H. P. 22
  Harriet 6
  Harriet S. 82
  Henry P. 85
  Huldah 105
  James 20, 80, 99
  James N. 37
  Jane 22
  Jane D. 77
  Jesse 117, 119
  Jno. 18, 66
  John 7, 57

Harrison (cont.)
  John L. 45, 74
  John P. 8, 23, 43, 95,
    102, 119
  Lewis 92
  Louisa M. 34
  Mary 6
  Mary E. 92
  Mary W. 119
  Matilda 117
  Mildred L. 43
  Nancey 84
  Nancey L. 8
  Nancy 45, 64, 87
  Patsey 119
  Polly K. 97
  S. S. 12, 16, 20, 97,
    99, 103
  Saml. 125
  Saml. S. 22, 107
  Samuel S. 43, 47, 60
  Sarah 94
  Susan 58
  T. S. 54, 55
  Tho. S. 109
  Thomas 80
  Thomas (Jr.) 88
  Thomas D. 18, 34
  Thomas P. 34
  Thomas S. 61, 63, 90,
    97, 102, 103
  Virginia C. 44
  Virginia S. 59
Harriss, Edey 119
Harriway, Kitty 7
Hart, Alexander 20, 81
  Betsey A. 11
  David 20
  Elizabeth 81
  Emily F. 113
  Jacob A. 11
  Lucy 47
  Mildred A. 103
  Patsey 44
  Polley 47, 106
  Susannah 20
Harton, Bashebe 53
Harvel, Jincy 69
Harvell, Elizabeth 105
  Levina 44
  Winney 41
Harvey, Jno. C. 39
  John C. 14, 22, 37,
    38, 40, 54, 56, 61,
    84, 95, 97, 116,
    119, 121
  Sally 106
Harvill, Patin 119
  William 20, 44
  Wm. 110
Harville, Eliza 102
Harvy, Thomas P. 103
Harwell, Nancey 42
Haskin, Betty 43
Hasten, Amy 45
Hastin, Biddy 57
  Eldridge 67
  Nanny 67
  Peggy 99
Hatcher, Benjn. 2
  Elizabeth 46
Hatchet, Harriet 56
Hatchett, Bettie 58
  Clarender F. 73
  Elizabeth A. 53
  Elizabeth C. 123
  Ephraim 63
  Jn. T. 108

Hatchett (cont.)
  Lucy W. 103
  Margaret 123
  Mary C. 117
  Mary N. 41
  Mildred R. 109
  Sarah 45
  Thomas R. 86
  Wm. 118
Hatchitt, Martha N. 70
  Nancy M. 71
Hawken, Thomas S. 111
Hawker, Philip 11
  Thomas S. 32
Hawkins, Alice V. 36
  Elizabeth 85
  Ellen (Mrs.) 124
  Ephraim 124
  Mary A. 61
  Mary E. 124
  Nancey Ann 89
  Nancy 117
  Sarah J. 98
Hawks, William 30
Hawl, Charles 30
Hawly, Kissiah 53
Hayes, Elizabeth C. 61
  James 11
  Polly 124
  Thomas S. 61
Haynie, William 44
Hays, Elizabeth 122
  James 14
  Polley 106
Headspeth, William 98
Hearndon, Clarey 74
Heathcock, Elijah 53
Hedgcock, Lucey 114
Heggie, James 66, 106
Hemphill, Hugh 71
Henderson, Albert G. 60,
    71
  Betsey 43
  Byron 48
  Elizabeth 32, 59, 117
  Elizabeth A. 124
  Frances A. 40
  Frances M. 15
  Hannah 48
  Harriott E. 28
  Hiram 27, 46
  Jacob 32, 33, 103
  James S. 28
  John N. 42, 45
  Joseph 45, 114
  Julia Ann 3, 96
  Ludolphus 30
  Martha 83
  Mary B. 89
  Mary W. 15
  Minerva Ann 40
  Nancey 48
  Pirzila 49
  Polley 56
  Priscilla 30
  Priscilla J. 55
  Priscilla M. 103
  Samuel 114
  Sarah 41
  Susan P. 70
  Thomas 58
  William 45
  Woodly 3
Hendren, L. L. 19, 35,
    123
Hendrick, Adelade R. 98
  Charles 30, 114
  Crecy 24

Hendrick (cont.)
  Lucinda 59
  Rhody 34
  Sophia 86
  Sophia J. 36
  William H. 17, 53
Hendrix, Elijah 45
Hendshaw, Frances 11
Henrick, Virginia 81
Henshaw, Mary 30
  Thomas 60
Hensle, Sally 4
Henslee, David 54, 77
  Elizabeth 67, 82
  Enoch 36, 57
  Frankey 36
  John 45, 50, 80
  Kessiah 86
  Lucinda 79
  Richard 58
  Sarah 82
  Thomas 45, 82, 92
  William 3, 52, 82, 101
Hensley, Addison 45
  Ann 80
  Artelia 15
  Dorithy 3
  Elizabeth Y. 74
  Ellionar 86
  Frances 67
  Levi 88
  Mary 67
  Mary J. 57
  Rachael 65
  Sarah 67
  Sidney L. 74
Heritage, William 16
Herman, John 57
Herndon, Elizabeth 98
  Frances 36
  George 36, 60, 95, 112
  Martha 7
  Sally 78
  William 10
Herring, James 71
  Mary 125
  William 87
  Wm. 107
Hester, Eliza 39
  Margaret 46
  Mary C. 54
  Robert H. 115
  Sarah 115
  Sarah C. 89
  William 12
Heston, Lucy 9
Hewbank, Priscilla 64
Hewell, Elizabeth A. 88
Hewlet, Susannah 46
Hews, Lydia 25
Heydon, Samuel F. 46, 97
  Thomas 4
Heygood, Mary 68
Hickman, Betsey 37
  Mary 107
Hicks, Daniel 46
  Ellenor 65
  Frances 27
  Levina 77
  Lucy (Mrs.) 42
  Rebecca C. 107
  Sophia 34
Higgason, Jane C. 23
Higginbottom, James A.
    39
Hightower, Agniss 15, 56
  Betsey 104
  Charnel 59

143

Hightower (cont.)
  Daniel 46, 114
  Delilah 32
  Deverex 78
  Edward 117
  Eliza 82
  Elizabeth 34, 53
  Epaphroditus 15, 56, 59
  Fanny 59
  Frances 101
  Frances T. 54
  Gregory 59
  Isabella 88
  Jane 47
  Joseph M. 123
  Joshua 20, 29, 34, 52, 97
  Lettice 80
  Martha 7
  Martha P. 97
  Mary 11, 59, 75
  Mary C. 113
  Nancey 21, 52
  Nancy 59
  Nancy W. 34
  Nicholas 76
  Permelia 114
  Rebecca S. 59
  Robert 101
  Sally 61, 112
  Sarah 15, 99
  Sarah L. 2
  Susan 79
  Susanah 22
  Thomas 77
  William 2, 22, 59, 61, 101, 107
Hill, Elizabeth 91
  Fanny M. 35
  H. G. 106
  John R. 107
  Leanna 89
  Lewis 21
  Lucinda B. 91
  Mary 120
  Saml. P. 10, 37, 74
  Samuel P. 115, 116
  Sarah F. 89
  Thomas D. 24
  Virginia C. 24
  Zachary 67
Hilliard, Lucy 10
Hilton, Mary 18
Hines, B. 64
  Benjamin 1
  Elizabeth B. 71
  Saml. H. 32
  Samuel H. 42, 65
Hinton, Adalaide 77
  Betsey 25
  Bill 1
  Christopher 64
  Eliza A. 120
  Henritta M. 109
  John 18, 50, 72, 122
  Mary 86
  Mary E. 1
  Nancy 50
  Polly 98
  William 124
Hipworth, John 122
Hite, Matilda 7
Hitower, A. L. 46
Hix, Artemesia 27
  Elizabeth 26, 121
  Hannah 102
  Nancy 105

Hobbs, Edy 85
  Kitty 4
  Lucy 33
Hobson, Rachel 50
Hodge, Catharine 125
  David 25, 47, 113
  Elisabeth 93
  Hannah 27
  Judath 4
  Louisa 92
  Mary 62
  Polly 5
  Sally 54
  Samuel 47, 54, 62, 77
  Sina 47
  Susan A. 17
  Washington T. 47
Hodges, Bettie 109
  Eliza 36
  Ellen T. 28
  H. E. 47, 66, 84, 86, 109, 118
  Henry E. 47
  J. A. 13, 28, 66, 92
  James 10
  James A. 73
  James M. 1
  Jas. A. 76
  John T. 10, 28
  Julia 1
  Kesiah A. 2
  Martha W. 97
  Mary 36, 117
  Mary F. 8
  Milton 47
  Nancey M. 41
  Nelson 86
  Robert 41
  Susan M. (wid) 44
  Susanah C. 108
  Thomas J. 55
  Washington T. 14, 35
  William H. 13
  Yuel F. 92
Hodnett, Caroline 70
  Daniel H. 110
  James 47
  Jancey 47
  Lucinda A. 125
  P. 43, 71, 92, 94
  Philip 33, 45, 60, 63, 78
Hoge, Louisa 23
  Matilda (Mrs.) 23
  Wm. 23
Hogg, Juda 36
Holcom, Elizabeth 28
  George 48
  William (Jr.) 28
Holcomb, John 77
  Martha M. 77
  Mary 21
  Perry 55
  Salley 23
  Sarah A. 124
Holden, E. B. 17, 64, 74, 98
  Henry N. 15, 17, 60, 99
  James 20
  Mary E. 109
Holder, James 17
  S. B. 14
  Samuel B. 3, 30, 44, 61, 80
  Sarah P. 47
  Susan 51
Holderby, Ann 45

Holderby (cont.)
  George H. 104
  M. C. 20
Holderness, Martha 20
  Robert 8, 104, 116
  Salley 9
  Simon 72
Holladay, Harriot 35
Holles, Elemore 29
Hollis, Jesse 10
Holloway, Betsey 77
  Jenny 114
  Joanna 26
  John 14, 15, 26, 62, 112
  Nathan 25, 46, 77
  Nathaniel 110
  Patsey 13
  Polley 51
  Sally 16, 94
  Whitefield 94
  William 13, 114
Holmes, Malinda 89
Holoway, John 3
  Susan 3
Holsonback, Liddy 115
Holt, John O. 48
  Sarah 25
  Washington 70
  William 95
  Williamson 124
Holycross, Sarah 110
Hood, Lotty 25
Hoofman, Sarah E. 52
Hooper, Ann L. 77
  Barbara 30
  Benjamin 43
  Daniel 78
  Deleware 37
  Eliza L. 51
  Elizabeth 41, 104, 114
  Elizabeth J. 47
  Elizabeth L. V. 24
  Emily 40
  Frances 47
  Frances G. 117
  H. 12
  Henry 43, 83
  Jane 20
  Jesse 7
  Jno. T. 65
  John 73, 123
  John C. 57
  John J. 97
  John T. 42
  Manerva A. 6
  Martha 27, 32, 73, 84
  Martha A. 45
  Martha J. 41, 69, 74
  Mary 31, 57
  Mary W. 19
  Nancy 8
  Nathl. 49
  Peter 57, 97
  Peter E. 11, 74
  Polley 91
  Polly 123
  Salley 14
  Sarah 42
  Susan 20
  Susanna 56
  Thomas 23
  William P. 47
  Winnie 6
  Wm. Y. 121
  Woodey 112
  Woodlief 48, 121
  Zachariah 5, 85

Hooper (cont.)
　Zachariah (Sr.) 103
　Zachariah L. 51
Hoopper, Benjamin 49
Hopkins, Wm. 71
Hopper, Winifred 5
Hornbuckle, Elisabeth 42
　Frances 41
　James P. 68
　Milley 122
　Nancey 49
　Richard E. 23
　Susanah 122
Horsley, Susannah 68
Horton, Elizabeth 83
　Leanah 70
　Martha 15
　Mary 1
Hostler, Richard 84
House, Henderson 2, 11,
　　14, 39, 40, 47, 52,
　　53, 63, 70, 81
　Mary J. 1
　Nancy 86
Howard, Alanson 35, 49
　Ann 3, 57
　Anne 52
　Betsey 79
　C. A. 58
　Caroline M. T. 74
　Cary A. 6, 50
　Cattie F. 58
　Charlotte F. (Mrs.) 84
　Elizabeth 65
　Elizabeth S. (Mrs.) 58
　Francis 71, 123
　Groves 38, 49, 67
　Henry W. 61
　Horace 28
　Isabella S. 38
　Iverson 79
　Jane S. 58
　Julia 118
　Lucy A. 74
　Margarett S. 84
　Martha E. 35
　Mary 49
　Mary (Mrs.) 35
　Nancey 49
　Thomas J. 84
　William 15
Howel, Hanner 42
　Nancey 37
Howell, Benjamin 37
　Thomas 53
Hubbard, A. D. 8
　Archibald D. 37
　Charles 47
　Freeman 42, 86
　Henry 47, 50
　Malinda 51
　Malinda (Mrs.) 8
　Martha 96
　Martha J. 8
　Mary 23, 30, 49, 97
　Mary (wid) 5
　Mildred 60
　Nancy 10, 87, 114
　Nancy (Mrs.) 47
　Phineas 83
　Polley 92
　Rhody 36
　Sally 98
　Susan 25
　Thomas D. 63
　Virginia 99
　William 50, 83, 104
Hubbird, Patsey 85

Hubbird (cont.)
　Polly 14
Hucherson, John L. 61
Hudgins, Susan A. 32
　Thomas H. 14
Hudson, Ann 20
　Betsey 90
　James M. 82
　Lafayette 70
　Peggy 37
　Sarah 96
　Shadrack 36, 81
　Thomas A. 74
　Thos. A. 4, 116
Hughes, Ann T. 91
　Betsey 67
　Elisabeth 81
　Elizabeth 8
　James 33
　John 36
　Lucy 50
　Margaret 61
　Mary 33
　R. W. 61
　Saml. 50
Hughs, Andrew 67
　Elizabeth Ann 95
　Henry 90
　Joice 70
　Louisa Rivers 91
　Malinda 41
　Martha 29, 105
　Mary 66
　Rosetta 102
　Sarah 27
　William 94
Hughston, Anna 103
　Elizabeth 88
　Jenney 12
Hulett, Samuel 28
Humeston, Hannah L. 117
Humphrey, Benjamin 104
　Lotte W. 49
Humphreys, Colmore 93
　Elizabeth 27
　J. B. 65
　John 112
　John H. 95
　Margaret C. 84
　Nancey 93
　Nancy 17
Humphries, Nancy 69
Humphrys, Henry 64
Hunley, Mary 38
Hunly, Mary H. 28
Hunt, Adolphus 51
　Armstead 22, 51
　Armsteard 120
　D. 120
　E. 22, 24, 25, 28, 40,
　　46, 48, 51, 61, 62,
　　63, 70, 92, 101,
　　105, 106, 108, 113,
　　116, 117, 118
　E. H. 119
　Ellen 73
　Emily 14
　Essex 14
　Eustace 35, 73, 107,
　　114
　Hannah 90
　Johnson 25
　L. T. 17
　Lewis 25
　Louisa 51
　Lucinda 48
　M. 51
　Mary 22

Hunt (cont.)
　Mary Jane 28
　Milly 116
　Precilla 51
　Rachel 115
　Salley 56
　Samuel 49
　Vina 48
　Viney 116
　Windsor 51
Hunter, Elizabeth 97
　Jane L. 34
　Marey 52
　Patsey 13
　Rebecca 83
Huntington, M. P. 4, 29,
　　32, 46, 55, 75, 77,
　　81, 100, 122, 123,
　　124
Hurdle, Ann (wid) 54
　B. F. 112
　Jacob 68
Hurley, Ann 73
Huskins, Mary 97
Hustin, George 51
Huston, Agness 54
　Betsey 50
　Eldridge 52
　Geo. 43
　George 35
　Jane 43
　Jonathan 12
　Rebecca 23
Hutchison, James 115
Hutson, Joshay 90
Inge, P. H. 35
Ingram, Benjamin 28, 52,
　　124
　Betsy 15
　Clary 37
　Elisha 2, 52, 61
　Elizabeth 2, 50
　Fanny 97
　James 30, 77, 81, 102,
　　124
　Mary N. 108
　Priscilla 1, 108
　Sarah E. 95
　Susanah 80
　Talley 113
　Thomas E. 114
　Tirzah 108
　Walter 122
Ingrom, Morning 42
Irby, Mary 122
　Sarah 90
Irp, Wesley 86
Irvine, Alexander 16
　Jennie 52
　Mary 43
　Silvey 52
Ivey, Stinceon 92
Jackson, (?) 51
　Agness 76
　Batt 68
　Catharine 69
　Cloe 30
　Corban 19
　Daniel 52
　Delilah 68
　Elisa 96
　Eliza (wid) 122
　Elizabeth D. 68
　Frances 15
　George 53
　Huldah 7
　J. B. 19, 41, 56, 62,
　　70, 72, 75, 81, 91,

Jackson (cont.)
  105, 125
  James B. 82
  John 9, 25
  Julia W. (wid) 105
  Margret J. 3
  Martha 41
  Mary 46
  Mary E. 28
  Mildred 72
  Nancey 51
  Nancy F. 91
  Priscilla 12
  Richard 10
  Robert 69
  Robert H. 52, 107
  Robert H. (Sr.) 52
  S. C. 106
  Salley 98
  Sarah 68
  Shadrack 70
  Soriah 117
  Spencer 9
  Susan 46
  Susanah 54
  Thomas 44, 52, 117
  Thomas (Jr.) 98
Jacob, Nancy 34
James, Amy 8
  Granville 123
  J. J. 26, 80
  J. W. 71
  James W. 72, 81
  Jane 123
  Nancy 46
  Virginia 82
Jay, James 73
  Salley 73
Jean, Nathan 87
Jeffers, Isabela 58
  John 8
  Susanah 117
Jeffres, Lewis 53
Jeffreys, A. W. 16
  Archibald W. 17, 109
  Bedford 43
  Betsy 106
  Cornelia 64
  Elizabeth Jane 35
  Elizabeth M. 64
  Geo. W. 63
  Geo. Washington 33
  George W. 113
  Harriett A. 67
  Helen E. 82
  Isabella 51
  Iverson 16
  James W. 10
  Jane 5
  John 15, 21, 27, 54
  John G. 34
  Johnston 55
  Joshua 114
  Lydia 26
  Martha 15
  Mary 10, 94
  Mary E. 51
  Melissa 53
  Mildred 40
  Mildred W. 70
  Nancy 41
  Osborn (Jr.) 90
  Richard 53
  Susan 16
  Tho. 7
  Thomas 3, 24, 63, 116
  Thomas (Jr.) 21
  Thos. 23

Jeffreys (cont.)
  Traverse 51
  Virginia A. 52
  William 25, 49
Jeffrys, Patty 36
Jenings, Mary E. 35
Jenkins, Sarah A. 119
  William 71
Jennings, Elizabeth M. 41
  Emma J. 65
  J. 28, 63, 81, 97, 112, 116, 117
  J. J. 103
  Joseph 31, 58
  Mary 64
  Saml. B. 108
  Samuella 60
Jerrill, Willie L. 18
Jimison, Latitia Alice 114
  Wiley 114
Johnagain, Faithey 57
Johns, Elizabeth 58
  Happy 117
  Isaac 58
  Polly 58
Johnson, Allen 54
  Ann 14
  Anness 22
  Coleman 101
  Frances 73
  George W. 47, 123
  Isaac 91
  James 28
  Mary P. 10
  Rosa Ann 118
  Thomas 14
  William 52
  William D. 104
Johnston, Adaline M. 31
  Aderline W. 121
  Alfred 54, 62, 120
  Alfred B. 5
  Ann 101
  Anna 34
  Anne 81
  Benjamin 86
  Betsey 16
  Caleb A. 3, 71, 120
  Catherine 54
  Charlotte 21
  Daniel 124
  David S. 120
  Elisabeth 122
  Eliza 22
  Eliza (Mrs.) 120
  Fannie 96
  Fanny 99
  Frances 66
  Hampton 75
  James 3
  Jane 3
  Jane E. 56
  Jno. Miles 102
  John 12, 47, 99
  John (Jr.) 70
  John B. 122
  John M. 120
  L. T. 56, 83
  Lancelot 13, 30, 46, 58, 73, 91, 93, 104, 112
  Lancelot T. 44
  Lancelott T. 24, 62
  Malinda 46
  Maranda 120
  Mary S. 73

Johnston (cont.)
  Mildred 43
  Milissa 44
  Nancy R. 29
  Nannie M. 121
  Pheobe 17
  Polly 1, 28, 29, 114
  Rebeca 9
  Rebecca 13
  Rebecca L. 45
  Sally 48, 101
  Saml. (Jr.) 34
  Samuel 7
  Sarah 62
  Sarah P. 101
  Susana 3
  Susannah 37
  Thomas 1, 122
  Thomas D. 21, 45, 63, 118
  Thos. D. 23
  Vina 46
  William 125
  William H. 46
  Zelphah 124
Jones, A. M. 31
  Aaron (Jr.) 37
  Agness 5
  Amandar 77
  Ann 111
  Ann P. (wid) 33
  Barbara 11
  Benjamin 41, 53
  Betsey 60
  Calvin 26
  Catharine L. 102
  Celia 20
  Clayton 29
  Cyntha 53
  Daniel 116
  E. M. 92
  Ed 41
  Edward D. 28
  Edward M. 68, 88
  Edward O. 96
  Eliza 104
  Elizabeth 34, 75, 86
  Elizabeth A. 2
  Ellen 54
  Ellin 26
  Ezekiel 94
  Ezekiel D. 64
  Ezekiel P. 72
  F. H. 105
  Fannie 122
  Fanny 70
  Frances 45, 70
  Frances A. 2
  George 49
  Georgian 47
  Hanry 55
  Hester 59
  J. J. 16, 21, 22, 28, 30, 32, 35, 36, 42, 46, 47, 48, 52, 53, 56, 58, 59, 63, 64, 71, 72, 73, 74, 75, 77, 79, 82, 83, 84, 87, 95, 96, 101, 105, 107, 108, 109, 110, 111, 116, 119, 125
  James 30, 54, 75, 102
  Jane 55
  Jane W. 63
  Jenny 112
  Jeremiah 33
  Jincey 13

Jones (cont.)
  Joel 77
  John 76, 90
  John E. 56, 116
  John J. 15, 33, 35,
    41, 42, 50, 51, 53,
    61, 69, 81, 85, 86,
    90, 91, 94, 95, 98,
    101, 109, 112, 119,
    122
  Julia 3
  Laura A. 116
  Leana 40, 57
  Lucy 3, 77
  Maria 55
  Martha 62, 85
  Martha A. (Mrs.) 40
  Martha J. 112
  Mary 48
  Mary (Mrs.) 116
  Mary A. 40
  Mary Ann 96
  Mildred 63
  Milly 98
  Minerva (Mrs.) 57
  Moses 57
  Nancey 95
  Peter 52
  Philip 9
  Phillip 54
  Polly 2
  Pricila 97
  R. H. 40
  Rachel 121
  Rebecca (Mrs.) 116
  Richard 11, 54, 62, 90
  Richd. 45
  Robt. B. 93
  Salley 10, 66, 101
  Sallie 116
  Sally 42
  Sarah 124
  Suckey 14
  Susan 69
  Thomas J. 28
  Thos. 55
  Titus 55
  Wila 79
  William 14, 63, 122
  Willie (Dr.) 9
  Wm. 55, 105
  Yancey 28, 80, 112
  Zalman J. 21
Jopling, Catherine 99
Jordan, F. M. 80
  Will. M. 43
Jordon, F. M. 51
  Mary 80
Jouet, Nancey 87
Jouett, Thomas 6
Jouette, Polley 25
Jouit, Susannah D. 91
Jourdon, Martha 17
Jurdin, Enus 102
Justice, Benjamin W. 103
  J. W. 91
  John W. 79
  Martha Jane 79
Kannon, James 41
  William 18, 56
Kearn, Rawley 75
Kearney, Joshua 118
Keen, John 32, 74, 87
  Mary E. 50
  Nancey 95
  Polley 64
  Susannah 51
Keesee, Jno. D. 80, 85,

Keesee (cont.)
  107, 118, 123
  John D. 15, 27, 30,
    84, 90, 116
  Louisa T. 103
  Paulina Ann 2
Keling, William 56
Kelley, Elisabeth 37
  Elizabeth 55
  George 55
  James 115
  Joseph 36
  Nancey 115
Kelly, Allen 5
  George 57
  Margret 99
  Rebecca J. 117
Kemp, Barnet 103
  Barnett 66
  Elizabeth 99
  Matilda 45
Kendall, Jesse C. 103
Kendrick, Elizabeth 60
  Mildred 74
  Samuel 23
  Thos. 91
Kennaday, Joannah 16
Kennebrew, Elizabeth 4
  William 4
Kennon, Abel 73
  Anne 83
  Anney 23
  Eveline 50
  Frances 21
  J. B. 121
  Jane 25
  Janey 56
  John 85
  Joseph B. 105
  Polly 103
  Reubin 94
  Richard R. 26, 103
  Sally 73
  Thomas 56
  Thursday Ann 7
Kent, Ann 82
  Charles C. 56
  Rob. L. 60
  Sally 105
  Stairling S. 50, 83,
    121
  Sterling S. 81
Kerby, Jeremiah 56
Kermichael, Duncan 16
  Leminah 17
  Sarah 100
Kernal, Mary 12
Kernall, Milley 77
Kerr, Anne 101
  Betsey 82
  Fannie L. 68
  Francis A. (wid) 38
  Frankey 3
  Isbel 9
  James 53
  Jno. 58
  Jno. (Jr.) 1
  John 44
  John (Jr.) 18, 56, 58
  Lucy 124
  Martha 98
  Mary P. 59
  Nancey 59
  Nancy 59
  Polley 59
  Polly 118
  William 10, 59
  Zephaniah T. 10, 57

Kersey, James 57
  James A. 18
  Juliann 10
  Ursley 79
  William H. 12
Key, Phoebe 20
  Sarah 43
Kiersey, Alexander 27,
    55
  Alexr. 111
  Lucy 102
  Nancey 117
  Polley 54
  Ritta 64
  Salley 2
  William 79
Kile, Betcey 47
Kilgore, Lydia 125
Killgore, Thomas 121
Kimbro, Andrew J. 48
  Azariah G. 15, 29, 38,
    39
  Elijah G. 67, 88
  Hannah 1
  Isbel 18
  James 76
  Margaret 109
  Mary J. 15
  Sarah 109
  Susannah 57
  Thomas K. 121
  Thomas R. 20, 47, 99
  William 37, 124
  William (Sr.) 73
  William N. 121
  William N. (Jr.) 78
Kimbrogh, Susan S. 125
Kimbrou, William 57
Kimbrough, Andrew 105
  Andrew J. 92
  Charity 1
  Elizabeth J. 24
  Elmira 107
  James 109
  John (Jr.) 38
  John S. 57
  Mary 84
  Miles 38
  Nancey 86
  Nancey G. 29
  Nancy 57
  Patsey 18, 107
  Rebecca 105
  Robert 86
  Salley 18
  Tabitha 48, 100
  Wm. N. 57
Kindrick, Sally 72
King, A. E. 124
  Ailcey 37
  Betsey 33
  Celia 116
  Clara (Mrs.) 116
  Edward 50
  Elizabeth 29
  Elizabeth E. 17
  Elvira J. 45
  Frances 6
  Henry 55
  Jane 117
  Joseph 57
  Lucy 57
  Matilda (Mrs.) 6
  Minerva 44
  Moses 116
  Nancy 33, 37
  Polley 88
  Rachel 78

King (cont.)
  Rebecca J. 18
  Robert Joseph 3
  Rogers 6
  Saml. 57
  Sarah 42
  Wilie 114
  William 8, 57
Kinnebrugh, John 34
Kirby, Ann R. 122
  Benjamin W. 2
  Fanny H. 2
  Henry 91
Kirk, Isaac 93
  Pamilia 12
Kirkpatrick, M. E. 75
Kirsey, Dicy 55
Kitchen, Elizabeth 94, 97
  Ester 58
  James 57
  John 48
  Salley 5
  Stephen 50, 57
Knight, Benja 24
  Franklin 14
  Jno. R. 85
  Joseph Jno. 57
  L. 85
  Margaret 47
  Margrett E. 108
  Martha 48
  Robert 2
  William 58, 62
  William M. 43
Knighten, Mary 47
Knott, D. 32, 60, 61
Kursey, Sarah 11
Kyle, David 56
  Jane 56
Lackey, Robert 33
Lacy, J. H. 85
  Jno. H. 64, 86, 109, 125
  John H. 88, 99
Laftis, Martha A. 123
Lamb, Martha 18
Lambert, Clayton 74
Lamkin, George W. 83, 111
  Susan 111
Lampkin, Jane T. 2
  Nancey 39
  Richard G. 72
  Sarah 36
  Sophia W. 68
Land, Sophia A. 32
  William H. 124
Landers, Abr. 19, 58
  Abraham 21
  James N. 19
  Jno. 82
  L. A. 70
  Larkin 58
  Larkin A. 55, 90
  Nancey 21
  Rachel 55
Landrum, Elgy 81
  Sarah A. 121
Lane, Ann P. 26
  Levy 58
  Mary E. 26
Langhorn, Elizabeth 100
Langley, Alcey 105
  John 9
  Joseph 12, 22, 88, 105
  Mary 9
  Moses 9, 12, 71, 93

Langley (cont.)
  Thomas 57
Langwell, Timothy 91
Lanier, Jane B. 13
Lannom, Tabitha 83
Lansdown, Elizabeth H. 7
Lashly, Harriet J. 14
Lawson, Cabe 48
  David 103
  Elisabeth 43
  Francis 36, 59
  Jane B. 124
  John 59, 74
  Joseph J. 110
  Kate 99
  Nancey 74
  Nancey B. 123
  R. W. (Jr.) 40
  Robert W. (Jr.) 38
  Rowland 118
  Salley 103
  Silvey 31
  Sina B. 124
  William B. 124
Lay, George 111
  Patsey 125
  Polly 10
  Sarah 111
Lea, Aaron V. 29
  Alanson M. 46
  Anna R. 39
  Annis 89
  Anniss 65, 119
  Archibald 86
  Aron V. 29, 94
  Arrimenta 40
  Ashley G. 21
  Barbara 44
  Barnett 89
  Benjamin 59
  Betsey 30, 66
  Betty 14
  C. (Maj.) 59, 96
  Caroline 88
  Celestia 3
  Charles 111
  Cornelia K. 101
  Delilah 38, 107
  Dicey 64
  Dilly Ann 120
  E. C. 114
  Eda 116
  Edmund 59
  Eliza G. 10
  Eliza K. 120
  Elizabeth 29, 38, 63, 80
  Eunicey 46
  Frances 64
  Gabl. R. 29
  Gabriel (Jr.) 65
  Gabriel B. 44
  George 18, 59, 64, 97
  Harrison 10
  Hearndon 46
  Henrietta 107
  Henry 102
  James 59, 77, 125
  James (Jr.) 30
  James K. 16, 20, 22, 29, 77, 89, 109, 110, 119
  James M. 61
  James W. 36, 68
  Jas. K. 120
  Jeremiah 59, 60, 73
  Jno. 59
  John 14, 59, 64, 73

Lea (cont.)
  John F. 59
  Jonathan 53
  Judith 77
  Laurence 41
  Law 53
  Lawrence 107
  Lemuel 60
  Maggie R. 38
  Marianne 28
  Martha Ann 112
  Mary 120
  Mary H. 10
  Mary J. 22
  Matilda 29, 77
  Nancey 124
  Nancy 77, 107, 125
  Nathaniel 30
  Nathl. 32
  Nicey 26
  Owen 14
  Phebe 8, 110
  Pheby 57
  Polley 73
  Polly 68, 121
  Prudence 106
  Rebecca S. 120
  Rebecca V. 35
  Richard 45, 60
  Rosanah 53
  Salley 60, 101
  Sarah 2, 4, 88
  Sarah H. 39
  Sidney S. 38
  Sopha A. 121
  Spencer 120
  Stephen 103
  Susan C. V. 111
  Susan J. 60
  T. L. 11
  Theo. L. 15
  Tho. L. 23, 36, 98, 105, 109, 118
  Thomas 46, 97
  Thomas A. 114
  Thomas L. 84
  Thos. L. 19
  Unice 57
  Vincent 110
  Virginia 50
  Virginia E. 46
  Will 30
  William 26, 60, 65
  William (Jr.) 59
  William A. 13, 59, 64
  Wm. 29
Leachman, John 51
  Thomas 32
Leachmond, Elizabeth 6
Leak, William (Sr.) 60
Leath, Chany 121
  Eliza 121
  Ephraim 121
  Frances 76
  Freeman (Jr.) 114
  George 28
  J. F. 60, 86
  James 9
  Joel 24, 60, 66, 85
  John A. 16
  John F. 51, 68
  Mary E. 56
  Rebecah 54
  Sarah 85
  Susan 7
Ledford, Catherine 11
Lee, Anne 91
  J. M. 20

Lee (cont.)
　Mary 116
　Polley 68
　Thomas J. 20
Legans, Letsy 118
Legrand, Mary 102
Legrant, Nancy 57
Leigh, David G. 36
Lemorns, Anne 30
Lennox, John 5
Lenox, Elizabeth 61
　John 23, 107
Leonard, Elizabeth 110
Lester, John R. 25
　Mary C. 82
Levy, Caroline E. 13
Lewis, Anderson 120
　Anny 115
　Antny 17
　Elijah 19
　Eliza 9
　Eliza (Mrs.) 17
　Elizabeth 53
　Elizabeth (wid) 60
　Elizabeth M. 120
　Ellen 17
　Henrietta 105
　Hiram 60
　J. W. 100, 102, 125
　Jno. 106
　Jno. E. 15, 35, 51, 98
　Jno. W. 14, 26, 88,
　　90, 101, 110
　John E. 112
　John W. 31, 44, 45, 68
　Joseph 27
　Lethy 101
　Lorenzo 118
　Louis 61, 63
　Lucy (Mrs.) 81
　Lucy M. 112
　Mary Ann 52
　Merriwether 61
　Milly 101
　Minnie 61
　N. J. 113
　N. M. 14, 20, 27, 29,
　　30, 34, 42, 47, 49,
　　51, 52, 55, 56, 60,
　　61, 63, 64, 66, 70,
　　74, 75, 79, 81, 82,
　　83, 84, 85, 89, 92,
　　93, 95, 96, 105,
　　107, 109, 110, 114,
　　115, 117, 118, 119,
　　121, 122, 125
　Nancy 17, 91
　Nicholas M. 111
　Pheby Ann 56
　Robin 81
　Sally 106
　Shadrack 33
　Temple 20
Lindsay, Julia Ann 114
Lindsey, Dorcas 101
　Harriet 113
　Henry 101
　Joseph T. 46, 61
　Mary 101
　Mollie E. 59
Link, Betsey 57
Linn, William 75
　Wm. 39, 74
Lipscomb, Charlott T. 17
　Henry 62
　John J. 28
　L. D. 60
　Mary 31

Lipscombe, Mary C. 108
Lisberger, Lucinda 64
Lloyd, George 4
Loafman, Anne 94
　Edward 61, 94
　Jincey 3
Lockard, Andrew J. 21
　Hiram 11, 61, 62
　Mary J. 21
　Rufus A. 11
　Sarah T. 124
Locket, Caroline 34
　Margaret 87
Lockett, Isabella R. 27
　Laura A. 48
　Th. Alexander 69
　W. Alex. 42
　Zachariah 90, 102
Lockhart, Julia C. 63
　Nancy 55
　William 12, 21, 45, 65
　Wm. 45
Loftis, Martha A. 123
Logan, Cathrine 30
　Henry 24
　Mecay 24
London, Sarah 75
　William 62
Long, (?) (Maj.) 59
　Agness 68
　Banjamin 71
　Edmund 7
　Elizabeth G. 89
　Fanny 93
　Frankie 123
　Hannah 102
　Henry W. 71, 76
　Isaac 123
　Jane 110
　Jno. 40
　John 62, 85
　John D. 12, 68, 81, 89
　Joseph 107
　Lea 60
　Margaret 79
　Marian 122
　Mary 89
　Nancy 17
　Robert 34, 62, 110
　Sally 47, 62
　Wm. 97
Longwell, David 3, 64
Loot, Mary 39
Love, Dicys 91
　Elisabeth 65
　Elizabeth 68
　Esther 70
　Jane 13, 93
　John 13, 68, 93
　John C. 27, 67
　Kitty 67
　Lewis 41, 44
　Margarett 72
　Martha 70
　Mary 49, 62, 65
　Nancey 22, 44
　Rebeccah 3
　Robert 72
　Salley 57
　Samuel 44, 65, 117
　Samuel (Jr.) 22, 27,
　　68
　Zilphah 17
Lovelace, Barnett 17
　James 18
　Joseph 73
　Libba 62
　Lucind 54

Lovelace (cont.)
　Lucinda 103
　Mary 17, 20
　Matilda 62
　Nancy 73
　Nancy F. 100
　Nelly 100
　Phoebe 18
　Pryor 62
　Sarah 73
Lovelass, Cloeyann 81
　Louisa 68
Loveless, Brewis 62
　Harriett A. 125
　James 112
　Matilda J. 112
Lovins, William H. 25
Lovlace, Jemima A. P. 85
Low, John 48, 49, 53, 54
Lowell, Margarett 46
　Thomas L. 46
Lownes, B. 40
　Birket 100
Lowns, Isabella C. 104
Loyd, Elizabeth 86, 108
　James G. 40
Loyed, Margaret 112
Lucas, Charles 14
　Martin 98
Lumpkin, Nancy 5, 79
Lumpkins, Elizabeth 21
Lunsford, C. W. 83
　Elizabeth (Mrs.) 83
　James 24
　Martha 69
　Mary 69
　Mary A. 52
　Payton L. 27
　Sarah E. 83
　Walter H. 81
　Warner J. 52
　Weldon H. 8, 81
Lydnar, Ailcey 3
Lyn, Sam 72
Lynch, Celah 88
　Cynthia 31
　James B. 2
Lyon, Edmund 75
　Elizabeth F. 90
　Frances 10, 15
　Francis 5
　Henry 63
　July 49
　Margarett 47
　Martha W. 116
　Mary 69
　Mary E. 30
　Noel W. 3
　Polley 41
　Rebeccah 58
　Robert 23
　Tempy 83
　William 10, 14, 64, 84
　William W. 10
　Wm. F. 56
　Wm. W. (Jr.) 14
Mabrey, Mary 104
Madden, Stanly 65
Madding, Jane E. 40
　Robert 3, 17
Madison, Thomas E. 86
Mahan, Jane 61
　Mary 54
Maho, Byrd 34
Mallary, Dianah 14
　Thomas 14
Mallory, Ann 14
　James 54, 60

Mallory (cont.)
  Nancy 24
  Rebecca 54
  Salley 94
  Sally 82
  Stephen 14, 66
  Susan 117
  Tho. 82
  Zebba 11
Malone, Albert A. 11, 44, 74
  Alfred A. 7
  Bartlet Y. 89
  Bennet 15
  Chloe 86
  Daniel 66
  Deloney 74
  Dicey 29
  Eliza 9
  Eliza B. 12
  Frances 62
  Henrietta 111
  James 54, 67, 82, 87, 123
  Jas. 46, 91
  Judy (Mrs.) 30
  Lewis 6, 19, 54, 66
  Margaret 20
  Margaret J. 44
  Mary 23, 74
  Mary J. 30
  Minerva 71
  Nancy 73
  Nathaniel 87
  Polly 69
  Rebecca 22
  Robert 11, 122
  Robt. 110
  Sally 102, 115
  Senia 94
  Sidney B. 55
  Tempy 99
  Thomas (Jr.) 91
  Violet 88
  William 66, 73
Malory, Nancey 94
Man, Jenny 46
Mangram, Eliza 85
  William 2
Mangum, Margaret 4
  Martha 23
Manley, Elacy 40
  Henrietta 46
  Ibba 33
  Ibby 43
  Lucy 33
  Mary 78
Manly, George W. 56, 57
  Matilda 73
  Polly 85
  Thomas M. 66
  William 88
Mann, Elizabeth 13
  Joel 26
  William 66, 103
  William (Sr.) 66
  William B. 124
Mannen, Susannah 36
  Titia 116
Manning, Susannah 92
Mansfield, Amy J. 17
  John 99
  Lucy T. 119
  Thomas 37, 119
Marable, Fannie 51
Marain, John 66
Marit, Eliza 82
Marler, Salley 104

Marlow, Nancey 104
Marr, Elizabeth 75
  Lucy T. 31
  Margaret 85
  Priscilla 26
Marriable, Elizabeth 6
  Nancy (Mrs.) 6
Marritt, Solomon 41
Marshall, David 125
  Elizabeth 86
  Mary A. 85
  Rebeccah 31
Martin, Baley 18
  Bettie 118
  Elijah 29, 73
  Elizabeth 40
  Frances 37, 94
  Francis 113
  George 67, 73
  George W. 67
  Hetta C. 73
  Jas. 46
  John 108
  Lucinda S. 26
  Lucindy (Mrs.) 105
  Lucy F. 105
  Malinda 94
  Martha 8
  Martha C. 96
  Mary 7, 111
  Nancy 62, 77
  Polley 77
  Polly 29
  Robert 39, 77
  Sarah Jane 53
  Sue F. 89
  Thomas 27, 48
  Wesley 105
  William P. 71
  Zenas 33
Mase, Joseph W. 68
  Martha 68
  William H. 68
Mason, Ann 112
  Betsy 95
  E. W. 87
  Elizabeth 95
  Grief G. 103, 106
  Jean 113
  Margarett 114
  Moris 30
  Partrick 89
  Patsy 68
  Robert W. 85
  S. G. 35, 36, 38, 39, 40, 41, 43, 45, 49, 53, 55, 59, 61, 64, 70, 74, 79, 83, 88, 92, 93, 98, 100, 102, 105, 118, 119, 120, 121, 124, 125
  Salley 37
  Sam. F. 99
  Saml. G. 38
  Sarah 115
  Thomas 48
Massee, John 10
Massey, Biddy 10
  Elie 4
  James W. 18
  John 2
  Margarett 67
  Mary Ann 92
  Nancey 2
  Nancy 6
  Nowell 4
  Rainey 45
  Thomas 67, 96

Massey (cont.)
  Will. H. 67
  William 2, 101
Massie, Nathan 6
Massy, Aggy 9
Match, Nancy 27
Mathews, Drury 22
  Matilda 22
  Salley L. 125
  Susan L. 106
  Thomas 125
Mathis, Charles 112
  John 23, 68, 110
  Patience 34
  Susannah 110
  Vines 22, 68
  William 68
Mathison, Christian 9
Matkins, Dennis 112
  John W. 68
  Joseph 97
  Martha E. 9
  Thomas 68
Matlock, Agness 46
  B. L. 68
  Barbara 21
  Benjamin 68
  Betsy 27
  Elizabeth 114
  Frances 30
  James 23, 56, 68
  John 68, 72
  Judah 72
  Leathy 99
  Lucy 71
  Mary 29, 56
  Nancy 61
  Sarah 71
  Susan 113
  William 9
Matthews, Alx. 58
  Ann M. 52
  Betsey 37
  Luke 24
  Martha 24
Mattox, Sarah J. 119, 120
Maughan, Archable 61
Maurice, John 69
Mayer, Jacob C. 44
Mayho, Henry 34
Maynard, H. A. 13
  John H. 75
  Merry 76
  Merryman 64
  W. 90
Mayo, Benjamin 56
  Darthey C. 72
  Hannah 67
  James 67
Maze, George 68
  Samuel 100
McAdams, Joseph 64
  Richard 15
McAden, B. Y. 16, 42, 48, 79
  Bartlett Y. 24, 102
  Caroline 89
  Cathrine 30
  Cynthia 42
  Henry 16, 73, 94
  Henry (Dr.) 39, 43
  Jno. 49
  John 30, 36, 91
  John H. (Jr.) 30
  Mary 49
  Nancy G. 25
  Sally M. 91

McAden (cont.)
　Sarah G. 54
　William 63, 112
　Wm. 80
McAdin, Mary J. 8
McAleer, Owen 3, 5, 40,
　　45, 48, 49, 63, 81,
　　84, 90, 91, 111,
　　113, 119, 123
McAlpin, A. 52, 56, 124
　Alex. 22, 92
　Alexander 18, 37, 50,
　　53, 58, 70, 87, 90,
　　106, 117
　And. J. 34
　C. A. 108
　Caroline 62
　Daniel L. 40
　Mary Jack 80
　Narcissa G. 110
McBride, Wm. 120
McCaddams, Hugh 30
McCadden, Juda 122
McCain, America L. 91
　Bettie A. 97
　Charlotte 121
　Clinton 71
　Elizabeth 83
　Elizabeth S. 55
　John 28, 63, 64, 115
　Joseph 4, 21, 73, 91,
　　114
　Joseph N. 63
　Mary 96
　Mary Ann 119
　Mary C. 123
　Matilda 107
　Nancey 91
　Nancy (wid) 19
　Samuel D. 28
　Sarah A. 74
　Susan (Mrs.) 71
　Tillitson 111
　Tillotson 58, 60, 91
　William 65
　William P. 63
McCalips, Jane 56
McCallum, Isaac 64
McCampbell, Nancy Jane
　　17
McCane, John 111
McCarty, C. C. 125
McCarver, Grussey 117
McClarney, Denishia 85
　James 31, 34, 35
　Polley 111
McClary, Polley 79
McClenehan, Lucy J. 108
McCoy, Unity 18
McCubbins, Dolly 124
McCulley, Nancy 101
　Rufus W. 95
McCulloch, Andrew 62
　Joseph 115
　Narsissus 82
　Rufus W. 82
McDade, Ashel 64
McDaniel, Elisabeth 23
　Elvira A. 47
　Joel A. 86, 112
　John 2, 10, 16, 49,
　　69, 77
　Louisa M. 43
　Mary 60
　Roterick 32
　Sally 42
　Sarah 84
　Susan W. 84

McDaniel (cont.)
　Susannah 34
　Wm. P. 43
McDaniels, Jane (wid) 48
McDowell, A. 33, 98
　Joseph 61, 68, 76
McFarland, Daniel 86
　Fanny 86
　Francis 87
　John 93
　Margurete 3
　Nancy 105
　Polly 57
McFarlin, Julia 86
McFarling, Zachariah 63,
　　121
McGehee, Elisabeth 71
　Oney 116
　William M. 102
　Wm. M. 55
McGhe, Mumford 71
McGhee, Martha 73
　Sarah 101
McGill, A. B. 80
McGilvery, Daniel 100
McGinnis, Betsey 72
McGonnigil, Samuel 125
McHaney, Julia A. 30
McIntosh, Benjamin 1
　Charles 36
　Nimrod 74
　William 5, 73
McKee, J. L. 20, 26, 28,
　　30, 39, 92, 96, 106
　James L. 12
　Jos. L. 33
　Mary 56
　Polley 11
　Robert 28, 46, 56
McKenney, Eliz. 80
McKinney, Elizabeth 24
　Iverson 94
　Lucy 89
　Martha 112
　Martha A. 68
　Martha J. 94
　Mary 2
　Mary F. 102
　Mary J. 90
　Patsy 109
　Peter 65, 72
　Sarah 72
　Susan 95
　Thomas W. 101
　William 73
　Wm. T. 65
McKinnney, William 70
McKinny, P. A. 107
　Susan 84
　William R. 87
McKissack, Thompson 5
McKissock, Priscilla 61
McKnight, Andrew 40
　Mary 21
McLaughan, Sally H. 1
McLaughlan, Daniel 107
　Rawley 81
McLean, Jesse R. 52
McMenamy, James M. 7
　Robeson 19
McMenemy, Salley 13
McMennamy, Robeson 19,
　　58
McMinamy, Sarah 73
McMullan, John 70
McMullen, Jane 39
McMullin, Elizabeth 110
　James 46, 77, 86

McMullin (cont.)
　John 90
　John W. C. 87
　Margarett 100
　Margret 44
　Polley 46
　Rebeccah 9
McMurry, J. W. 76
　V. 66
McMury, Madison 72
McNab, John 31
　Phebe 31
McNeel, Mary E. 72
　Ursula G. 75
McNeeley, Polley 54
McNeely, G. W. 58
　George W. 61
　Rachel 33
McNeil, Ann (Mrs.) 76
　Elizabeth 88
　Mack 120
　Margaret J. 71
　Milissa V. 109
　Nancy 111
　Stephen 76
McNeill, Emma L. 119
　Julia A. 83
　Lois 27
　Patty Hubbard 59
　Thomas 27
McNiel, Frances 56
McNiell, Henry 2
McNight, Andrew 25
McNutt, Elizabeth L. 96
　William 23, 61, 70, 82
　William H. C. 68
　Wm. 111
McOrmick, Catherine 32
McReynolds, Joseph 3,
　　10, 21
Meachum, Paulina F.
　　(wid) 124
Meadors, Jesse 28
　John D. 68, 125
Meadows, Bettie 103
　Mary 67
Means, Polley 95
Mebane, Emma C. 69
　Harriet 63
　Henrietta Virginia 90
　James 24, 31
　James (Jr.) 69
　Jane 107
　Jeremiah 69
　Sarah 26
Medley, Isaac 58
Medlin, Sidney 87
Medors, Joab 113
Melone, Elizabeth 114
　Isabella 115
　Mary A. 102
　Sarah 87
Melton, David 1
　Littleberry W. 26
　Mary 2
　Patsey 1
Meredith, Elisabeth 50
Meritt, Daniel 108
Merony, Mary 7
Merricks, Polly 47
Merritt, Benj. 93
　Daniel 65, 69
　Danl. T. 79
　Freelove 41
　James 86
　Lucy M. 36
　Mary 60
　Solomon 41, 81, 83

Merritt (cont.)
  Susannah 98
Messer, James 36
  Mime 36
Michel, Nancy 94
Michell, David 98
Midkiff, Mary J. 18
Midlebrook, Isaac 114
Midleton, Mary 14
Milam, Elizabeth 72
Miles, Abner 94, 115
  Abraham 88
  Aleander 74
  Alexander 69, 96, 115
  Amos 82
  Ann 115
  Bidsey 18
  Dolly 111
  Eliza (Mrs.) 82
  Elizabeth 33, 57, 83, 111
  Elizabeth J. 7
  Fanny 90
  Henry 111
  Huldah 70
  James 45, 97
  James (Jr.) 69, 110
  John 75, 95
  John S. 69, 111
  Leah 111
  Lucy 14
  Martha E. 83
  Martha R. 55
  Mary A. 8
  Nancey 100
  Nancy R. 26
  Patcey 40
  Peggy 105
  Polly 89
  R. 67
  Rhody 95
  Richard 69, 79, 100
  Richd. 26
  Sally 82
  Susan 20
  T. H. 20, 33, 78, 81, 107, 112, 121
  T. M. 44
  Tho. H. 65, 67
  Thomas C. 69
  Thomas H. 55
  Thos. H. 50, 101
  William 12
Miller, Elisabeth 121
  Henry 40
  James 45
  Joseph 21
  Robert 119
  Sarah E. 119
Millner, Martha A. 123
Mills, Ann 61
  George 14
  Thos. J. 6
Mils, Carolin 111
Milton, Daniel 29
  Elizabeth B. 45
  James 29, 101
  Nancy 57
Mimms, Drury A. 116
  Fannie 88
Mims, Charlotte 23
  Dury A. 95
  Eleanor W. 48
  Frances 45
  J. W. (Jr.) 69
  Jno. W. 55, 73
  John W. (Sr.) 70
  Martha J. 55

Mims (cont.)
  Martin 99
  Mary Ann 96, 116
  Mary Jane 79
  Matilda B. 73
  Sarah F. 100
  Thomas B. 23
Mitchel, Arthur 96
  Catharine 119
  Cisily 33
  Ellioner 90
  Jenny 83
  John 40, 101
  Lavina 40
  Peggy (Mrs.) 40
  Thos. 15
  Vilette 119
Mitchell, A. A. 49, 85, 119, 120
  A. J. 37
  Alfred A. 2, 24
  Andrew J. 37
  Betsey 84
  Betty A. 21
  Caty 104
  Charles G. 34
  Chatherine 46
  Coleman L. 23
  Colemon L. 96
  Cornelia 50
  David 4, 94
  Elizabeth 28, 37
  Elizabeth A. 22
  Frances 68
  Harriet R. 121
  Henry 14, 70
  Huldath 9
  J. B. 70
  James 19, 45
  James T. 35, 36, 37, 40
  Jane 56
  Jinney 118
  John 48, 68
  Julia (Mrs.) 70
  Julia Ann 22
  Lucinda 48
  Lucy A. 43
  Martha 70
  Martha J. 117
  Mary 88
  Mary A. 33, 115
  Milton P. 55
  Mirine 94
  Nancey 6
  Nancy 6
  Nancy S. 100
  Penny 70
  Polly 101
  Richard 6
  Robert D. 82
  Samuel 65
  Sarah 58
  Sina E. 124
  Susannah 44
  Vilet 40
  William 7, 46, 54, 57
  Wm. C. 20
Mohr, John A. 9
Montgomery, A. D. 19
  Alexander 41, 71
  Anne 40
  David 32, 71, 85, 109
  Edward 41
  Eliza C. 70
  Elizabeth 16, 57
  Elvira 92
  Harriett E. 44

Montgomery (cont.)
  J. N. 83
  J. W. 120
  Jame 23
  James H. 26
  James N. 98, 111
  Jas. N. 123
  John 71, 96
  Mary 113
  Mary A. 62
  Polly 49
  Rebecca 36, 74
  Robt. A. 117
  Sally 33
  Sarah L. 7
  Sary 70
Moor, Frances 73
  Maria 14
Moore, Adeline S. J. 23
  Alcey 60
  Alexander 62, 101
  Alexr. 109
  Amanda 48
  Anne 90
  Betsey 84
  Betsy 27
  Blanche A. 99
  Brittain 11
  Delpha 30
  Demcey 31
  Elijah 118
  Elizabeth 65
  Elizabeth E. 75
  Elizabeth Lightfoot 125
  Emily 109
  Frances 25
  Isabella G. 1
  James 64, 71
  Jammimah 106
  Jefferson 24
  Jesse 81
  John 62, 65, 71, 95, 97, 104, 119
  John E. 110
  Judith 108
  Louisa Ann E. 75
  Lucey 13
  Malinda 23
  Margaret 68
  Martha 88, 109
  Martha F. 101
  Mary 11, 29, 90
  Mary A. 17
  Mary R. 1
  Matilda 19
  Melesia 9
  Menerva 70
  Mildred 109
  Nancy 11, 114
  Olive 115
  Olive Ann 22
  Pennelope 33
  Polly 64, 88, 105
  R. A. 35, 59, 63, 89
  R. F. 62
  Rachel 62
  Rebecca H. 66
  Richard 63
  Richard F. 55
  Robert 17, 27, 62, 84, 86, 101
  Robt. 109
  Roxey 63
  Sally 88
  Saml. 13, 95
  Samuel P. 32
  Sarah 11, 62, 122

Moore (cont.)
  Sarah A. 120
  Scecily 19
  Sophronia 34
  Susan 4
  Tabitha 47
  Thomas 16, 79
  Thompson 118
  Viney (Mrs.) 63
  W. 111
  Will C. 72
  William 11, 19, 36, 40, 93, 98, 111, 117
  William W. 45
  Williamson 23, 72
  Wm. 30
  Wm. J. 16, 36, 37, 50, 107, 117
  Wm. V. B. 109
More, John 82
Morehead, Jas. M. 122
Morgain, John 42
Morgan, A. 88
  Addison 27, 72
  Benjamin F. 72
  Elizabeth 59, 117
  Irena (Mrs.) 78
  Jubila 78
  LaFayette 18
  Louisa J. 78
  Martin 43, 59
  Mary 83
  Nancy 63, 101
  Polly 122
  Reubin 79
  Sally 122
  Susin 89
  William 17
Moris, John 78
Morison, Alexander 24
Morris, Eliza 69
  Mary 66
  Smith L. 89
  Susannah 25
  Woodson 89
Morrison, Malinda A. 84
Morriss, Edward J. 1
Morrow, Robert 97
  William 73, 93
Morton, A. B. 52, 73
  Abb 7, 80
  Abraham B. 13, 76
  Avey 61
  Azariah 29
  Barbary 4
  Betsey 61
  Elijah 73
  Elizabeth 7, 21
  Ellen 84
  Francis 9
  Hezekiah 68
  Jesse 61
  John 33, 61, 83
  Josephsiah (Jr.) 67
  Lewis 15
  Lewis S. 5
  Maranda R. 62
  Marguret 8
  Martha 56
  Mary 10
  Mary F. 43
  Meshack 73
  Nancey 88
  Payton (Jr.) 73
  Polley 67, 68
  Polly 29
  Samuel (Jr.) 73, 118
  Samuel (Sr.) 26

Morton (cont.)
  Step 61
  Vina 107
Moseley, Agnes 61
  C. H. 53
  Harry 73
Moss, Catherine 104
  Nancey 53
  Polly 66
  R. H. 23
  Susannah 39
Motheral, Joseph 73
  Margret 26
  Mary 26
  Robert 113
Motley, George C. 118
  Isaac 108
  Joel F. 58, 123
  Nathaniel C. 53
  Virginia 108
Moton, Polly 29
Mott, Phebe M. 104
Muchmore, Hannah 36
Muirhead, Elisabeth 113
Mullens, Rilla 10
Mullin, William 80
Mullins, Robert 73
Murphey, Ald. 24, 94
  Alex. 8, 38, 42, 45, 71, 94, 95, 117, 119, 124
  Alexander 14, 24, 65, 74
  Alexr. 29
  Archibald 42, 59, 84
  Archld. 13
  Bazel 53
  Betsey 4, 63
  Betsy 30
  Dudley Y. 44
  Elbert 71
  Elizabeth 17, 49
  Elizabeth F. 64
  Frances 4
  Gabriel 73, 115
  Gabriel (Jr.) 74
  Harriet A. 89
  J. G. 83
  James 43, 49, 73
  Jane 16, 29, 67
  Jno. Green 52
  John G. 32, 56
  Jona. 59
  Jonathan 70, 74, 115
  Joseph 115
  Lilla 29
  Lucy 23
  Margaret 70
  Martha 4
  Mary 1, 42, 56, 67
  Mary Ann 114
  Mary M. 11
  Maryan 10
  Matilda A. 16
  Nancey 24, 64, 91, 115
  Nancey S. 107
  Nancy 124
  Permilia A. 73
  Sena 96
  Sm. 18
  Smith 13, 48, 74, 86, 89
  Stephen 73
Murphy, Dudley Y. 98
  Elizabeth 60
  James 79
  John 5
  Lucinda 98

Murphy (cont.)
  Susan 93
Murray, David M. 4
  David R. 73
  Eliza 69, 118
  Francis T. 74
  G. 88
  John S. 109
  Mary Ann 43
  Mary F. 81
  Nancy 83
  William J. 102
Murrey, John 95
Murrie, Charles 74
  James M. 59
Murry, Franky 92
  Martha M. 23
  Sarah C. 69
  Walter 39
  Wm. Walter 23
Muse, Frances E. 89
Musick, Pheby 29
Mustain, William J. 7
Musting, Rachel 45
Mustion, Sinai 102
Muze, Sarah 3
Muzle, Frances 59
Muzzal, Fnces 100
Muzzall, Elizabeth 4
  Math. G. 13
  Nancy 70
  William 46
Muzzle, Jane 66
Nance, Clement 5
  Elizabeth 32
  Isabella G. (wid) 4
  Jared W. 32
  John T. 74
  Mildred (Mrs.) 32
  Wm. H. 75, 76
  Wm. M. 100
  Wm. M. (Jr.) 56, 61
Nash, Alfred M. 10, 14, 51, 69, 78
  Cornelia 32
  Eliza 65
  Eliza E. 69
  Farmesia 38
  Minerva A. 122
  Nancy 29
  Viney 108
  William J. 38
Neal, Becky 117
  Cynthia A. 92
  Elizabeth 38
  Emeline 45
  F. M. 76
  Felix M. 66
  Herett A. E. 52
  James M. 6, 7, 33, 55, 76, 121
  Jas. M. 74, 106
  Mary A. 70
  Mary P. 98
  Philemon 33
  Philemon H. 38, 76, 79
  Philemon M. 110
  Rebecca M. 63
  Rufus 54
  Sebilla (Mrs.) 98
  Stephen 7, 16, 25, 29, 33, 35, 41, 42, 43, 49, 54, 57, 60, 66, 68, 73, 76, 79, 84, 85, 92, 93, 99, 102, 103, 104, 108, 109, 110, 111, 116, 119, 120, 121, 122

Neal (cont.)
    Thomas P. 76
    Thos. P. 11
    Virginia Ema 63
    William D. 32
    William R. 74
    Wm. D. 98
Neblett, James H. M. 75
Needham, William 94
Neeley, Joseph 19
    Nelley 86
    Nicey 115
Neely, James 9
Nellson, Phebe 8
Nelson, Azariah 72
    Benja. B. 106
    Harriet 102
    John A. 41
    Martha B. 72
    Mary A. 47
    Mary C. V. 4
    Nancey 58
    Permelia 10
    Polley 79
    Rebeccah 77
    Salley 107
    Samuel 75
    Stephen C. 75
    Willey 15
New, Susan 112
Newbell, Martha 50
    Parthena E. 98
    R. A. 5, 16, 34, 40,
        56, 62, 65, 75, 76,
        81, 82, 91, 106, 110
    R. W. 106
    Richard A. 11, 50, 66
Newell, R. A. 15
Newman, Robert 31
Newton, Cathrine 113
    Rachel 25
    Reuben 95
    Reubin 25, 62
Nichols, Betsey 67
    Brockman 4
    David 87
    David A. 31
    Nancy J. 87
    Polly 57
    Susan (Mrs.) 87
Nicholson, Martha 95
    Nancy D. 7
Nickels, Sarah 63
Nickleson, Betsey 13
Nipper, Eliza 37
Noel, Ephraim 7
    Tabitha 118
Noles, William 76
Norcutt, Wm. D. H. 81
Norfleet, Jean 74
    M. W. 89, 90
    Maramduke 77
    Marmaduke 11
    N. W. 86
Norflet, Julia A. 23
Norflett, Fannie P. 8
Norman, Alfred 76
    Anny 75
    Betsy 118
    John 76
    Maria 49
    Mary S. 75
    Nancy 51
    Westly 75
    William 42
Norris, Catharine J. 83
North, Polly 17
Northington, David 14

Norton, Elizabeth 79
    William 47, 79
Norwood, Parthena 56
Nowel, Mary 102
Nowell, Elizabeth 50
    Marthy 118
Nowles, Holly 26
    Nancy 87
    Patsey 81
    William 81
Nowlin, Frances A. 48
Nunn, A. Nelson 95
    Admiral N. 100
    Ary 73
    Martha 66
    Mary 5
    Mary J. (wid) 105
    Miller 16
    Nancey 43, 62
Nunnally, Agness J. 114
    Archelaus 91
    Elmira J. 6
    Hesteran 61
    Jim 30
    John 73
    Martha E. 74
    Mary P. 104
    William H. 17, 64
Nunnaly, Martha 17
Nunnary, Alexr. 4
    Polly 4
Nutt, Absalom 26
    Cornelia Ann 60
    William 32
O'Brian, Jno. M. 82
    John M. 53
    Mary Ann 9
ONeill, Mary 91
Oakely, Sarah 10
Oakes, T. C. 79
Oakley, Arrena 71
    Cornelia F. 71
    F. L. 16, 18, 37, 46,
        66, 68, 78, 90, 92,
        96, 97, 114
    H. 71
    Jeen 24
    L. 115
    Nathan 78, 123
    Thomas P. 71
Oakly, Thomas 3
    Thomas P. 67
Oaks, Benjamin F. 47
Oan, Frances 69
Obrion, Hanner 110
Ogilby, Richard 64
Oglesby, John S. 4, 39,
    76
Oldham, Amey 12
    Jesse 43
Oliver, Alva 60
    Ann C. 49
    Bevin D. 30, 75
    Caroline 112
    Damaris R. 125
    Douglas 25
    Frances 1
    Iverson L. 57
    Jno. J. 1, 29, 98
    John 30
    John G. 1, 77
    Linsey 74
    Louvina 59
    M. 27
    Mary E. 35
    Matilda 123
    Monroe 99
    Nancy (wid) 74

Oliver (cont.)
    Nicholas P. 79
    Patsey 83
    Robert F. 84
    Stephen H. C. 115
    William A. 5, 77
    Yancy 83
Olliver, Catherine 115
Olridg, Sally 22
Orander, Thomas 18
Orr, Betsy 62
    Ezekiel 102
    Ezekiel J. 17
    James 77
    Jesse 62
    Nancey 86
    Nelley 51
    Robert 77
    Samuel 86
    William 77
Orrich, Lucy A. 61
Overby, Elizabeth 47
    Frances 27
    Nancy 51
    Rebecca 47
    Saluda 62
    Susanah 27
    Thomas 41, 47, 56
    Virginia 27
Overstreet, Mary 77
    William 77
Overton, Richard C. 11,
    99
Owen, Adeline A. 29
    Ann 30
    Caroline 19
    Edith 72
    Jas. H. 98, 105
    Jesse 4, 11, 91, 93
    Lucy 41
    Lucy Ann 123
    Martha 77, 87
    Martha A. 30
    Mary 41
    Mary A. E. 74
    Mary P. 50
    Nannie W. 60
    Reubin P. 87
    Sally K. 76
    Sherwood 63
    Susannah 106
    Tabitha 87
    Theodore 77
    Thomas W. 75
    William 115
Owens, Margarett 75
    Parthena 65
Page, B. J. 78
    Bentley W. 98
    Betsy 111
    Daniel J. 31, 62
    Deborah 94
    Delila 78
    Elizabeth 78
    Ester 116
    Frances 92
    H. 78
    Henritta 78
    James 1, 30, 37, 78,
        80
    James P. 7
    Jane 88
    Jennie 116
    Jesse C. 57, 78
    John 66, 78
    Josiah 10, 99
    Levi C. 15, 76, 78
    Lucinda 7

154

Page (cont.)
　Lucy 66
　Martha 31
　Mary 4, 66, 78
　Mary C. 93
　Milley 34
　Milton 78
　Nancey 29
　Noah 81, 82
　Pamelia Frances 57
　Rachael J. 31
　Rachel 26
　Sally 62
　Sally Ann 31
　Samuel 40, 73
　Sarah A. 56
　Stephen 78, 82, 109, 111
　Susan 32
　Susan M. 29
　Thomas 78
　W. C. 90
　Washington D. 31
　Whitehead 18, 62, 78
　William C. 15, 25, 35, 83
　William L. 16, 78
　Zachariah 29, 121
　Zeneth 33
　Zenith 78
Paine, Ransom 41
　Robert 70
　Sally (Mrs.) 41
Palmer, Edward 19
　Elizabeth 40
　Hettie 39
　Lucie L. 69
　Lucy Ann 94
　M. J. 75
　Mary 84
　N. J. 19, 33, 37, 83, 87, 123
　Sarah 111
　Thomas 117
　Thos. 96
　Willie J. 105
Pamplet, James 26
Pamplin, Virginia H. 77
Pane, Polly 70
Panton, Alexander 31
　Isabella 31
　Rhoda (Mrs.) 31
Parish, Harriott 88
　Mary J. 90
　W. Thomas 65
　William T. 79
Park, Jno. S. 70, 88
Parker, Ann 65
　Byrd G. 37
　David 79
　Edey 110
　Elisabeth 117
　Elizabeth 19
　Jephtha 110, 118
　P. W. 100
　Solomon 55
　William 116
Parkes, Susanna 23
　Williamson 22
Parks, Alfred 75
　Artilia 45
　Celey 66
　Celia 99
　Drady 10
　Elisabeth 83
　Eliza 45
　Hariet 7
　Hiram 79

Parks (cont.)
　Hirem 95
　James N. 9
　Jepthah 21, 85
　Mary 58
　Milly 112
　Nancy 20
　Rachel 10
　Sarah T. 113
　Solomon 10, 24, 46, 83, 90, 110
Parrish, Eliza E. 79
　Elizabeth 94
　Martha 75
　Polley 37
　S. T. 28
Parsons, Mary 98
Partee, Marshaw 54
Paschael, Frances 95
　Nancy 79
　Susan 13
Paschal, A. R. 9, 114
　Alexander R. 99
　China 35
　E. L. 69
　Ezekiel 13
　Ezekiel D. 90
　Rebecca H. 9
　Sally 35
　William 27
Paschall, Catharine 77
　Elisha 79
　Eliza 104
　Hannah 27
　John 74
　Mary Ann 27
　Nancey 84
　Polly 100
　Reliance 72
　Sarah 100
　Selma 62
　Susanna 51
　William 62, 100
　William D. 84, 122
Paschell, William 79
Paskell, Sarah 100
Paskill, Nancy 51
Pass, Elizabeth 88
　Ellis 105
　Fanny 105
　Geo. 10
　Holloway 5, 88
　Jane 34
　Jemima 120
　John 45, 69
　John A. 53, 80
　Katharine 122
　Lucy 86
　Martha 36
　Mary 81
　Nathaniel 71, 120
　Nathaniel W. 36, 96
　Nathl. 1, 12, 85
　Rachel M. 125
　Rebeccah 35
　Salley 71
　Sarah 81
　Thomas C. 28, 46, 102, 124
　Thomas Y. 122
Pate, Richard A. 74
Patellor, Frances H. 22
Patillo, A. A. 27, 47
　Elizabeth B. 4
　Lewis A. 30
Patite, Adaline 49
Patterson, Cassanda 104
　Cassandia Caroline 39

Patterson (cont.)
　David 69
　Elizabeth 69
　Fanney 104
　Isaac 29
　Jane 25
　Martha A. 91
　Mary 8
　Pelina 1
　Turner 4
　William 26, 39
　Wm. B. 1
Pattillo, A. A. 26, 40, 54, 80, 83, 89, 116, 121
　Ann E. 57
　Bob 5
　George 38
　M. V. 80
　William H. 61, 86
　Wm. H. 80
　Zachariah P. 79
Paul, Betsy 114
　Elizabeth 24
　James 50
　Patsey 5
　Rackael 18
　Robert 80
　Saml. 5, 91
　Samuel 18, 80
Paxton, William C. 20, 70
Paylor, Jno. D. 71
　Manda 85
Payne, Ann V. 64
　Betsey 100
　Caty 89, 92
　Clary 19
　Curtis 66, 99
　Daniel 122
　Elizabeth B. 38
　Elizabeth C. 103
　Frances 75
　Greenwood 19
　John 33
　Joseph 11, 13, 25, 56
　Lucinda 24
　Martha 99
　Mary 33
　Missouri F. 60
　Polly 43
　Priscilla 12
　Thomas 84
Paynor, Eleanor 93
Peabody, James B. 36
Peak, Jno. J. 103
Pearce, Delilah 28
　Joseph M. 100
　Philadelphia 11
Pearman, Jonathan 33
　Pleasant 33
Pearson, John 63
Pendergrass, Mary 95
Penick, Barbara Jane 68
　Danl. A. 28, 38, 120
　Elizabeth A. 62
　Frances 6
　Sallie A. 65
　Thomas 84, 85
　W. S. 80
　Wm. G. 6
Penix, Prudence 25
Pennick, Sarah B. 3
Peoples, Ursley D. 77
Perkins, Betsey 78
　David 30
　Dicey 18
　Elizabeth 33, 50

155

Perkins (cont.)
　Francis 114
　James 81
　John 81, 102
　Lucy 38
　Lucy A. 15
　Malinda C. 75
　Mary A. (wid) 87
　Nancey 61
　Polley 57
　Rachel 57
　Robert 33, 47
　Salley 33, 61
　Sarah 120
　William G. 50
Perry, Eliza Jane 119
　Jenny 11
　Mary 119
Person, James 25
Persons, Helena 99
Peterson, Blanche 42
　Delilah 5
　John 69, 91
　John L. 113
　Joseph 101
　Joseph (Sr.) 81
　Martha 93
　Nancy 101
　Nicy L. 105
　Polly 6, 81
　Susan 78
　Susannah 73
　Vincent 37, 80
　William 52
　Williamson 21
Pettifoot, Eliza 67
Pettiford, Frances 21
Pettigru, John A. 93
Pettigrue, John A. 81
Petty, Mariah A. 50
Phelps, Betty W. 5
　Delphia 89
　Dennis 107
　Frances 11
　Larking 81, 100
　Lucy 100
　Nancy 89
　Nicey M. 77
　Rachael 93
　Rebeckah 46
　Reubin 89
　Robert C. 112, 117
　Thomas 46
　William 115
Phifer, Caleb 86
Philips, Adeline 37
　Ann 89
　Frances 84
　Irby 65
　Mahala 56
　Mary 65
　Mildred Ann 76
　Nancy 21
　Polly 108
　Susan 62, 82
Phillips, Celly 54
　Eliza 40
　Fedrick 54
　Francis 64
　Franklin 105
　Irby 81
　Mary 7
Pickard, J. H. 79
　John H. 15, 17, 18,
　　20, 28, 30, 48, 56,
　　66, 73, 75, 79, 83,
　　108, 113
Pickel, Jean 116

Picken, John H. 78
Pickens, John H. 31
Picknel, William 3
Pierce, Nancey 40
Pierson, Jane 65
Pike, Joshua 112
　Nancy 63
Piles, Eliza 90
　Henry 94
　Jane 19, 34
Pinchback, Adaline 121
　Gracy 120
Pindexter, Nancy 3
Pinick, Jane M. 108
Pinix, Alexander 36
　Judeth 13
　Sarah 101
　Tabitha F. 71
Pinnix, George W. 9
　J. C. 24
　Jane 76
　Jno. C. 78
　John 52
　John C. 45
　Jos. C. 51
　Joseph 68
　Joseph C. 4
　Louisa 77
　Margaret 77
　Martha 82
　Mary A. 24
　Mary E. 109
　Mary J. 9
　Sallie A. 65
　Stephen 109
Pinson, Elizabeth 40
　Frances 78
　John 15, 16, 71
　Joseph 78
　Lucy (Mrs.) 78
　Rebeccah 82
　Rhody 13
　Susanah 18
　Thomas 24, 94
Piper, Catherine 106
Pirant, Abner 83
　Charles 5
　Rebecca 5
Pirkins, Nancy 33
　Usrly 13
Pistole, Patsey 124
　Wm. R. 124
Pitman, Emsey H. 64
Pittard, Anne 125
　Davis 67
　Frances 67
　Humphry 66
　Jno. 82
　John 71
　Nancey 41
　Rebecca 66
　Saml. 71
　Samuel 22, 23, 29, 86
Pitts, Susan 10
Pleasant, A. L. 63
　Aartesia 74
　Betsey 101
　Buford 45
　Dolly 69
　Elizabeth 25, 38
　Herry 86
　John 109, 119
　Leatha 115
　Louisa 114
　Lucy 1, 39, 109
　Martha 86
　Martha A. 78
　Mary M. 32

Pleasant (cont.)
　Mary Milberey 45
　Micajah (Jr.) 1
　Nancey 5
　Patcey 32
　Patty 5
　Polly 111
　Ruffin 5
　Sarah A. 110
　Silviah 101
Pleasants, A. L. 3
　Artelia S. 65
　Pleppa, Susanah 75
Pogue, Fanny 91
　Hanner 31
　John 3
　Rhodan 91
Poindexter, Eliza 11
Poinor, Sally 67
Polston, Elizabeth 98
Pond, Benjamin 17
Ponds, Benjamin 104
　Betsey 14
　Salley 118
Ponsonby, Elizabeth 111
Pool, Annis 68
　Caroline 27
　John T. 31
　Matilda M. 31
Poore, Betty 30
　J. S. 50
　T. S. 29, 66, 96, 106, 118
　Thomas S. 56, 70
　Thos. S. 123
Pope, Mary R. 91
Porter, Polley 6
　Sally 37
Poston, Betsey 99
　Jere 54
　Jeremiah 12
　Jeri 77
　Priscilla 25
　Rebeccah 54
　William 99
Poteat, Jack Wmson. 8
　James 29, 57, 75
　John 54
　Leaned 8
　Liley A. 98
　Martha 8
　Nancy (wid) 93
　Ransom 83
　Sallie E. 61
　Sarah 42
　Tempa 64
　Thomas 50
　V. E. 11
　William 83
Poteate, Cindy 83
　Elisabeth 69
　George 118
Poteet, Betsy 83
　John (Jr.) 87
　Miles 66, 83
　Nancey 73, 84
Pound, Nancy 124
Pounds, Meshac 50
　Meshack 70
Powel, Eliza Ann 49
　George 17
Powell, Adaline 122
　Amy 124
　Ann Catharine 34
　Anna 14
　Araminta A. 64
　Ary W. 24
　Carter 50

Powell (cont.)
  David 3
  Elizabeth 78
  Elizabeth A. 45
  Fanny 1
  Hannah 2
  Harriett E. 109
  James 2
  James M. 70
  Jemima 17
  John B. 33, 34
  Kesiah 85
  Leah 80
  M. E. (wid) 37
  M. J. 36
  Margaret E. 37
  Mary A. 81
  Mary C. 49, 81
  Mary G. 28
  Mary Jane 98
  Mastin J. 14
  Matilda 18
  Meriah A. 94
  Nancy (Mrs.) 33
  Nancy M. 15
  Nannie W. 119
  Oliver 77
  Polly 43, 72
  Rebecca F. 36
  Susann 100
  Thomas 1
  Thomas A. 30
  Virginia V. 33
  William 83
  William B. 61
Poyner, David 67
  John 11
  Sally 88
  Sarah 11
Prather, Elizabeth W. 42
  Leonard D. 73
  Margarett 20
  Martha A. 2
  Mary W. 30
  Robert R. 120
Prendergast, C. W. 14
  Caroline 3
  Elizabeth 58
  G. W. 67, 82, 99, 101, 107
  George 79
  Harriotte 75
  Luke 30, 84
  Nancey 15
  Thomas 30
Price, Abram 72
  Ann W. 84
  Daniel S. 27, 74, 77, 90, 91, 103, 108, 118, 122, 125
  Elizabeth 12
  Fannie 5
  Geo. W. 27, 44
  George W. 27, 71
  Haskue 32
  Isbel 5
  Janie 111
  Joel 66
  John 85
  John (Jr.) 13, 50
  John P. 84
  John S. 6
  Louisa 84
  Maraday 37
  Margaret A. 117
  Martha A. 24
  Mary 109
  Mary A. 123

Price (cont.)
  Mary J. 15
  Mary M. 64
  Mary S. 5
  Matilda 85
  Matthew 65
  Nancy 76, 79
  Robert M. 84
  Robt. M. 6
  Sarepta W. 47
  Susan C. 15
  Susanna B. 43
  William 84
  William W. 17, 19, 37, 70, 73
Pride, Woolsey 32, 39
Prior, Joseph L. 67
Pruett, Frances 79
  Robert 85
Pruitt, Emily 108
  Joseph 24
Pryor, Elizabeth W. 59
  John H. 34, 64, 117
  Pleasant 43
  Tabitha 112
Pucket, Agnes 110
Puckett, Polly 95
Pugh, Martha 1
  Mary E. 85
Pulhim, Agniss 33
Pullham, Jane Allin 9
Pilliam, James 120
  Susannah 48
Pullium, Ann 28
Purkins, Francis 119
  Julia Ann 10
  Mary J. 50
Puryear, William H. 50
  William M. 20
Puttery, Salley 11
Pyrant, Mary 110
  Nelly 38
  Subrina 83
Pyron, Elenor 21
  Frances 56
  Jane 42
  John 36
  Margery 29
  Will. 42
Qualls, Abner 95
Quarles, Nancey 50
Quine, Benjamin 85
  Betsey 101
  Henry 20, 30, 85
  Jacob 41
  Nelly 23
  Sarah 14
Ragland, Anne W. 107
  Martha S. 31
  Orphie (wid) 87
  William 13
Ragsdale, Elex 8
  Elizabeth 36
  John 82
  Leander 8
  Lewis 64
  Martha Ann 46
  Mary (Mrs.) 8
  Mary E. 25
  Thomas 58
  William (Jr.) 69, 86
Rahen, A. J. 21
Raimey, Catherine 43
  Delilah L. 48
  Elizabeth 49
  Salley 10
  Susan H. 26
Raine, H. M. 84

Rainey, Ann S. 88
  Bridget (Mrs.) 122
  Bristor 122
  Dabney 60, 70, 77
  Elizabeth 54
  Elizabeth H. 54
  Elizabeth S. 25
  Isaac 25, 39, 42, 54, 65, 74, 75, 91, 106, 111, 115
  James 22, 38, 54, 74, 86
  Jane 27
  Jno. P. (Jr.) 35
  John P. 55
  Josiah 21, 44, 100
  Leml. 25
  Lemuel 21
  Polley 117
  Sarah A. 40
  Thomas 93
  Thomas M. 99
  Thomas W. 69
  William 23, 26, 27, 37, 54, 56, 59, 87, 101, 113, 121, 122
  Wm. 47
Rainy, Fanny 48
  Virgil M. 74
Ramey, Daniel 124
  H. N. 86, 124
  John W. 124
  Margaret L. 124
  Rufus 47
  Susan 86
Ramsour, A. A. 1
Randal, James 81
  James (Jr.) 117
  Nancy 117
Randolph, Betsey 51
  James 27
  James (Jr.) 86, 99
  Robert 114
  William 50, 51
Rankin, Vittory 110
Ranndolph, James 86
Ransom, Betsy 3
Rasberry, Betsey 46
Rasco, Henry T. 108, 112
  Nancy (Mrs.) 86
  Smith 86
Rascoe, Ethelbert S. 84
  William 86
Rawley, David J. 117
Rawlins, Jas. M. 31
  Martha A. 31
Ray, Francis 8
  Jordan 25
  Mary 3, 116
  Rachel 85
  Sarah 8
  Susannah 98
Rayl, W. W. 108
Raynolds, Lelia S. 105
Rea, Sarah 71
Read, Mary 102
Reamy, Edwin 35
Reany, Edwin 96
Rear, Lucy R. 44
Rease, Elizabeth 29
Reason, Mary 32
Reaves, Mary E. 36
Redden, Catherine 68
Reed, Clarissa H. 99
  George 26
  Haley 3
  Isaac 53
  John 3

Reed (cont.)
  Lucy 105
  Nancy 38, 122
  Noel 107
  Noles 124
  Rebeccah 8
  Thomas 76, 80
  William 14
Reid, A. L. 78
  Amy (Mrs.) 11
  Eliza W. 89
  Frances 107
  Isabella V. 65
  Laura 80
  Letetia J. 23
  Mary 85, 86
  Mary Ann 38
  Mary E. 52
  Millie 11
  Nick 11
  Sarah 98
  Silvey 91
  Thomas 87, 105
  Thos. J. 57
Rend, Mary J. 34
Renolds, Daniel B. 86
Rew, Nannie 40
Reylye, James 99
Reynolds, Elijah 93
  Lucy 118
  Sarah 41
  Theodotia 118
Rhoades, Mary 91
Ricaud, T. Page 28, 30, 45
Rice, Ann 119
  Anne 77
  Archabald 34
  Archibald 5, 52
  Betsey 16, 97
  Charles R. 116
  Darothey C. 116
  Delphia 13
  Edmond 88
  Eliza 104
  Elizabeth 59, 111
  Elizabeth B. 41
  Frances B. 121
  Harriet 121
  Henrietta 87, 88
  Hezekiah 15, 77
  Ibzan 3
  Ibzan (Jr.) 116
  Isabella 5
  James 87, 107, 111
  Jephthah 104
  John 55
  Julia Ann 68
  Kerin H. 2
  Leroy 20
  Liddey 13
  Marey 117
  Martha G. 122
  Marthy E. 44
  Mary F. 106
  Milley 15
  Minerva J. 2
  Nancy 5, 69
  Nancy E. 4
  Nathan 27, 120
  Nathaniel 88
  Patcey 94
  Polley 94
  Polly 112
  Rebecah 74
  S. A. 114
  Salley 58
  Sally 6

Rice (cont.)
  Sarah 17
  Sarah M. 2
  Stephen 88
  Susan 112
  Susannah 125
  Thomas 97
  William 32, 33, 55, 80, 88
  William H. 87, 90
  Williamson 87
  Willy 31
  Wm. H. 122
  Z. 59
  Zadok 40, 41
  Ze. 93
  Zeri 50
  Ziba 121
  Zilpah 55
  Ziza 10, 41
Rich, Nancy V. 96
Richards, Derritt 12
  Durrett 27, 47
Richardson, Elisabeth 19
  Elizabeth 37
  Frances 50
  George 27
  Harriet M. 35
  James 64
  Lawrence 41, 84
  Louisa 89
  Lucy 36, 53
  Mary 4, 84
  Mary A. 123
  Mary S. 100
  Nancy P. 95
  Prudence 43
  Rachel 66
  Susan 102
  Susannah 65, 67
  Thomas 19, 36, 66
  Thoms. 19
  Unity 9
  William M. 81
  William W. 12, 103
  Wm. W. 43
Richmon, Susan 75
Richmond, Adams S. 34
  Agness S. 12, 82
  Ann 63
  Anne 68
  Burley 75
  C. H. 13, 51, 72, 80, 84, 99, 106, 115
  C. J. 41, 48, 65, 88, 114, 122
  Calvin J. 70, 115
  Catharine A. 67
  Elizabeth 26, 86
  Ellen 86
  Fannie 83
  Fanny 113
  Frances 123
  George 111
  H. A. 22, 68, 117
  Henry A. 23, 63, 123
  Hulday A. 99
  J. H. 52
  James 26
  Jane 22, 26
  Jinny C. 31
  Joel 88
  John 88, 89, 93, 118
  John L. 88
  John Lea 72
  John M. 1, 88, 89, 107, 116
  John W. 66

Richmond (cont.)
  Joseph 75, 90
  Joshua 26
  Margarett C. 66
  Martha W. 87
  Mary 7, 72
  Mary A. 111
  Mary Ann 10
  Mary D. 42
  Mat 49
  Minerva 123
  Miranda 89
  Nancy 73
  Peggy 12
  Phebe 61
  Sallie J. 87
  Sallie L. 97
  Sarah 15, 54, 74, 75, 87
  Sina 111
  Susan A. 82
  Susan T. (wid) 88
  Vilet 26
  Violet 89
  Virginia C. 31
  William A. 27, 63, 64
  Yancey 74
Rickettes, James 94
  Nancey D. 94
Rickman, Agniss 89
Riddle, Polley 115
Riffetoe, David 86
  Liewvinia E. 86
Riggs, A. 89
  Drusis 89
  Elizabeth 3
  George W. 1
  Polly 89
Right, Eliza A. 6
Rigney, Talitha J. 1
Riley, John W. 89
Rines, Jane 58
Roan, Anness 39
  Asanath 103
  Eliza 48
  Elizabeth 123
  Fanny 107
  J. W. 65, 123
  James 39, 48, 89
  Jno. W. 13
  John 46
  John W. 55, 60, 88, 89, 91, 123
  Justin 103
  Margaret A. 77
  Martha J. 55
  Mary 75
  Mourning 59
  N. M. 55, 120
  N. M. (Dr.) 89
  Nancey 48
  Nancy 103
  Nathaniel M. 19, 48, 62, 69, 88
  Nathl. M. 107
  Nathl. M. (Dr.) 22
  Patsey 72
  Preston 45
  Sarah 23, 89
  Thomas 89
  Virginia 59
Roark, Benjamin 44
  Dolly 44
Robards, Susann 108
Roberson, Hannah 95
  Mary 95
  Pleasant 122
  Thomas 89

Roberts, Bashaba 94
  Betsey 123
  Bettie 56
  Comfort 102
  David 90
  Edmond 65
  Elijah 116
  Eliza 31
  Eliza F. 92
  Elizabeth 46
  Elizabeth M. 58
  Faithey 54
  Frances 102
  Franklin 38
  Hannah 17
  Henrietta 57
  Humphrey 10
  Isabella G. 83
  James 26, 65
  James L. 63
  Jamima 84
  Jane 61
  John (Jr.) 83
  John L. 45
  Judith 3
  Kittey 97
  Layton T. 50
  Leavin 106
  Lidy 114
  Lindsay 20
  Lindsey 4
  Lucinda 109
  Lucy 87
  Lucy Ann 93
  Marry A. 61
  Martha J. 44
  Mary 47, 114
  Nancy 115
  Phebe 114
  Pheby 89
  Philip 111
  Polley 100, 102
  Roland 9
  Salley 41
  Sally Ann 125
  Sarah 67, 110
  Shadrack 116
  Simon 7
  Stacia 96
  Stephen 97
  Thomas 90
  Vincent 84
  William A. 90
Robertson, Alex. 103
  Amy 54
  Ann S. 27
  Chrs. 21
  Dilly 18
  Dolly 59
  Eady 78
  Edward H. 56
  Eleanor 21
  Elizabeth B. 18
  Emily 105
  Francis 106
  George 9
  Giden 91
  Green 92
  Jack 55
  John 107
  John E. 59, 110
  Joseph 31
  Mariah 111
  Mary R. 1
  Pathena 124
  Pinkney 118
  Thompson 96
  William 91

Robinson, Chaney 106
  Ester 36
  Henry 98
  James 8, 19, 47, 64, 79
  Kiziah 79
  Nelly 13
  Patsey 101
  Peninah 42
  Polley 10, 113
  Thos. 107
Robson, William G. 64
Rodden, Henry E. 34
Rodenhizer, Martha E. 20
  R. C. 4
Roe, Joseph 10, 51
  Mary 98
  Robert 32, 39
  Sally P. 94
  Susanna 39
  Susannah 93
Rogers, George C. 112
  John (Jr.) 15
  John C. 95
Roland, Henry 100
  Susan H. 93
Rolen, Jessy 91
  Lucrasey F. 28
Rolley, Martha 103
Rone, Anne 23
Roper, Allice W. 12
  Ann 11
  Ann Eliza 28
  Arreminta 54
  Frances C. 9
  Henry 88, 92
  Isabella C. 50
  Jane F. 93
  Jane N. 80
  Jno. 11
  John E. 49
  Mary L. (wid) 8
  Mary M. 87
  Patsy 64
  Rachel R. 5
  Sarah 19
Ropper, James 125
  Jemima 125
Rose, Henry 25, 33, 70, 107
  Jane 39
  Martha Stout 38
  Polley 14
Rosebrough, Jane 34
Rosson, Abner 58
Rowark, Polly 77
Rowe, Mary 98
Rowland, Henry 98
  Mary 19
  Mary R. 98
Rowlet, Patience 109
Rowlett, Saludia 69
  Viveldi 39
Royal, Betsey 47
  George 51
Royester, Lou F. 87
Royster, Elizabeth 53
  Henry 23
  William 122
Rozes, Jno. 86
Ruark, Edward 84
  Henry 113
  John 62
  Polley 62
Rucker, Amelia Ann 1
  Lavina (Mrs.) 49
  Stephen 102
  Thomas 49

Rucks, Virginia M. 36
Rudd, Aldridge 67, 69
  Bethel 3
  Betsey 31
  Boza 101
  Celestia F. 113
  David 46, 57, 92
  Elisha 18, 33, 92
  Elizabeth 104
  Elizabeth F. 65
  Emily 118
  Frances 33
  Frances A. 76
  Hezekiah 92
  Irrena 69
  James 50, 60, 67, 86, 104, 123
  James C. 90
  Jere 101
  Jeremiah 39, 54, 73, 80, 87, 92, 99
  Joshua 92
  Judy 92
  Julia 109
  Lizzie 38
  Luther Y. 80, 90
  Malinda 69
  Margaret 90
  Martha 83
  Mary A. 98
  Nancy 122
  Patience 33
  Pleasant 73
  Polly 109
  Rufus A. 69, 100
  Sabine 3
  Sarah J. 90
  Susan A. 16
  Thomas H. 16
  Thomas L. 76, 92
  Vienna 5
  W. C. 125
  William 31
Rudder, Jane (Mrs.) 80
  Mildred 91
  Sally 80
  William H. 92
Ruffin, Wm. K. 56
Runnalds, Patsey 48
Runnells, Sally 83
Runnels, Dudley Y. 92
Rush, Betsey 32
Russel, Ann 118
  Elizabeth 26
  Jno. T. 44
  John T. 94
  Judiah 20
  Mary N. 46
Russell, Charles G. 92
  Eliza J. 35
  Elizabeth 12
  Emily T. 20
  Jerome B. 24
  Jno. T. 42
  John T. 115
  Joseph M. 48, 108
  Judy 12
  Martha 44
  Martha J. 14
  Rebecca 98
  Sarah E. 22
  William 40, 92
  William M. 7
  Wm. 45
Saddler, Martha L. 25
Sadler, Edward 56
  James W. 76
  Mary 24

Sadler (cont.)
  Sally 56
  William M. 75
Sailes, Permela F. 32
Samuel, Anne 21, 101
  Archd. 93
  Betsy Pain 2
  Elizabeth 82
  George 42, 125
  James 64, 109
  James (Jr.) 11
  Jenny 86
  Jeremiah 122
  Josiah 5
  Letty 73
  Lucy 93
  Mary 93
  Milley 73
  Patsey 91
  Robert 65
  Sally 93
  Susannah 93
Samuell, Anthony 93
  Fanney 23
  George 93
  Harnden 93
  Josiah 88, 93
  Judith 93
  Nancey 32
  Rowzee 32
Samuels, Nancy 80
Sanders, Adams 96
  Aggy 93
  Ann P. 93
  Anna 99
  Anne 37
  Betsy 3
  Delpha 29
  Elizabeth 25, 67, 114
  George 67
  Ida V. 38
  Jas. 29
  Jemima 4
  Jess 4
  Jesse 112
  John H. 1
  Leroy 4, 19
  Lyda 124
  Manerva 65
  Mary 16
  Mason 112
  Obadiah 68
  Omah 93
  Patcey 79
  Patsey 71
  Polly 93
  Ransome 4
  Richard P. 20
  Robert 62, 73
  Romulus M. 59
  Susan 19, 93
  William 65, 71, 93, 95
  Wm. 99
Sargant, Sarah 97
Sargent, Anne 113
  Dready 111
  Elizabeth 26, 79, 97
  James 89, 100, 123
  Mary 34
  Phebe 59
  Rachal 110
  Ruth 26
  Sarah 113
  Stephen (Jr.) 34, 110
  Thomas 29
  William 113
Sarrett, John 65
Sartain, Elisha 106

Sartin, Anna 76
  Elisha 36
  Elizabeth 65
  Emma C. 65
  Mary 92
  Mary A. 100
  Matilda P. 36
  Nancy A. 108
  Thomas J. 93
Saterfield, Adalade 115
  Jno. 93
  John 93
  Nancy 14
Satterfield, Amos 12
  Bedford A. 50
  John 18
Saunders, Annie 16
  Susan 25
  W. L. 92
  William 53
Sawyer, Dicey 81
  Elizabeth 81, 110
  Ezekiel 2, 13, 25, 33,
    88, 91
  H. 23
  Henry 77
  James 94
  John 16, 33, 94
  Martha Ann 39
  Mary 11, 25
  Nancey 19, 52
  Sally 110
  Thomas 32
  William 102, 119
  Wm. 110
  Zibby 91
Sawyers, Anthy 79
  Betsey 98
  Elizabeth 119
  Ezekiel 117
  Jane 52
  Levi 10
  Martha 70
  Moses 94
  Nancey 102
  Polly 48
  Sarah 92
Scarlet, Mary Ann 103
Scarlett, Jane 78
Schavers, Sally 68
Scoggin, Johnston 60
  William 44
Scoggins, Ann 72
  Francis 12
  Johnson 34
  Milton G. 58
  Rachel 2
Scott, Allen 10, 85
  Amanda 87
  Annie (Mrs.) 22
  Asa 25, 41
  Azariah 66
  Bartlett 94, 95
  Betsey 48
  Daniel 95
  Deby (Mrs.) 25
  Delila 102
  Fanny 70
  Frances 40, 42, 102
  Harbert 95
  Harrison 47
  Hugh 1
  James 9, 94
  Jane 116
  John 12, 94, 95, 102
  John (Jr.) 37
  Joseph 106
  Lucey 3

Scott (cont.)
  Martha F. 25
  Martha R. 29
  Mary 50
  Mary F. 33
  Mial 53
  Nancy 22
  Nanny 83
  Polly 6, 103
  Rachal 95
  Rebecca 9
  Robert (Jr.) 100
  Sarah 8
  Silvy 18
  Susanna 91
  Van 79
  Vaughn 79
  W. R. 40
  William 10, 22
Seal, Rebecca 75
Seamore, Robert 95
  Susy 95
Seates, Harriett F. 30
Self, Sarah J. 105
Sergant, Polly 3
Sergeant, William 112
Sergent, Daniel 122
  Margaret D. 59
Sertain, Elisha 93
Settle, Elizabeth G. 49
Sewell, Daniel 2
  Polley 2
Seymour, Robert 55
Shacford, Elizabeth 4
  Nance (wid) 4
Shackelford, Absalom 48
  Ann A. 5
  Elizabeth 113
  Luzeta 120
  William 118
Shackleford, F. A. 111
  Francis 114
  Garland 95
  John T. 5
  Mary H. 5
  Mildred 21
  Nancy 20
  Sally 10
  William 114
Shacklford, Anna 20
  Anne 5
  William 20
Shalton, James 43
Shaman, Thomas 96
Shankes, Sophia 37
Shanks, Elizabeth 24
  Robert 95
  Thomas 32, 64
Shapard, Booker 87
  Lewis 25
Shappard, Lewis 14
Sharp, William 108
Sharpe, Matilda H. 43
Shaw, Ben 120
  John S. 64
  Letta 95
  Nancy 87
  Urcillia P. 116
  William 16
  Wm. A. 119
Shearman, Charles 55
  Heathy 11
  Tempi 113
Shell, Lemmon 31
Shelton, Caroline M. 63
  David 86
  Drucilla 73
  Eliza 114

Shelton (cont.)
 Eliza M. 5
 Elizabeth 37, 61
 Henry 43, 77
 Jane 113
 Louisa 118
 Margret 87
 Martha 14
 Mary 9
 Mary Ann Mariah 96
 O. P. 52
 Patsey 94
 Pinkney N. 66
 Sally 43, 74
 Samuel 18
 Susan 25
 Susan S. 49
 Susannah 21
 W. M. 91
 Wesley 96
 William 10
 William C. 96
 Willoughby N. 119
Shemcy, Catherine 108
Sheon, Misura E. 2
Shepard, Elizabeth 78
 James 95
 Susanna 6
Sheperd, Salley 71
Shepherd, Martha 69
Sheppard, Elisabeth 40
 Frances 99
 Joannah 13
 Mary 84
 Susan W. 12
Shermon, Elisabeth 11
Shields, John 33
 Johnston 105
 Joseph 33
 Mary (Mrs.) 105
 Sally A. 105
 Susan P. 47
Shirly, Susanna P. 27
Shocklee, Polly 80
 Robert B. 80
Short, John 96
Shreve, Robt. 76
Shuemaker, Ann 125
Shumaker, Lindsey M. 12
Shy, Marthy 30
 Nancy 29
 Polly 111
 Robert 29
 Sally 29
 Samuel 111
Siddall, Ira 104
 Isaac B. 107
 John 94
Siddel, Job 37
 Sarah 76
Siddle, Cloe 17
 J. B. 6
 J. Bedford 6
 Martha E. 6
 Mary 7
 Nancy 104
 Parthena 101
 Sarah 94
Sidebottom, James H. 26
Sikes, James F. 7
 Mary 96
Simmons, Avis 32
 George 92
 Hannah 60
 Isaac 67, 96, 97, 98, 107
 Issac 29
 James 90

Simmons (cont.)
 Kesiah 125
 Levina 24
 Margaret 87
 Martha 60
 Nancey 96
 Presilla 105
 Rebeca H. 46
 Ritta 107
 S. T. 90
 Salina 113
 Sally 2
 Thomas 72
Simms, Alletha 94
 Frances 66
 Henrietta 10
 Lornah 66
 Zuriah 88
Simpson, A. 19
 Almeda 82
 Anice 111
 Annie 45
 Calvin 81
 Celenis B. 9
 Charles 84
 Citty 7
 D. W. 29, 31, 66, 75, 81, 97
 Deby (Mrs.) 122
 Delphia 47
 Dililah 19
 Duke W. 99
 Elizabeth 45
 Francis L. 97
 Geo. W. 8
 George W. 12
 Hannah Ann 7
 J. P. 87
 J. T. 7
 Jacob 107
 James 105
 James P. 28, 41, 79
 Jas. P. 19, 24, 35, 45, 53, 102, 107, 114, 117
 John 122
 John H. 9
 Lewis 4
 Louisa 68
 Martha A. 111
 Martha G. (wid) 86
 Mary W. 70
 Massay 111
 Matilda 6
 Matilda (Mrs.) 82
 Moses 11
 Moses S. 32
 Nancey 10, 74
 Nannie L. 78
 Nanny 7
 Oliver 74, 97
 Penelope 38
 Polley 42
 Priscilla 97
 Rachel 122
 Richard 36
 Richd. 12, 87
 S. 78
 Sandford M. 97
 Silas 32
 Susan B. 39
 Susanna 12
 Susannah 97
 William 49, 82, 113
Sims, Edward 7
 George 70
 George (Jr.) 10
 Mary 7

Sims (cont.)
 Nancey 67
 Zilpah 28
Sinard, Jonathan 57
Singleton, Anne 108
 Catherine 116
 Robert 91, 92, 94, 100
 Robt. 109
Sisson, Mary 39
Skeen, Hannah 62
Slade, A. 1, 2, 15, 20, 34, 46, 76, 77, 94, 109
 Abisha 16, 26, 41, 47, 54, 104, 109
 Abishai 95
 Adeline H. 44
 Bartlett Y. 13
 Cherry 120
 Daniel 97
 Delilah 46
 Elias 110
 Elias D. 97, 111
 Elizabeth 17
 Ezekiel 31
 Hannah 59
 Hannah M. 45
 Harriet 43
 Isbella 92
 James 88
 Jesse F. 92
 John 28
 Josephine 84
 Josiah 122
 Lucinda 71
 Margaret 97
 Martha 120
 Martha G. 95
 Martha L. 28
 Mary Ann 109
 Mary C. 21
 Mary J. 116
 Nancy 101, 102
 Nancy G. 12
 Phebe (Mrs.) 97
 Polley 38
 Stephen 43
 Tho. 14, 51, 99
 Thomas 74, 98
 Thomas (Jr.) 15, 36, 43
 Thomas L. 69, 70, 103, 105
 Thos. 28
 Thos. (Sr.) 97
 Virginia E. 47
Slaten, Eliza F. 46
Slaughter, Samuel 55
Slayden, Frances K. 4
Slayton, Judith T. 28
 Martha J. 3
 Mary 8
Slaytor, Richard A. 42
Sledge, Catharine A. 119
 Cranford 119
Smith, Absolem Burton H. 41
 Almedia 4
 Amanda 90
 Anderson R. 92
 Ann R. 108
 Anna 78
 Anne 95, 122
 Arrela S. 107
 Beney 2
 Betsey 28, 29
 Betsy 29, 90, 97
 Cathrine 12

161

Smith (cont.)
  Christopher 83
  Daniel 98
  E. M. 45
  Elisabeth 49, 115
  Eliza A. 9
  Elizabeth 20, 112
  Elizabeth A. 5
  Elizabeth M. 3
  Ellen 70
  Ellennor 70
  Ewell 103
  F. E. 12
  Fed 116
  Frances 15, 29, 83
  Francis 5, 90, 99, 116
  Geo. A. 106, 114, 121
  George 7, 12, 45, 90, 94, 98
  George A. 101
  H. 31
  Henry F. 90, 100
  Henry L. 84
  Herrod 20
  Isabella 29, 83, 100
  J. 41, 62, 80, 92
  J. M. (Jr.) 41, 61
  James 42, 82
  James M. 14
  Jane 24, 97
  Jas. 21
  Jenney 52
  Jerry 12, 27, 53, 74, 77, 82, 83, 85, 89, 92, 98, 102, 107, 117, 118, 124
  Jirilla 76
  Jno. 29, 43
  Joannah 51
  John 24, 52
  John A. 7
  John C. 117
  John R. 118
  Jonathan 62
  Joseph 11
  Keziah 19
  Larkin 113
  Lewis 32
  Malissa 69
  Manerva 104
  Martha 71
  Martha Ann 97
  Mary 10, 87, 118
  Mary F. 3
  Mary K. 21
  Mary W. 55
  Mimy 91
  Moses 56
  Nancey 5, 46, 117, 120
  Nancy 19, 107
  Nancy B. 36
  Patsey 6
  Patsy 82
  Peter 17
  Polley 3, 66, 73
  Polly 52, 96
  Richard 2, 36, 70, 82
  Richard J. (Jr.) 29
  Richd. S. 4
  Robert 18, 46, 122
  Robert K. 125
  S. Jane 76
  Salley 14, 115
  Sally 40
  Sally J. 121
  Samuel H. 72
  Sandy L. 46
  Sarah 29, 70

Smith (cont.)
  Sarah Frances 18
  Sarah Jane 69
  Stephen 98
  Susan 18
  Susan Ann L. 74
  Susan F. 107
  Susana 17
  Susanna 82
  Teby 92
  Thomas 1, 14, 94, 118
  Thomas B. 10, 76
  Virginia 47, 81
  W. 17
  William 31, 37, 51, 54, 89, 94, 117
  William (Sr.) 107
  William B. 12
  William F. 71
  William T. 50, 59, 66, 95
  William W. 49
  Willis B. 81
  Wm. F. 28, 110
  Wm. T. 83
Smither, Julia C. 30
Smithey, Anne 115
  Elizabeth 1, 100
  John 100, 115
  Nicy 113
  Samuel 1, 115
Smithson, Hezh. P. 14
Smithy, James 100
  John 62
  Martha E. 100
  Nancy 24
  Sarah (Mrs.) 100
  Sarah Jane 4
Smyth, Samuel 100
Smythe, Samuel 24, 115
Snead, Alexander 100
  Benjamin 61
  Benjn. 22
Sneed, Annis 2
  Catherine 58
  Elizabeth 22
  Frances N. 21
  Mary 120
  Sarah 61
  Susan 120
  William A. 36
Snipes, Anderson 62
  Caroline 117
  Cornelia 74
  Elizabeth L. 97
  Frances 82
  Hannah 82
  Nancey 46
  Nici 45
  Sarah J. 117
  Teletha 115
Snody, Elizabeth 11
Snow, Tilman 62
  Tilmon 28, 62, 108
  William G. 100
Soes, Joshua (?) 53
Solomon, Thomas 8
Somer, John 100
Somers, Abijah 124
  Catherine 60
  Frances J. 1
  Henry 122
  Jemima Ann 119
  John 93, 99, 100, 124
  Mary 113
  Mary Ann 2
  Nancy 7
  Sarah 68

Somers (cont.)
  Susan 93
  William 2
  William A. 100
Sommers, Zera 13
Sotherland, Susan 85
Sourtherd, Matilda 16
  William 16
Southard, Lithy 62
  Mary 74
  Nancy M. 33
  William 62, 115
Southerland, Patsey 58
Spain, Edward M. 25
  Elizabeth 72
  Martha R. 119
Sparks, Milton 42
  S. T. 10
Sparrow, C. G. 103
  Eliza C. 52
  Nancey 63
  Willy 83
Spaulding, Robert E. 41
Speed, Spencer 21
Spence, Caroline 76
Spencer, Barbary 82
  Elizabeth 101
  Francis 52
  James 52
  Mary 101
  Mary P. 121
  Thomas 54
Spratten, Elizabeth 6
  George 6
Spratton, George 123
Squire, Sina 50
Stacey, Hennritta 77
Stacy, Elizabeth 10
  Fannie E. 21
  John 104
  Thomas 10
Stadler, Elizabeth 10
  John 6, 10, 12, 20, 31, 32, 48, 51, 56, 57, 65, 67, 69, 70, 73, 74, 76, 78, 79, 100, 112, 115
  John T. 1, 15, 46, 65, 97, 101, 102
  Lidia 32
  Martha F. 65
  Mary C. 10
  Nancy A. 1
  Polley 68
  Polly 67
  R. E. 37, 101
  Reece E. 67
  Robert 1, 18, 57, 67, 115
  Stephen C. 88
  Susan A. 115
  Susannah 2
  William B. 2
Stafford, Adam 101
  Barnet 117
  Betsey 42, 117
  Cynthia 8
  Delilah 19
  Elizabeth 118
  Jese B. 118
  John 33, 91
  Nelley 33
  Phoebe 29
  Saml. 14
  Sarah 2
  Sinty 81
  Tho. 101
  Thomas 19

Stafford (cont.)
　William 101
Stainback, Forester 79
　Forister 63
　Mary 7
　Parthenia (Mrs.) 114
　Susan A. 114
　W. H. 114
Stalcup, Silviah 78
Staler, John 108
Stallings, Wiley P. 108
Stamps, Anna 49
　Claracy 107
　Edward R. 47
　Eliza (Mrs.) 75
　Jane 16, 75
　Jno. 101
　Jno. (Jr.) 48
　John 117
　July 8
　Lucinda 45, 61
　Mary 46
　Mary E. 85
　Milly 107
　Rufus 21
　Thomas J. 84
　Warner 75
Stanback, Betsy 122
　Martha 76
　Mary Frances 12
Standbury, Elisabeth 83
Standfield, Elizabeth A. 88
　Henderson 29
　Martha T. 9
Standley, Richard 102
Standsbury, Rachel 14
Stanfield, Ann M. 96
　Anna 52
　Benj. F. 25
　Durrett 101
　Frances 24
　Harrison 48
　Henderson 64
　Isaac O. 77
　Jno. 109
　Jno. L. 119
　Joseph M. 75
　Josiah A. 119
　Marion P. 102
　Mary L. 82
　Mumford 100
　Munford 86
　Nanny 15
　S. A. 16, 17, 18, 42, 49, 51, 60, 77, 90, 109, 122
　Sarah J. 40, 92
　Susan 64
　William A. 23
Stanley, Alfred G. 76
　Edgar 50
　Elisha 102
　Joel 81
　Martha J. 108
　Mary F. 10
　Nancey 102
　William R. 10, 102, 108
Stanly, Alpheus 84
　Fr. 114
Stansbury, Saml. 102
Starkey, Elisabeth 24
　Elizabeth 87
　John 1, 17
　Jonathan 24
　Judith 39
Starky, Jonathan 98

Starky (cont.)
　Rebeckah 98
Steel, Nancy E. 20
Stegall, Rebecca A. 32
Stenson, Nancey 72
Stephen, Nancy 33
Stephens, Abarilla 121
　Algernon D. 32, 89, 117
　Alginon D. 102
　Andrew 102
　Andrew W. 77, 80
　Ann 63
　Barbarah 102
　Benjamin 72, 103, 117
　Benjamin F. 41
　Betsey 89
　Betsy 19, 53
　Catey 46
　Catharine 41
　Charles 34, 102
　Elizabeth 41, 63
　George 79, 102
　Iverson G. 121
　John 102
　John C. 1
　John W. 26
　Malinda 59, 121
　Mary 59
　Mary C. 117
　Matt 102
　Nancey 50
　Nancy 90
　Patsey 63
　Polley 57
　Rebecca 89
　Rebeckah 67
　Sarah 92
　Susan 107
　W. G. 97
　William 72, 102
Williamson M. 23, 102
Stevens, A. G. 121
　Martha J. 94
　Matilda 63
　Temperance 81
　William 102
Steward, Betsey 103
　Elizabeth 29
　Mildred C. 31
Stewart, Adeline T. 75
　Frances A. 106
　Jane 23
　Lydia Ann 31
　Mary R. 72
Stewert, Rachel 48
Stimpson, William 11
Stinson, Lucy P. 9
Stokes, (?) 36
　Allen Y. 84
　Betsy 8
　Dudley G. 41, 84, 117
　Dudly G. 111
　Eliza F. 84
　Elizabeth 39
　Jesse 90
　John Y. 64, 108
　Lettice 109
　Mace 64
　Martha 43
　Mary 103
　Mathis Moore 11
　Nancey 105
　Nancy 81
　Nannie 90
　Peggy 11
　Rebecca 113
　Sally 36

Stokes (cont.)
　Silvanus 37
　Silvs. 36
　Susannah B. 85
　William Y. 103
Stone, (?) (wid) 119
　Ann 103
　Bettie M. 123
　C. 50
　Ellen J. 28
　Henry 4
　Jos. 85
　Lucy 27, 33
　Mary L. 111
　Nancey 4
　Priscilla 69
　Sarah 27
　Sarah A. 29
　Susan A. C. 103
　Thomas R. 103
　William (Jr.) 33
Stoner, Polly 45
Storks, Salley 44
Stovall, Benjamin 37
　George 37, 78
Stowers, John 41
Strader, C. 56
　Celia 112
　Christian 80, 97
　David 58, 80, 103, 112, 124
　Henry 90
　John 103
　Lydia Marget 90
　Mary 37
　Mary Ann 27
　Rachel 58
　Sarah J. 80
　Seluda 8
　Susan 26
Strador, Betsey 6
　Christian 6, 33, 103
　Christian (Jr.) 109
　David 34
　Delilah Ann Juda 113
　Esther 33
　James 27
　Mahala 34
　Martha 27
　Susannah 109
　Zeporiah 33
Strange, Andrew J. 72
Stratton, Lenorah H. 124
Street, Martha 41
　Polley 10
　Salley 95
Stringer, James 104
　Maryann 87
Strother, Conrod 103
Stuart, Aggy 11
　Edward G. 98
　Hannah 55
　James 103
Stubblefield, Alice 6
　Catharine 123
　Edmund 110
　Geo. W. 6
　Nancy 80
　Rebecca H. 70
　Susanna 6
　Theo 104
　Theodorick 48
　William 70
　Wyatt 80, 123
Stublefield, Patsey 73
Sullivant, Russell 124
　Susannah 124
Sumers, Zeri 104

Summers, Catharine 112
  Elizabeth 13, 96
  William 1
Suthard, Elizabeth 17
Sutherland, Philena 84
Sutherlin, Bird G. 99
Sutton, Smith 13
Swain, Martha A. 67
Swainey, Margret 11
Swan, Arree 14
  Danl. W. 18
  Mahaley 111
  Milley 83
  Peggy 113
  Sarah W. 18
Swann, Adaline 104
  Benj. 104
  Betsey 111
  Burch 38
  Daniel W. 42, 51
  Elizabeth F. 32
  Huldah 66
  J. J. 27
  James 113
  John A. 89
  John M. 8, 91, 94
  Joseph 64
  Louisa A. 94
  Lucrecia 1
  Lucy 15
  Matilda J. 1
  Peggy 90
  Penciselia 120
  Pensey 21
  Sarah C. 108
  Susan B. 76
  Thomas (Jr.) 111
  W. B. 16, 27, 65, 80,
    82, 84, 85, 97, 100,
    108, 110, 114, 124
  William 16, 26
  William B. 66
  Wm. B. 23
Sweaney, John 11
Swepson, Geo. W. 77
Swift, Anthony 87
  Anthony W. 31
  Betsey 96
  Caroline 59
  Emeline 100
  Frances 53, 77
  Frances M. 55
  Frances T. 105
  George A. 84, 91
  Harvey 69, 105
  Joseph M. 41
  Margaret 46
  Mary 67
  Mary H. 104
  Nancey 77, 95
  Nancy 30
  Polley 59
  Polly 105
  Robert 7, 99
  Sally 83
  Sarah 92
  Sarah S. 88
  Susanah 43
  Susanna W. 32
  Thomas 40, 55, 96, 104
  Thomas S. 34
  Wesley 96
Sykes, Jas. P. 106
Taber, Elizabeth 97
Tabor, Polly 43
Tabour, Lucy Ann 44
Tait, Edy 83
  Elizabeth 125

Tait (cont.)
  Fanny 32
  Henry 18, 31
  Huldah 18
  Isabell 31
  Jenney 98
  Lidia 10
  Mary S. 84
  Polly 56
  Sarah 104
Taite, Mary A. 2
Talbert, Joseph 114
  Sarah 114
Tallaw, Joicy 11
Talley, James H. 122
Tally, Eliza E. 96
  Lodrick E. 114
  Mary C. 66
Tanner, Mary J. 86
  Newton 117
  Patsey A. 25
Tapley, Hosea 31, 44
  John 75
  Milley 79
  Salley 90
  Sarah Moore 30
  Susanah 83
Tapp, Sophia 53
Tapscott, Edney 122
  Henry C. 7
  Luscinda 112
Tarpley, Janey 37
  Thomas O. 105
  Thos. 105
  William 90, 94, 107
Tarwater, Edward A. 48, 96
Tate, Adeline 81
  Allen 105
  Elizabeth 79
  Hannah 55
  James 90
  James M. 69
  Jobe 85
  Lemuel R. 3
  Lucinda 50
  Patsey 37
  Sarah 53
  Susannah 36
  William 92, 105
  William S. 12, 117
  Zaccheus 98
  Zachariah 10
Tatom, A. 64, 97
  Abner 34
  Absalom 111, 112, 120
Taylor, Abel 105
  Charles 3
  Charles D. 36
  Charles M. K. 108
  Fanny 125
  Frances 42
  George 105, 106
  George W. 76, 105
  Henry 42, 50, 106
  Hiram 3
  James 10, 42, 106
  Jane 109
  Joseph A. 76
  Joyce 26
  Leathy 5
  Lucinda 33
  Margaret C. 64
  Margarett 3
  Martha 49, 75
  Mary Ann 80
  Mary M. 81
  Mary W. 53

Taylor (cont.)
  Moses 105
  Nancey 3
  Napoleon B. 69
  Patsey 42
  Peggy 52
  Polly 28
  Reubin 48
  Robert 105
  Ruth 53
  Salley 53
  Samuel W. 3
  Sarah L. 106
  Septimus 8
  Thomas 26
  W. H. 105
  William 33
  William W. 1, 72
  Willis L. 101
  Willm. 86
  Wm. H. 106
  Wm. W. 81, 110
Tenneson, Ignatius 2
Tennesson, Creasy 96
  Elizabeth 33
  Sarah 2
Tennison, Ignatius 2
Tennisson, Celia 80
Levy 80
Terel, Lucy 74
Terell, John 21
  William M. 77
Terpin, Anderson 68
Terrel, James 75
  Mercy 75
Terrell, Ann 72
  Betsy 9
  Frances 115
  Henderson 21
  James 10
  Jane 116
  Jonathan 4
  Joseph J. 31
  Lucy 28, 78, 82
  Margret 70
  Martha 115
  Patsey 73
  Paul 106, 116
  Salley 66
  Sarah 73
  Tabitha 16
  William 29
Terrill, Elizabeth 46
Terry, Abner R. 43
  Barton 32
  Barton (Jr.) 94
  Dabney 96
  Elizabeth A. 125
  Harriet 32
  Julia A. 69
  Lettice W. 52
  Martha 54
  Mary A. 66
  Mathew 27
  Narcesia B. 84
  O. F. 10
  Sarah A. 31
Tery, David 107
  Milly 107
Thacker, Martha A. 66
  William 63
Tharp, John 6
  Patsey 39
Thaxton, Amandy 107
  Thomas 17
  Thos. 106
  William 39
Thomas, Allice 35

Thomas (cont.)
  Betsey 124
  Catharine 42
  Celia A. 28
  Daniel 57
  Daniel C. 107
  Danl. 107
  David 107
  Dianna 102
  Dicey 102
  Elisabeth 9
  Frances 98
  George 106
  Henry 11, 86, 107
  James 75
  Jinsey 83
  Joel P. 107
  John 46, 101
  M. C. 89
  Margaret 55
  Margaret (wid) 107
  Martha 96
  Martha A. E. 96
  Martha J. 14
  Mildred 77
  Nancey 56
  Phillip 60
  Polley 30, 46
  Sally (wid) 22
  Sarah 41
  Susan B. 87
  Susan V. 55
  Thomas 9
  Thomas J. 107
  Wm. 3
  Woodlief 47, 98
Thompson, Andres J. 29
  Ann E. 7
  Ann Eliza 119
  Anthony 119
  Betsey 32
  Eveline 107
  Frances P. 121
  Geo. W. 35, 41, 50, 82, 106, 113
  George W. 27, 71, 75
  James C. 107
  James H. 42, 107
  John 107
  Justina L. 119
  Mary 5
  Nancey 26
  Nannie 12
  Robert 29
  Sarah S. 60
  Susan C. 29
  Thomas M. 7
Thorn, Kitty C. 5
Thornton, Adaline 48
  D. R. 38
  Fannie 98
  Felix F. 34, 91
  Joseph 90
  Millie (Mrs.) 48
  Ret 48
  Robert B. 33
  Sallie F. 53
  Susan E. 33
  Susan J. 51
Thorp, Louisa 74
Tillinghast, S. T. 55
Timberlake, Augustine 108
Tindal, Elizabeth 115
  Thomas 39
Tindil, Thomas 91
Tirpin, Susan R. 23
  Thomas V. 23

Tobey, Tho. W. 116
  Thomas W. 23, 24, 38, 62, 68, 80, 82, 83, 87, 103, 104, 111, 122, 123
Todd, Elisabeth 103
  Priscilla 62
Tolbert, Elisabeth 69
  Jeremiah 4
  John 69
  Martha 4
  Nancy 114
Toler, Mary 27
Tolloh, Frances 91
Tomson, Salley 83
Toney, John 62
  Lucy (Mrs.) 62
  Mary 40
  Nancy 62
  Sarah 67
Torian, George L. 124
  Mandy 92
  Nathaniel 111
  Robert A. 46
Totten, Emeline 87
  J. S. 18, 34, 41, 42, 48, 62, 89, 94, 112
  John C. 51, 93, 112, 124
  Joseph S. 1, 44
  Mary A. 79
  Parthena A. 79
Totton, Nancy W. 110
Townes, Edward 98
Townley, Robert 103
Tracey, Jenney M. 97
Trammell, Crosha 37
  Elizabeth 109
Travis, Alcey S. 23
  Aryann 73
  Eliza A. 101
  Ellis 108
  Elzey W. 23, 58
  Geo. A. 108
  Isaac 108
  Isaac H. 108
  James 108
  James S. 108
  Jno. W. P. 108
  John 1, 52, 55, 108
  Polley 55
  Purlina 58
  Stephen 85
Traylor, Elisabeth 9
Traynham, David 84
Traywig, Jane 63
Trice, Henry 76
Tricky, Anness 26
  Giles 26
Trigg, Betsey 13
  Teletha 2
  William 2
  William B. 64, 69
Trim, Frances 25
Trotter, Thomas 79
True, John 108
  Nancy 42
  Ozza 93
Tuck, Louisania C. 99
Tucker, H. T. 35
  John W. 30
  Perlina 77
  Robert 76
  Sallie P. 76
Tulloh, William 31
Tunks, Frances 24
Turner, Chesley 109
  Elisabeth F. 93

Turner (cont.)
  Elizabeth 61, 97
  Elizabeth T. 30
  Ephraim 37
  Fanney 60
  Frances 67
  Frances A. 74
  George 110
  Henry 37, 65, 109
  Henry D. 39
  Isham 109
  James 34, 67, 109
  James C. 109
  James H. 109
  John 69, 109
  John A. 93
  John F. 20
  Letty 11
  Louisa 94
  M. A. 36, 38, 59, 79, 92, 93, 109, 120
  Maria 110
  Martha M. 111
  Mary 98
  Mary (wid) 37
  Mary A. 1, 110
  Mary F. 28
  Matilda 109
  Milly 117
  Nancey 28, 32, 111
  Nancy 57, 121
  P. 90
  Patrick 119
  Peter 31
  S. E. 33
  Salley 34
  Sallie 115
  Sally 71
  Sarah 7
  Susannah 26
  Thomas 32, 41, 57, 61, 119
  Thomas (Jr.) 97
  William A. 4
Tyre, Martha 27
Tyree, David 19
  Mary 64
Tyrrell, Isbell 71
Underwood, Annis 45
  Artelia 16
  Margarett 16
  Sarah E. 94
Upton, Edd. 95
  Edward 33
  Edwd. 95
  William 22, 52
Vaden, Amanda 68
  Patsy 1
Valone, Bennet 66
VanHook, Elizabeth L. 117
  G. W. 33, 39
  G. W. G. 17
  Geo. W. 20, 22, 41, 123
  George W. G. 49
  Jacob T. 110
  Marcus A. 25
Vanhook, Araminta D. 72
  Betsey 23
  Bridget 42
  Isaac 8, 104, 125
  Isaac V. 23
  Jacob 54
  Jesse 54
  John 91
  Kindal 19
  Laurence 42

165

Vanhook (cont.)
  Marcus A. 88
  Penelope M. 77
  Polly 91
  Susannah 55
Vaser, Nathaniel 6
Vaughan, Betsey 57
  Elizabeth 57, 59
  Frances 45
  James 16
  James (Sr.) 80
  John 45, 53, 69, 94,
    95, 111
  Lucy 62
  Maurice 93
  Nancey 87
  Nancy 5, 95
  Priscilla 57
  Richard 106
  Sterling F. 3
  Thomas 40, 111
  William 2, 46
Vaughn, Eddy 55
  Eliza 30
  Lucy 79
  Maurice 54
  Nancey 78
  Patsey 95
  Richard 73, 79
  Sarah J. 70
  Susanah 96
  Thomas 100
Vermillion, Mary J. 78
  Nancy 6
  Wilson 34
Vernon, C. D. 28, 52
  Calvin D. 21, 60, 82
  Edith A. 24
  Marinda C. 78
  Mary J. 39
  Narcissa 104
  Robert T. 3, 44, 95
  W. A. 24, 28, 76, 90,
    92
  Wm. (Cpt.) 48
  Wm. A. 51
Verser, John A. 119
  Martha 44
Vershear, Ammy 43
Vincen, Charity 5
Vincent, Alexander 103
  Anne 103
  James 13
  Levi A. 5
  Sarah J. 7
Vinson, Mary F. 113
Virloins, Elizabeth 115
Voss, Greenbeary 38
  Greenbury 16, 21, 51
  Kitty 45
  Paschal 90
  Philip P. 93
  Sarah E. 104
  Stephen T. 99
Vowell, Susan 95
Waddell, Nancey 113
  Patience 5
Waddill, Pleasant 40
Wade, Ann 111
  Ann R. 50
  Elisabeth 73
  Elizabeth W. 99
  John J. 50
  Robert D. 44, 110
Wadleton, Sina 72
Wadlington, Francis 84
Wagstaff, Ester 119
Waid, Betsey 46

Waite, Wm. 112
Walden, Mildred 122
Waldrope, Ann 55
Walf, Lucy Ann Elizabeth
  103
Walker, Virginia A. 2
  A. B. 53, 69, 112,
    115, 119
  Abner 112
  Abner (Jr.) 36, 88
  Alijah 26
  Ashford 31
  Barbara 113
  Barbary 40
  Betsey 11
  Catharine 40
  Catherine 51
  Celie 62
  D. A. 32
  David 23, 51, 85
  Elisabeth 11
  Eliza 88
  Eliza (Mrs.) 82
  Eliza A. 27, 101
  Elizabeth 99, 100
  Frances 58, 64
  G. G. 22, 31, 39, 97,
    112
  George 69, 99
  George G. 70
  Henry A. 112
  Hugh 97
  Jacob G. 21, 111, 117
  James 29, 86, 91, 112
  James M. 92
  Jane 5, 91, 100, 112,
    113
  Jane E. 58
  Jefferson H. 32, 65
  Jefferson M. 45
  Jemima 15
  Jethro J. 37, 100, 113
  Jimima 104
  Jinnie (Mrs.) 111
  John M. 5, 17, 54, 112
  L. L. 114
  Leticia 75
  Levi 112
  Lucinda 112
  Lydia 32
  M. C. 51
  Malinda 51, 79
  Margaret F. 51
  Margarett 19
  Martha 14, 36, 62
  Martha F. 17, 105
  Mary 10, 12, 73, 112
  Mary (Mrs.) 86
  Mary A. 35
  Mary C. 69
  Mary E. 112
  Mitchell 7
  N. L. 35, 60
  Nancey 18, 54, 64
  Nancy 29, 62
  Nancy J. 64
  Peggy 75
  Philip 113
  Polly 104, 122
  Priscilla 82
  Rachel 91
  Rachiel 21
  Rebecca J. 68
  Samuel 75
  Sarah 36, 96
  Sarah A. 68
  Scott 53
  Squire 89

Walker (cont.)
  Stephen 96, 111
  Thomas J. 80, 104, 113
  William 5, 58, 113
  Willy 112
  Wm. 82
  Wm. A. 113
  Wm. S. 7
Wall, Byrd 102
  Catherine 113
  Jincy 46
  Nancy 47
Wallace, James 99
  Nancey 49
  Parthena 80
  Sarah 51
Waller, Lydia 118
Wallis, (?) (Maj.) 49
  Allen 80
  Elizabeth 8, 34
  James 72, 113
  John 34
  Rachel 60
Walters, Ann E. 113
  Archer 32
  Azariah G. 113
  Berry 113
  Charles H. 95
  Cloe 53
  Davy 113
  Elizabeth 32, 37
  Elizabeth (Mrs.) 1
  Fanuel 56
  Henry 6
  Iverson B. 113
  John 42, 74
  Julia J. 1
  Leathy M. 81
  Louisiana 15
  Lucy 23
  Martha 65
  Martha A. 97
  Martha B. 16
  Mary F. 37
  Mary J. 42
  Matilda 14
  Nancy 123
  Paul 113
  Polley 37
  Robert 106
  Sally 29
  Thos. 122
  William 1
Walton, Candis J. 13
  Loftin 114
  Robert 62
  Thomas 63
Ward, Betsy 121
  Elizabeth Jane 90
  John 51, 114
  Letitia 4
  Louisa 67
  Nancy 89
  Q. A. 97
  R. H. 61
  Richard 62
  Salley 52
  Susanna 51
  William J. 114
Ware, Ansel 63, 125
  Aryann 47
  C. E. 121
  Celia 110
  Charlotte 63
  Elizabeth 50
  Frances 119
  Francis 25
  Hannah 77

Ware (cont.)
  Harriet 12
  Huldy 40
  John (Jr.) 52
  Louisa 49
  Martha 4, 37, 64
  Mary 60
  Nancey 108, 114, 118
  Patcey 122
  Rody 45
  Salley 22
  Silas 60
  Stephen 114
  Talbert 37
  Thomas 53
  Thomas (Jr.) 14
  William 77, 85
  Wm. 114
Waren, Fanny 2
Warf, Atkinson 114
  Elisa 24
  Elizabeth 23
  John 114
  Kezziah 24
  Richard 25
Warner, James 87
  Mary 87
Warren, Agness 12
  Ann 42
  Bartemas H. 60
  Benjamin 115
  Betsey 66, 90
  Bluford 11, 64
  Bozzel 49
  Catharine A. 56
  F. L. 73, 74, 113
  Fanney 19
  Frances 54
  Franklin L. 76
  Granderson 51
  Henry 115
  Iverson G. 99
  James 89
  James R. 36, 104
  James S. 55
  Jas. R. 114
  John 34, 52, 115
  Joseph N. 56
  Leatha 10
  Lucy 66, 101
  Mary A. 12, 20
  Mary C. 55
  Mehala 98
  Nancey 20, 124
  Nancy 73
  Permelia 46
  Rachel 27
  Saml. (Jr.) 115
  Sarah 21, 107
  Starling 59
  Thomas 90, 118
  Thomas M. 109
  Viney 69
  Westley 19
  William 19, 48
  William (Jr.) 74
  Yancey G. 39, 69
  Yerbey 21
Warrick, John 57, 107
  Nancy 23
Warrin, Anness 14
  Betsey 47
  Bluford 30, 84
  Elisabeth 63
  Francis 74
  Frankey 14
  Hedgman 47
  Jane 81

Warrin (cont.)
  Jeremiah 115
  John 115
  Larkin 117
  Nancey 100
  Nathaniel 47
Warsham, Mary 108
Warson, Elizabeth 83
Warwick, Elizabeth 102
  Marguret 107
  Polley 57
Washburn, Recey 39
Washington, Lucy 3
Waterfield, Elizabeth 72
Waters, Anna 93
  Mary Jane 76
Watkins, Anna S. 51
  Berryman 21
  Glenn 119
  Isaac 70
  James 26
  Jane 46
  King 82, 86
  Logan S. 116
  Mollie 49
  S. D. 16, 58
  Samuel 48, 52, 80
  Stephen D. 31, 51, 82, 92, 122
Watlington, Ann P. 83
  Armistead 9
  Armstead 41
  Edward 84
  Elizabeth 7
  Frances 5
  Francis 94
  George 41
  Hiram A. 97
  Isaac 49
  James 9, 48, 116
  Jane (Mrs.) 118
  Jas. M. 68
  Jonathan B. 9
  Julius C. 10
  Kiziah B. 53
  Letitia 123
  Louisiana (Mrs.) 49
  Martha A. 116
  Mary 55, 94
  Mary A. 94
  Mary B. 9
  Mary C. 90
  Mary E. 88
  Melissa 7
  Mildred 48
  Nancey 84
  Paul 116, 118
  Penelope 111
  Phillis 41
  Rebecca 116
  Sallie 118
  Sarah L. 108
  Victoria 120
  William P. 38, 109
Watson, David 80
  J. B. 36
  Jessey 86
  Joseph I. 24
  Nancey A. 92
  Polley 48
  Sarah 64
  Susan E. 87
  W. E. 116
Watterfield, Polley 102
Watts, Albertis L. 51
  Martha S. 95
  William H. 121
Wattson, Anny 47

Wattson (cont.)
  Nancey 37
Waurren, William 115
Wealsh, Samuel 117
Weastbrook, Jane 60
Weatherford, Elizabeth 22
  Fannie 6
  John 117
  Mary Ann 22
  Nancy 70
  Polly 103
  Robert 6
  Thomas 22
  Warren 122
  William 54, 103
  William (Jr.) 32
Webb, William S. 5, 18, 110, 111
  Wm. S. 91
Webster, Charles 59, 117
  Charly H. 55
  John 117
  Malbon C. 117
  Mary 44
  Nancey 44
  Sallie Ann 8
Wedding, Jereney 9
  Sarah 72
Weeden, Luisia 94
  Mary A. 42
Weire, Bettie J. 102
Weldon, Johnathan 98
  Marthany 98
Wells, B. 44, 105
  Benj. 16, 19, 23, 32, 44, 55, 64, 66, 81, 85, 89, 115
  Duppe 117
  James M. 117
  Mary 16, 115
  Miles 117
  Miles (Jr.) 8, 45, 117
  Prisilla 45
  Sarah 15, 122
Wemple, J. D. 49
  Laura 49
  Polly (Mrs.) 49
Wesley, John 39
West, Ann 103
  B. C. 53, 81, 122, 125
  B. C. (Sr.) 2, 12, 20, 26, 58, 60, 72, 110, 117
  Benj. C. 77, 83, 118
  Benj. C. (Sr.) 26, 87, 124
  Benj. Clabon 79
  Benjamin C. 32, 124
  Benjamin C. (Jr.) 77, 78, 108
  C. 20
  C. W. 108, 118
  Cary W. 1, 36, 47, 77, 99, 117, 122, 125
  Catharine 46
  Cornelius 24, 74
  Crawford 105, 124
  Elizabeth 124
  Isaac 104
  J. A. 73
  Judeth 91
  Louisa J. 7
  Mahaley J. 77
  Margaret 46
  Martha Ann 12
  Martha T. 42
  Mary 65

West (cont.)
  Mary B. 108
  Milcey 76
  R. J. 79, 81
  R. James 108
  Robert 65, 124
  Robert J. 92
  Sarah E. 116
Westbrook, Peggy 60
Westbrooks, Caroline 72
  Frances 117
  Granderson F. 121
  John 44
  Malinda 66
Westly, Elionar 27
Whalebone, Sina 13
Wharton, Julia 14
Whealer, Frances 59
Wheeler, Elsey 9
  Susannah 93
Whelton, William 6
White, Celia 1
  Clary (Mrs.) 8
  Hugh 8
  James F. 123
  Jincey 79
  John W. 109
  Louisa D. 56
  Mary 108
  Mildred 75
  Molly A. 101
  Polley 18
  Rachel 24
  Robert 92
  Sally 86
  Sarah 45
  William 111
Whited, Catherine M.
  (wid) 38
Whitehead, Ebenezer 72
  Nancey 78
  Page 18
Whiteheart, Chordy 93
Whitemore, Eliza K. 73
Whitescarver, B. F. 43
Whitfield, W. A. 37, 94, 96
Whitlock, Nancey 96
  Taylor 48
  Winnie (Mrs.) 48
Whitloe, Ursley 122
Whitlow, Caty 14
  Fanny 101
  Jesse 72
  John 31, 89
  Mary 117
  Nancy 101
  Solomon 34, 64
  William 46, 122
Whitmore, Charles 98
  Jemima J. 58
  Richard 114
  Salley 98
Whitt, John A. 110
Whittemore, Aniva E. 6
  Gower 25
  Lewis V. 4
  William L. 67
Whittrow, Susan C. 49
Whrey, Thomas 87
Wier, Bell 113
  Thomas 113
Wild, Luke 24
Wilder, William V. 32, 113
Wilds, Thomas 6
Wiles, Robert R. 81
Wiley, Adaline W. 118

Wiley (cont.)
  Albert G. 15
  Alexander 15, 22, 39, 46, 50, 107, 118
  Eleanor 27
  Esther 9
  F. A. 4, 104
  Franklin A. 119
  George 83
  Jincey 22
  John 27, 58, 118
  John H. 22, 23
  Julia 15
  Lucinda R. 39
  Margret 39
  Mary 48
  Nancey 15
  Robert H. 15
  Robert M. 23, 39, 89
  Robert W. 118
  Woody 118
Wilkerson, Edey 106
  Hazelwood 65
  Jane 66
  Marthy E. 3
  Parthana F. 20
  Polly 65
  Puritha 77
  Rachel 24
  Rhody 77
  William 53, 70, 73
  Wm. 57, 73, 98, 117
Wilkes, Lucy Ann 17
Wilkins, Patsy 109
  Stephen D. 54
Wilkinson, D. W. 80
  E. S. 101
  John E. 43
  R. W. 3
  S. T. 89
  Sarah W. 53
  Simon T. 4
  William 33, 72
  William H. 61
  Wm. 13, 15, 16, 36, 45, 94, 112
  William, Downs 26
Williams, Aggy 36
  Ann 121
  Ann R. 18
  Betsey 79
  Craftin (Jr.) 119
  Crafton 44
  Duke 43, 46, 59, 119
  Eliza G. 20
  Elizabeth 14, 49, 64
  Elizabeth Ann 114
  Henry 3, 6, 37, 88, 97
  James 53
  James M. 4, 102
  James M. (Jr.) 50, 63
  Jenney 37
  Jno. 51
  John 79
  John D. 120
  John M. 37
  John McNeill 82
  John Mdk. 110
  Judith C. 66
  Letitia F. 112
  Martha 50
  Mary 97, 107
  Mildred A. 114
  Nancey 121
  Nancy 31
  Nathan 66
  Phebe O. 60
  Robert 119

Williams (cont.)
  Sally 53
  Sarah 14, 75
  Sophia 2
  Susan Ann 106
  Tobias 42, 87
  Ursly Duke 80
  Warren 22
  William 19, 35, 81, 103
Williamson, A. S. 16
  Abram 120
  Adaline H. 23
  Addison A. 78
  Alfred 105
  Ann E. 32
  Azariah 92
  Benj. 34
  Benjamin F. 38, 41
  Candice 5
  Cornelia A. 99
  Dick 109
  Edmond 22
  Elisabeth 71, 118
  Elizabeth 99
  Ellick 2
  Emily 1
  Emily A. 48
  Emily G. 38
  Frances 20, 84
  George 10, 33, 59, 104, 120
  George O. 5
  Hannoh 112
  Henry E. 39
  Isabella 59, 92
  Isabella M. 38
  James 8, 82
  James C. 35
  James E. 19
  John 20
  John D. 119
  John L. 74
  Julia 5
  Leath 118
  Leatha 120
  Lethe 109
  Lindsay 5
  Littie 20
  Louisa 26
  Lucey 10
  Lucinda 118
  Margaret 2
  Maria 49
  Marth 120
  Martha 43, 105
  Mary 48, 58
  Mary P. 43
  Mintus (Mrs.) 118
  Moore 78
  Nancy 43
  Nathan 104
  Peggy 97
  Polley 8
  Pulliam 26
  Rachael 54
  Randy 112
  Robert H. 55
  Sarah 73
  Sarah F. 123
  Silvy 77
  Thomas 6
  Thos. J. 41
  Virginia F. 120
  Winny 60
Willingham, John 81
Willis, Anderson 15, 121
  Benjamin 116

Willis (cont.)
  Betsey 98
  Ebby 3
  Elizabeth B. 80
  George W. 102
  Hannah (Mrs.) 7
  Henry 43, 57, 67
  James H. 16
  James T. 121
  John W. 58, 99
  Joicey 21
  Joicy 15
  Joseph 121
  Judah F. 34
  Kizziah W. 122
  Laura A. 39
  Malissa 69
  Malissa Rose 7
  Margaret 47
  Marshall 10
  Martha A. 110
  Martha Ann 77
  Mary 56, 78
  Nancey 39, 99
  Nancy E. 90
  Peter 7
  Polly 45
  Sterling 38
  Thomas 121
  William 42, 121
  Wm. 121
Willson, Abbarellah 30
  Agness 104
  Betsey 72
  C. 88
  Ch. 28, 113, 122
  Cha. 70
  Charles 7, 27, 61, 90, 121
  Chs. 61, 77
  Geo. M. 28, 42
  George 22, 88, 93
  James 12, 104, 121
  Jno. G. 60
  Jos. 96
  Margret 4
  Mary L. 60
  Mathew 120
  Rebecca 103
  Robert 36, 44
  William 30, 37, 95, 121, 123
Wilmouth, Nancey 118
Wilson, Abner 101
  Ann 53
  Annie E. 18
  Betsy 122
  Betsy Ann 100
  Candis 35
  Cathrine 81
  Ch. 29
  Dafney 101
  Dennis 20
  Edward 2
  Elizabeth 60
  Ellen 51
  Franklin J. 36
  George 111
  Henry 113
  Henry W. 101
  Huldah G. 26
  J. M. 105
  James 6, 18, 39, 90
  John 104
  Johnston 47, 117
  Joseph 123
  Keziah 47
  L. L. 10

Wilson (cont.)
  Lucindy (Mrs.) 81
  Lucy 81
  Martha 41, 47
  Martin 66
  Mary 60
  Mike 81
  N. M. D. 36
  N. W. 58
  Pensy C. 112
  Polly 87, 111
  Rebecke 104
  Robert 46
  Viney 98
  William 81, 92
  Wimbus, Nancy 111
Windsor, Eliza J. 58
  Elizabeth 34
  Felix 100
  Frances 122
  Jerry 49
  John (Jr.) 88
  Joseph 7, 56, 122
  Martha A. 31
  Ned 35
  Paul 2, 10
  Rebecca 7
  Sarah 105
  Susan 10
  Thomas 85
Winfre, Harden 28
Winn, Sarah F. 50
Winne, William B. 124
Winningham, John 11, 16
Winstead, Alexander 71, 75
  Contance 122
  Daniel D. 117
  Dianah 59
  George 39
  George T. 72
Winsted, Ailse 125
Winters, Elizabeth 32, 93
  Mary 47
  Polley 108
  Rachel 64
Wisdom, Catharine 39
  Lewis 53
  Mary 115
  Nancey 115
  Rachel 103
  Salley 90
  Sally 53
  Wm. 34
Wiseman, Martin 101
Witchel, (?) (Dr.) 47
Witcher, Julina F. 2
Withers, Alice 124
  E. B. 3
  E. K. 19, 79, 93, 96
  Elijah 29, 34, 37, 51, 75, 76, 80, 122
  Eliza 6
  Elizabeth A. 27
  Jamima Jane 3
  John A. 103
  Lewis W. 6, 96
  Nancy B. 6
  Susan L. 76
  Sytha Anne 76
  William M. 62
Withhers, E. B. 121
Woff, Sally 106
Wolters, William H. 113
Womack, Cisley 64
  David 52
  David G. 16, 50

Womack (cont.)
  Elizabeth G. 38
  Elizabeth S. 55
  Elizer A. 44
  Green P. 59, 103
  Henry A. 38
  J. 18, 19, 21, 24, 29, 36, 50, 63
  James H. 74
  Jno G. 25
  Jno. 44, 71
  Jno. C. 96
  Jno. G. 17, 35, 40, 49, 70, 108
  Jno. P. 34
  John 30, 110, 120
  John G. 49
  Joseph B. 123
  Josiah 4
  Lafayette 6
  Lewis P. 94
  Lucy 52
  Luke 97
  Martha 8
  Martha Jane 92
  Mary Ann 94
  Mary Jane 19
  Mary P. (wid) 1
  Nancey 52, 122
  Nancy 6
  P. H. 14
  Pleasant H. 54
  Sarah 14
  Sinna 8
  Susan A. 93
  Vashti 40
  William P. 25, 50
  William W. 91
  Wm. P. 50, 123
Womble, James 62
  Sarah E. F. 36
  Susannah F. 32
Wommack, Adline 39
  Bristo 39
  Delila 69
Wonycott, J. W. 55
Wood, Betsey 9
  Joshua J. 85, 113
  Thomas 113
Woodall, James 13
Woodey, Judith 65
  Thomas 123
Woodie, Jno. 37
Wooding, Nathaniel 35
  Susan T. 80
Woods, A. M. 64, 67, 89, 106
  Andy M. 89
  Ann E. 1
  Archibald S. 15
  Betsey 6
  Cornelius E. 96
  John 33
  Margaret A. 15
  Margret 89
  Martha 95
  Mary 72
  Mary J. 72
  Nancy M. 64
  Polley 50
  Samuel 8, 103
  Sarah A. E. 32
  Thomas 50
  William 10
Woody, Frances 113
  John 118
  John G. 75
  Nancy 8

Wootson, Bettie S. 24
Word, Fleming 81
  John 106
  M. C. 91
  Thomas 8
  Virginia 9
Worsham, Archibald W. 16
  Emily 108
  John 10
  Lucy 45
  Ludwell 5, 83
  Mary R. 45
Wray, Milly 47
  Pinckney J. 119
  Salley 3, 33
  Thomas (Sr.) 124
Wrenn, Jno. F. 43
  John F. 58
  Wm. 124
Wright, Abram M. 113
  Adaline W. 42
  Ann B. 60
  Betsey 18, 78
  Easter Jane 107
  Esa 38
  George W. 110
  Henny 2
  Isaac 62, 100
  Jacob 30
  Jacob (Jr.) 50
  Jno. 86
  Joshua 78
  Laura V. 61
  Martha 122
  Martha Jane 84
  Mary J. 73
  Molley 86
  Nancey 72
  Nancy 30, 59
  Polley 30
  Polly 97
  Priscilla 52
  Providence 41
  R. L. 6, 124
  Rebecah 100
  Rufus 86
  Rufus L. 73, 96
  Sarah E. 31, 59
  Susannah 59
  Ursley 38
  Zachariah 7
  Zacharias 124
Wyatt, Hannah 54
  Manerva J. 48
  Polly 53
Wyles, Thomas 40
Wyne, Cathrina 14
Wynn, Charles W. 1
  Jerusha 4
  Sarah C. 52
Wynne, Charity 74
  Polly 39
Yancey, A. G. 43, 74
  Algernon S. 38
  Ann E. 35, 123
  Anna 1
  Bartlett 47
  Caroline L. 69
  Elizabeth 8, 40, 43, 97
  Fanney 118
  Frances W. 63
  J. 100
  James 57, 65, 67, 78, 87, 96, 115, 125
  Jas. 18, 71
  Jno. 87
  John 32, 105

Yancey (cont.)
  Mary C. 69
  Mildred A. 66
  Nancey 86
  Nancy 54
  Nathan 85, 116
  Polly 38
  Precilla 50
  Salley 87
  Saml. 125
  Thomas 2, 125
  Tryon 124
  Virginia B. 104
  Wylie 94
Yancy, Elizabeth 65
  James 125
  Wylie 5
Yarbrough, David 98
  John 12
  Joseph J. 66, 125
  Martha 106
  Mary N. 84
  Matilda 98
  Mendah (Mrs.) 98
  Miranda 125
  Richard 36, 46, 72, 125
  Sally B. 106
  Sarah 93
  Temperance D. 44
  William S. 8, 53
Yates, Betsey 119
  Celia 64
  Dolley 104
  Elijah 111
  Elizabeth 106
  Geo. 4
  Henry 125
  Jackson 25
  Joycey 104
  Kiziah 91
  L. W. 125
  Lawson 125
  Mary B. 69
  Nancy 76
  Polly 65, 81
  Sally 115
  Sarah 110
  Thomas 125
Yeats, John 91
  Thomas 57
Young, Jesse C. 5
  Martha S. 122
  Mary L. 41
  Polly 116
  Sally 26
  Susan A. 90
Yuille, Susan S. 12
Zachary, Polly 14
  Priscilla 112
  Prudence 11
  Robert 90
Zachory, Judah 73
Zigler, Martha Jane 28